A HISTORY OF HONG KONG

A History of
HONG KONG

G. B. ENDACOTT

'Another illustration of "The Art of Colonisation" . . . and what is curious—the success is such as to show the flexibility of the present system or want of system.'

> *Minute on the Hong Kong Government's Annual Report for 1861 by Sir Frederick Rogers, Permanent Under-Secretary at the Colonial Office.*

HONG KONG

OXFORD UNIVERSITY PRESS

LONDON   NEW YORK

Oxford University Press

OXFORD LONDON GLASGOW
NEW YORK TORONTO MELBOURNE AUCKLAND
KUALA LUMPUR SINGAPORE HONG KONG TOKYO
DELHI BOMBAY CALCUTTA MADRAS KARACHI
NAIROBI DAR ES SALAAM CAPE TOWN
and associated companies in
BEIRUT BERLIN IBADAN MEXICO CITY NICOSIA

First published 1958
Reissued in Oxford in Asia Paperbacks 1964
Revised edition 1973
Seventh impression 1983

ISBN 0 19 638264 5

Set in Great Britain by The Bowering Press, Plymouth
Printed by Ko's Arts Printing Co., 16-18 Westlands Road, Quarry Bay, Hong Kong
Published by Oxford University Press, Warwick House, Quarry Bay, Hong Kong

To

George and John

PREFACE

This book is an introduction to the History of Hong Kong. It does not claim to be definitive. It is based on a study of the Colonial Office records consisting of the dispatches of the governors and the replies from the Colonial Office, reports of local commissions and committees of enquiry, sessional papers and other information sent home by the governors, correspondence between the Colonial Office and other departments, annual Blue Books of statistics relating to the colony, minutes of the Executive and Legislative Councils, Hong Kong Government Gazettes, and Hong Kong Ordinances. The records of the Foreign Office, Admiralty, War Office and Board of Trade were also consulted. In addition various sources, such as the local newspapers which date to a period twelve years preceding the birth of the colony, gazetteers and memoirs, and such Chinese material as has been available in translation have been used. But the story of Hong Kong has been told mainly as seen through the eyes of the governors and the Colonial Office.

This has the advantage of substantial accuracy on matters of fact despite the tendency of officials to write up their policies and to point with pride to their achievements. If a governor took a pardonably prejudiced view of his own proceedings, his successor could be relied upon generally to supply a corrective. Still, the author has been aware of the danger of relying on official sources.

Governors of Hong Kong usually commented that Hong Kong was a peculiar colony, unlike any other, and this peculiarity was recognized by the Colonial Office in its earliest instructions to Pottinger. It was not a settlement, to which British migrated to make their homes; it was a 'factory' in the Indian sense, a mercantile station, in which length of residence was determined almost entirely by economic considerations. A permanent resident community grew up only slowly. Yet, looking back, the history of Hong Kong was not peculiar, but very typical of British overseas activity of the early Victorian epoch. What was sought was a commercial and not a territorial empire, and the island was taken over reluctantly, primarily for the purpose of establishing the necessary organs of law and order and administration, free from Chinese intervention or control. Its function was no different from that of the settlements in the

treaty ports in which the British Consul could supervise trade and
settle disputes, free from interference. A healthy trade demanded
settled conditions, suppression of robbery, guarantee of contract
and of impartial justice. Since the Chinese were thought to be
unable to provide these conditions, the British had to provide
them. This is fundamental to any understanding of the history
of Hong Kong. The colony was not thought of in terms of
territorial gain, but as the minimum space required for what
were thought to be the necessary British institutions. Its function
was to be the headquarters of British trade, administration and
general influence in the Far East. It remained linked with the
control of diplomacy in China until the Elgin Mission of 1857
during the Second Anglo-Chinese War, and with the control
of trade until the retirement of Bowring in 1859.

Three main problems are posed for the historian of the colony.
First, was there on the island a real community with an internal
life of its own or was the life of the colony subordinated to that
of British activity on the China coast.taken as a whole? It must
be confessed that the present volume does less than justice to
the relations between the colony and the treaty ports. British
activity in China was regarded as a whole, and should be
looked at as a whole, but the fact that the Chinese crowded
into the colony did give it quite early a separate existence and
created problems independent of those relating to the broader
position on the China coast. It has been argued that Hong
Kong never developed into a community, but remained a
trading post inhabited by a succession of traders and their
dependants. In fact, a fairly strong community feeling developed
in a society which was abnormal only in the relatively short
'expectation of life' as far as residence in Hong Kong was concerned. What mattered was that people did remain in the
island sufficiently long to absorb its spirit and outlook.

Secondly, all Hong Kong history is economic history in the
sense that the birth and growth of the colony were shaped by
economic forces, and the problem is to balance this economic
aspect against other more conventional aspects. It will be felt
by many that this history does less than justice to the economic
life of the colony; the explanation is that Hong Kong was a
free port and trade figures are not readily available. Much
material not yet worked over exists, but the author felt that

to incorporate this would bring this work beyond the scope of a single volume and would delay the publication of a general history based on government records which were of sufficient scope and interest to justify publication. A more detailed history is needed.

Thirdly, there is the problem of bringing the story of Hong Kong up to date. Over a hundred and more years, the colony has changed physically and in spirit; the issues that face the modern Hong Kong differ in substance from those of a century ago. The climate of ideas is different. To deal adequately with modern Hong Kong one needs a fresh starting point. Even if this were not so, the difficulty remains of dealing objectively with events which are too recent to permit of the necessary perspective. I considered that a history of the colony ought to be brought 'up to date', and in the final chapter treating of events within the memory of many of us, I have tried to relate the great changes that have occurred in international affairs to those that have taken place in the internal economic and social life of Hong Kong. Paradoxically, here is continuity, for during the whole of its history, the colony has been strongly influenced by events outside, and beyond its control.

The rendering of Chinese names in English is always a problem. I have adopted the Wade System of romanization, and in the case of Chinese of national standing the Mandarin form has been given; the Cantonese form has been retained in the case of those Chinese who were prominent only locally, and for whom therefore the Mandarin form would be unrecognizable and pedantic. Exceptionally, in each case, common usage has been retained.

I wish to thank Professor Gerald Graham and my colleagues, Professor Brian Harrison, Mr. Jack Gray and Mr. J. L. Cranmer-Byng for reading the script and giving me the benefit of their comments, Professor F. Drake for help with the romanization of Chinese names, and Mr. L. Berry for advice and assistance with the maps. I gratefully acknowledge my debt to Miss Margery Perham, the script of whose biography of Lord Lugard I was privileged to see.

The shortcomings of the book remain entirely my own.

G.B.E.

Hong Kong, 10 October 1957

PREFACE TO THE SECOND EDITION

THIS book was written nearly fifteen years ago just when Hong Kong's astonishing transformation into an important industrial centre was gaining momentum and beginning to bring profound changes to all sides of Hong Kong life. On the basis that the present has grown out of the past, a Hong Kong historian must record and attempt to explain those changes if he is to fulfil one of his functions, that of giving an up-to-date picture of the society to which his history points. Hence this second edition. The text has been retained with but minor amendments, except for the latter part of the last chapter dealing with the war and post-war periods, which has been re-written and expanded.

1 September 1971, Hong Kong   G.B. Endacott

CONTENTS

LIST OF ILLUSTRATIONS

MAPS

CHAPTER I

INTRODUCTION

*'And men had to come from the Far West to give it a name
in the history of the East.'*

E. J. Eitel, *Europe in China*, 1895.

HONG KONG is a British colony situated on the south-east coast
of China. It comprises the island of that name which was
obtained from China in 1841, the small district of Kowloon on
the mainland just opposite, which, together with Stonecutters
Island, was secured in 1860, and a larger area of the mainland,
called the New Territories, which was leased for ninety-nine
years in 1898. This leased territory covers an area of 355 square
miles and is in the form of a peninsula with its northern boundary roughly along the Shum Chun River from Deep Bay to the
northern shore of Mirs Bay; it includes 235 islands, the biggest
being Lantau, Lamma and Cheung Chau. The island
of Hong Kong from which the colony takes its name is less than
one-tenth of the size of the New Territories, having an area of
thirty-two square miles; Kowloon is again only a tenth of the
size of the island, being only three and a half square miles.

Hong Kong lies just within the tropics, at the mouth of the
Pearl River. It has a monsoon type of climate; the north-east
winds blow steadily from October to May, bringing generally
dry and cool conditions, and occasionally, in winter, when the
wind is from the north, from the land mass of Asia, the temperature drops suddenly. From May to October the south-west
monsoon brings great heat and humidity and most of the annual
rainfall averaging eighty-five inches falls in this season. This geo-
graphical factor of the monsoons dominated the navigation of
the China Sea by the early western traders, and as long as ships
carried sail its influence was always important. Hong Kong also
lies within the typhoon zone. Its climate, with its high humidity,
extremes of temperature and threat of typhoons, is therefore
trying for about half the year.

Geologically, the colony is similar to the neighbouring land mass of which it is an integral part. The coastline is deeply indented and provides ideal shelter for shipping, and from it the hills rise steeply up to nearly 2,000 feet on the island, and to just over 3,000 feet in the leased territories; these are often bare, and even barren from the effect of erosion, though it must be added that much of the barrenness has been caused by human agency, and slopes of thick vegetation are not infrequent. These hills rise so abruptly as to leave little or no margin of level cultivable land at sea-level, and agricultural land is to be found only in the many small and narrow alluvial valleys devoted to rice and vegetables. Sharp ridges and granite outcroppings limit the amount of land that can be taken in by terracing, and the number of people who gain their livelihood from the soil has been and still is limited.

This area now has a population of over four million people, living chiefly in two great urban centres, the northern shore of the island, and Kowloon. This is astonishing, because it will be apparent from what has been said that the area is incapable of supporting this number from its own resources. Hong Kong's most valuable asset is not its land, but its water; between the island and the mainland, only a quarter of a mile away at its narrowest part, lies a magnificent harbour, almost landlocked and an ideal anchorage for shipping. Hong Kong is the product of its harbour; shipping has been and still is its life blood.

The island has a very favourable position geographically, just at the mouth of the Pearl River, at the head of which, seventy-six miles away to the north-west, stands Canton, a great commercial centre and the capital city of Kwangtung province. The Pearl River is the most important outlet to the sea of the Si Kiang, the chief river of south-east China, its highways serving the whole hinterland beyond Canton. The island is therefore geographically favoured as a trading centre, and its real story begins with the trading relations between China and the West, which had been centred mainly at Canton since the end of the seventeenth century, and solely there from 1757 to the birth of the colony.

Recent archaeological investigation has shown that the island was inhabited from primitive times, but it has also failed to reveal evidence of the existence of any previous centre of population. All that it would be safe to conclude is that in the early migration of peoples along the Pacific coast, an island with a plentiful water supply and some cultivable land would naturally attract permanent or temporary settlement. Up to the nineteenth century it remained sparsely populated. Small villages maintained a livelihood by fishing, by cultivation of the scanty soil available, and by casual preying on coastal shipping. Shaukiwan and Chek Pai Wan (Aberdeen) were traditionally noted as being the haunt of pirates from the time of the Mongol Dynasty.

The barren islands off the coast hardly invited additional settlement until there was pressure on the soil further inland.

The discovery of an early Han Dynasty tomb at Li Cheng Uk, in Kowloon, provides some evidence of Chinese penetration of the south, but it would be rash to assume any general Chinese military or commercial settlement before the T'ang Dynasty. The history of the peopling of the island and mainland around Hong Kong is partly conjectural, but Cantonese migrants called Puntis, from the Cantonese *poon tei* meaning local inhabitants, probably began increasingly to settle there about the fourteenth century and were followed not long after by the Hakka, or 'guest people', and any local primitive indigenous people either disappeared or were absorbed. Before the close of the Ming Dynasty, a third group of Chinese settled in the area, the Hoklos. These people were less numerous than the other two, they came from the coastal district further north, and spoke a Fukien dialect. They were a seafaring people, and, because of a greater leaning towards piracy than the other two groups, had a reputation for ferocity and daring which made them the terror of the coast.

During the fighting which followed the fall of the Ming Dynasty and its supersession by the Ch'ing Dynasty of the Manchus, the Ming forces were driven to Hong Kong, and the Emperor K'ang-hsi ordered all the inhabitants to withdraw 50 li inland, in order to starve out the last resistance groups.

Generally, the conclusion must be that this area had little part in the main current of Chinese history. Besides the Han tomb, the only other historical monument still existing is the Sung Wang T'ai,[1] a big granite boulder overlooking the village

---

[1] Sung Wong T'oi, in Cantonese.

of Ma Tau Chung, its name inscribed on it in three Chinese characters to commemorate the flight to the Kowloon area, of the last boy emperor of the Sung Dynasty, after his defeat by the Mongols in 1279, and his temporary refuge there before being driven further west to his final defeat and death.

One authority[1] has cited the Wong Kwu Fan[2] as an ancient monument. This is the grave of the 'Emperor's Aunt' and consists 'of a stretch of hill side sloping to the sea, having for boundary stones two granite pillars set fifty yards apart'. Here, according to tradition was buried an aunt of one of the Sung emperors.

The history of Hong Kong really begins with the coming of the British in 1841, which arose out of the trade between the merchants of Western Europe and China, and to these traders we must now turn.

CHAPTER II

THE EUROPEAN TRADERS AT CANTON
1833–39

'It is not by force and violence that His Majesty intends to establish a commercial intercourse between his subjects and China; but by the other conciliatory measures so strongly inculcated in all the instructions which you have received.'
Wellington to Lord Napier, 2 February 1835.

THE opening of the sea routes by the Portuguese in the sixteenth century ushered in a new era in the relations between China and the West. They settled at Macao in 1557, and were followed by Spaniards, Dutch, English and French, all seeking trade, lured by the fable of the riches of Cathay. There was little that Europe could export to China, but much that it wanted to import, particularly tea and silk. During the eighteenth century the commerce between China and the West had largely passed into British hands, partly because the British were able to make the products of India and the East Indies available, and partly because they had become a nation of

[1] G. R. Sayer, *Hong Kong, Birth, Adolescence and Coming of Age*, 1937, p. 5.
[2] Wang Ku Fên, in Mandarin.

tea-drinkers, and so were China's best customers. A monopoly of trade on the British side was exercised by the Honourable East India Company, but the Company had confined itself to the tea trade for some years, and had found it increasingly convenient to allow private merchants to share the remaining trade under its control. Unfortunately, the conditions under which the trade was carried on gave rise to much dissatisfaction, out of which the colony of Hong Kong eventually arose.

Some efforts to establish centres of western trade at Amoy and Ningpo had been made before Canton secured its monopoly in 1757. At the same time another monopoly was set up; the westerners could have commercial dealings only with a loosely organized group of Hong merchants, usually called by the foreigners the Co-Hong. This group owned the 'factories' situated on the river just outside the south-western corner of the city, where the foreigners lived during the trading season. They varied in number, but after their reorganization in 1782 there were thirteen. For their privileged position they had to pay heavily, since it was partly through this monopoly that the Imperial government collected its share of the profits of the lucrative overseas trade. The commerce was strictly controlled by means of regulations, which were normally eight in number, but were not all applied all the time, and tended to vary in phrasing each time they were promulgated. Briefly they restricted freedom to pass in and out of the factory area, and forbade entry into the city. Residence was permitted only during the trading season, October to May. The foreign merchants were not allowed direct access to the local mandarins, all communication with them had to take the form of a petition sent through the Co-Hong, and any reply came by the same channel. Nor were they allowed to learn the Chinese language, and though this regulation was not strictly enforced, only the official Chinese linguists were recognized by the Chinese government. The use of sedan chairs and the employment of Chinese servants was nominally forbidden, but generally allowed. European women were not allowed into the factories, the possession of firearms was forbidden, and no warship might pass the Bogue, the narrow channel leading to Canton. The merchants were allowed to cross the river to the Fati gardens three times a month, in small parties and accompanied by a linguist; otherwise they were confined to the factories. There was nothing very strange or unusual about these regulations, yet they were felt to be irksome and restrictive; they were enforced by the Chinese only spasmodically, and were always in reserve for use on those occasions when pressure upon the Europeans was judged to be necessary.

Regulations were not the only grievances. Customs duties on the trade were varied arbitrarily; port dues levied on the ships, after they had been measured at Whampoa, were regarded as excessive; and the Co-Hong monopoly did not allow the western merchants to ascertain prices in the open market, which knowledge would have allowed them to bargain more effectively. The Europeans were called barbarians, and treated as such, and were regarded as in need of continual guidance and occasional correction. Assumption of superiority by the Chinese was irritating to foreigners who were equally confident of their own superiority. The Chinese failed to realize that an intellectual and scientific revolution in Europe had completely outmoded what had earlier been a fairly justifiable Chinese claim to dispense civilization to the rest of the world.

The Chinese attitude was clear and consistent. China had no need of European products, it was the westerners and not the Chinese who sought the trade which was a favour granted to them on Chinese terms. Besides, if merchants came to China they must clearly obey Chinese laws; 'Obey and remain, disobey and depart; there are no two ways,' said Governor Lu K'u just before his death in 1835. This, it must be added, was the normal rule in all countries.

Except for the great Jesuit mission in Peking, the contacts between China and the West were almost completely commercial. This was unfortunate, because the European seamen adventurers were not the best representatives of European culture, and because the merchant's calling was not highly regarded by the Chinese. The term 'merchant prince', implying esteem, would have been incomprehensible to them. It was therefore quite normal that the Canton officials should insist upon foreign merchants dealing only with the Chinese merchants. Besides, the Chinese had no tradition of diplomatic relations with other countries on a level of equality, if the occasional dealings with Russia are excepted, and there was

therefore no precedent for the diplomatic or consular representation of the interests of the foreign merchant, or for the
negotiation of any trade treaty on equal terms. The Chinese
contempt for the westerner made the relations worse. 'But the
barbarians are by nature insatiably avaricious and the more
forbearance and indulgence are shown to them the more do they
become proud and overbearing,' reported Lu in September
1834, and concerning the English in particular, the view was
that 'the common disposition of the English barbarians is
ferocious, and what they trust in are the strength of their ships
and the effectiveness of their guns.'

For the Europeans, life in the factories was reasonably pleas-
ant, even opulent. Relations with the Co-Hong merchants were
cordial; there was mutual trust, all the more noteworthy in that
all contracts were verbal. One observer summed up the general
feeling about the Chinese in these terms: 'We found them
honourable and reliable in all their dealings, faithful to their
contracts and large-minded.' Yet because of the restrictive
nature of the relations, discontent grew, and with it a demand
for changes by which the commerce should be extended, subjected to less restriction, and regularized by a commercial
treaty. In 1833 the English East India Company lost its
monopoly. The British merchants who had been in Canton on
sufferance had largely been instrumental in securing this success
for free trade and open market principles, and having secured
the abolition of one monopoly, they were now eager to get rid
of the other on the Chinese side. They wanted to open the
whole of China to trade, primarily to make their fortunes in
the shortest time, and were not unnaturally impatient when
the Chinese showed little appreciation of the blessings of unrestricted trade.

Lord Napier was sent out in 1834 as Chief Superintendent
of Trade. The British government pursued a correct policy
towards the Chinese. The new British representative was told
to abstain from 'all such conduct, language, and demeanour
as might needlessly excite jealousy or distrust'; he was to
impress constantly on the British merchants 'the duty of con-
forming to the laws and usages of the Chinese Empire'. The
policy was to maintain a friendly attitude as far as possible, and
to establish direct relations between the government officials as

a means of solving all difficulties. It was precisely this diplomatic contact that the Chinese would not agree to, since they would not admit the British claim to equality. Unfortunately, Napier's instructions to proceed direct to Canton and announce his arrival to the Viceroy by letter were contrary to the Chinese regulations, and placed him from the start in a false position. The Chinese refused to deal with him and stopped trade; Napier ordered two warships to Canton, and they forced the passage of the Bogue. Sick with fever, he retired to Macao and died there on 11 October 1834. His successors established themselves there, and they too were unable to set up direct relations with Chinese officialdom, though Captain Charles Elliot, who became Superintendent of Trade in December 1836, won a limited measure of recognition.

The failure of Napier and the growing discontent caused the position of the foreigners at Canton to be fully debated locally in Canton and amongst those interested in the China Trade in Britain. In December 1834 a petition to the Home government was presented by the British merchants in Canton, in which it was argued that the most dangerous course was that of quiet submission to insult, and that if Napier had been given the requisite powers backed by force 'the present degraded and insecure' position would have been avoided. The restrictions on the trade were condemned on the ground that they prevented 'almost entirely that interchange of thought and those kind offices of humanity which the Almighty has vouchsafed to his creatures as their birthright.' The petitioners asked that a plenipotentiary should be sent out to China armed with adequate power and backed by the necessary force, to demand reparation for the insult to the British representative and compensation to the merchants for loss of trade, to negotiate the removal of trade restrictions and 'the arbitrary and irregular exactions to which it is exposed', and to challenge 'the arrogant assumption of supremacy' claimed by the Chinese.

From this discussion on the position of the foreigners in Canton arose the question of securing an island or islands off the Chinese coast to replace Canton as the centre of the trade and so avoid the difficulties which had arisen there. It was out of this debate that Hong Kong was born. The Bonin Islands, Lantau, Hong Kong and Formosa were all suggested as suitable sites, but many were strongly against the acquisition of any territory from China. Lord Napier had suggested in 1834 the desirability of occupying Hong Kong; he thought that the Chinese would never agree to a commercial treaty without the threat of force. Later Superintendents argued the same way, and the feeling was that it was better to have the British Superintendent established on an island under British control than have him force his way to Canton, and maintain himself there by armed strength.

There were four views on the desirability of an island off the Chinese coast. The first view was that already mentioned; Canton had become too difficult, and rather than attempt to secure the desired trading position in Canton, it would be better to retire to some island, obtained by negotiation or purchase, and so eliminate some of the main grievances. The second was strategic. Many believed that the Chinese would never improve the conditions of trade except under force, and the application of force meant primarily naval action, and this was practicable over a long period only if a handy naval base could be secured. The third view was that an island off the coast handling the coastal trade would, on the analogy of Bombay and Singapore, become a great emporium of trade. This was the view of Sir Henry Pottinger, who later negotiated the cession of Hong Kong in the Treaty of Nanking. Finally there was the 'law and order' view. Under the English system, government action can be taken only in accordance with law, and in case of dispute can be enforced only in a court of law. The weakness of the British Superintendents was that they had very little real authority over the merchants, and no method of making it effective. The abolition of the East India Company's monopoly had brought to Canton an undesirable type of merchant, enterprising, aggressive, out to make money, and resentful of restraint. If control were to be effective clearly a law court would have to be established, and since a British court could not be set up on foreign soil, the flag should be raised over a small island to serve this purpose. Neither in Canton nor in Britain was there a desire for territorial aggrandizement against China. The demand was for a secure and ordered trade, free from exorbitant charges and arbitrary arrangements; for law and order and for courts of justice in which the merchant had confidence. The

British merchants argued that if the Chinese could not provide the requisite conditions in which trade could flourish, the British must. The demand for an island station was therefore a regrettable necessity, and its size was immaterial; the important thing was its function in providing those necessary conditions in which trade should flourish. When hostilities with China unfortunately began in 1839, one result was to make this question of an island trading centre an immediate and practical issue.

The situation at Canton after 1834 was serious; its deterioration into open war was due primarily to opium. Opium as a medicinal drug had been known and used in China at least since the T'ang Dynasty. The practice of smoking opium was more recent, and from its introduction in the seventeenth century it gradually became a serious national problem.

The poppy was grown in China, but the supply of opium came mainly from India, and because of British influence there, the opium trade fell predominantly into British hands and by 1832 brought the considerable annual revenue of £1 million to the Indian government at Calcutta. In the eighteenth century the Chinese government passed edicts against the smoking of opium and in 1800 completely prohibited its importation. The trade was therefore contraband, carried on in defiance of Chinese law; so there were no customs or measurement charges; it was usually a cash trade, in which the Chinese buyer met all incidental costs. Lintin Island in the Pearl River estuary became the centre of this nefarious traffic which attracted the adventurers to Canton. The demand for opium was such that the trade increased rapidly. In the early eighteenth century the annual import was about 200 chests; between 1800 and 1821 it remained steady at about 5,000 chests; ten years later the import was 16,500 chests. With the abolition of the Company's monopoly in 1833, the import increased rapidly to nearly 40,000 chests in the 1838-9 season. The effect was to reverse the terms of trade with China. Silver that had flowed into China to pay for tea and silk now flowed out to pay for the imported opium.

The Chinese court took the reasonable view that the drug was harmful and should be suppressed, that foreigners coming to China should obey Chinese laws, and should not engage in an illegal and pernicious traffic which destroyed men and, by the drain of silver, was to the economic disadvantage of the country. Unfortunately, the Chinese were powerless to stop the traffic. No efficient preventive service was organized; the local officials found it profitable to turn a blind eye, and the fast smuggling boats that were later employed were heavily armed. It is not surprising therefore that the anti-opium edicts were defied. Most of the foreign merchants in Canton were involved: some defended opium as 'a harmless luxury and a precious medicine except to those who abuse it'; more took the simple line that if they refused to import opium, this lucrative trade would only fall into other hands. The trade had been allowed so long that few thought the opium edicts would be rigorously applied. The argument was also raised that the Indian government could not afford to lose the revenue from the opium trade. But in general the attitude was that the question was purely commercial, a matter of economic supply and demand and not one of morals; if the Chinese wanted opium and were ready to pay for it, the merchants were prepared to sell it.

The British government adopted a very correct attitude. The Chinese government was entitled to issue what laws it liked in its own country, but it had the onus of making them effective. The British merchants were told they must expect no protection from the British government if they engaged in contraband trade; the British Superintendents of Trade were told they had no authority to interfere with the activities of the British merchants. The British government took the view that it was no part of its duty to undertake responsibility for the execution of the laws of China. It had sent out a Superintendent of Trade to deal with the Chinese officials, and this mission had been refused recognition, and all equality denied. The Chinese had refused the opportunity to negotiate over difficulties on a diplomatic level, and the British government felt itself justified in refusing to take any positive action until its mission had been received in Canton and given proper recognition. This equality of status between the two governments the Chinese were never willing to concede; their answer was again unequivocal and clear; traders who go to a foreign country should obey its laws as a matter of course. To the Chinese it was a relatively simple matter for the British officials to suppress the opium traffic.

They did not understand that British officials could be sued in the courts if they acted outside the law, and that legislation by Parliament would have been necessary. Evangelical opinion in England which had just abolished slavery might have been more effectively mobilized against the evils of opium had it not been for the hostile Chinese attitude towards Christian missions. Official opinion in England was antagonized by the refusal of the Chinese to accept the trade mission. And so the opium question drifted to an inevitable tragedy.

Lin Tsê-hsu was appointed a special Imperial Commissioner for the suppression of the opium trade and arrived in Canton on 10 March 1839. His plans had already been prepared and the rapidity and decision with which he struck took the British by surprise. They expected some temporary difficulty, after which the trade would gradually drift back to its former comfortable state, in which the edicts would continue to be ignored. That Lin would act with decision, energy, and devotion to the interests of China, was quite unexpected. On 18 March, he ordered all opium in the possession of foreign merchants to be given up, and a bond to be signed by each individual that no opium would be imported in future on penalty of death; sixteen of the more notorious offenders were to be handed over as hostages. To enforce these terms the Europeans were to be detained in the factories and deprived of the usual domestic services. Captain Charles Elliot, the British Superintendent of Trade, managed to get through to the factories from Macao; he discovered the factory area in a state of siege, and assumed control. After an offer of a few chests had been made and contemptuously refused by Lin, Elliot agreed to the surrender of all the opium in British hands. He met the difficulty that much of the opium was not the property of the merchants, but was held by them for sale on a commission basis, by promising that the British government would be responsible. When 20,291 chests had been handed over, the British were free to leave. Elliot refused to agree to the bond or to continue the trade at Canton, and withdrew all the British to Macao—to the astonishment of Lin, who had believed that once the opium had been disposed of, there would be nothing to prevent the resumption of good relations. Elliot had reported the proceedings to London and Calcutta, and asked for military intervention. Lin now threatened the British by exerting pressure on the Portuguese in Macao; Elliot offered British forces for its defence and even contemplated taking over Macao. But the Portuguese did not want to be drawn into the dispute, and Elliot withdrew the British community to merchant ships and proceeded to anchor in Hong Kong harbour. Soon after, in July 1839, a Chinese, Lin Wei Hi, was killed by a British shore party in an affray, and Commissioner Lin now demanded that the murderer should be handed over. The British had for long distrusted Chinese judicial procedure, and even if it had been possible to solve the difficulty of finding the culprit, it is probable that he would not have been given up. The British ships were now attacked by fire-rafts, and a British expedition was on its way; hostilities had begun.

To sum up, the British were dissatisfied with the conditions of trade at Canton; but as a tribute to the efficiency of the Chinese controls, it must be added that the surprising thing is not that there was dissatisfaction, but that there was not much more. When trouble had arisen, trade was stopped and then resumed after some common-sense solution had been adopted. By 1839 conditions had changed. The British merchants had secured the abolition of the Company's monopoly and had become more vocal in their complaints about restrictions. The Chinese were faced with the great problem of the increasing opium trade. The British attitude had hardened. Britain had now established herself as a great trading nation; she controlled much of India, her national life was becoming industrialized, her merchants had established markets for themselves in nearly every country in the world and had shown unparalleled enterprise and energy in opening up new commercial fields. The old methods of solving disputes between the two countries were becoming no longer acceptable, and since the Chinese would not open diplomatic negotiations or recognize the British government as anything but normally tributary, it followed that any serious incident would easily lead to war. There was no acceptable alternative.

CHAPTER III

THE BIRTH OF THE COLONY

'There can be neither safety nor honour for either government until Her Majesty's flag flies on these coasts in a secure position.'
Captain Charles Elliot, 6 April 1839.

THE underlying causes of the so-called Opium War may be summarized as follows: (1) The British merchants at Canton were dissatisfied with the regulations governing trade and with the arbitrary customs duties and port charges. (2) They generally believed that the Chinese would never alter these regulations and charges except by force. (3) They wanted to abolish the Co-Hong and Canton monopolies and open all China to European trade. (4) The British government wanted to negotiate with the Chinese government for the settlement of all outstanding questions; this assumed an equality between the two governments which the Chinese would not admit. (5) Europeans were treated as barbarians by Chinese officials, with whom direct communication was forbidden. (6) The Chinese adopted a rigid attitude; if the Europeans did not like the conditions, or did not wish to obey Chinese laws, they could return home, because China was self-sufficient and had no need of the products of any other country. (7) The growth of an illegal opium trade carried on in defiance of the Chinese government created a dangerous situation, and the consequent outflow of silver created internal economic difficulties.

War, which might have come in 1834 after the Napier episode, was delayed until 1840 and became associated with the discreditable opium trade.

On the news of the action of Commissioner Lin against the foreign community at Canton, the British government at last took up the cause of the merchants with the intention of securing a settlement of the Canton difficulties. Lord Palmerston, the Foreign Secretary, had pursued a 'correct' policy towards China and continued to do so. He did not wish to force opium on the Chinese people, nor did he question the right of the Chinese government to seize the opium being smuggled into the country. Palmerston set out the views of the British government in a long letter to the 'Minister to the Emperor of China', in which he argued that the opium laws should have been enforced against Chinese and foreigners alike. There would have been no complaint if the Chinese 'after giving notice of its altered intentions' had seized all the opium they could find in Chinese territory, but, instead of doing this, the Chinese 'determined to seize peaceable British merchants instead of seizing the contraband opium' and made the British Superintendent 'the agent for carrying out the laws of China with which he had nothing to do'. The British merchants had been compelled to surrender opium under physical duress, yet the opium did not necessarily belong to them, and Elliot had given it up only 'in order to save the lives of his imprisoned fellow country-men'.

Palmerston summed up his demands as 'satisfaction for the past and security for the future'. The value of the opium 'exacted as ransom for the lives of the imprisoned British merchants' was to be refunded, and he demanded satisfaction for the affront to the British Crown by the imprisonment of its representative, and the payment of the expenses of the expedition. As security for the future he demanded the cession of 'one or more sufficiently large and properly situated islands' where 'British subjects should not again be exposed to violence'.

The cession of an island was not however to be an essential demand. The plenipotentiaries were told that if the Chinese government agreed to a treaty giving security and freedom of commerce to British subjects in China, 'the British government would, in that case, forego the permanent possession of any island'. This was to be a matter of negotiation, and the suggested alternative did not appear in Palmerston's letter to the Chinese. The aim of the war was security for the merchant, either by territorial cession or by a commercial treaty with adequate guarantees. Pending negotiations, the 'one or more islands' were to be occupied, and were to be chosen by the Naval Commander and the Superintendent; they were to be 'conveniently situated for commercial intercourse, not merely with Canton', have good harbours, 'afford natural facilities for defence, and be easily provisioned'.

An expedition was prepared; Captain Charles Elliot and his

cousin, Rear-Admiral George Elliot, were appointed Plenipotentiaries. They were instructed to blockade the Canton
River, occupy the Chusan Islands, from which to blockade the
mouth of the Yangtze, proceed to the Peiho River, and at each
place try to deliver a copy of Palmerston's letter, and to attempt
to open negotiations. War was not declared, and the sending
of the expedition was referred to as 'hostilities'.

The aim of the expedition, then, was not all-out war, but
the use of sufficient force for an effective blockade, which should
induce the Chinese to come to terms. It was June 1840 before
the expedition was ready to leave Macao for the north. Chusan
Island was occupied, and the Peiho River was reached in
August. There, at an interview with Keshen, it was agreed to
resume negotiations at Canton, and the Plenipotentiaries
returned to Macao, arriving in October. Shortly afterwards,
the Admiral retired through ill-health, leaving Commodore
Sir J. J. Gordon Bremer as Senior Naval Officer, and Captain
Charles Elliot as the sole Plenipotentiary, in charge of the
negotiations.

Captain Charles Elliot had come out with Napier in 1834
in a junior post. He had been highly recommended by J. F.
Davis, Napier's successor, and had been Superintendent of Trade
since December 1836. Until the arrival of Lin he had consistently
advised and pursued a policy of conciliation and caution. He
thought the British Trade Commission should not be forced on
the Chinese, nor should a man of high rank and great pretension
be sent out. He judged that the interest of both countries lay
in maintaining cordial trade relations, that the Chinese would
of their own accord recognize and treat with the British on an
official plane, and that, until then, it was better to abide by
the regulations. Accordingly he sent communications through
the Co-Hong headed 'petition', until he was reprimanded by
Palmerston. He was against the opium trade, particularly in
the confined waters of Canton, as a direct provocation of the
Chinese. He had no doubt that the Chinese could be defeated
in war, but the danger was that the whole Chinese political
fabric might crumble. His aim was to limit the use of force to
the Canton area, and to induce the local officials there to accept
new relations on a basis of common interests. In the hostilities,
as before, his policy was still conciliatory.

In the negotiations at Canton, Keshen refused most of the demands, and there followed a period of tortuous negotiation, which early in January 1841 broke down. Elliot moved against Canton and occupied the Bogue forts; a truce was arranged three days later, and after resumed negotiations an agreement was reached, generally referred to as the Convention of Chuenpi. The two men arranged to meet at Chuenpi on 20 January 1841 to sign the agreement, but Keshen raised difficulties, and the final meeting arranged for 12 February did not take place. The Convention in fact was never signed; it was disavowed by each government, and both Keshen and Elliot were recalled.

Elliot had prematurely announced the terms of the settlement on 20 January 1841. Under it, Chusan was to be evacuated; there was to be free access to Canton; Hong Kong Island was to be ceded but Chinese customs charges were to be allowed there as if the trade were at Whampoa. Arrangements were to be made for the mutual rendition of criminals, for drawing up trade regulations, equality between officials, and for compensation for the opium seized.

It was in virtue of this so-called Convention that Hong Kong was occupied on 26 January 1841 by a naval force under Bremer which landed and raised the flag at Possession Point. Almost two and a half years were to elapse before the British government recognized this as the birth of a new colony.

Elliot's conciliatory policy was clearly shown by the terms of the Convention. He took a long-term view and aimed rather at an enduring settlement than at immediate advantages imposed by superior force. He thought the trade would continue to be concentrated in the Canton area, and so did not press for the opening of treaty ports. He chose Hong Kong Island to be the insular trading station because, on his view, it had to be near Canton, and he envisaged a continuation of the Canton trading system with the only difference that the foreign merchants would now live at Hong Kong under the security of the British flag; but he had no desire to deprive the Chinese of their customs revenue. The island station would have the additional advantage of enabling control over the lawless British element which had gathered in the area.

Having failed to get Keshen to sign the agreement, Elliot renewed hostilities, and in March 1841 the Bogue forts were again occupied, and Canton threatened. A truce was again made, to allow the merchant vessels at Whampoa to complete the season's shipment of tea, for Elliot was always anxious that hostilities should not interfere with trade. He continued to attempt negotiation, but on harder terms, and the Chinese proved more unyielding, for Keshen had been removed from the scene and sent to Peking in chains. In May 1841, on the night of the completion of the loading of the last British ship, the Chinese attacked shipping in the Canton area by fire-rafts and the armistice came to an end. The factories were reoccupied, and while preparations were being made to assault the city, the Chinese again asked for terms. Elliot hoped to win Chinese good-will by sparing Canton a military occupation, and much to their disgust, he refused to allow the military to enter. A ransom of six million dollars was imposed; Chinese forces were to be withdrawn from the city and British forces from the Bogue.

Elliot now prepared to carry hostilities to the north, but on 29 July 1841 he received official notice of his recall; such was the efficiency of commercial intelligence that the news of his recall had appeared in the local press five days before.

At home, Palmerston received the news of the Chuenpi agreement with disappointment and disapproval. 'You have disobeyed and neglected your instructions,' he told Elliot. 'You seem to have considered that my instructions were waste paper which you might treat with entire disregard, and that you were at full liberty to deal with the interests of your country according to your own fancy.' The Foreign Secretary accused Elliot of having settled with the Chinese for much less than he had been told to demand, 'without the full employment of that force which was sent to you expressly for the purpose of enabling you to use compulsion, if persuasion should fail.' 'I cannot understand why you omitted to employ that force for the very purpose for which it was sent,' Palmerston complained.

He was not impressed by the cession of Hong Kong, 'a barren island with hardly a house upon it', and clogged by conditions which made it doubtful if it was a cession in full sovereignty. Palmerston did not believe that Hong Kong would become the mart of trade, any more than Macao had, and thought that trading conditions would be little altered. The merchants would continue to trade at Canton and be at the mercy of the Chinese;

the only change was that now they could retire to Hong Kong instead of Macao for the summer months. The proclamation declaring Hong Kong annexed to the British Crown was 'entirely premature', since no formal treaty had been signed, and in any case, even if a treaty had been signed, no formal cession could take place until ratified by the Chinese Emperor. Elliot was recalled, and replaced by Sir Henry Pottinger. Perhaps it may be said of Elliot that his methods and policy might have put relations with China on a better permanent footing than was ultimately to be the case, and the legacy of Chinese hostility to the West avoided.

But the hostilities entered a new phase in which the future of Hong Kong lay in the balance.

CHAPTER IV

UNWILLING RECOGNITION

'A secure and well-regulated trade is all we desire; and you will constantly bear in mind that we seek for no exclusive advantages, and demand nothing we shall not willingly see enjoyed by the subjects of all other states.'
Lord Aberdeen to Sir Henry Pottinger, 4 November 1841.

POTTINGER had been sent out to secure the full British demands. In his instructions Palmerston dealt with the question of an island station off the China coast in more explicit terms. He said that 'four or five principal commercial towns' were to be made accessible to British trade, and for this to be effectual, either British subjects and British consuls should be allowed to reside there, or alternatively some island 'on the East coast' should be ceded, but with the important stipulation 'that free commercial intercourse should be permitted between that island and the towns on the mainland'. Pottinger was told not to give up the island of Hong Kong unless it could be exchanged for another island near Canton 'better adapted' for the purposes in view, and he was to examine the suitability of Hong Kong. Palmerston added that since Hong Kong could not for a great length of time afford any new facilities for trading with the

C

northern ports, its possession did not supersede the necessity of
either securing another insular station on the east coast, or of
securing for British subjects permission to reside in the ports
to be opened. In other words, Hong Kong was not the insular
station Palmerston was looking for. He did not object to the
arrangement which he understood Elliot had made, by which
trade at Hong Kong should be liable to Chinese customs duties,
after paying which, merchandise could be freely exported to
any Chinese port; he thought it would be anomalous to have
Chinese customs officers on British soil, yet he said there were
precedents in some European countries for such an arrangement
and it might check exorbitant and illegal duties; but all
arrangements must be included in the treaty. Writing five
weeks later, on 5 June 1841, Palmerston stated more definitely
that the island of Hong Kong ought to be retained.

Sir Henry Pottinger arrived at Macao on 10 August 1841.
He had returned home the previous year after an exciting and
notable career in India, and the calculation that he would pursue
the British demands more energetically proved well founded.
With a decisiveness much to the liking of the military and naval
officers, he set out for the North within ten days of his arrival,
and in just over twelve months he brought the hostilities to a
successful conclusion. The campaign need be noticed only very
briefly here. Admiral Sir William Parker, who had gone out
with Pottinger, was in command, with General Sir Hugh Gough
in charge of a military force, numbering 2,500 men. Amoy was
taken; on 1 October Tinghai fell, and Chusan Island was once
more in British hands; shortly after, the capture of Chinhai
and Ningpo brought the season's campaign to a close, and in
December, Pottinger returned to Macao.

In the spring of 1842 news arrived of the fall of the Whig
government in Britain. Peel's new Tory administration, with
Lord Aberdeen as Foreign Secretary, maintained the general
British demands in China and decided to make all preparations
'to carry on the ensuing campaign with vigour and effect'.
Aberdeen's instructions to Pottinger contained some important
modifications, by which the latter was to have more discretionary power in negotiation. The most important change
was in the matter of securing an island station. Aberdeen laid
it down that acquisitions of territory made in the course of the

war, 'were not to be regarded in the light of a permanent conquest'; the government's aim was commercial intercourse, secured by means of a treaty, which would open four or five additional ports in which British consuls could be stationed. The demand for an island station, as an alternative to the opening of more ports, under safeguards, was now dropped. Aberdeen regarded such islands as had been seized as useful military bases, and as pawns in negotiations, but did not intend that they should be retained. He argued that they would be expensive, and the amount of commercial benefit to be derived from them would be doubtful if they were retained against the wish of the Chinese government, and that there was the danger that Britain might be drawn into Chinese politics.

Before these amended instructions arrived, Pottinger had become convinced that Hong Kong ought to be retained. He was impressed by its growth, and in March 1842 moved the headquarters of the Superintendency of Trade there from Macao, at the same time declaring it a free port. The belief that the occupation was to be permanent was thus given some official encouragement, despite the fact that the home government had not yet declared British sovereignty over the island.

When Aberdeen's new instructions did arrive, Pottinger wrote home that 'this settlement has already advanced too far to admit of its being restored to the authority of the Emperor consistently with the honour . . . of Her Majesty's Crown'. In accordance with his revised instructions, he forbade all further building and grants of land, but there can be little doubt that he returned to the North in June 1842 for the resumption of negotiations with a strong feeling in favour of retaining the island.

The campaign had been renewed in March 1842 by the repulse of a Chinese attack on Ningpo. The Woosung Forts at the mouth of the Yangtze were taken in June, and Shanghai was occupied; the fleet proceeded up the river, and after seizing Chinkiang and blockading the Grand Canal, arrived at Nanking early in August. Pottinger was adamant in refusing all compromise. 'The basis on which alone peace between the two countries can be negotiated, has been too repeatedly notified by Her Majesty's Plenipotentiary to be misunderstood, and it remains unchanged,' the Chinese were told, and he prepared to attack Nanking. To save the city, the Chinese accepted his terms and on 29 August 1842 the hostilities were concluded by the Treaty of Nanking.

The treaty was not a full settlement of the differences between the two countries, and much was left for further discussion. Each side was eager not to delay the treaty by prolonged negotiation; the British feared being drawn into an all-out war with China, and the Chinese were willing to free the river from the invader on almost any terms. The terms of the Treaty of Nanking may be briefly summarized. China agreed to pay twenty-one million dollars as compensation for the opium destroyed for the Co-Hong debts and for the expenses of the expedition. The Canton monopoly was broken by the opening of four additional ports, Amoy, Foochow, Ningpo and Shanghai, at which British subjects and British consuls could reside. An agreed tariff was to be arranged, there was to be mutual release of prisoners, and the recognition of diplomatic equality between the two countries.

The treaty also provided for the cession in perpetuity of the island of Hong Kong, on the ground that it was necessary for the British to have 'a port whereat they may careen and refit their ships'. In securing Hong Kong, Pottinger exceeded his instructions. He had secured both the opening of treaty ports and the cession of an island. In defence of his action he later wrote, '. . . the retention of Hong Kong is the only single point in which I intentionally exceeded my modified instructions, but every single hour I have passed in this superb country has convinced me of the necessity and desirability of our possessing such a settlement as an emporium for our trade and a place from which Her Majesty's subjects in China may be alike protected and controlled.'

The news of the treaty was received at home with great satisfaction, but the government viewed the cession of Hong Kong without enthusiasm, and maintained its correct attitude by refusing to make any pronouncement or to set up any definitive administration until assured that the Peking government accepted the cession. Ratifications of the treaty were exchanged in Hong Kong on 26 June 1843, and only then was the island declared a British colony with Sir Henry Pottinger as its first Governor.

This hesitation in assuming colonial responsibilities in China was typical of the early Victorian era. The mercantilist ideas underlying colonization in the seventeenth and eighteenth centuries had been discredited by the loss of the American colonies; the new free trade theories were making the old mercantilist conceptions of trade protection outmoded. The free traders tended to be anti-colonial because, theoretically at least, there was little room for preferential tariffs and other forms of colonial trade protection within the free trade system. Thus the men who were successful in destroying the East India Company's monopoly in Canton were of the new industrial age; they were chiefly interested in a commercial empire, not a territorial one, to be built by the unrestricted enterprise of merchants, not by the state. If the flag was raised, as at Hong Kong, it was to give the merchant the security he needed. In the event, as so often in the history of British overseas expansion, it was not the home government, but the man on the spot who raised the flag.

The Treaty of Nanking had left much still to be settled. On the British side, the clear assumption was that having secured diplomatic recognition on a basis of equality, all outstanding questions could be the subject of future negotiation. Opium, exterritoriality, the position of other Europeans, the tariff, inland transit duties, trade regulations, were important issues that were left over to be decided. There was also the question of Hong Kong's relations with the Chinese mainland.

These points were dealt with by the Supplementary Treaty of the Bogue, signed at Hu Men Chai, on 8 October 1843. A tariff of customs duties which the Chinese government was allowed to charge on British goods was agreed to, and commercial regulations dealing with such subjects as shipping and trade in the open ports, the functions of the consuls, and the settlement of commercial disputes were drawn up; and this tariff and the regulations were embodied in the Supplementary Treaty. This also dealt with exterritoriality, conditions of residence in the open ports, and the mutual handing over of fugitive criminals. On the opium question, the treaty was silent; the British government refused to negotiate officially on this, on the ground that as long as the import of opium was prohibited, it was purely a domestic matter to make that prohibition effective.

Commercial relations between Hong Kong and the mainland were carefully regulated and restricted, much to the annoyance of the British merchants. Palmerston had clearly seen the problem that if an island were ceded, it could never become a great emporium of trade unless unrestricted commercial intercourse with the mainland were provided for, and he had envisaged an arrangement by which Chinese customs duties having been paid at Hong Kong, goods could be freely sent to any port in China. The Chinese demanded, not unnaturally, that all foreign trade should be confined to the five open ports in accordance with the Treaty of Nanking. By the Treaty of the Bogue, Hong Kong was to be open to trade from the five Chinese open ports on payment of the customs duties and on obtaining a customs clearance from the ports. All natives of China wishing to come to Hong Kong to make purchases of goods were to have free and full permission to come, but any Chinese vessel used for carrying away purchases must have a pass or port clearance from the Chinese port from which she might sail. An English officer was to be appointed at Hong Kong to examine all Chinese vessels, and any such vessel without a pass was to be regarded as a smuggler and debarred from trade. Provision was made for information on all Chinese ships and cargoes leaving the five open ports to be sent to Canton, and the English officer at Hong Kong was to make a similar return to Canton of all arrivals and departures of Chinese vessels at Hong Kong together with the nature of their cargoes. An 'additional article' contained a concession to British small craft such as schooners and lorchas which had been accustomed to plying between Canton and Hong Kong and Macao. On entering Whampoa, they were, if under 150 tons, to pay tonnage dues of one mace per ton, instead of the five mace laid down for British shipping. This arrangement was confined to Canton, since the other four open ports 'had none of this intercourse'. To these arrangements was added a declaration against smuggling.

The effect of these stipulations of the Treaty of the Bogue was, in the absence of any treaty limitation of Chinese discretion in the issue of passes and port clearances, to hand over complete control of all native shipping visiting Hong Kong to the Chinese, and even to use a British officer to assist in making that control effective.

1. Conference at Chusan, 1840.
(Chromo-lithograph by Sir H. Darell from *The Chater Collection*, by James Orange. Thornton Butterworth.)

2. Signing the Treaty at Nanking, 1842.
(Engraving by Captain John Platt from *The Chater Collection* by James Orange. Thornton Butterworth.)

3. North-east view of Victoria.

(Aquatint by J. Prendergast from *The Chater Collection* by James Orange. Thornton Butterworth.)

4. View of Jardine Matheson's looking north-west from Causeway Bay.

(By M. Bruce, from the private collection of J. R. Jones, Esq.)

There was a great outcry in the colony against these arrangements. The British merchants argued that they directly contra-
vened the freedom of the port which Pottinger himself had
proclaimed; Pottinger was strongly attacked for betraying the
interests of the colony, and his popularity vanished.

Unfortunately, a version of the treaty had been published in
which these restrictive clauses did not appear, and the Hong
Kong merchants had learnt of them from the Chinese version.
This led to an accusation that Pottinger had been duped by
the Manchu Kiying, who had been the chief negotiator on
behalf of China and who, it was alleged, had had these articles
inserted in the treaty without Pottinger's knowledge. Pottinger
later explained that his published version was not intended to
be complete. The whole incident is a little obscure. The British
merchants wanted the junk trade to be uncontrolled, and thus
in effect to give the Hong Kong junk trade access to all Chinese
ports; this would have successfully by-passed the open port
system as arranged for in the Treaty of Nanking. Pottinger
acted in accordance with the treaty, but he was blamed at home
and in the colony for having achieved an island trading station
and yet failed to protect its trade by adequate treaty concessions. Opposition to this interference with the freedom of the
port was so strong that on the British side the restrictive clauses
of the Treaty of the Bogue were abandoned, and no British
officer was ever appointed to examine junk passes and clearances
from Chinese ports or to make returns to Canton.

The relations between the colony and the mainland were
left in this unsatisfactory state, to the detriment of legal trade.

CHAPTER V

THE EARLY YEARS OF THE SETTLEMENT, JANUARY 1841 TO JUNE 1843

'A barren island with hardly a house upon it.'
Lord Palmerston, 21 April 1841.

FROM 26 January 1841, the day on which Sir Gordon Bremer,
the Naval Commodore, had proclaimed British sovereignty over
Hong Kong, difficulties arose in the effective occupation of the

island, some of which have already been described. The renewal of hostilities against China, the refusal of Palmerston to accept the Convention in virtue of which the occupation had been effected, the refusal of Lord Aberdeen to countenance any permanent cession of Chinese territory, made it difficult to guess the future of the island. There was little doubt about the outcome of the war, but for two and a half years, until 26 June 1843, when it was formally declared a British colony following the ratification of the Treaty of Nanking, there was great doubt about its future as an island station. In the absence of a regular colonial government, makeshift expedients and temporary measures inevitably led to administrative chaos and uncertainty; under these conditions the growth of the settlement could not be systematically fostered.

In announcing the terms of the Chuenpi agreement to the British at Macao on 20 January 1841, Elliot admitted that the 'details remain a matter of negotiations', and paid tribute to Keshen, 'the very eminent person with whom negotiations are still pending'. He thought there was no doubt that the main terms of the settlement, including the cession of Hong Kong, had been accepted and he and many others thought the war was over; Captain Belcher of H.M.S. *Sulphur*, after completing the first survey of the island, wrote, 'the Commodore had released me, in the full belief that the war in China was at an end,' and prepared to sail home.

After his formal declaration of British sovereignty over Hong Kong on 26 January 1841, Elliot began to arrange for its administration. A proclamation dated 29 January 1841 vested the government of the island in the Chief Superintendent of Trade. All natives of the island and all natives of China resorting thereto, were to be governed according to the laws of China, 'every description of torture excepted'. All British subjects and foreigners were to be given full security and protection according to British law. A further proclamation by Bremer and Elliot, dated 1 February 1841, announced that the island had become part of the dominions of the Queen 'by clear public agreement between the high officers of the Celestial and British Courts'. The inhabitants to whom it was addressed were promised protection against all enemies, and 'further secured in the free exercise of their religious rites, ceremonies and social customs. . . . They will be governed, pending Her Majesty's further pleasure, according to the laws customs and usages of the Chinese . . . by the Elders of Villages, subject to the control of a British magistrate; and any person having complaint to prefer of ill-usage or injustice against any Englishman or foreigner, will quickly make report to the nearest officer, to the end that full justice may be done.' All Chinese trade was to be exempted from any charge or duty of any kind to the British government; and all heads of villages were to be held responsible that the commands of the government were observed.

These proclamations gave a clear invitation to Chinese and foreign merchants to regard the island as the centre of the trade, and showed that from the first Elliot intended it to become a permanent trading station. In the next month, February 1841, foreign merchants began visiting Hong Kong with a view to setting up their establishments there, but they generally played safe by arranging to maintain houses in Macao or Canton also. In addition, Elliot had expressly declared in the notification of 20 January 1841 at Macao, that the British government wanted no exclusive privileges in China, and that protection would be given to the subjects, citizens and ships of all foreign powers that may resort to Hong Kong. With these blandishments, therefore, the settlement began to grow, in spite of the break-down of the agreement with Keshen. Elliot further encouraged its growth by declaring in a proclamation dated 7 June 1841, that all traders and merchants would be able to resort to and trade at the port of Hong Kong freely; that no duties would be levied on trade at the port, and that an embargo on Canton and other large Chinese ports would be put into operation if there was any obstruction to its freedom.

By April the haphazard building of wooden or matshed structures, sometimes with stone or brick foundations, began, and the question of surveying and marking out allotments of land for buildings and provision for roads and other public works became urgent. Elliot was not able to proceed very far with these arrangements before the agreement with Keshen broke down and hostilities were renewed. The campaign against Canton and the preparations for carrying the war to the north took up much of his attention, and also of those military and naval officers who might otherwise have been available to

undertake the organization of the colony. Captain Belcher of
H.M.S. *Sulphur* surveyed the coast and calculated the heights
of the main peaks, and is said to have been responsible for
naming them. A road was planned and early put in hand
following a well-marked track facing the harbour along the
northern shore; it was named Queen's Road and became the
main thoroughfare of the settlement.

The disposal of land was the main problem. Sites were being
appropriated and buildings begun without reference to any
authority, and land was being sold by Chinese inhabitants
without a proper enquiry into the title by the purchasers. The
security of the British flag was not the only attraction. Many
merchants wanted land for building, but many saw that if Hong
Kong became a British colony, land would become valuable,
and there was competition to get good sites partly as a speculation. Some control was necessary to bring order into this
situation to ensure that land would be available for public
needs, and to safeguard future development. In May 1841 the
principles of land disposal were announced. Allotments were
to be made at public auctions to the highest bidders for the
payment of an annual rent, this rent being the subject of the
bidding. Elliot safeguarded the rights of the Crown, but promised that land holders would be allowed to purchase their
allotments in freehold if the home government agreed; and
purchasers of town lots could buy suburban or country lots
with choice of site. The first land sales were announced to take
place on 12 June: 'the dimensions of the respective lots will be
specified and defined on the spot by the commanding officer
of Engineers to whom the parties are referred for further particulars'. Buildings of a certain minimum value fixed at $1,000
had to be built on the plots, within a time limit, and a deposit
of $500 had to be made, the rate being fixed at 4s. 4d. to the
dollar. It was intended to offer one hundred marine lots facing
Queen's Road on the seaward side, and one hundred suburban
lots the opposite side of the road. There were difficulties in
getting the plots surveyed, and although the sale was postponed
two days to 14 June, only fifty marine lots were then ready for
sale, each having one hundred feet frontage along Queen's
Road, and varying in depth to the shore according to the shape
of the coastline. Elliot also warned all those who had already

begun buildings that all sales of land had to be made through an officer of the government, and all native inhabitants claiming land would be required to prove their claims.

In the event, competition for the limited number of lots available was keen, and prices varied from £20 to £265 a lot according to depth to the sea. But Elliot had been too eager to get the merchants to begin to reside in the island; the proceedings were hurried and the lots were later found to have been inaccurately surveyed and marked out, and this was to be a source of dissension and difficulty later. Soon after the first sales, Elliot wrote to the two principal merchants, Jardine and Dent, saying that he would urge the home government to allow the land to pass to the purchasers outright on payment of one or two years' purchase, or else at a nominal quit rent, and asked them to circulate his letter to those interested. He was no doubt anxious to encourage the merchant firms to come, but he led them to think they were getting grants of land on much more favourable terms than he had authority to offer. The home government later refused to concede these terms, causing much discontent since the purchasers alleged that Elliot's promises had been dishonoured.

The main result of the land sales was to create the impression of permanency, and to attract people to the island; for it must be remembered that it was against a background of alternate war and negotiation that the merchants had to make up their minds in the summer of 1841, whether to move to Hong Kong or not. The beginnings of a colonial government were made. Elliot himself took responsibility as Superintendent of Trade, and on 30 April 1841 he made his first appointment; Captain William Caine, of the 26th Regiment of Infantry, was selected to be magistrate, with wide judicial authority, but limited powers of punishment, mainly directed to maintaining the peace. Those accused of more serious crimes were to be reported to the head of the government; all non-Chinese were to be tried according to English law; the magistrate's jurisdiction over Chinese was to be in accordance with Chinese law, usage and custom, and his power to punish Chinese was limited to $400 fine, three months' imprisonment or a flogging of 100 lashes; criminals meriting greater punishment were to be handed over to Elliot. Caine also became superintendent of the jail which was subsequently built.

On 22 June, as Elliot prepared to go north with the expedition, he arranged for A. R. Johnston, the Deputy-Superintendent of Trade, to be left in charge of the colony; other appointments made at this time were Lt. W. Pedder, R.N., of the steamer *Nemesis*, as harbour-master and marine magistrate, his assistant called Lena, and J. R. Bird as clerk of works with the task of organizing a public works department. The military established themselves at Sai Ying Pun, West Point, and also in the central district, on the east side of a nullah (now Garden Road). These civil officials and the military occupied rough matsheds until more permanent buildings could be erected.

Disasters very early attacked the infant colony. The preparation of sites led to a severe epidemic of fever and considerable mortality; a cemetery became necessary, for which a piece of ground, just to the east of the central military area, had to be made available. On 21 July, a violent typhoon flattened all the insubstantial housing and damaged shipping; a second less severe visitation struck the colony four days later. In this typhoon, Elliot and Bremer were caught on their way to Hong Kong from Macao in the cutter *Louisa*. Elliot assumed control of the ship and showed great seamanship in beaching it on an island, where it was completely wrecked. There was a price of 100,000 dollars on Elliot's head, but he managed to induce a Chinese to take him back to Macao for 3,000, fortunate to be alive. Then on 12 August a fire consumed the makeshift huts of Chinese artisans and labourers who had been attracted to the island in increasing numbers.

With the arrival of Sir Henry Pottinger on 10 August 1841 came the news of the recall of Elliot and the disavowal of his policy. The attitude of the home government produced uncertainty as to the future of the island.

Pottinger issued a notification two days after his arrival saying that the arrangements which Elliot had made regarding Hong Kong should remain in force until Her Majesty's pleasure regarding that island should be received. The result was that Johnston remained in charge and the other official appointments already made were allowed to continue. The new Plenipotentiary regarded the successful prosecution of the war as the main task and thought the question of Hong Kong could very well wait. He arrived in the harbour in the steamer *Queen* on the afternoon of 20 August, on his way to the north, landed, and came ashore again the following morning. He appeared to be impressed with the progress of the settlement, but it was a cursory visit of less than twenty-four hours, during much of which he was occupied with plans for the campaign. He left behind orders forbidding any further allotments of land and halting all further development pending a decision on the island's future, and agreed only to the continuance of work of military importance. He ordered the evacuation of Kowloon by British troops, and the guns there to be moved to Kellett Island in the harbour; he agreed to a military road to Tai Tam, and to the building of barracks.

A. R. Johnston, either from a misunderstanding or because he was unable to resist the pressure of the merchants, continued to act on the assumption that the colony was permanent. In October 1841 he announced that 'it is now found desirable that persons applying for lots of land for the purpose of building upon, should be at once accommodated upon terms which will be made known to them by application in person to the land officer', a Captain G. F. Mylius, who had been appointed just before Elliot had left. A fairly comprehensive scheme was adopted of classifying sites at appropriate prices into marine, town, and suburban, and a notification was made in November 1841 that purchasers of lots who failed to abide by the conditions would forfeit their deposits as well as their allotments. Marine lots were defined as those within a maximum distance of two hundred feet from high water; town lots as certain specified areas in Hong Kong, Wong Nei Chong (Happy Valley), Chek Chu (Stanley) and Chek Pai Wan (Aberdeen); suburban lots were all the rest. In addition some areas were marked out as bazaars to serve the Chinese population.

Pottinger received the news of these additional sales with disapproval, and told Johnston that he had entirely exceeded his authority and had acted in direct opposition to his orders that all was to remain precisely as it was until instructions had been received from home. He again explicitly forbade further sales of land without his express sanction. Pottinger had agreed to some military works, but other than this his policy was that the arrangements of Elliot should be unchanged until the wishes of the home government were known. 'I have no personal predilection in its favour,' he wrote in November from the north, 'but I must provide for immediate tranquillity and good government for all persons genuinely residing in the settlement.' Whether Johnston misunderstood the position or not is difficult to say. He behaved as if he were the governor and corresponded directly with the Governor-General of India until Pottinger sent him orders to cease. In November 1841 he sent Pottinger a long account of progress already made. He reported that the road (soon to be named Queen's Road) was good from Cantonment Hill Barracks to the Bazaar, but between there and the West Barracks it was as it had been left by the Engineers. The prison was completed, the Magistracy nearly so, and a 'Record Office' was in rapid progress for the Land Officer. A bridle path had been cut up the hill towards Chek Pai Wan (Aberdeen) and wooden barracks were being built at Stanley. Houses were being erected in the Chinese areas so rapidly that some regulations had become necessary. Streets twenty feet broad were laid out, straight and regular (as they still are in that area), buildings were to be at least five feet from the edge of the street with permission to have a veranda; each Chinese occupier was to have one vote for the election of the three commissioners or headmen, who were to make regulations for the good conduct of the bazaar.

In December 1841 Pottinger returned to the south, but it was not until February that he was able to give the island his attention. He discovered that much progress in the creation of a settlement had been made during the six months he had been away; Queen's Road had been completed, more houses and a government 'Record Office' built, and, more particularly, there were now over 12,000 Chinese living on the island, mostly workers attracted by the employment available and shopkeepers to attend to their needs.

Pottinger's instructions to Johnston had not been free from ambiguity, and Johnston's explanations were accepted by Pottinger on the ground that Johnston was best fitted to judge what it had been necessary to do to deal with the influx of Chinese and provide for immediate tranquillity. In March Pottinger himself took two decisive steps. He declared Hong

Kong and Chusan to be free ports, open to all ships without discrimination, and announced that 'in the improbable event' of the troops being withdrawn, merchants would be given time 'to remove their goods and adjust their accounts'. This was the first open indication that he thought Hong Kong should be retained. Later in the month, as already mentioned (see page 21) he took the important step of removing the headquarters of the Superintendent of Trade from Macao to Hong Kong.

In spite of his criticism of Johnston, Pottinger found himself obliged to continue to make some grants of land to the leading officials, to religious organizations and to educational bodies. He also had to mark out new locations to provide for the influx of Chinese who were anxious to settle. He reserved much more formally and explicitly the rights of the Crown, including the principle that all land in Hong Kong was vested in the Queen.

He set up a land committee to deal with all private claims to land and with that required for public purposes; and issued a general warning against unauthorized purchases, encroachments, and illicit reclamations of the foreshore. No sales of land were to be valid without the knowledge of the land officer and they had to be registered by him. An Anglican Church was suggested and Pottinger agreed to a subscription list being circulated for its building, and promised government assistance. An assistant land officer, E. G. Reynolds, was appointed to help with the increased work. Pottinger dealt with the currency and fixed the parities at two and a half Company rupees to the dollar, both being made equivalent to twelve hundred Chinese copper cash. It is true that Pottinger made no further grants of land to the merchant firms or to private individuals outside the government, and defended what grants he made on the ground of absolute necessity, but it is evident that he was acting in the belief that the occupation of the island was to be permanent.

In May 1842 he received the home government's disapproval of the offices of Land Officer, Surveyor and Colonial Surgeon, and these appointments ceased from 31 May. In May, he also received the new instructions from Lord Aberdeen refusing to countenance any cessions of territory at the expense of China. In acknowledging the receipt of these instructions, he said that the only step taken that could have been avoided was the removal of the Superintendency of Trade from Macao to the island. He defended this by saying: 'but I may declare that even that was forced on me by the extraordinary and unparalleled progress which this settlement had made.' He added: 'I had no predilection for raising a colony at Hong Kong or at any other place in China,' but it was impossible to set aside Elliot's work, and he urged, 'this settlement has already advanced too far to admit of its ever being restored to the authority of the Emperor.' On the receipt of the new instructions, Johnston was asked for a full explanation of his motives in granting lands, and Pottinger had replied, 'I am also aware of the difficulties you had to contend with, and well satisfied with your motives for acting as you did.'

Pottinger instructed Johnston to make no further grants of land 'on any pretence', to make no new appointments, and to undertake no further public works except barracks and any roads or bridges already begun. Reynolds became land and roads inspector with the duty of preventing encroachments, and with that, Pottinger left for the north in the second week in June. A few weeks later, after the Treaty of Nanking, he wrote to Johnston that the cession of Hong Kong, which had been arranged, would make land in the island much more valuable, and he was to 'decline to listen to any applications for allotments'.

It has already been shown that Pottinger was faced with much negotiation after the Treaty of Nanking, which occupied him until the Treaty of the Bogue in October 1843. In addition he now had the task of organizing the new colony of Hong Kong, to which he returned in December 1842.

The cession was accepted by the home government in spite of its declared opposition to any acquisitions of territory, and the Colonial Office was now brought in to advise on the organization of the new colony. The ratifications of the treaty were exchanged at Hong Kong on 26 June 1843, during a ceremonial visit by Kiying, and on the same day Hong Kong with its dependencies was declared a British colony, with Sir Henry Pottinger as its first Governor.

CHAPTER VI

BLUE PRINT FOR A NEW COLONY

'It follows that methods of proceeding unknown in other British Colonies must be followed at Hong Kong.'
Lord Stanley to Sir Henry Pottinger, 3 June 1843.

It now remains in this chapter to give an account of the shaping of the Hong Kong government and of the problems that were involved, and to review the part played by Sir Henry Pottinger during the short period in which he remained in charge of the affairs of the colony as its first Governor, until his departure in May 1844.

The island was not declared a British colony until 26 June 1843, and until then, the Foreign Office in London was in control. The officials of the Colonial Office, at that time under the Secretary of State for War and the Colonies, were called in to advise on its establishment as a colony, but Pottinger could not communicate with them direct until he became Governor in name as well as in fact. In the next place, the intention was to make the island the British administrative, military and commercial centre in the Far East. Organizing the colony and organizing the China trade were seen as two sides of the same problem. Hong Kong was not to be a colony in the usual sense, but a 'factory' similar to the old establishments of the East India Company in India. From the outset, therefore, it was decided that the man who controlled the trade relations with China should control the colony. The three offices of Plenipotentiary and Minister Extraordinary, Chief Superintendent of the Trade, and Governor of Hong Kong were to be held by one person, the first two remaining under the Foreign Office, and the third being placed under the Colonial Office. The Governor of the colony therefore had to serve two masters and continued to do so until 1859.

The immediate problem was to make temporary arrangements for the administration of the island until a more permanent constitution could be created, and this was done in a series of nine instruments comprising dispatches, orders and

D

commissions, all dated 4 January 1843. In these the principle was laid down that the offices of Superintendent of Trade and the Governor of Hong Kong were to be held by the same person; they made provision for the government of the island until it could be declared a British colony, for possible vacancies in the governorship, and for meeting its expenses from the proceeds of the indemnity demanded from China. They also established a law court for British offenders in Hong Kong and China, of which the Superintendent was to be the judge, and dealt with the claims of holders of land allotted before the cession was recognized. If the Emperor should fail to ratify the treaty or should recede from his engagements, Hong Kong was to be retained, but in that case its proclamation as a British colony was to be issued in an amended form. The Governor was instructed to correspond with Lord Stanley, Secretary of State for War and the Colonies, on all matters affecting the administration of the island, and with Lord Aberdeen, Foreign Secretary, on those affecting trade and relations with China. He was given much advice on the opium question, the status of Hong Kong as a free port was agreed to, but Pottinger was told 'not to allow any exaggerated expectations to be founded on that term', and to give no undertaking not to levy customs on articles for internal consumption in order to safeguard possible revenue. If the Chinese attempted to fortify Kowloon from which to threaten Hong Kong, they were to be told that such an action would 'have a tendency to interrupt the good understanding which it is so much the interest of both countries to maintain'. The naval and military commanders were to be guided by him in the disposition of their forces. It was decided not to place Hong Kong under the control of the British authorities in India, but the Governor-General there was to be kept informed.

On two matters Pottinger was asked to report in fullest detail and with 'the utmost unreserve'. One was the constitution, especially the powers of the Governor and the mode of appointment of the Legislative Council. The other was the judicial establishment, and particularly the framing of laws and police regulations so as to satisfy the requirements of the British and yet 'best conciliate the respect and fall in with the manners of Her Majesty's Chinese subjects'.

The virtual merging of the offices of Superintendent of Trade and Governor of the colony was opposed by the Colonial Office. Sir James Stephen, Permanent Under-Secretary, remarked that it was an assumption 'which I could not justify by what could appear to myself good reasons, but I have no doubt there are very good reasons for it.' The intention was that Hong Kong should be the administrative centre to which British communities in the open ports, even though they lived on Chinese soil, should be amenable. The general view was that Hong Kong would develop into the great emporium of English trade in the Far East, and no one foresaw the spectacular growth of Shanghai.

The constitution for the colony was laid down in the so-called Hong Kong 'Charter' of 5 April 1843; it was read publicly on 26 June 1843, following the proclamation of the island as a British colony after the exchange of ratifications of the Treaty of Nanking. It erected the island 'and its dependencies' into the separate colony of Hong Kong; the Governor, with the advice of the Legislative Council, had power to make laws, for its peace, order and good government, in accordance with instructions and subject to the power of disallowance by the Crown. The Governor, assisted and advised by an Executive Council, was to keep the seal of the colony, make grants of land, make temporary appointments and suspend public officers until Her Majesty's pleasure should be made known. He was empowered to exercise the royal prerogative of pardon of convicted criminals, and also had a limited temporary power of remission or suspension of fines. In case of absence or other inability to carry out his duties, authority devolved on the Lieutenant-Governor, or if no Lieutenant-Governor had been appointed, then on the person holding the office of Colonial Secretary.

Sir Henry Pottinger was given additional guidance on the working of the constitution and on general administration, in his instructions from Lord Stanley, dated 6 April 1843. He was told in regard to the powers of the Legislative Council, that 'in the very peculiar circumstances of Hong Kong, H.M. Government have thought it right to confer upon you the extra-ordinary power of passing laws independently of their assent should the necessity for such a proceeding arise.' In such a case the members of the Council had the right to send home their reasons for dissent. Further instructions of 3 June 1843 provided more detailed guidance. The island was occupied 'not with a view of colonisation, but for diplomatic, military and commercial purposes.' Since the Governor had three separate functions: (1) To negotiate with the Emperor, (2) To super-intend the trade of British subjects in China and (3) To regulate the internal economy of the settlement, 'it follows that methods of proceeding unknown in other British Colonies must be followed at Hong Kong'. The doctrine of repugnancy, by which a British Colonial legislature was normally forbidden to pass any law contrary to British law, was not to be applied strictly to Hong Kong, where special legislation repugnant to British laws might prove necessary. The Legislature was to have power to pass ordinances covering a wide variety of subjects such as administration of the criminal law, police, gaols, land and transfers of land, including the authority to vote taxes. It could create other governmental agencies, such as a supreme court; an Order in Council had earlier been passed setting up a law court, but it was now felt preferable, on the recommenda-tion of Sir James Stephen, that this should be created by the local legislature.

The two Councils were deliberately kept small, not more than three each in number besides the Governor, and in practice confined to men holding high official positions, familiar with the day-to-day problems of government, and in close personal con-tact with the Governor; in this way, the Governor was enabled more easily to maintain his personal influence. No elective element was included for the same reason. Members were to be chosen by the Governor, but the actual appointment rested with the home government, and they held office during the Queen's pleasure. Some form of municipal self-government seems to have been intended from the start; Pottinger had been informed that he should levy rates on town property for muni-cipal and police purposes, 'confiding to the house-holders the power and the obligation to assess themselves and each other'.

The instructions provided that Chinese in Hong Kong should be subject to Chinese law, in these terms: '. . . in Hong Kong it will be necessary that for the government of the Chinese residing there, the laws and customs of China should supersede the laws and customs of England,' except where a Chinese law was 'repugnant to those immutable principles of morality which Christians must regard as binding on themselves at all times and in all places. . . .' No English person was to be subject to Chinese law or called before a Chinese court. Property and succession to property were to be in accordance with English law.

Regarding finance, 'an annual plan' or budget of expenditure and ways and means of meeting it were to be laid before the Legislative Council and published for all to see. The principle was stated that 'H.M. Government expect that the local revenue will be adequate to defray . . . all the . . . expenses of the government of Hong Kong,' and the necessity 'for a strict observance of an enlightened frugality in every branch . . . of the local government' was pointed out.

The Secretary of State in London was, of course, firmly in control; he issued instructions, laid down general principles, called for information and from time to time gave direct orders on local questions. The Governor was expected to assume the initiative in local legislation, take administrative action, and supply information, but he had always to report his actions for comment and approval from home.

One interesting constitutional problem was that of making the new colony the administrative centre from which British subjects living in the new Treaty ports should be controlled. Up to 1843 the authority of the Superintendent of Trade derived from an act of 1833 and various orders in council made under it. On 4 January 1843, an Order in Council transferred to Hong Kong the law court set up under that act, and on 24 February, the same year, by another Order in Council, British subjects in China were restricted to the five open ports. But to provide legislative authority over British subjects living in China, a new act was passed, giving the Queen-in-Council power to originate laws governing them, and delegating this power to the Superintendent of Trade and the Legislative Council at Hong Kong.

Commenting on this power the Foreign Secretary, Lord Aberdeen, pointed out the difficulty of operating laws in a foreign country where they could not be enforced by officers of the Crown, but he thought that there would always be some respect for law; and some laws would be willingly accepted, or accepted because breach of the law might result in civil actions, but all problems could not be solved, and only the hazard of leaving British subjects uncontrolled justified such an innovation and anomaly. 'The trust is of a very peculiar and critical nature,' he said, but the risks could be avoided by the 'care which you will constantly employ to promulgate no law which could give any just or plausible ground of offence to the Chinese authorities.' Pottinger was to be guided by the laws he made for the colony, but the two sets of ordinances were to be kept separate, and reported to different Secretaries of State; the one to be promulgated by the Governor of Hong Kong, the other by the Superintendent of Trade. Hong Kong Justices of the Peace were given authority by their Commissions over all British subjects in China as well as in the colony.

A second constitutional problem concerned the application of Chinese law and custom to the Chinese living in the colony. Elliot had promised that the Chinese would be governed in accordance with their own laws and usages, and Pottinger had agreed to this in principle during the negotiations that followed the Treaty of Nanking. He reported in October 1842 that the Chinese plenipotentiaries had shown great anxiety in the matter of jurisdiction over the Chinese at Hong Kong. They always referred to Hong Kong as given to the British 'as a place of residence', and had demanded the principle that Chinese should be tried by Chinese and English by English. In January 1843 Pottinger reported to Aberdeen that he had agreed that Hong Kong Chinese 'should be governed by their own laws, and Mandarins were to be stationed at Kowloong for that purpose,' but that the British must retain police control over the colony, a concession which caused some consternation at home before it was discovered that 'Kowloong' was not on the island, but in Chinese territory across the harbour. But the Colonial Office criticized the concession, on the ground that it required parliamentary action to implement it, that the Chinese government would claim that Hong Kong had been transferred 'in occupancy and not in sovereignty', and that no distinction had been made between permanent residents and Chinese visitors. The Foreign Office replied that since British were wholly exempt from Chinese courts, it was difficult to resist the Chinese claim, and suggested that a Chinese magistrate might reside on the island to dispense Chinese law to Chinese visitors; as for Hong Kong Chinese residents who had become British subjects by the cession, they might be subject to Chinese law, administered in the name of the Queen by one or more judicial authorities to be employed by the Hong Kong government. Sir James Stephen was against any distinction between transient and domiciled Chinese, and thought the question of jurisdiction over the Hong Kong Chinese should be left to the local legislature. The law officers of the Crown advised against any form of jurisdiction in Hong Kong by the Emperor's appointees, and thought that the inhabitants should be 'subject to the English government and to the laws which the Crown of this country think it right to declare'.

After much debate Pottinger was instructed, in April 1843, to treat with the plenipotentiaries on the basis that the Chinese in Hong Kong were to have Chinese law and custom, with a Chinese judge resident in Hong Kong. This was in accord with Colonial Office advice. Meanwhile, and before these instructions arrived, Pottinger seems to have had second thoughts; writing in June 1843 to Aberdeen he enclosed a memorandum to the Chinese plenipotentiaries, Elepo and Kiying, in which he declared that Hong Kong must be subject to British jurisdiction. To this Kiying sent a dignified protest that the principle that Chinese were to be subject to Chinese law had already been agreed to and that Pottinger was changing his ground. He argued that the Chinese unwillingness to obey the laws of England was exactly the same as the refusal of the English to be forcibly ruled by the laws of China. The Colonial Office at home were annoyed at the change. '. . . it seems to me the Chinese High Commissioner has the best of the argument,' Sir James Stephen remarked, and added that it was a Foreign Office matter and Lord Aberdeen should decide. Lord Stanley agreed, and commented, 'I do not see that my intervention would be productive of anything but confusion.' There the matter rested. It was agreed that Chinese should be subject to Chinese law, but it was left to the Legislative Council to make the arrangements; the Treaty of the Bogue was silent on this question and provided only for the mutual rendition of fugitive criminals.

The next task was to decide on the colony's civil establishment, the government officers and their departmental staffs, and on ways of defraying the cost of government. The chief departmental officers were the Colonial Secretary, the Colonial Treasurer, the Auditor-General who combined his duties with those of the Clerk of the Councils, a Surveyor-General in charge of public works and collection of land rents with an engineer assistant, and a Harbour-Master with an assistant. For the Supreme Court to be set up by the Legislative Council, provision was made for a Chief Justice, a registrar and interpreter; for the police court there was to be a Magistrate and an interpreter; and as the law officer of the government, an Attorney-General. There was to be a Colonial Chaplain, giving the Church of England an official status and endowment; no other section of the Christian Church was helped in this way. Pottinger had recommended a Colonial Surgeon, but the office was not allowed. There were also officials attached to the office of Superintendent of Trade, who, though prominent men in the colony, were not part of the colonial establishment.

Appointments were to be made by the Governor on a temporary basis until approved from home, and the first senior officers who were appointed from home did not arrive until May 1844 with the new Governor, Sir John Davis. Pottinger made temporary appointments from army and other personnel available locally. Major William Caine, formerly of the Cameronians, continued as Magistrate, Lt. Pedder, R.N., as Harbour-Master with Lena as his assistant, and A. T. Gordon as Land Officer and Civil Engineer. Lt.-Colonel G. A. Malcolm, who had taken the Treaty of Nanking home and returned with the ratification, became Colonial Secretary. An army surgeon, R. W. Woosnam, was pressed to act as assistant and private secretary to Pottinger and proved invaluable. A Bombay lawyer, R. Burgass, 'happening to be in China', became legal adviser, Charles E. Stewart was appointed Colonial Treasurer, and Lt. G. T. Brooke was appointed the Governor's A.D.C. and Military Secretary.

Two additional appointments soon proved necessary. Because of so much lawlessness at Chek Chu (Stanley) on the south of the island C. B. Hillier, a former ship's mate, became Assistant Magistrate there; and Charles St. George Cleverly became assistant surveyor. Two early appointments were made by Lord Stanley; the Reverend Vincent Stanton arrived to assume the Colonial Chaplaincy in charge of a matshed church on the parade ground; he had earlier been British Chaplain at Macao, and had been captured by the Chinese in August 1840 and held in Canton in chains. Major-General D'Aguilar came out as General Officer Commanding. Because of his rank, he was given a dormant commission as Lieutenant-Governor to act in place of the Governor if required; normally, in the absence of a high-ranking military officer, the Colonial Secretary deputised. J. R. Morrison was appointed Chinese Secretary to the Superintendent of Trade 'and to act as such' for the government of Hong Kong. Unfortunately, he died almost immediately he was appointed, in August 1843, at Macao. He had been a very competent linguist; his loss was a severe blow to the whole British administration on the China coast, and reduced Pottinger to despair. He had tried to set up the Councils in July 1843, Johnston, Caine and J. R. Morrison forming the Legislative Council. Morrison died, Johnston was granted sick leave, and owing to the difficulty of finding men, the Councils were not properly constituted until early in 1844.

One pressing problem was that of opium. The British government's policy was set out in a dispatch to Pottinger of January 1843. The British opium smuggler must receive no protection or support, and all officials must hold aloof 'from so discreditable a traffic.' 'H.M. Government . . . have not the power to put a stop to this trade . . . but they may perhaps impede it in some degree by preventing the Island of Hong Kong or its neighbouring waters from being used as the point from whence British smugglers shall depart on their illegal adventures.' The import of opium into the colony could not be prevented, but when the island was declared a British colony, Pottinger would then have power to prohibit the import of opium intended for export, or its deposit on board receiving vessels in the harbour. It was agreed that this action would do little to mitigate the evil, and Pottinger was to consider measures which would have the effect of putting the trade on a less discreditable footing. He was to urge legalization, even if it meant confining the trade to one port, Canton, in which case the British government would assist in making the restriction effective. As long as there was total prohibition the British could only prevent Hong Kong from being a resort and a market. Pottinger was against the trade, but replied that to deny Hong Kong to the opium smugglers would only add to the evils by driving the trade elsewhere, and that he hoped still to induce the Chinese to legalize it. In November 1843 the Foreign Office in consultation with the Colonial Office agreed to suspend the exclusion of opium ships from the harbour. The opium traders took the precaution of moving the opium store ships away from Hong Kong to the outer anchorages, Kap Sui Mun and Namoa, and Pottinger therefore had solid grounds for believing that any official action taken against the trade at Hong Kong would be circumvented.

Another urgent problem was the question of the allocation of land for building and public purposes. Conditions were chaotic. Elliot had sold allotments on ambiguous terms and Johnston had made further sales contrary to his instructions. There were many squatters, both Chinese and European, who had never troubled to obtain legal title to the land they occupied, and some merchants holding marine allotments were extending their areas by private reclamations of their own. Pottinger had in the spring of 1842, set up a land committee to tackle the problem, but as the home government had decided against retaining Hong Kong and had ordered all further building, except for military purposes, to cease, the committee was unable to proceed with its work.

After the Treaty of Nanking Pottinger sent home a complete account of the land situation and asked for instructions. In reply, he was told that land must not be granted 'either in perpetuity or for a greater length of time than may be necessary to induce the tenants to erect substantial buildings.' All land must be leased and not sold outright, and the term of the lease was fixed at seventy-five years, and in the case of land not required for building, for only twenty-one years; renewals were to be at the discretion of the government. Grants of land were to be made by auction, an allotment being awarded to the person who bid the highest amount as annual payment for the lease. It was also pointed out that no one had any right to grant lands in the island before its cession was recognized by the home government, and no grants made before 26 June 1843, the date

the colony was proclaimed, would be recognized as of right and
no land rents would be claimed except from that date. Pottinger
had made grants of land to some of the high officials because
there was nowhere for them to live unless they built their own
houses, but this concession was strongly condemned. It was
realized to be impossible to make a clean start from 26 June
1843 because buildings had been erected on the grants of land
that had already been made. In these cases, it was left to
Pottinger to decide as a matter of equity what ought to be done.
The home government thought the holders should not suffer
because of the improvements they had effected, and even went
as far as to say that they 'would be disposed to deal more
liberally with these people than with others and thus afford
them at least such compensation for the disappointment of the
expectations which they had been led to entertain.'

The situation was further complicated by the fact that before
these instructions arrived Pottinger had already attempted to
deal with some of the abuses himself. A notification of 10 April
1843 called for a full statement and proof of claims to land from
each holder, and announced that the land officer had been told
to prevent the commencement of any further building or the
clearance of any site until after final arrangements had been
made; all building at whatever stage was to be stopped if proof
of ownership of the land was not satisfactory. All encroachments
on the future line of roads and streets were to be prevented,
and 'all persons were to confine themselves to the exact dimensions of the lots which were originally allotted to them.' In
August 1843 Pottinger set up a Land Committee to investigate
all claims, fix the rents and arrange for further sales of plots.
There was considerable delay in settling the issues, partly due
to a dispute between Pottinger and the army over the extent
of the military lands, which held up decisions on roads and the
amount of land available, and partly due to discussion of the
lay-out of the town. Gordon, the Land Officer and Colonial
Engineer, wanted the town to be sited in the Wong Nei Chong
Valley (now Happy Valley) with various quays for shipping
linked to the sea by a canal, and Jardine Matheson, the chief
merchant firm in the colony, had offered to dig a canal fifteen
feet deep, but this project was abandoned, chiefly because the
valley was found to be unhealthy. Another cause of delay in

the preparation of deeds and the planning of roads was the severe outbreak of fever in the summer of 1843. At one time every official in the Land and Engineer department was sick, though only one, De Havilland, died. There was, too, much speculation in land by merchants, government officials and army officers, and Pottinger was left virtually alone in attempting to protect the public interest amidst so much self-seeking. The Land Committee finally reported in January 1844, and recommended that all marine lot holders should retain their lots on a seventy-five year lease; it also found that much of the land sold by Johnston had been sold well below its real value and suggested a revaluation, but on this Pottinger delayed taking any positive step. In March 1844, the chief merchants who were holders of most of the original allotments complained strongly against the new conditions and the seventy-five year leases. Pottinger showed them little sympathy and complained to Lord Stanley at home that 'not one individual in twenty of the purchasers of land at the sales or grants authorised by Captain Elliot or Mr. Johnston had fulfilled the prescribed terms' and that such allotments should have been forfeited and re-auctioned. The merchants continued to protest and later they were to secure substantial concessions; meanwhile the continued delay in settling the land question favoured the land jobbers.

Pottinger quarrelled with the army over the area they claimed for military purposes, and this affected land, roads and the general siting of the settlement. General Gough, before he left for India, had suggested a garrison of 4,500 men; Pottinger thought there was no intention on the part of the Chinese to violate the treaty, and that 1,000 men would be enough. Pottinger was not popular with the army; he had severely criticized the handling of the troops in Hong Kong during the fever outbreak of 1842, alleging that they were allowed to bathe in the sea for excessive periods and to drink excessively, and there had been a court of enquiry. After the Treaty of Nanking the War Office sent Major Aldrich out specially to prepare a scheme for the garrison, fortifications and military accommodation. Aldrich proposed a grandiose plan, with a large cantonment for the military, to be permanently defended; this included not only the present military area, but much of the west side of the present Garden Road covered now by government buildings and the Botanical Gardens; the navy was also to be provided for in this area. Pottinger strongly opposed this because it would make 'the face of the Island a mere military position in lieu of . . . a vast emporium of commerce and wealth.' He was willing to give the military all the land they needed at West Point, but wanted to cut down the military area in the centre and to preserve the frontage of Queen's Road for the community. The matter was not determined until after Pottinger had left, and eventually a great part of the west side of the nullah, now Garden Road, was saved for civilian purposes. There was trouble with the navy too. The area of Belcher's Creek (also called Navy Bay), near the western military area, had been chosen by the navy as the site for a naval base, but Admiral Parker had taken possession of a central location adjoining Queen's Road for naval stores, and refused to move them, much to Pottinger's annoyance and to the hindrance of his plans for laying out the settlement. Pottinger named the settlement Victoria and wrote in August 1843 asking for approval; before that it had been referred to as Queen's Town.

The problem of maintaining law and order demanded continuous attention. Crime was prevalent, piracy on the sea, robbery and burglary on the island. This was due largely to the influx of a labouring artisan class, living in primitive conditions in which the normal restraints of family and community life were absent, and eager to make enough money to go back to their native villages. There was some truth, too, in the view of the English officials that the colony attracted a criminal class, 'the scum of Canton'. In any case it was all too easy for a criminal to escape into Chinese territory just across the harbour. The merchants took their own measures; they carried arms for self-defence, and hired watchmen to protect their property. What was needed was an efficient police force. Caine, the chief magistrate, had been authorized by Elliot to recruit soldiers as police, and, later, Indians were added; but soldiers proved unsatisfactory, and Pottinger suggested a standing police force of fifty men and four inspectors, to be recruited and trained in England for service in the colony. Lord Stanley thought this too expensive and suggested that the officers only should be sent from England, and a force of Malays raised locally. Pottinger had recruited selected soldiers for police duties, and a Captain Haly of the Madras Native Infantry was made Superintendent of Police. After some delay the home government agreed to send out a superintendent and two inspectors to train and organize a local force. In the meantime lawlessness continued. Caine and his assistant Hillier used to patrol the streets in person on occasion, in an effort to check crime, and began to inflict heavy corporal punishment when it was discovered that the Chinese did not regard imprisonment as a severe penalty; their standard of living was so low that a spell in prison was not without its attraction.

Pottinger also suggested a system of registration of Chinese for 'mutual security and responsibility'. In April 1843 he set up a 'registry committee' to deal with the policing and general organization of the Chinese community. The committee was asked to consider the exclusion of certain undesirable classes of Chinese from the colony, registering of boatmen and controlling their charges, licensing and security of shops and bazaars, and the regulation of coolie hire. It was left to his successor to carry out this scheme.

Financial organization was necessarily chaotic until the Legislative Council began to function, and enact taxation ordinances. Sir James Stephen remarked in November 1843, 'I can't help feeling that Sir Henry Pottinger acts as if he had an unlimited fund to draw upon.' Pottinger had been told to use for government expenses sums received from China and remit the balance to Calcutta; he had assumed financial responsibility for the government of the island from the date of the treaty, whereas the Treasury considered its cost should be treated as part of the war expenses until it was proclaimed a colony. Pottinger was not able to provide any estimates because 'work flowed in' and it was again left to his successor to place the finances on a definite footing. When Pottinger left in May 1844, no revenue whatever had been collected from the residents.

The Executive and Legislative Councils began to function early in 1844, and the latter passed a series of ordinances, loosely phrased in the absence of a law officer in the colony, 'and must, I presume, be judged very leniently,' as a Colonial Office official at home remarked. It stands to Pottinger's credit that the first ordinance passed in Hong Kong forbade all forms of slavery in the colony, though because the British law against slavery was held to apply to Hong Kong as part of the Queen's dominions, it was disallowed. Another ordinance providing for seven years' transportation for some classes of crime, was also disallowed, on the ground that there were no arrangements for the reception of Chinese criminals in Australia. One ordinance was described by Stanley as 'unintelligible without some report explanatory of the motives and of the results anticipated from it.' In most, considerable amendments were suggested.

Sir Henry Pottinger was in fact overwhelmed by the variety and complexity of the problems of founding the new colony and of organizing the new pattern of relations with China, and by delays caused by the need to refer all questions of principle to the home government. On every issue he was confronted with self-seeking, for by general consent Hong Kong was destined to become the great emporium of trade in the east; it was clearly a time of great opportunity. He was alone in upholding the public interest in the infant colony, and his stand involved him in a series of conflicts in which his great popularity vanished and he was driven into social isolation.

He quarrelled with the army, when it claimed an excessive amount of land in the centre of the settlement, and when d'Aguilar wanted a large allotment on the sea front for a military hospital he resisted the claim in the interest of social and commercial development. He quarrelled with the navy for its refusal to move its stores from this central area. He quarrelled with the merchants over land and over the clauses of the Treaty of the Bogue and he had to check illegal reclamation and illegal holdings. Army officers and high officials, including Caine and Johnston, speculated in land; he was faced with a general absence of public spirit and a disregard for the public needs. He was grossly overworked, and it is impossible not to feel sympathy for him. 'I have stood alone,' he wrote to Lord Stanley just before he left, and complained that he had had to act on his 'unassisted judgement', and yet was unfairly blamed 'as the originator and approver of all public mistakes and oversights'.

He resigned in July 1843, shortly after the proclamation of the colony, but it was not until May 1844 that his successor, Sir John Davis, arrived and enabled him to return to England with a pension. He became Governor of the Cape of Good Hope, and shortly afterwards secured the post he most wanted, the governorship of the Madras Presidency.

CHAPTER VII

EARLY GOVERNMENT UNDER
SIR JOHN DAVIS, 1844-48

'*It is a much easier task to govern the twenty thousand Chinese inhabitants of this Colony, than the few hundreds of English.*'

Sir John Davis to Lord Stanley, 6 November 1844.

POTTINGER had settled for the time being the relations between the British and China. He had secured the cession of Hong Kong by treaty, but without that necessary condition of its economic prosperity which Palmerston had seen to be essential, namely unrestricted trade between the island and the mainland. The form of government had been laid down and a number of decisions on matters of principle taken, but he had been so preoccupied with the negotiations that little had been done to implement the decisions, and he did not remain long enough to see the result of his labours.

It was left to Sir John Davis to create an effective government, to organize the public finances, to institute the judicial system, and generally to make the administrative machinery function. This brought him into bitter conflict with merchant opinion and he became the most hated Governor the island has had.

Sir John Davis had had long experience of China with the English East India Company. He came to Canton in 1813 and soon showed an interest in the Chinese people and language. He accompanied the Amherst Mission to Peking in 1816, and rose to be chairman of the Company's Select Committee in China, the highest post in the Company's service in the Far East, and published many works on the Chinese, and some translations. When the Company's monopoly was abolished in 1833 and Lord Napier was sent out in the following year as Chief Superintendent of Trade, Davis accepted the post of

Second Superintendent under him, and on the death of Napier in October 1834, succeeded him as Chief Superintendent, but resigned after three months and left for home in January 1835. He explained later, in a letter written in December 1843 just before coming out as Governor, that the Chief Superintendent of Trade had had too little power to control 'the ill-conduct of British subjects in China', and this 'imperfect and impracticable state of its functions' had brought him home 'in despair' in 1835. He had been brought up under the regime of the Company, and there is no doubt that he saw the passing of the Company's control at Canton with regret, and that he disliked the new free-trade regime, of which Hong Kong was the outward visible sign. It was not surprising therefore that he incurred the hatred of the merchants.

After leaving Canton Sir John Davis had continued to study Chinese, and, having just published a scholarly and authoritative work on China, he appeared to be eminently qualified to succeed Pottinger. He was appointed to the combined offices of H.M. Plenipotentiary for the purpose of carrying on any negotiations with the Chinese government, H.M. Superintendent of Trade with the task of supervising the work of the consuls and looking after the interests of British trade in the five treaty ports, both subject to the Foreign Office, and of Governor of Hong Kong, subject to the Colonial Office. This dualism in the position of the Governor made Hong Kong unique, in the sense that the Colonial Office had not complete control over it.

He landed on 7 May 1844, accompanied by officials who had been recruited in England to take up important posts under him. Frederic Bruce who later became first minister to China, was Colonial Secretary, R. Montgomery Martin was Colonial Treasurer, and there was also Davis's young nephew, W. T. Mercer, as his private secretary. R. D. Cay, Registrar of the Supreme Court, and J. Pope, civil engineer, also arrived, and the Chief Justice, J. W. Hulme, came a month later. A. E. Shelley arrived from England too with some vague recommendation from Lord Stanley, and was made Auditor-General, though Stanley later denied that he had given any encouragement to Shelley, who had come out entirely on his own. Paul Ivy Sterling assumed the post of Attorney-General in July.

E

Almost immediately Davis enlarged the size of the Legislative and Executive Councils. The instructions were that each was to contain three members besides the Governor, and he interpreted this as meaning a minimum of three. He increased the Legislative Council to five—the Major General Commanding, Chief Justice, Colonial Secretary, Colonial Treasurer and Chief Magistrate; and the Executive Council to four—the Major General, Colonial Secretary, Attorney-General and Chief Magistrate. Lord Stanley refused to accept this, since the Councils had been deliberately made small to strengthen the Governor's position, and in 1845 Davis had to reconstitute them. The Major General, Chief Justice and Attorney-General now made up the Legislative Council, and the Major General, Colonial Secretary and Chief Magistrate composed the Executive Council, with the Governor as chairman of each.

Finance was the most urgent question. No one in the colony had paid any taxes from its foundation, and the home government was bearing the total expenses of defence, administration, and of the public works under construction. Parliamentary opinion was much averse to the British tax-payer having to bear the cost of colonial government. The free-traders, and they were influential, objected to the colonies as useless burdens, and thought that free trade, not the development of overseas territories, was the policy most conducive to Britain's industrial and commercial prosperity. There was a small group of radicals who interested themselves in colonial problems, particularly in emigration, and who urged colonial self-government on the basis of colonial governments being financially self-supporting. Both sections united in criticizing grants towards colonial expenses, though for very different reasons. The general principle was laid down that the home government would expect the Hong Kong government to meet its own expenses, but it realized that a new colony could not be self-supporting at first, and it agreed to undertake the cost of defence, chiefly the cost of the garrison, and also to make an annual grant equivalent to the cost of the establishment, that is, the salaries of the officials. The necessary public works, civilian and military, were to be met from local taxation. Davis was told to cease using the China indemnity funds for the colony's expenses, which were to be met from local resources supplemented by the Parliamentary vote.

The difficulty was how to raise a local revenue. Customs duties on imported goods could not be levied because Hong Kong had been declared a free port. Davis solved the problem by commencing the collection of the land rents from which he anticipated receiving the greater proportion of the revenue, and he supplemented this source by a system of monopolies farmed out to the highest bidder and by the sale of licences. Monopolies for the sale of opium, the quarrying of stone and the handling of salt were created, and each market was made a monopoly and similarly let. Licences for the sale of wines and spirits were introduced, pawnbrokers, auctioneers and billiard-table proprietors were licensed and a percentage tax on all goods sold under auction was also imposed. He proposed a tonnage duty on all ships entering the port, but this was dropped; he wanted to impose a tax on the consumption of wines and spirits, but was opposed by every member of the Legislative Council, and so abandoned the plan, though, as he pointed out, it would have been the only one of the new taxes which the wealthier foreign merchants would have had to pay. In 1845 a rate on all property was levied to pay for the police.

This assessment for rates on all the occupiers of property caused great resentment because the home government's intention was that the residents should assess themselves through some form of municipal organization. Davis found it politic to reduce the assessments by forty per cent from a total of $325,840 to $195,520, seriously reducing the yield.

Rent from land was the main source of revenue. Disposal of land in all British colonies produced difficulties, largely through speculation; Hong Kong was no exception. The home government had imposed seventy-five-year leases, and Davis incurred the odium of having to enforce this unpopular decision. He tried in various ways to increase the rents from land. Roads and streets were developed to open up new sites; he provided locations for the Chinese in an attempt to stop squatters; he invited Australian colonists to take land in the south of the island for sheep and cattle grazing, until the home government forbade it. He found that many allotments were held by speculators who had no intention of building; no deposit had been charged and no penalty exacted if the allotments were renounced, and this absence of risk encouraged speculation.

Davis put an end to it by demanding ten per cent deposit on all sales, and arrears of rent if the land was surrendered.

These financial measures made Davis unpopular, though in fact he was carrying out the home government's policy that a colony could not depend upon the British tax-payer for its support. Davis intended that the colony should pay its way, once the initial necessary public works were completed, and continued his financial policy in the face of bitter opposition.

During the calendar year 1845 the revenue collected amounted to £22,242. By 1847 it had increased to £31,078. The main increases were land rents £5,313 to £13,996; opium farm from £2,384 to £3,183; police rate £529 to £2,239, and Supreme Court fees and fines £1,343 to £2,418. Expenditure in 1845 was £72,841; but by 1847 it was reduced to £50,959. The deficit was made up by a vote from the British Parliament, the sums being £49,000 in 1845, £36,900 in 1846, £31,000 in 1847 and £25,000 in 1848. 'This promises to be a very expensive colony,' Sir James Stephen remarked, and for a few years it was so indeed.

The problem of the administration of justice and of maintaining law and order was pressing, and one of Davis's early tasks was to organize a police force. Pottinger's plan of recruiting a police force in England had been rejected on grounds of expense, and he was not able to make much headway in securing efficient police personnel. The soldiers proved unreliable, and sailors waiting to join their ships were even less so. Meanwhile, robberies and burglaries were rife, and general insecurity of persons and property continued.

In November 1844 one havildar, two serjeants and twenty men from the Indian troops were added to the police for night patrol work, and sickness amongst the European contingent necessitated further increases.

After urgent requests, the home government sent out in the spring of 1845 a London police officer, Charles May, to be Superintendent of Police, accompanied by two inspectors. May found only 47 remaining of the original force of 90 Europeans, and he selected 41 of these, added 30 army men, and created a force of 71 Europeans, 46 Indians and 51 Chinese, a total of 168. He recommended more generous pay and pensions, and better accommodation for the Indians, and he organized water police to patrol the harbour. The organization of an efficient police force remained a problem for many years because there was continual pressure from home to economize in personnel and administration. The high cost of pensions was objected to, and when the men were offered pensions on half-pay after fifteen years or a twenty per cent rise in pay, they all elected the pay increase, and the rapid turnover of men continued. Pay at $14 a month for a European constable was too low to attract the right men, and the police force remained for many years noted for its inefficiency, corruption and drunkenness. In 1848 an official notification was issued warning all the inhabitants that it was unsafe to move outside the town after dark except in company. It must be borne in mind that the establishment of police forces was quite an innovation in England; there was not much experience to go on, and in some respects Hong Kong was even ahead of some English counties.

Two incidents arose out of the police question. Pottinger had already suggested that a system of registration would be a valuable check on Chinese criminal elements, but it was left to Davis to introduce it mainly as a police measure. He thought that it would be less invidious to apply a registration system to all residents of the colony, irrespective of nationality, and an ordinance of August 1844 ordered this universal registration. It produced a storm of protest among the European community, and the Chinese adopted a passive resistance, closed their shops, withdrew their labour, and some slight rioting occurred in the bazaar. The ordinance was not announced until 19 October and was to take effect on 1 November. The vehemence of the protest was due to the fact that so little time remained, as much as to the proposal itself. There was also resentment against Davis's financial measures. The Europeans sent a strongly worded memorial which Davis returned because of its disrespectful language; and two amended versions were also rejected; the Chinese also sent a memorial and were told that it would not be considered until they had opened their shops and resumed their occupations. Pressure of public opinion forced Davis to modify the plan, and a new registration ordinance in December 1844 applied only to those who could not produce $500, largely the Chinese, and cancelled the annual registration fee of one dollar.

The establishment of the police force was related to the question of municipal government. Following English precedent the intention was to give control of the police and other services to the residents with the obligation to pay the cost. Davis reported that he intended to appoint local commissioners from among the principal inhabitants to be responsible for police, roads and sewers, and empowered by ordinance to levy the necessary rates. Because of the prevailing lawlessness and the difficulty of recruiting an efficient police force, Davis changed his mind, and determined to have the police under his own control. The ordinance of August 1845 levying a police rate placed the assessments and collection directly under the government and not the local inhabitants as had been promised, and there was an immediate outcry against it. Davis had feared this resentment, and had delayed the ordinance to make sure of its legality. He tried to disarm criticism by reducing the assessments by forty per cent, ostensibly because of the inflated value of land in the colony, and said that he still intended to place roads and sewers under local commissioners.

In August 1845 the Hong Kong merchants sent a further memorial to the home government in which opportunity was taken to range over the whole field of grievances. They condemned the rates ordinance as unconstitutional and illegal; and complained that they had been encouraged to move to the island and then in spite of their protests, seventy-five-year leases had been imposed on their purchases of land, and they alleged it would have been cheaper to stay in Macao. But 'the measures of the existing government of the island have still further aggravated the evils,' since every description of trade and commerce was 'a subject of taxation, a source of revenue or of monopoly.' They asked for the abolition of the opium farm, auction duties and other 'harrassing taxation', and they asked for a municipal body 'with power to decide on the appropriation of monies raised.'

They argued that the Hong Kong administration was designed to serve the open ports as well as the island, and that therefore the cost should not fall on the island alone. They said: '. . . such a settlement as Hong Kong was never really required by the British merchants,' and that it was inexpedient and unjust in practice to call on the civil part of a community for any large portion of the expense of the colony 'which is held rather as a naval and military station.' The China trade benefited the home country and it was proper that it should contribute to the cost of the island from which that trade was controlled and defended.

Gladstone, who had just become Secretary of State, rejected these demands and supported the Governor. He said the circumstances of Hong Kong being different from those of England, he could not accept the view that rates should be levied only by a municipal body, or that there was any constitutional objection to the government's levying of rates. He upheld Davis's financial measures and rejected the merchants' argument that Hong Kong was held as a military and naval station. 'The mercantile body have altogether mistaken the object of Great Britain in the occupation of Hong Kong. . . . Hong Kong except for the security of commerce is unnecessary.' Sir James Stephen advised strongly against a municipal government in Hong Kong on the ground that the English minority could hardly be entrusted with the powers it would give them over the Chinese, and it would be 'incompatible with that decisiveness and energy which is necessary'. The municipal project was thrust into the background. So the Governor's policy was upheld and, as a mark of confidence, he was created a baronet.

Davis was confronted immediately with the problem of the maintenance of law and order, that prime duty of Victorian government. Chinese crime was linked with the existence of Triad societies, which Davis regarded as patriotic combinations against the rule of the foreigner; he concluded therefore that the Chinese ought to be controlled through their own people in the way that Elliot had envisaged. An ordinance of May 1844 created Chinese officials, Paouchong and Paouken; these were essentially police or 'peace' officers, elective and unpaid; their function was to help the police, assist with the registration scheme, and provide information of breaches of the peace in their own areas. The step was approved after some doubts, but the experiment was not successful, for Chinese could not be expected to assume responsibility without more clearly marked status and reward. The application of Chinese law to the Chinese had been left in some obscurity. Pottinger, on one occasion, had refused to hand over seven Chinese accused of murder, because of no proof of guilt, and he informed Lord Aberdeen that the Chinese government had now waived the right to try Chinese subjects. Aberdeen doubted this, and in March 1844 asked Davis for a further report.

Davis felt that the Chinese in Hong Kong should be subject to British law because they were coming to the island in increasing numbers to seek the security and protection of British law. The ordinance of 1844 setting up the Supreme Court did give that court power to punish the Chinese in accordance with the laws of China, and a similar clause appeared in the ordinance of 1844 defining the summary jurisdiction of magistrates. In defence, Davis said that Chinese punishments such as loss of queue, the cangue and blows with the cane had already been used in Hong Kong and that the Chinese were too poor to pay fines, and prison sentences had little deterrent effect. The Colonial Office agreed to the principle, but not without great misgivings. 'The dilemma is between ruling Chinese people by English law and requiring judges to administer in H.M.'s name the law of China', Sir James Stephen wrote, but he felt that 'effective restraint' and 'a government not to be trifled with' were so important that they ought to be secured 'even at the expense of adopting a policy the most opposed to our own feelings and prepossessions'.

There the matter rested. In spite of the home government's declaration to Pottinger that there would be in the island 'a large body of Chinese persons to whom the law of England would be a rule of action and a measure of right equally unintelligible and vexatious,' the administration of the law was kept firmly in British hands, and the liberal principle of giving the Chinese their own law and customs was only partially adopted. The Chinese were left alone and their customs and usages were respected, as far as was consistent with the needs of law and order and of the criminal law, but the adoption of Chinese punishments provided the excuse for savage penalties which appeared to be demanded by the prevailing lawlessness. As long as the main function of the state was the maintenance of law and order, no great difficulty arose, but when the state began to improve social and economic conditions, the treatment of the Chinese created a serious problem. Davis attempted to stem the crime wave by heavy penalties; his proposed transportation of criminals to the Australian colonies was forbidden, but he secured transportation to the Straits Settlements by permission of the Indian Government. By an ordinance passed in January 1845 members of Triad societies were, on second conviction, to be branded on the right cheek and expelled, but Lord Stanley asked that this severe though painless penalty should be amended. Kiying protested against the transportation of Chinese and renewed the claim that Chinese should be judged by Chinese officials; but Davis replied that no one was compelled to live in Hong Kong, and if Chinese committed crimes in Hong Kong, they must expect the same treatment as British subjects, just as they could expect the same protection and privileges.

The Chinese government did not renounce their claim to control the Chinese living in the colony. In December 1844 a Chinese official was discovered collecting land rents at Stanley on the south side of the island. Davis made a strong protest and kept the official in custody until Kiying had given a definite undertaking that China disclaimed any such right. In October 1845 an attempt by Chinese officials to seize wanted Chinese suspects in Hong Kong was resisted, and one of the former was given a month's imprisonment. A similar incident occurred a year later, and Davis again demanded that a Chinese officer who had landed and seized a Chinese should be punished.

As in the case of Chinese law for the Chinese, so in the case of opium, the liberal sentiments professed by the British were forced by circumstances into the background. Peel had declared in Parliament that the opium trade would not be countenanced at Hong Kong; and Davis wrote to Stanley just before sailing to say he entirely agreed. British policy remained that China ought to legalize and control a trade which she could not prevent; the British government could not undertake to secure the proper execution of Chinese laws, at the same time it was anxious that good relations should not be jeopardized by opium smuggling.

Davis, like Pottinger, urged legalization of opium on the Chinese without result; the trade was allowed to drift into its old channels, and the Chinese virtually gave up the uneven struggle against it. In June 1844 Davis reported home that 'opium is now tacitly tolerated by the Chinese government even at the ports of regular trade.' He decided therefore to use an opium monopoly as a source of revenue in the colony, following the example of Singapore. In December 1844 he wrote home that all scruples regarding opium were now gone, and that Kiying 'in his last communication to me' had admitted that the Chinese official opium policy could be disregarded. Davis added that opium was now in general trade along the whole coast, and that 'under these altered circumstances any scruples on our part within our own colony, appear to me to be more than superfluous'.

Davis therefore permitted the import of opium into Hong Kong for internal consumption, and indeed he saw clearly that it would have been illogical to request the Chinese to legalize opium and at the same time forbid it in Hong Kong; it must also be remembered that the Indian government was opposed to any interference with a trade from which it derived so much revenue. To control it, Davis created a monopoly for the sale of the drug for all amounts less than one chest, and this mono-poly was farmed out to the highest bidder, so making its contribution to the colony's revenue. The step met with much opposition, chiefly from the opium merchants who objected to any taxation and to any form of monopolistic control. There were some like R. Montgomery Martin, the Colonial Treasurer, who objected to the principle of taxing vice for revenue, and Martin became a bitter opponent of the Governor. Davis was upheld by the home authorities, and in March 1845 the monopoly was sold for one year for 8,520 dollars to George Duddell, and regulations for the sale of opium under the opium ordinance were promulgated. The monopoly was not a success. Opium for export was excluded from the monopoly, which covered only opium sold in Hong Kong, and Chinese dealers were able to avoid it by purchasing opium avowedly for export, but in fact for sale in Hong Kong. The ordinance had to be amended and the farm was bought in 1845 by a group of Chinese for £4,275. Even they found it almost impossible to enforce their monopoly in spite of employing a corps of men and an armed boat, and the value of the monopoly declined. In 1847 Davis decided to abolish it, and set up a licensing system in its place. A monthly fee of thirty dollars was charged for a licence to sell raw opium, of twenty dollars for refining and selling prepared opium, and of ten dollars for a licence to open an opium-smoking shop.

The Governor was not fortunate in some of the men appointed to fill the higher posts; the island had a reputation for fever which made recruitment difficult. It was almost impossible to fill the post of Chief Justice, and the salary had to be raised to £3,000 before Hulme was obtained, and he proved to have an excessive weakness for conviviality. Frederic Bruce left soon to become Lieutenant-Governor of Newfoundland, and was replaced as Colonial Secretary by Caine, Hillier being then promoted to be Chief Magistrate, and a junior official, William Holdforth was made Assistant Magistrate. Shelley, the Auditor, and bosom friend of Hulme, was reported by Davis as dissipated, negligent, unreliable and in debt.

The Colonial Treasurer, Robert Montgomery Martin, gave serious trouble. He took a despondent view of the prospects of Hong Kong; he estimated the annual expenses as £50,000, exclusive of defence and public works, and the income as £5,880, and angered Davis by financial proposals based on the prospect of a permanent deficit. He thought the colony would never become an emporium because trade would go to the open ports, and called Hong Kong 'a small barren unhealthy and valueless island' to which Chusan was much to be preferred. In July 1844 he addressed a long memorandum to Lord Stanley criticizing the choice of the island in every respect, and wrote privately to the Colonial Office making an even stronger attack and asking to be relieved of his post. Davis made the mistake of sending on the memorandum without a serious attempt to answer the objections. The Colonial Office realized that Martin's censures were hasty since he had been in the colony only a few weeks, yet it was perturbed because it was under pressure in the Commons over the Hong Kong vote.

Davis rejected Martin's financial proposals and a bitter quarrel ensued, particularly over the opium monopoly. In June 1845 matters came to a head. During his frequent visits to the Treaty ports, Martin became convinced that the whole China policy was on the wrong lines, and that Chusan ought to be retained. He decided to return to place his views in person to the home government; he appeared to think that he had been specially selected as Treasurer to collect useful information on conditions in China. Davis refused him leave and said the consuls were there to provide information and complained to Lord Stanley that he was 'an inefficient and troublesome person'. In June 1845 Martin left on his own responsibility and was held to have resigned, and was replaced as Treasurer by Mercer. He failed to move the home government, but his continued crusade against the island, coming on top of the memorial of the merchants against Davis, was one of the factors which led to the Parliamentary Select Committee of Enquiry into the China Trade of 1847.

A quarrel with Hulme brought about the trial of the Chief Justice on a charge of drunkenness, and the downfall of the Governor. The two men had travelled out together in 1844 as far as Bombay, where the judge and his numerous family were left behind because of insufficient accommodation in the warship which was to bring the party to the colony, and he was put to the expense of finding his own passage. Hulme drew up the rules of the Supreme Court to give himself what Davis thought was an excessive vacation of six months, from June to December. This vacation applied only to the court's criminal jurisdiction, but Davis insisted on cutting it down; an open quarrel in the Legislative Council resulted and the dispute was referred home. Hulme was rightly jealous of the independence of his court against interference by the executive, and wanted complete control of the court, including the appointment of all court officials, but the Governor felt he was responsible for the good working of all departments of government. He regarded the magistrates as administrative officials and when he gave them instructions, Hulme protested that they were law officers and subject to his own guidance in the performance of their duties.

When the Vice-admiralty court was set up in 1847, the Governor, who was nominally vice-admiral of the port, fixed the sessions with complete disregard for the convenience of Hulme, who was the court's presiding judge. There followed bitter personal charges in the course of which Davis challenged the right of the judge to be styled 'His lordship'.

The Compton case of 1846 brought matters to a head. Compton, a British merchant at Canton, had been found guilty of provoking a riot and was fined £100 by the consul, at Davis's direction. Compton appealed to the Supreme Court and Hulme quashed this verdict, remitted the fine, and passed strictures on the irregularity of the consular proceedings. The real issue between Davis and Hulme, stripped of personalities, was that the Governor thought that in the circumstances of the China Coast, British control would be most effectively secured by strong administrative action; the judge was for the full application of the law.

In January 1847 Davis determined to get rid of Hulme, and wrote a long condemnation to the Colonial Office based on the allegation that the judge had defied the Legislative Council over the question of the vacation. He confidently expected that the Secretary of State, Earl Grey, would call for Hulme's resignation. In order to strengthen his case, he sent a private letter to the Foreign Secretary, Lord Palmerston, making the accusation that Hulme was an habitual drunkard. The result was the opposite of what Davis had calculated. In reply to his formal complaint, Earl Grey censured both Governor and judge. His private letter to Palmerston was treated as an official communication and sent to Grey, who demanded that Davis should hold a public enquiry into the accusation it contained, and if the judge were found guilty he was to be suspended. Davis, who naturally shrank from holding any such enquiry, wrote a long and involved letter attempting to explain away the charges, pointing out that his letter had been a private one and arguing against the undesirable publicity which would result. Earl Grey refused to give way and instructed the enquiry to be held. In August 1847, in face of these rebuffs, Davis resigned.

In November 1847 a public enquiry was held before the Executive Council. Davis was very much chagrined, but as he had already resigned he took little personal interest in the proceedings which were conducted perfunctorily and with considerable irregularity. The charges against Hulme referred to incidents in 1845 and 1846 and to habitual drunkenness. He was found guilty on one count and suspended. The home government reversed the decision and Hulme returned the following year, his character completely vindicated.

In May 1848 Davis left, and the residents studiously ignored his departure. For some time he had lived isolated from the community which detested him. Yet he should not be condemned because of his unpopularity, which was partly the product of resentment at the failure of the colony to become the emporium it was expected to be; no Governor could have been popular. It is true that in his treatment of Hulme he committed an error of judgement, in his pronouncements he was too fond of parading his knowledge of the classics and of Chinese, and he found it difficult to disguise his contempt for the type of European he found living on the China Coast, but he was an able Governor and put the administration of the colony on a sound basis. It was his misfortune to have to take and carry out unpopular decisions in the face of unreasonable attitudes adopted by the merchants. He retired and continued his Chinese studies, founded a scholarship at Oxford for the study of Chinese, was honoured by the University with the degree of D.C.L., and lived to reach the age of ninety-five.

CHAPTER VIII

SOCIAL AND ECONOMIC CONDITIONS, 1841–47

'. . . and if any unfortunate individual in either of Her Majesty's services be compelled to come by duty, just let him have a stout heart, and a lively trust in God's mercy.'

H. C. Sirr, *China and the Chinese*, 1849.

PROGRESS during these early years was uneven. On the one hand there was rapid social development to meet the needs of a newly created settlement, on the other economic progress was disappointing. At first optimism prevailed, but with the coming of peace came also a realization that the early expectations of rapid economic prosperity would not be fulfilled.

Population, the first condition of success, increased rapidly at first and then much more slowly. The settlement attracted the foreign merchant who sought the security of the British flag, beachcombers out to make money easily and ready for any venture, as well as Chinese who came because there was a demand for labour. Estimates of population vary, and, before the registration scheme of 1844 was working, must be largely guesswork. The Hong Kong Government *Gazette* of May 1841 gave the figure as 7,450, made up of 4,350 in the villages, 2,000 boat people, the rest being visiting labourers and vendors. But one village was said to have 2,000, and it is probable this is a clerical error for 200, and so the estimate is perhaps properly 5,650. By October 1841 the population was estimated in the local press to be 15,000. Samuel Fearon, the first Registrar-General under the Registration Ordinance, issued a report on 24 June 1845 to show the working of the act during its first six months. He stated that at the cession, the population of the island was 4,000, of which 1,500 were engaged in agriculture and 2,000 in fishing; the latter are presumably the boat population since he does not mention these separately. He also stated that the British occupation drew some thousands of Chinese to the island, the majority being Hakka people, whom he describes as 'careless of moral obligations, unscrupulous, unrespected . . .'. Chinese registered under the ordinance numbered 9,900 and he calculated there were 2,150 boat people. His estimate of the total population was 23,817, made up as follows:

	Men	Women	Children	Total
Europeans	455	90	50	595
Indian	346	12	4	362
Chinese in Brick Buildings	6,000	960	500	7,460
Chinese in Boats	600	1,800	1,200	3,600
Labourers	10,000	—	—	10,000
Visitors	—	—	—	300
Chinese in the employ of Europeans	—	—	—	1,500
			Total	23,817

By 1847 the total population was given as 23,872, exclusive of the troops of the garrison, of which 618 were Europeans. These figures suggest that there was a great influx of Chinese after the British assumed control, and that thereafter the annual growth was small. It must also be admitted that the figures do not reveal the turnover of population, for incessant coming and going was a feature of the island's life from the start, and that therefore they are more relevant to the growth of economic activity than to the growth of the settlement as a community.

Since only 9,900 had registered out of this total the figures can only be approximate, and when the figure for 1846 showed a decrease, the Governor, Sir John Davis, attributed it to a more efficient registration. Yet the figures given above do give some picture of the colony at that time. There is a clear male preponderance except among the boat people, but among these the men would in many cases find better employment ashore and be reckoned accordingly.

Building never really ceased in spite of the home government's interdict of 1841, but after the treaty there was a great increase, and it was reported in October 1844 that one hundred houses were in process of erection. The Registrar-General's first report in 1845 gave the number of stone and brick buildings as 264 European and 436 Chinese. Even then the housing shortage was acute and Pottinger, before he left, built a block of four houses called the Albany, for the chief government officials. The home government objected to this in principle and refused to agree to any further provision of housing for officials, who were expected to fend for themselves on the same terms as the rest of the community. Murray Barracks and buildings for the Commissariat and Engineer department were built. The military had a further camp at West Point (Sai Ying Pun—Western Military Camp) occupied largely by Indian troops, though some Indian troops were still in matsheds in the centre of the town in 1845. Quite early, detachments of troops were stationed at Chek Pai Wan (Aberdeen) and Chek Chu (Stanley) on the south side of the island, and at Sai Wan on the east. Reference to the map opposite page 54 will show the general layout of the new settlement. Murray Parade Ground was hewn out of the hill-side and used also as the site of the temporary Anglican Church.

Government House was early fixed approximately in its present position. Pottinger had lived in a house owned by A. R. Johnston, lying on a piece of high ground overlooking Queen's Road and adjoining the Parade Ground. Davis, who had left his family in England, had also taken over Johnston's house, but not liking to have the military as such close neighbours, he moved to a small house further up the hill. This was a three-roomed building hastily built to receive Kiying in June 1843, for the ceremony of exchanging ratifications of the treaty, and it served for some years as Government House.

Pottinger embarked on a large programme of public works which was continued and developed by Davis. Johnston's house was earmarked for use as a Supreme Court building, but a large structure built by Dent & Co. as an exchange was purchased for this purpose. Both Pottinger and Davis incurred the displeasure of the home government by setting on foot public works which were not sanctioned, but which they regarded as necessary, and on one occasion Davis was told 'the mere fact of a public work being necessary does not constitute a justification for its commencement'. Davis was anxious that the public works specially required for the founding of the settlement should all be completed quickly and that there should then follow a period of more normal recurrent expenditure to be met out of income. His aim was to make the colony self-sufficient. By 1844 bridle 'roads' had been made to Stanley and Aberdeen, and roads to Sai Wan and from there to Stanley, were being constructed, and roads were planned making a complete circuit of the island. They were badly constructed, and it was difficult to prevent the tropical summer rains from washing them away and the wooden bridges over the nullahs gave similar trouble. Davis reported that Gordon was not very competent and that a great improvement had resulted while he was away on sick leave. Police stations at Victoria, Aberdeen and Stanley were built, a cemetery was laid out in the Happy Valley in 1845, with a chapel. A jail was completed consisting of one large room 'where the chain gang is confined during the night', four small rooms for prisoners committed for trial, and eleven cells for those sentenced to death or to solitary confinement and for debtors. Two suits of clothing were allowed to each prisoner but no bedding. The chain gang was responsible for much of the road-making and repair.

Epidemics of fever, which visited the colony each summer, retarded its development and gave it an evil reputation for insalubrity. 1841 and 1842 had been bad summers, but 1843 was even worse. Pottinger reported in July of that year that the colony was 'visited by a great deal of most severe and fatal sickness', which caused much mortality and alarm; and one regiment alone, at West Point, lost a hundred men between June and the middle of August. Fever carried off J. R. Morrison, one of the more competent of the early interpreters and a man

F

difficult to replace. This reputation as 'a haunt of fever' made
it more difficult to recruit able men into the public service of
the colony. Pottinger defended the new colony and believed
1843 was just an exceptionally bad year and that with better
housing, more drainage and cleanliness, Hong Kong would be
no worse than any other tropical colony. A Committee of Public
Health was established during the summer to create and
enforce a code of sanitary rules for the protection of health, but
it did little. Drainage and the end of a period of intensely rapid
building brought some relief. 1845, for example, was remarkably
healthy, but fever remained endemic. The early severe outbreaks filled the community with despondency. The Wong Nei
Chong Valley, with considerable paddy, was soon found to be
unhealthy, and many houses built in what at first seemed the
most attractive part of the colony became untenanted. In 1846
the cultivators were bought out, the valley drained, and a road
constructed around it for recreational purposes.

The fever necessitated hospitals. Even in the old Canton days,
provision had been made at Whampoa for sickness among seamen, and an American, Dr. Peter Parker, had charge of an
eye hospital, chiefly for Chinese. Soon after the founding of the
colony, a Parsee merchant, Hermusjee Rustomjee, offered
$12,000 for a seamen's hospital, and a committee of manage-
ment was appointed. The contribution was never made as
Rustomjee became bankrupt, but other merchant firms, notably
Jardine Matheson, came forward with subscriptions, and in
1844 a hospital was established and later given a new building
on an eminence near Morrison Hill overlooking the Happy
Valley. A military hospital was proposed in 1844 on the north
side of Queen's Road opposite the cantonment, much to Pottinger's annoyance. He considered the site much too valuable,
and wanted the military hospital built on higher ground within
the military area. The Medical Missionary Society of Canton
established a hospital near Morrison Hill. Pottinger strongly
urged the need of a Colonial Surgeon and appointed a Dr. Dill
temporarily, but the home government refused and argued that
the lower grades of government civil servants, entitled to free
medical treatment, who also needed hospital treatment, should
obtain it in some private hospital already in existence and
should contribute to their maintenance by deductions from

their pay. Davis was never able to extract more than grudging agreement from home, that the provision of a hospital could be helped from colonial funds only if 'the Colonial revenue were sufficient', and if he were first assured that 'private benevolence would do the rest', and that the institution would be able to maintain itself. In the meantime, Dr. A. Anderson was employed to treat the police and lower grades of civil servants.

Provision for religious worship was another feature of the early life of the colony. The American protestant missionaries were particularly active at Macao and Canton, and along the whole China coast. In Hong Kong the American Baptists built the first Christian place of worship, in 1842, the Baptist Chapel in Queen's Road, in the charge of Rev. J. L. Schuck. This was soon followed by the Catholic Church of the Immaculate Conception, in Wellington Street. The London Missionary Society, under the great Chinese scholar Dr. James Legge, built the Union Chapel, in Hollywood Road in 1845. The Muslims erected a mosque above Caine Road, and a little later in 1845 the Chinese began a new temple off Hollywood Road in the Tai Ping Shan district.

The Anglican Church lagged well behind in the matter of building largely because its position and finances were bound up with the Colonial Government. The other Christian churches had to fend for themselves financially, and so were able to proceed with their plans.

The home government appointed a Colonial Chaplain, of the Church of England, as part of the establishment, despite Pottinger's omission to recommend it, and in December 1842 the Rev. Vincent Stanton arrived as Colonial Chaplain. There had been talk of joining the Anglicans and Presbyterians in one organization, a Union Church, but the Secretary of State did not approve. Anglican church services were first held in a temporary matshed church on the Murray parade ground, and later in one of the rooms of the Law Courts. A public subscription was raised to meet the cost of a church; at that time it was customary to assist the building of Anglican churches in the colonies from public funds, and the home government agreed that in Hong Kong the colony finances should provide two-thirds of its cost. There was great delay because the plans which were sent to England for approval were refused as too costly.

Designs sent from England were rejected by Davis on ground of unsuitability, and it was not until 1847 that building was begun by the Governor himself laying the foundation stone. The cost had been seriously underestimated, and the tower had to be omitted; it was added later, but the home government refused to sanction any additional official contribution towards it. On the establishment of the Anglican Bishopric of Victoria, in 1849, the church became the cathedral church of the new diocese.

The European community developed a strong social life; an amateur dramatic corps came into being in 1844, though its life was brief, and the Hong Kong Club came into existence in 1846. In 1847, chiefly under the patronage of Davis, a China branch of the Royal Asiatic Society was founded. Life was made pleasanter by an ice-house set up by public subscription, for which the government gave a free grant of land in what came to be known as Ice House Street. These activities were confined to the comparatively few wealthy foreigners by whom the colony was dominated. There was no attempt to build a community. There were in fact many communities having nothing in common except sharing the small island. Apart from the wealthy Europeans, there were the poor Europeans, seamen, and the usual off-scourings of the port; some made good in a hard competitive world, but many were failures, frequenting the numerous taverns. The Parsee community was considerable, and had its own cemetery at West Point. The Chinese were despised and treated with contempt as inferior beings, though this was partly a result of the prevalence of crime among them, and their reputed unreliability except where their own interest was involved. There was no social mixing, and each community went its separate way in pursuit of the objects that had brought it to Hong Kong.

The official attitude towards the Chinese was liberal enough in theory, but much of the legislation providing for law and order discriminated against them. A strict curfew was imposed; Chinese could not walk abroad after nine o'clock in the evening without a note from their employers, and had to carry lanterns after dark. An ordinance to make membership of a Triad society punishable by branding was not accepted by the home government. In the administration of justice, punishments were heavy; for the Chinese, flogging and the cutting of the queue were normal additions to prison sentences, since detention in jail was not regarded as a sufficient deterrent to people with a low standard of life. A protest against the excessive floggings imposed in Hong Kong was raised in the British parliament by Dr. John Bowring, who later became Governor. The incident which gave rise to this protest may be briefly recounted as typical. In April 1846, a policeman had arrested a Chinese who was carrying some timber, on the suspicion that it was stolen. Passing some Chinese houses on the way to the police station, he had been stoned, and the Chinese suspect had escaped. A detachment of police was sent to the scene, and being unable to discover those who had earlier assaulted the constable, they arrested all the Chinese they found without registration tickets. These were fined five dollars each, or in default sentenced to receive twenty strokes with the rattan and have their queues cut. Fifty-four were unable to produce the five dollars, and were publicly flogged. This action aroused the protests of the Chinese community, who usually passively accepted their conditions unless they became intolerable.

The registration ordinance, which in effect applied only to the Chinese and was conceived as a police measure to control the movement of population, was administered oppressively.

George Smith, an anglican missionary and first Bishop of Victoria, who came out to the East on an exploratory visit during the years 1844–46, gave a depressing picture of life in the colony, which he judged quite unsuited to become the centre of the intended missionary effort. The foreigners were hated for their 'moral improprieties and insolent behaviour', and he complained of the frequent scenes in the streets which brought discredit upon the British. Of the Chinese, he said, 'the lowest dregs of native society flock to the British settlement in the hope of gain or plunder', and they were 'treated as a degraded race of people'. Some Chinese Christians expressed 'the most impassioned indignation when speaking of the harsh treatment to which they are exposed.' In defence of this severity it must be admitted that the Chinese proved to be difficult and not readily amenable to British ideas of law and order, and all too often in the courts their testimony was proved quite unreliable. The suppression of crime was a formidable problem.

A later Attorney-General found much evidence of irregularity in the magistrates' courts, and though there were no cases of deliberate perversion of justice, the temptation was to treat the Chinese too summarily.

At the end of the war, it was confidently expected that the new settlement would rapidly expand and become the centre of British trade in China. 'Within six months of Hong Kong being declared to have become a permanent Colony, it will be a vast emporium of commerce and wealth,' Pottinger had written in the spring of 1842. This expectation was not and could not have been fulfilled. There were many reasons for the failure to visualize the pattern of British commercial development in China.

In the first place no one knew how the five new open ports would develop as far as residence and British trade were concerned. No one foresaw that the mud flats of Shanghai, near the mouth of the Yangtze River, would grow into the wealthy and populous International Settlement, or that Ningpo would fail to show any development. Many thought that the cession of Hong Kong was a mistake and that it should be exchanged for the island of Chusan off the mouth of the Yangtze, which was much more suited for the China trade. The subsequent growth of Shanghai shows this view to have been substantially correct. As British trade grew, ships naturally sailed to the five treaty ports to avoid the expense of transhipment at Hong Kong. No one knew what living conditions would be like at the open ports; residence was allowed by the Treaty of Nanking, but by the Treaty of the Bogue had been hedged in by restrictions, and events were to prove that the Chinese interpretation of residence at the open ports differed from that of the British. Besides, by long tradition, residence had been interpreted as residence during the trading season only. In part, the hopes of Hong Kong were built on the assumption that the Canton area would retain its monopoly of the foreign trade, with the difference that Hong Kong would replace Canton as its centre. This was the view of Elliot, and led him to demand the cession of the island. The British demand for the opening of the five treaty ports really undermined Elliot's policy. Hong Kong could only become an emporium by being the centre of an unrestricted trade with the neighbouring coast. This was barred by treaty obligations, and much of its early trade was therefore necessarily illicit.

Despite the British government's desire to discourage it, the island became the great centre of the opium trade. Davis had reported soon after his arrival in 1844, that 'almost every person possessed of capital who is not connected with government employment, is employed in the opium trade', and later in the year said that opium was in general trade along the whole coast. The opium merchants recovered from their fright over possible action by the home government against the opium trade, and the outer anchorages of Namoa and Kap Sui Mun were given up for the greater security of the colony. Opium could be stored more cheaply in its godowns or in hulks in the harbour, and the hazards of the open anchorages were avoided; this allowed lower insurance charges. Prices were openly announced in the press.

Shelley, the Auditor-General, in a report to Davis written in the autumn of 1845, said there were 80 clippers engaged in the trade, and named 71; of these 19 belonged to Jardine Matheson, 13 to Dent & Co., and 'several small schooners belonged to Duus, Scott and others'. Shelley was not a very reliable person, but presumably wrote from some personal knowledge. The annual government report for 1845 referred to opium as the big export and to its transhipment at Hong Kong to smaller vessels adapted for the coastal trade, which then returned to the island with specie.

The opium farm set up by Davis was attacked by the merchants, who wanted the whole trade under their control, and was accepted by the Colonial Office only on the recommendation of the Board of Trade; Earl Grey said in 1846, 'I confess I have still great doubts if the decision of the Board of Trade is wise,' but thought it must be accepted, though it was directly at variance with the 'written testimony of the largest house engaged in the trade of those ports.'

In 1845, Davis told Lord Aberdeen that two difficulties had arisen in dealing with the opium merchants. They had assumed consular appointments in the service of other nations, to the annoyance of Davis who thought they would put themselves alongside the British consuls, and that this practice 'might increase the disposition of the rich opium merchants, already sufficiently inflated and independent', to disobey the laws; and they went north of latitude 32 degrees, contrary to the Order in Council, by using ships of foreign registry. Grey advised in reply that there was no legal objection to either course.

Hong Kong did not make its livelihood from opium alone. Chinese junks used the island to circumvent the Chinese salt monopoly. Salt was transferred to small fast rowing boats and sold on the mainland at less than the official price. Gutzlaff, reporting on the native junk trade in 1845, said the salt junks came from Hachong and Kweishen, but he said, 'this had always been a thriving business', as if it had always existed. The junk captains took opium and piece goods with the proceeds from the sale of the salt in Hong Kong.

Smuggling was not confined to opium and salt. British and Chinese alike had no scruple about turning the island's immunity from Chinese control to their own advantage, and Davis wrote in 1845 that lorchas used to come from Canton bringing little except tea 'not passed through the Chinese customs house'.

Legitimate trade grew slowly, handicapped by the treaty stipulations which confined Chinese commerce with the island to the five open ports, and in practice this meant largely to the Canton river delta. Davis reported in 1845 that the advantage of Hong Kong was that goods could now be placed in 'insurable' godowns, to await a favourable market. In December 1846 Davis said this system of having goods for the Canton market warehoused at Hong Kong until actually sold or until there was prospect of a prompt sale, was an important element in the prosperity of the colony.

Precise figures for the colony's trade and shipping cannot be obtained, because Hong Kong was a free port and there existed no machinery for recording imports and exports. Shipping returns were provided by the Harbour-master, but since ships called for stores, orders or the latest advices, as well as for trade, they give only an indication of the commerce carried on, and the information was admitted not to be full or accurate. In 1844, 538 ships having a tonnage of 189,257 entered the port, and in 1847 the figures were 694 and 229,465 tons. The chief countries from which they came in 1847 were Great Britain, 53 ships of 21,173 tons; India 114, of 66,259 tons; Australia 33, of 10,364 tons; N. America 16, of 8,175 tons; S. America, Pacific Islands, and East Indies 56, of 15,800 tons; China Coast 139, of 24,337 tons and the Canton River 283, of 83,287 tons. The chief increases were with India, Australia and N. America. The number of ships from England showed some decline, and the Manila trade, important in the early years for rope, timber, and tobacco, had almost disappeared.

Imports from Great Britain were chiefly beer, gin, wines, earthenware, cotton goods, coal, hams, and iron bars. India sent chiefly cotton and opium. Figures for opium in 1846 were given as 9,348 chests, an amount adequate for Hong Kong's needs and as a stock to cushion market fluctuations; some opium intended for China would be sent direct, but would be accounted for in the island.

Entrepôt trade took some time to develop. The attempt to make Hong Kong a centre of the tea trade collapsed with heavy losses; the large building erected by Dent as an exchange remained unused until it was taken for the Supreme Court. The junk trade, a good index of entrepôt progress, developed very slowly. In 1847 imports of goods into Hong Kong in Chinese vessels was valued at £498,239, of which sugar at £196,350, rice at £152,750 and nut oil at £121,000 were the chief. Exports were valued at £226,130, of which £195,625 was for opium. The sugar trade which had grown up in 1847 was carried in British ships and so would not be shown. Gutzlaff, the Chinese Secretary in the office of the Superintendent of Trade, who interviewed junk owners, reported that the failure of Hong Kong to become an emporium was due to the opening of the treaty ports, and not, as was too often alleged, to the Treaty of the Bogue. He also reported that he did not receive a single complaint from any junk master of interference by the Chinese government, nor had he heard of a single instance of seizure or confiscation by the Chinese customs. In his report for 1845 Gutzlaff summarized the reasons why Hong Kong did not develop as an emporium: (1) Piracy hindered trade. (2) It was more economic to trade directly at the open ports. (3) Chinese products were not saleable in Hong Kong—tea, alum, rhubarb, sulphur were all tried unsuccessfully; the British merchants got all they needed direct from the open ports. (4) The Chinese used British ships for imports from the Straits and other neighbouring countries, because they were cheaper and safer; this helped the British carrying trade, but did not help Hong Kong. (5) No important Chinese merchants came to the island because it was more advantageous to be at Canton.

The island was important economically because it was an administrative and military centre and the headquarters of important merchant houses. It developed shipping services which became the basis of its economy. Repair services were in demand and firms tried to secure land on the cheap to build patent slips for this work.

Piracy was endemic and every junk ran the risk of capture if it did not buy its immunity. Pottinger had refused to assist in the suppression of piracy because of the danger of incidents which might hamper the good relations he wanted to establish with China; the navy did not like police work, and there was the difficulty of operating in Chinese territorial waters. The Chinese authorities took no action, and Davis reported more than once that piracy was becoming a serious menace. In 1844, 12,000 rupees of army pay were pirated off Chek Chu. Davis urged naval action, but the Admiral, Cochrane, replied that it was impossible to distinguish a pirate, that naval vessels were unsuitable for inshore work, and suggested disarmament of Chinese vessels and the organization of convoys, and complained that many pirates actually came into the harbour where accomplices supplied the necessary information. Chinese merchants in Hong Kong offered to subscribe towards the cost of two lorchas which Davis wanted for local anti-piracy work, but he complained afterwards that 'they evaded the subject when it was pressed upon them'. Davis had one lorcha built for this work, but little effective action was taken until the navy changed its policy and organized expeditions against the pirate fleets.

Currency produced some difficulty too, as the Chinese were very fastidious over coins, preferring Spanish dollars to Mexican though the two were identical in silver content, but generally accepting silver only by weight and touch. The copper cash was their most popular coin. In May 1845 a proclamation made the following coins legal tender in addition to British coins and fixed their sterling equivalents: the East India Company's gold mohur at 29s. 2d.; the rupee at 1s. 10d. and the half, quarter, and one-eighth rupees, pro rata; the dollar of Spain, Mexico and any South American state at 4s. 2d. and the Chinese copper cash at 288 for one shilling. In April 1845 a branch of the Oriental Bank was established in the colony, and its note circulation in August 1847 was reported as $58,305.

The colony had many detractors and few defenders. The violent criticisms of R. M. Martin, the strong memorial of the Hong Kong merchants against Davis's new taxation, the necessity of voting annual sums towards the expenses of Hong Kong and the consular establishments in the five Treaty Ports, together with disappointment at the failure of the China trade to show the spectacular growth that had been anticipated, all led to the appointment in March 1847 of a Select Committee of Parliament to 'enquire into the present state of the commercial relations between Great Britain and China'.

So far as Hong Kong was concerned, the Committee pointed out in its report that no great commercial advantage had been derived from it. The treaty arrangements debarred it from performing its natural function as an entrepôt for the neighbouring coasts. In addition 'to these natural and necessary disadvantages it appears to have laboured under others, created by a system of monopolies and farms and petty regulations, peculiarly unsuited to its position and prejudicial to its progress.' This course of action was a result of the attempt to maintain order and security 'in the midst of a vagabond and piratical population', and also of the desire to raise a revenue adequate to the maintenance of its civil government, and was contrary to the true interest of the settlement, which demanded the greatest freedom of intercourse and traffic consistent with the treaty obligations. The report continued 'Nor do we think it right that the burden of maintaining that which is rather a post of general trade in the China seas, than a colony in the ordinary sense, should be thrown in any great degree on the merchants or other persons who may be resident upon it.' The Committee recommended the government to revise the whole system of administration which was unnecessarily expensive in relation to the colony's needs. It criticized the arrangement by which the Governor was responsible to the Colonial Office as Governor and was under the Foreign Office as Superintendent of Trade and Plenipotentiary. It suggested a short code of law should be drawn up to assist in the adminstration of justice, more teaching of the Chinese language should be done in Hong Kong and schools for the Chinese should be encouraged. The Committee referred to the petition sent home by the merchants and expressed a guarded sympathy with their complaint that tenure of land was limited to seventy-five years, adding that certain vague assurances of a more permanent tenure appeared to justify their feelings that there had been a breach of faith. The Committee recommended 'that a share in the administration of the ordinary and local affairs of the island should be given, by some system of municipal government, to the British residents.' The Committee felt it necessary to remind the British in China that the best interests of commerce were best served 'by studying a conciliatory demeanour' and showing good will.

The Committee's report was a triumph for the merchants, and so indirectly a censure upon Sir John Davis, though the Hong Kong government's point of view does not appear to have been asked for until it was requested to comment on the findings. For the next few years administrative policy in the island was dominated by the Committee's recommendations.

CHAPTER IX

SIR GEORGE BONHAM, 1848–54

'Stringent measures must be made to reduce expenditure at whatever inconvenience and sacrifice.'
Earl Grey to Bonham, 21 September 1848.

SAMUEL GEORGE BONHAM had risen in the service of the East India Company to become, at the early age of thirty-four, Governor of the Straits Settlements, then administered by the Company; ten years later, in 1847 he was selected to succeed Sir John Davis as Governor of Hong Kong, and Plenipotentiary and Superintendent of Trade in China; he was knighted in 1851 and made a baronet in the following year. He proved to be a popular and successful Governor in spite of the difficulties which faced him on his arrival in March 1848 and which continued during the period of his administration. The colony had failed to develop economically as expected, with the result that the value of land declined, and there were renewed protests by the merchants against the taxation imposed by Davis designed to hasten the day on which the colony would become self-supporting, and which the 1847 Parliamentary Select Committee had criticized. Quite apart from these two serious difficulties, a third appeared; there was a crisis in the colony's finances. The result was that Bonham came under considerable pressure to make economic and administrative adjustments to meet the island's diminished prospects, and was forced to adopt a crippling policy of the strictest economy and retrenchment.

The financial crisis was the most immediate problem. It emerged suddenly in the summer of 1848, and was the result of a number of factors. Bonham produced revised financial estimates showing less revenue and greater expenditure than had been anticipated by Davis, and consequently, a larger deficit to be made good by the parliamentary vote for Hong Kong. In September 1848 Grey replied that it was quite impossible to increase the vote for Hong Kong which had been fixed at £25,000, the same as for the year 1848, and that expenditure would have to be reduced 'at whatever inconvenience and sacrifice'. He said there would have to be 'a continuous and rapid diminution in the parliamentary vote in future years' and that the colony would have to rely for its civil support on its own resources.

At the same time a serious deficit in the colony's accounts was brought to light by the Board of Audit at home. This had arisen in the early days of the colony when Elliot and Pottinger had drawn on military funds to meet government expenses. A budget of income and expenditure should have been prepared and submitted to the Colonial Office for its consent, in June 1843 when the island was declared to be a British colony, but Pottinger had been overworked and in any case time was needed to prepare estimates and to organize the Legislative Council to vote the necessary taxation. Pottinger in fact continued to raid the military chest as an emergency measure. Davis arbitrarily disregarded his predecessor's financial arrangements and established the colony's finances on a new basis dating from his arrival. It took the Audit Department five years

to discover that expenditure amounting to some £23,000 incurred in that early period had never been accounted for. In
addition Pottinger had been asked to supply an estimate of all
expenses from 1 September 1843 to 31 March 1845; this was
not received in time for use in preparing the Hong Kong vote
to be presented to Parliament in 1844. The Colonial Office on
12 June 1844, submitted an estimate, 'based on conjectural
grounds', asking for £30,000, a sum which proved to be completely inadequate. The Audit Department therefore raised an
awkward and obscure issue, causing anxiety to a Colonial
Office already troubled by the cost of Hong Kong. There was
a further complication that estimates for public works were put
at their total cost regardless of what could be spent in any one
year, and the Treasury ruled that any unspent balances in one
financial year could not be made available as income in a subsequent year. These disclosures intensified the demand for
retrenchment.

Bonham received the demand for the curtailment of expenditure within the limit of the parliamentary vote of £25,000
with dismay. He complained that the financial year was well
advanced and that he was already committed to expenditure in
excess of income greater than could be made up by the parliamentary vote. He stopped all public works except those actually
in hand, held up the building of the urgently needed Government House, and only balanced his budget by delaying the payment of his own salary until the following financial year. This
financial stringency imposed on Bonham a completely negative
policy with regard to the development of the colony.

But the home government went even further. In December
1848, Grey ordered Bonham to carry out a thorough and comprehensive investigation into all branches of colonial expenditure, civil, military and naval, describing it as 'a particular task
calling for special powers', with the object of making permanent
economies in the establishment. T. F. Wade was sent out as his
Private Secretary for the purpose. As a result of his investigation Bonham recommended the abolition of the offices of
Treasurer, Surveyor-General, Registrar-General, Colonial Surgeon and Assistant Harbour-Master, and suggested that one
third of the Governor's salary should be met by the Foreign
Office for his work as Plenipotentiary and Superintendent of

Trade, that the Colonial Secretary was to combine his duties with those of the treasurership at a reduced salary, and the work of the Surveyor-General and Colonial Surgeon should be done by military officers on a part-time basis. The Chief Magistrate was to carry out the duties of Registrar-General with extra pay. There were also to be economies in the cost of the Police Force. Bonham described the judicial side of the administration as 'the most overpaid and underworked department of this colony', and suggested reducing the salary of the Chief Justice from £3,000 to £2,000 and that of the Attorney-General from £2,000 to £1,000. In addition, in each department a reduction in the number of minor offices was proposed. To prevent injustice, these changes were to be effected as vacancies occurred, but a few officers resigned in view of the uncertainty facing them. Inglis, the efficient Registrar-General and an able linguist, joined in the gold rush to California in 1849, with little success apparently, for he soon returned to the colony. The Treasurership was not in the end abolished, and the offices of Colonial Secretary and Auditor were combined instead. Many of these proposals proved unnecessary by the time vacancies occurred.

Bonham reviewed the military expenditure and in January 1849 suggested sweeping reductions. He considered six companies of British and three companies of Ceylon Rifles, totalling 1,200 men, would be an adequate garrison, and that a colonel might replace the major-general as the garrison commanding officer. He suggested big reductions in the Artillery, Engineer and Medical Departments, and reported that the Ordinance and Commissariat Departments were excessive, but that he did not have enough information to be able to suggest what reductions were possible. The reduction in the Engineer and Medical branches made it impossible to spare officers for part-time work on the civil side, and so nullified two of Bonham's proposed economies in the office of Surveyor-General and Colonial Surgeon.

The defence of Hong Kong, he thought, must rest ultimately on the navy, and a frigate and a steamer should be permanently stationed there. He advised that the navy maintained excessive stores, and recommended that some stores like ammunition and provisions should be merged with those of the army.

As a result of all these economies, the expenditure fell from

£62,658 in 1848 to £36,418 in 1853 and Bonham's estimates for 1854, the year he retired, were even reduced to £31,509. The parliamentary grant during his period of office was reduced from £25,000 in 1848 to £8,500 in 1853. Military expenses, which were entirely borne by the home government, fell from £80,778 in 1848 to £50,346 in 1853. The home government was still dissatisfied with the cost of Hong Kong, and on Bonham's retirement made a futile attempt to reduce the status and salary of the Governor, solely in the interest of economy.

Land was a pressing problem; many holders were giving up their lots, and revenue from rents suffered. In February 1848, before Bonham arrived, the merchants had presented a memorial to the Secretary of State on the subject of land, complaining that the rents were too high, owing to the insufficient number of lots put up at the first auction, a fact which produced un-natural competition and forced up the rents, and asking for a revision of the leases and a reduction of rents. They again pointed to the 'questionable policy' of making the few residents bear the cost of a colony maintained for the general benefit of British trade. Grey replied that any reduction of rents would be unfair to unsuccessful bidders at the auctions, and suggested for con-sideration an extension of the terms of the leases; in December 1848 he authorized Bonham to substitute 999-year leases, virtual perpetuity, for those of seventy-five years.

The merchants still imagined they were overtaxed and wrote to Bonham in January 1849 asking for tax reductions. There were still many cases of land being given up and Bonham re-ported that in December 1848 130 lots of land had reverted to government; of these 5 were resumed by government, 49 were purely speculative, and 76 had been held by genuine buyers who gave up the holdings because the colony had not progressed as anticipated. Revenue from land was reduced by a fifth, and full enquiry was decided upon.

A special Land Committee was set up in 1850 and all allot-ment holders who felt they were paying excessive rents were asked to bring their cases before the committee. In spite of all the fuss and protest of the merchants, only eleven did so, and half the amount of land involved belonged to one notorious speculator, George Duddell. Only five of the applicants had their claims recognized. The two unofficial members of the committee who were merchants, suggested a complete abolition of all land rents, and that the revenue should be made up by an increased Imperial grant and by a tax on the China trade; but this was hardly a practical suggestion. The outcome was that some relief was given in the rents of seven allotments, and arrangements were made for subdividing allotments to facilitate sale. A little later, a change in the conditions of auction was made; it was no longer to be for the annual rent, but for the payment of a single premium to secure the allotment at a fixed rent. The land now ceased to be a burning question, and by the end of Bonham's period of office land values began to recover as the mood of despondency gave way to better-founded calculations of the colony's future.

The report of the 1847 Select Committee on the China Trade had recommended easing the burden of taxation on the residents, but this was impracticable, since the demand in Parliament for a reduction in Imperial expenditure on Hong Kong was inconsistent with any real relief in local taxation. In January 1849 the merchants sent a petition to Parliament complaining that, except in the case of land, nothing had been done to implement the recommendations of the Select Committee, particularly in the matter of giving the residents a voice in the ordinary and local affairs of the island. The view was again strongly put that the island was necessary for the protection of the China trade as a whole, and that the cost of its administration should not fall on the firms who happened to be resident there, and that there should be some form of local self-government. The Supreme Court was criticized for its heavy fees, and for the lack of a simple code of law, two conditions which were considered to be frustrating the ends of justice in Hong Kong.

Bonham commented to Earl Grey that he had known about the petition only through the press, but he was quite willing to hand over the control of the police to municipal commissioners, if they were prepared to assume financial responsibility for it; but since the police cost £4,283 and the police rate amounted to no more than £2,500, he said he did not see what the merchants had to gain. He also proposed that the local inhabitants might be given a voice in government by the nomination of two of their number to each of the Legislative and Executive Councils. Grey accepted the suggested addition to the Legislative Council,

G

but not to the Executive Council, and Bonham was asked to nominate and submit the two names for approval. Bonham regularly consulted influential opinion in the colony and the practice was followed on this occasion. He asked the unofficial Justices of the Peace to nominate the two members, but it was an informal arrangement and the nominations remained technically his own. The Justices nominated Jardine and Edger, members of two of the leading merchant houses in the colony, and in June 1850 their warrants arrived and they were sworn in, being the first unofficial members of the Legislative Council.

The proposed introduction of municipal government did not materialize. Bonham consulted the Justices of the Peace, and offered them control of the police if they would raise additional revenue to make up the deficit in the police rate which amounted to only £2,500. He suggested taxes on carriages and chairs and offered additional assistance from the general colonial revenue for two years. The Justices refused, because increased taxation was the very condition they had objected to; they also argued that there had recently been economies in the police force which made it more inefficient than ever, and that much expense was needed to bring the police to the desired level of efficiency. The Justices said that the community were quite willing to undertake responsibility for police, roads and sewers if the government would provide the funds. On this simple issue, of who was to pay for the municipal administration, the talks broke down.

A final attempt was made to patch up the system of Chinese administration for the Chinese. They had found the Supreme Court procedure cumbrous and expensive, and their ignorance of the forms of law was exploited by some British lawyers. One abuse discovered was the extortion of money by resident Chinese from their newly-arrived compatriots by securing Supreme Court affidavits alleging some civil wrong such as debt. Chinese residents petitioned the Governor to be allowed to settle civil cases in which the parties were Chinese, in their own way, and in fact for six years no such civil case had come before the Supreme Court. There were 30,000 Chinese now in the colony, handling about a quarter of its trade, and Bonham thought it advisable to support them in this matter. An ordinance was passed extending the powers of the head-men to settle all civil disputes if the parties were willing to abide by their decisions, and arranging for salaries to be paid to them from special rates payable by the Chinese, who were to assess themselves. The ordinance was made voluntary in that it was to operate only in those districts which petitioned for it.

The colony continued to grow, despite the forebodings of the merchants. Bonham estimated the population had increased by 82½ per cent between 1848 and 1853; the number of Europeans had increased from 642 to 776, excluding troops, and the Chinese from 20,338 to over 38,000. The Taiping Movement created unsettled conditions and brought Chinese families to the island, and the murder of Amaral, the governor of Macao, in 1849, brought an influx of Portuguese. By 1853 there were 491 European and 2,416 Chinese houses. Retrenchment meant that public works were drastically reduced. Government House was built at a cost of £14,407, but the delay was so great that it was only just completed when Bonham left. The jail was improved as a result of the visit of an official from home and a prison wall was built; but much necessary public work was left for the future.

The health of the colony gradually improved and fever epidemics became rarer. The troops suffered more than the civilian population; in 1848, deaths among European troops rose to 20.43 per cent and among native troops to 5.14 per cent, but the mortality among Chinese civilians was 1.14 per cent only. The following year, 1849, the mortality among European troops was 7.90 per cent, among native troops 6.18 per cent, among European civilians 5.06 per cent and among Chinese only 0.61 per cent. But the next year was again a bad year for European troops with 23.94 per cent mortality compared with 10 per cent for the civilian population, which latter was swollen by the deaths of seamen. The home government had refused to set up a civil government hospital, but in 1848 Bonham reported that he had taken a house to serve as a civil hospital because of the 'present unhealthy state of the colony'. The lack of facilities for storing medicines and the distances separating the police stations made Dr. Morrison's task of attending the government personnel too difficult, and the hospital was agreed to. Morrison was the first to recommend residence on the Peak for health reasons.

A disastrous fire in December 1851 reduced much of the

Chinese part of the city and destroyed 458 Chinese houses. The army was called out to help fight it and two British artillery officers and twenty Chinese lost their lives, and one officer and one of his men were wounded while using gunpowder to demolish buildings in an attempt to stop it spreading. It had begun in a clothier's shop, the upper part of which was made of wood; it was the dry season and there was little water to fight the flames. Sheds were erected to house the homeless, food was supplied, and their ground rents for the second half of 1851 and their police rates for all of 1852 were remitted. To make up the deficiency in revenue, Bonham asked for an additional special parliamentary grant of £2,500 for the year 1852. In the rebuilding, all houses were to be of brick or stone, and new streets were laid out; opportunity was taken to use the rubble to fill in the adjoining creek on which to construct a good road, named Bonham Strand, the cost of the reclamation and supporting stone wall being borne by the holders of adjoining lots. This was the first of the reclamations which were to alter the face of the city.

The Anglican church was completed in 1849, and in the same year the Anglican bishopric was established by private endowment, and George Smith, C.M.S. missionary, became the first Anglican Bishop of Victoria, with the whole of China and Japan as his diocese. The church was accordingly elevated to the status of a cathedral. St. Paul's College for the training of Chinese candidates for the ministry which had been projected by Stanton, the Colonial Chaplain, was completed, and the Bishop took over control of the college and secured a grant from the Foreign Office for the training of interpreters for the consular service in China. The London Missionary Society and the Catholic Church set up similar institutions to serve their missionary work.

Bonham secured a period of home leave in 1852–53; he had sent in his resignation at the same time as his request for leave, and leave was given him as an exceptional case. During his absence, Major-General Jervois, took over the administration of the colony, as Lieutenant-Governor, and Dr. John Bowring left his consulate in Canton to act as Superintendent of Trade. The question of dividing the control of trade and British subjects in China from that of the colony now came to the fore, and while Bonham was home, it was decided to make some changes.

The Hong Kong Justices of the Peace had as early as 1844 lost their authority over British subjects in the treaty ports. In 1853 the Hong Kong Legislative Council lost its power to make ordinances controlling British subjects in China who were placed under the direct administrative control of the consuls, responsible to the Superintendent of Trade, as had been advocated by Davis. Henceforth the Council's authority was confined to the colony. The arrangement by which the Governor was also Plenipotentiary and Superintendent of Trade remained a few more years.

Bonham left in April 1854, and his departure was genuinely regretted. He was popular and friendly; he had avoided imposing additional taxation, and in attempting to carry out the policy of the 1847 Select Committee, had decreased expenditure. He gave it as his opinion that the inhabitants were let off lightly; 'were this Colony taxed in the same way as are the Settlements in the Straits, it could in a year or two be made to pay its own expenses.'

CHAPTER X

SIR JOHN BOWRING, 1854–59

'Hong Kong is always connected with some fatal pestilence, some doubtful war, or some discreditable internal squabble . . .'
The Times, 15 March 1859.

DR. JOHN BOWRING had had a remarkable career before his appointment to the combined office of Plenipotentiary, Superintendent of Trade in China, and Governor of Hong Kong. He was well travelled, a brilliant linguist, an economist, a politician closely associated with the Philosophical Radicals, a hymn writer, and President of the Peace Society, and had been Member of Parliament as a radical and supporter of the Whigs. The doctorate which he was fond of parading was an honorary one from Gröningen University granted in recognition of his services to European literature. Trade recession in 1849 brought about the failure of his business undertaking; he sought a government post and accepted that of consul at Canton. He had interested himself in Chinese affairs partly because his son was employed in Hong Kong in the merchant house of Jardine, Matheson. He acted as Superintendent of Trade while Bonham was on leave in 1852, and when Bonham returned, he himself returned home on leave and was appointed as Bonham's successor. He arrived in 1854, being then sixty-two years of age, eleven years older than the man who was retiring. He was a man of liberal ideas, in advance of his time; he had energy—he began learning Chinese at the age of fifty-six—but he was conceited, self-important and not of sufficiently strong character for high administrative office. The result was an inconsistency and lack of balance. This man who had talked peace, by his own high-handed action brought about the second Anglo-Chinese war. He produced a number of excellent schemes of reform for the colony, but failed to carry them out because he was quite unable to control his subordinates. He was liberal in principle and yet his period of office saw a wave of anti-Chinese legislation. Under this good and well-meaning man the administration of the colony sank to its lowest level.

The retirement of Bonham prompted the home government to attempt further economies in the island's establishment. The Colonial Office informed Bowring before he came out that 'the civil establishment of the Colony is larger than its means would justify or that its probable importance for the present requires, and in particular, that it is not expedient to maintain a governor on the scale hitherto adopted.' The home government also decided to separate the offices of Superintendent of Trade and Governor; a Lieutenant-Governor, at a much reduced salary, was now thought to be adequate as the chief executive of the colony, in view of his diminished responsibilities. It was proposed to make Caine the Lieutenant-Governor, at a salary of £2,000, and place the colonial secretaryship in the hands of the Portuguese chief clerk, J. M. D'Almada e Castro, on the understanding that Caine would himself undertake the more responsible duties attaching to this normally important office. There was strong local opposition to the appointment of D'Almada, on the ground that he was not a British subject, and William Mercer was given the post, his place as Colonial Treasurer being taken by Rienaecker, the chief clerk at the

Colonial Treasury, at a much reduced salary. It was found impossible to separate the offices of Governor of Hong Kong and Superintendent of Trade in China without special legislation, and the Foreign Office insisted on the Superintendent of Trade residing in the colony. The result was that when Bowring became Superintendent of Trade and Plenipotentiary, he had to be Governor as well. To overcome the difficulty it was arranged that he should be a purely nominal Governor of Hong Kong, without salary. His instructions reserved to him the power of intervening in the colony's affairs when he thought the interest and well-being of the British in the Far East required it, but this was little more than a saving clause, since he was the nominal Governor, and it was arranged that he should see all dispatches. Caine was to be Lieutenant-Governor at a salary of £2,500 and to be responsible for the administration of the colony, and be given 'the necessary amount of independence and discretion far beyond what he would have' if only acting during the Governor's absence. This cumbrous and unworkable arrangement broke down. Bowring fully understood what the position was, but he was not the man to agree to remain aloof from Hong Kong affairs, and was dissatisfied with receiving only half the salary of his predecessor. He occupied the new Government House which was ready soon after his arrival, a circumstance which may have made him feel that his governorship was more than nominal.

In April 1854 Caine assumed control of the government of Hong Kong in conformity with the new scheme. Bowring soon began interfering, and in February 1855 matters came to a head over the appointment of a temporary Colonial Chaplain. The Rev. William Baxter, who had just come out from England to assume the post, was discovered to be a fugitive debtor, and Bishop Smith would not licence him. An army chaplain, the Rev. M. C. Odell, was appointed to take over the chaplaincy temporarily, and this was announced in the Government Gazette. Bowring took exception and asked who had authorized the appointment; Caine replied that he had consulted the Bishop and members of the Executive Council and thought Bowring had agreed, and so he had announced it. There were also differences over the Legislative Council. Bowring thought he should always preside, and not only on those occasions when affairs relating to China were being discussed, as Caine argued. The main reason for the breakdown of the new arrangement was that Bowring had large schemes of reform for the colony and wanted to carry them out. The dispute was referred home and Palmerston agreed that Bowring's position was anomalous and impossible. He called it 'an administrative solecism' since it created a governor who was a nonentity, and in April 1855 Bowring was given the governorship with full power. Bowring suggested Caine should be retired, but this was refused since Caine had not been responsible for the muddle. The economy in the governorship did not materialize, indeed it involved the additional expense of a sinecure Lieutenant-Governor until Caine retired in 1859.

The news of the outbreak of war against Russia (the Crimean War 1854–56) followed soon after Bowring's arrival in 1854, and without delay he accompanied the Admiral, Sir James Stirling, on an expedition to the north to forestall possible Russian action in the Far East. Hong Kong was now seized with panic due to the fear of being left undefended; the fleet had sailed, and the army numbered 570 men instead of the 1,128 recommended by Bonham, and only 400 of these were fit for duty. Piracy flourished and a fleet of nineteen pirate vessels was believed to be ready to attack, and rumour had it that pirates murdered only British nationals. 'A Russian fleet, as was well-known, being in these seas,' as Caine put it, added to the fears. To the threats from without were added those from within, from 'a vagabond population with secret ties of association'.

In June 1854 Caine invited seven 'gentlemen of Hong Kong' to meet the Executive Council to advise on defence measures. They decided to man the colony's defences, to enrol auxiliary police, who soon numbered seventy-six, of which thirty-six were British, and to strengthen all police stations outside Victoria against attack. A volunteer corps was raised for the protection of the colony and the maintenance of order, and within a month it numbered 127, of which ninety-two were British, sixteen Portuguese and the remainder comprised various European nationalities. The war scare soon died away; the auxiliary police force was dissolved to save expense after a life of only six weeks; the volunteer corps lingered a little longer.

Sir John Bowring pursued a vigorous policy with regard to China and precipitated the war over the lorcha *Arrow* dispute in 1856. His policy displayed inherent contradiction. He held on the one hand the most liberal ideas; he had been president of a Peace Society advocating conciliation in the settlement of international disputes, and to the Chinese in Hong Kong he pursued a policy that was liberal and humane. On the other hand, he treated the Chinese government in a most high-handed way and was ready to use threats to secure concessions. The Treaty settlement had never worked satisfactorily at Canton, where attacks on Europeans were frequent, anti-foreign sentiment was strong, and the right of residence in Canton had been denied. Bowring had brought back with him a demand for treaty revision claimed on the most-favoured nation principle by a clause in the American Treaty of Wanghia of 1843. The Chinese High Commissioner at Canton, Yeh Ming-shên, made every excuse to avoid meeting Europeans, and in September 1856 Bowring with the French and United States representatives went to the Peiho River in an abortive attempt to negotiate direct with the Peking authorities.

The lorcha *Arrow* dispute brought about hostilities. In 1855 an ordinance was passed allowing Chinese shipowners who were lessees of Crown land in Hong Kong to secure the protection of the British flag by placing their ships on the colonial register. There was so much insecurity in neighbouring waters due to disturbances resulting from the Taiping rebellion that this protection became a valuable privilege. The *Arrow* was a Chinese-owned lorcha and was registered at Hong Kong, with a British master in command, though at the time of the incident the twelve months period covered by the registration had expired. In October 1856 the ship was boarded at Canton in the absence of the master, and the crew imprisoned on a charge of piracy. It was alleged that the British flag was hauled down, but this was denied. Bowring took a strong line and upheld the Consul's demand for an apology and the restoration of the crew, and when his ultimatum was not met, forces were assembled, and an assault on Canton was begun; an extremely trivial incident had led to war. Palmerston supported the action taken, but he was defeated in the Commons, where Bowring's policy was strongly condemned, even by many of his former friends. The defeat of the government led to a general election; Palmerston's Whig party was returned to power and the war against China, joined by the French, went forward. It is unnecessary here to follow the war in detail; the forces were insufficient to make an all-out attack on Canton, and Yeh did not succumb, as expected, to the bombardment and breach of the city walls. In 1857, the Indian Mutiny diverted to India the expedition intended for China, and it was not before December 1857 that the allies were ready to take Canton, which fell early in the new year, and Yeh was sent a prisoner to Calcutta. The war was taken to the north and concluded in June 1858 by the Treaty of Tientsin. The Chinese promised to open additional ports to trade, and to agree to receive a British diplomatic mission resident at Peking, though in view of great Chinese opposition, Lord Elgin, the British Plenipotentiary, undertook to recommend that it should be resident elsewhere than at the capital. Hostilities were renewed in 1860 because the British envoy found his passage to Peking barred at the Peiho River; Peking was occupied and the Convention of Peking of 1860 followed. But by this time Bowring had left.

The war vitally affected Hong Kong. In the first place the process, by which the island ceased to be the headquarters of British trade and administration in China was accelerated. Already in 1847 British subjects in China had lost the right of appeal to the Supreme Court in Hong Kong against consular decisions concerning the regulation of trade. In 1853 the Legislative Council had lost the power of concurrent legislation over the British subjects in the treaty ports. The Hong Kong Justices of the Peace had lost their authority over British subjects in China even earlier in 1844. It was now the turn of the Governor. He had come out in 1854 boasting of the vast area to which he had been accredited as British representative—'full of the importance of China and himself' it was said. He had taken a strong line with the Chinese over a trivial incident and brought hostilities; but this vigorous defence of what he conceived to be his country's interests did not bring him the credit he had hoped. The negotiations were taken out of his hands and Lord Elgin was sent out as Plenipotentiary in July 1857 and relieved him of this part of his duties. Bowring remained Superintendent of Trade until his retirement in 1859, when these duties were handed over to the resident British Minister to China, and henceforward the control of the colony was completely separated from that of relations with China and the Governor became responsible solely to the Colonial Office. In 1865, the Hong Kong Supreme Court lost its appellate juris-diction over civil cases from the Consular Courts, and from that date the severance was complete.

The second result of the war was an extension of territory of the colony by the cession of the Kowloon peninsula and Stone-cutters Island. Since this occurred in 1860 after Bowring had left, it will be dealt with in the next chapter.

Thirdly, the war brought once more conditions of insecurity, particularly when the attack on Canton was called off in November 1856, pending the arrival of more forces. Yeh hailed the withdrawal as a victory and ordered all Chinese to refuse to co-operate with the British. A price was put on their heads, the factories in Canton were burned down, and British wharves and port facilities at Whampoa were destroyed. The supply of food to Hong Kong was forbidden, though this embargo was not carried out, and placards appeared in Victoria urging all Chinese to join in the struggle against the enemy. In January 1857, on the orders of Chinese mandarins, an attempt was made to poison the foreigners in the colony by placing arsenic in the bread supplied by the E Sing Bakery in Wanchai. Fortunately the excessive amount used made detection easy and no great harm resulted. But the attempt inflamed the foreign com-munity. The police came in for the usual criticism, and strong measures against the Chinese vagrant population were urged, but Bowring, to his credit, resisted a widespread demand to have the suspects executed without a trial. Cheong A Lum, the owner of the bakery had gone to Macao that morning; he was brought back and tried, but was acquitted by a British jury because no real evidence against him could be produced. Fifty-two of his men were detained, and, the jail being full, they were confined from the fifteenth to the nineteenth of January in a room fifteen feet square at a police station; ten were then tried, but the remaining forty-two were kept in the same room until 3 February, when they were removed to the jail at the urgent instance of a local doctor. They were released, only to be seized again at the prison gate as suspected persons, while Bow-

ring referred the case home. Many British and Chinese petitioned against this detention, and the men were released on
condition they left the colony, and Cheong A Lum followed
them. News of the treatment of these men reached home through
the press, and to its credit, the British government demanded an
enquiry at which the facts were revealed. There were also mass
arrests; between 500 and 600 men were rounded up and 167
transported to Hainan, and on 24 January, 204 'suspicious looking characters' were arrested in Bonham Strand and 46 imprisoned; a further 146 men were arrested on secret information. Another bakery owned by Duddell was shortly afterwards
burned down, but tension soon subsided. Many Chinese sought
to avoid the conflict by emigration, and in 1857, 26,213 Chinese
passengers left Hong Kong mainly for the Pacific coast and
Australian colonies, compared to 14,130 in 1856.

   The war brought bitterness and insecurity; Bowring introduced harsh legislation against the Chinese, which was quite
at variance with his general policy, which was liberal and
humane. He was a reformer by inclination, and it was unfortunate that his programme of reform, which showed a deep
interest in the welfare of the Chinese, should have coincided
with a period of war and social tension, when it needed a period
of quiescence. Bowring brought the trouble on his own head,
and yet it is well to examine this other side of his character.

   Soon after his arrival Bowring reported that a 'system of fees,
extortion, favouritism and abuses in different shapes exists in
the colony, which ought not to exist,' and that he had received
many complaints from the Chinese 'to whom I am bound to
pay special attention as the sources of the present and future
prosperity of the Island.' He wanted to root out all irregularities,
and protect the Chinese from extortion and from rapacious
lawyers. He planned to broaden the Legislative Council by
adding an elective element, giving the vote to all registered
holders of Crown lands in Hong Kong, regardless of race, paying
a minimum annual rent of £10. He formulated ambitious
schemes of public works, land reclamation, the building of a
praya, the establishment of a Botanical Garden, and the improvement of the training of officials through a cadet scheme.
He particularly deplored the lack of schools for the poorer
sections, and wrote 'a large population of children of native

mothers by foreigners of all classes is beginning to ripen into a dangerous element out of the dunghill of neglect. They seem wholly uncared for.' He also saw that sanitary improvements were essential. Such were his ambitious and all-embracing plans for reform.

He was unable to carry out all this programme, but he initiated many developments for which his successor, Sir Hercules Robinson, got the credit. Strained conditions resulting from the war were against him. He himself was rather precipitate, and Russell, Colonial Secretary in 1855, remarked that Bowring 'was rather wild upon all subjects'. The strength of his personality did not seem commensurate with the scope of his ideas. One main difficulty was the personal bickering among his officials which brought the administration of the colony to its nadir.

Bowring set up a commission to enquire into extortion and the payment of illicit fees in the government departments, and to examine the question of all private fees. The enquiry was salutary, but ran up against the difficulty that the Chinese who expected to pay for access to government officials were unwilling to give evidence of actual cases. 'We rule in ignorance, they obey in blindness,' he said, and his solution was to push on with education to try and produce a new type of public servant to bridge the chasm between governors and governed; he thought the language problem was at the root of many evils; officials were needed who were not only honest and capable, but could overcome the language barrier as well. He got Foreign Office approval for a cadet scheme to supply the consular service in China with the necessary language training, and the essentials of this scheme were later adopted for the colony in 1861 by Robinson. Bonham had refused to promote officials who were competent in the Chinese language.

In order to help the Chinese understand the policy of the Hong Kong government, Bowring revived the office of Registrar-General which Bonham had abolished by his enforced economies, and added to it the title 'Protector of the Chinese', so that there should be an official to whom the Chinese could appeal for information and assistance; D. R. Caldwell, a brilliant linguist, was appointed, but not without misgivings at the Colonial Office.

Bowring also discussed the appointment of Chinese to positions of administrative responsibility in the government, as Justices of the Peace, for example. The Secretary of State agreed in principle, but advised caution, and no such appointments were in fact made.

Legal reforms were undertaken to give Chinese cheaper and more expeditious justice. In 1858 an ordinance was passed amalgamating the two branches of the legal profession; this allowed barristers to accept briefs direct from clients, avoiding the expense of an attorney. There had been exorbitant fees, sharp practice by dishonest lawyers exploiting Chinese ignorance, and agents were frequently employed to secure litigation on a commission basis. Now fees were regulated in the interest of litigants. Chinese were no longer debarred from serving as jurymen or from qualifying as legal practitioners. In various ways Sir John pursued his policy of alleviating Chinese conditions of life. It has already been mentioned that he allowed Chinese land-holders to register their ships under the British flag. In the matter of property, an ordinance was passed recognizing wills drawn up in accordance with Chinese usage as valid in the Court. Special burial grounds were set apart for the use of Chinese.

Bowring was concerned about sanitation and health. Smallpox was becoming serious, and the stench from drains was a matter of continuous outspoken comment. In 1854, following the death of Dr. William Morrison, J. Carroll Dempster, an army medical man, was appointed Colonial Surgeon, and he became an outspoken critic of the sanitary system of the colony. His first annual report for the year 1854 opened by regretting that 'Hong Kong should present so much filth and so many nuisances.' Tai Ping Shan contained 'cowsheds, pigsties, stagnant pools', the receptacles of every kind of filth. More drains, sewage, pavements and scavenging were needed: the houses, 'of which there is the greatest number in the smallest space', were faulty, and he suggested white-washing twice a year. Next year he reported nothing had been done except the building of a few dustbins, and he now thoroughly condemned the sanitary condition of the jail; he had often found up to sixteen men in a cell, and had had to have them separated. In the annual report for 1856, he made the most outspoken complaint because nothing had been done about his recommendations, though sanitation was most vital to the colony, and he complained that the invariable reply to all his representations was that the matter was 'under consideration' (underlined). In 1857 cholera appeared and was attributed to neglect of drainage and cleanliness.

Bowring did attempt to take some action. New drains, and bins for the deposit of garbage were built. Scavenging was carried out by convicts; the Surveyor-General defended himself in 1855 by saying that 4,826 convicts in all had been used under police supervision for scavenging during the previous year. While such arrangements existed no great improvement could be expected. Bowring grappled with the problem of nuisances, and passed a Building and Nuisances Ordinance in 1856. This met with the combined opposition of the Chinese who asked for no more than to be left alone, and of property owners who resented interference with property rights. The magistrate found difficulty in interpreting the ordinance, and, with the Justices, who opposed the measure, gave decisions contrary to the spirit of the act, much to Bowring's annoyance. This led to an open quarrel, for when Bowring remonstrated with the Justices for not administering the law as it was, they replied that interference with the administration of the law by the Executive was unconstitutional and that any guidance on the law should come from the Chief Justice in the Supreme Court, and not from the Governor. The dispute was referred home and the view of the Justices was broadly upheld. Perhaps the most significant of Bowring's actions in the field of sanitation was the appointment of an Inspector of Nuisances in 1859, the real beginning of the Sanitary Department; the Colonial Surgeon as yet bore no responsibility for the general health of the community, his duties being confined to attending the lower grades of government officials, the police and convicts in the jail. He had charge of a civil hospital, but it served the community only in accident cases.

The problem of sanitation included that of water supply, which became serious with the growth of the population. This increase, which was largely the result of unsettled conditions in China due to the Taiping Movement, had begun under Bonham and gathered momentum under Bowring. In 1853 the population was reported as 37,536. In 1854 it was 55,714, next year, 1855, it had jumped to 72,607, and after falling a little owing to the tension in the island in 1856, it grew to 85,330 in 1859. Water-supply was seriously defective; many houses had wells, but the Chinese poorer classes had no supply other than the open streams on the hillside. Bowring, rather surprisingly, took the line that it was not the function of the government to supply water; this was a matter for private enterprise, and he suggested a water company might be formed with power to make a charge. The Executive Council thought otherwise, and a plan was prepared to bring water from the south side of the island, but its execution had to wait some years.

Bowring came up against Chinese opinion in his attempt to control gambling, which he thought lay at the root of much of the colony's crime. He wanted to recognize the evil and license the gambling houses, but the home government would not permit this. Bowring did secure a Contagious Diseases Act providing for the recognition and licensing of brothels, but because of Chinese opposition, the ordinance was not made applicable to them.

Sir John Bowring wanted to reform the Legislative Council, by adding elected members. There were many reasons which led him to suggest this change. He was a radical in political life and a follower of Jeremy Bentham, the founder of Utilitarianism, which had become the dominant political philosophy of the period, and aimed at producing 'the greatest happiness of the greatest number' broadly by the democratic method of giving each man a vote. In view of his associations therefore, Bowring can hardly have caused surprise by wanting to introduce the vote into Hong Kong; besides, it was part of the colonial policy of the time to grant self-governing institutions to the colonies by setting up representative assemblies. What was surprising was that he was willing to give the vote to Chinese and foreigner on equal terms. Bowring wanted to use the Legislative Council as the agent of his reforms and therefore wanted it to be representative of opinion in the colony. He also thought that if the Legislative Council were made more representative, a scheme of municipal government which Bonham had attempted would become unnecessary. One other interesting argument used by Bowring was based upon finance. Bowring was able to write in July 1855 to say that he would not require any grant from the Imperial Parliament; the colony had become self-sufficient. He propounded the constitutional doctrine that if a colony were financially self-supporting, then it should have self-governing institutions, a doctrine that the Colonial Office did not accept. The colony made little contribution to military defence, and in any case Bowring had boasted too soon, for a heavy building and security programme forced him to appeal to the home government for grants in 1858 and 1859.

Bowring also said that the existing Legislative Council had been reduced to a nullity because Bonham had not consulted it about finances, and that Jardine, 'the only non-office holder of weight', had ceased to attend. The Council under Bonham had numbered six; three official, two unofficial members, and the Governor. The number was increased to seven when Bowring insisted on presiding, and Caine, who had also to attend as Lieutenant-Governor, was made 'senior member'. Bowring in August 1855 proposed a reconstruction of the Council by adding three official and three unofficial members. He also proposed that the five unofficials should be elected for three years by an electorate composed of all holders of un-divided lots of Crown lands with an annual rent of at least £10, and at least three out of the five were to be chosen from among the Justices of the Peace. He was anxious that all races should have the vote on equal terms 'as parts of the whole community', and gave the number of qualified holders as sixty-nine British, forty-two Chinese, and thirty other nationalities, but calculated that the electorate would be reduced to seventy-five when account was taken of holdings by partnerships and companies.

Labouchere, Secretary of State, minuted 'I have no wish to try the experiment' and rejected most of the scheme; he replied in July 1856 that 'the Chinese have not yet acquired a respect for the main principles on which social order rests,' and that since the British were few and remained only temporarily, it was not possible to give them power over the permanent residents. He went on to argue that elections would be suitable as a transitional step to giving the Legislative Council full power, but 'great commercial interests and the future progress of civilization throughout the East are to a great extent involved

H

in the maintenance of British rule and of orderly government in Hong Kong,' and to suggest that affairs in the colony could be conducted 'with the greatest regard to the feelings and interests of the Chinese population.' He made two proposals. Bowring could select competent Chinese for administrative posts or for the Legislative Council, and he agreed to an increase in the Legislative Council. The proposed elections were dropped. The Legislative Council was increased by the addition of two official members and one unofficial. The unofficial members were still to be appointed by the Crown on the nomination of the Governor, and Bowring continued Bonham's practice of allowing the Justices of the Peace to suggest the candidates for nomination. Bowring increased the number of the Legislative Council still further by adding two more official members, the Surveyor-General in 1857 and the Auditor-General in 1858, much to the annoyance of the three unofficial members who wanted their own element proportionately increased. Bowring's relations with the community had by then become strained, and gave him little incentive to approach the Colonial Office again. He began the practice of publishing the proceedings of the Legislative Council and in 1858 its meetings were opened to the public.

Bowring was fortunate in being free from the financial stringency which had so restricted Bonham. The mood of pessimism passed, and land values rose, stimulated in part by the influx of Chinese. The public revenue nearly doubled from £33,011 2s. 4d. in 1854 to £62,476 9s. 4½d. in 1858; the land rents improved during that period from £10,266 10s. 2½d. to £17,907 18s. 11d., and the expansion of sales brought increased income from the premiums realized at the auctions. The police rate improved in amount from £3,327 0s. 9d. to £13,281 4s. 4d., but this latter sum in 1858 included the proceeds of a new lighting rate. The legalization of opium in China followed the Treaty of Tientsin, and Bowring re-introduced the opium monopoly in 1858 which brought in £4,508 6s. 8d. But spirit licences in that year produced £4,760 14s. 7d., and indeed, 1859 was the first year since the abolition of the opium monopoly by Davis in 1848 in which the public revenue did not gain more from the European vice of alcohol than from the Chinese vice of opium. Expenditure showed a comparable increase from £34,035 0s. 1d. in 1854 to £62,979 9s. 1d. in 1858, due to increases in the establishment, and to a greatly increased programme of public works which flowed from the reforms and plans for development which Bowring put forward. There was considerable delay and expense over Government House because unsettled conditions in the Canton River held up supplies, and it was not ready for occupation until October 1855; a new debtor's jail was completed at about the same time. A new central police station was authorized, and additional police stations built in the western district as a result of the increased population. Strong criticism of the jail led to the building of a new jail, and new drains and garbage depots were built. The expansion of the population and of house-building meant increased expenditure on streets and roads. To meet the needs of these newcomers, a reclamation scheme between Happy Valley and the sea was carried out, and named 'Bowrington' after the Governor, the water from the valley being taken through the area in two open canals. Bowring was dissatisfied with the market monopolies and the construction of new markets was undertaken.

Two other schemes of economic value, but designed to embellish the city as well, stand to Bowring's personal credit. He was very keen to set up a public Botanic Garden, and lectured to the Royal Asiatic Society in Hong Kong on its value in spreading a knowledge of Chinese trees, woods and fibres. The Colonial Office remarked that any spare funds ought to be devoted to sanitation improvements, but Bowring persisted and to the enduring benefit of the colony the garden was established. Bowring was also the prime mover in a plan to construct a road along the whole sea front of the settlement, from Navy Bay to Causeway Bay; the scheme was referred to as the 'praya' scheme, tribute to the abiding Portuguese influence in the Canton delta area. The 'Bowring Praya', as it was to be called, was undertaken not only as an embellishment, but as an important development of economic value. From the early days, the lots of land had all fronted on Queen's Road and each marine lot holder had been left to provide a pier or effect any improvements on the sea front he chose. As shipping developed and the settlement grew, this lack of public access to the seashore became an anachronism. A praya scheme had been put forward by Gordon, the first Colonial Engineer, in 1843, but not until Bowring's time was it financially practicable, and even then, the Governor had to accumulate funds for the project by careful budgeting. The praya involved the construction of a sea wall and a measure of reclamation since it could not follow the uneven coast-line. On this question of reclamation Bowring came up against property rights of the large merchant houses, for the marine lot holders had already done some illicit reclamation on their own account; they had in fact more than doubled the size of their holdings, and the praya scheme was to them extremely unwelcome. The Surveyor-General produced a scheme which was announced in November 1855. The marine lot holders were to pay additional rent for the area added to their original holdings and to contribute to the cost of the sea wall and piers, the construction of which was to be undertaken by the government. Bowring threatened to resume the allotments, but did not allay the great opposition from European lot holders, who held a meeting of protest. The question was referred home, and the Governor's project was upheld. Chinese holders in the western area and some of the Europeans agreed to the plan. In these cases and where the government itself held marine lots, as at Bowrington, the work was begun. J. M. Dent, who held land between the central military cantonment and the town centre, and who led the opposition to the Governor, was among those who refused to give way, and in 1858 Bowring introduced an Ordinance to apply compulsory powers. To his intense surprise, the Legislative Council rejected the proposed ordinance; three of the official members joined the unofficial members in voting against the Governor. The praya scheme was thus delayed, so long indeed that it failed to attach to itself the name Bowring Praya as its originator intended.

The constitutional issue in this vote was an important one. Bowring, liberal as he was, did not object to the official members voting against him; he merely thought they should have indicated their opposition to him beforehand. The rule that official members must act and vote collectively on government legislation had not yet been laid down. Bowring thought that the merchant firms could bring pressure to bear on officials, and did do so on that occasion, and that the only solution was to remove the opportunity for such pressure by paying reasonable salaries, and doing away with the system of government officials receiving private fees. It is also true that Sir John had made himself unpopular with everybody by his liberalism to the Chinese and the extent of his reform projects. His departure was impending and the officials may well have calculated that a vote against him could do no harm.

While there was much in Sir John's policy and achievement that was admirable, he was unable to do as much as he proposed. He was singularly unfortunate in some of his officials, among whom there was bitter dissension; he lacked strength of personality, and the combination led to a virtual breakdown of his administration which has since served to obscure the value of his work in the colony.

Bowring made additional appointments as the financial situation made this possible. A Crown Solicitor was appointed in the Legal Department; in 1857 the Colonial Secretary was relieved of his audit duties by an Auditor-General, and the post of Registrar-General was revived. In 1856, a new Attorney-General arrived, T. Chisholm Anstey, a peculiar character, who outdid Bowring himself in his zest for reform and for rooting out abuse, malpractice and extortion, which he considered were rife in the colony. He was incorruptible and honest but lacking in balance, judgment and restraint. He forthwith attacked the Chief Justice, the Chief Magistrate, and eventually fell foul of Bowring, whose misfortune it was to be saddled with this quixotic man as his chief legal adviser. Anstey accused Caldwell of being unfit to hold the position of Justice of the Peace on the ground that he was financially interested in brothels and had consorted with pirates, and when the government took no action, Anstey forced the issue by resigning his commission as a Justice of the Peace. Bowring appointed a Committee of Enquiry which found that Caldwell, though not free from censure, should not be recommended for dismissal. Anstey's conduct in bringing unsubstantiated charges against his colleagues was now discussed by the Executive Council and on its recommendation he was suspended, and his dismissal was upheld by the home government. Unfortunately there were repercussions, and the Caldwell affair became a *cause célèbre*. Caldwell had been very friendly with a Chinese, Ma Chow Wong, who

in July 1857 was convicted for aiding pirates, and this association was at the root of Anstey's charges. It had leaked out that
when Ma Chow Wong's house had been searched, evidence
incriminating Caldwell had been found by Charles May, Police
Superintendent; this had been sent to the Acting Colonial
Secretary, Dr. W. T. Bridges, at whose orders it had then been
burnt. When the Caldwell enquiry resulted in Caldwell's
exoneration, suspicion fell at once on Bridges. Bridges was a
strong, unscrupulous character, a barrister who was brought
in as acting Attorney-General and Colonial Secretary while the
holders of those offices were on leave. He was a great supporter
of Caldwell. A local editor directly accused Bridges of burning
the evidence in order to save Caldwell; Bridges prosecuted him
for libel, but failed to win the action. The result was that in
the public mind, Caldwell was by no means cleared. The tale
of attacks and libel actions involving the press and many
government officials would take too long to chronicle here.
Bridges' own conduct over the new opium ordinance in 1858
did not escape censure from a committee of enquiry when he
accepted a retaining fee from the opium monopolist, though
acting as Colonial Secretary. Bowring was forced to send home a
massive number of papers and long dispatches relating to these
bickerings, and it was fairly clear that he had lost control. In
laying the mass of papers on the table of the House of Commons,
the Colonial Secretary said he would have preferred to lay the
table on them, and that they revealed 'hatred, malice and
uncharitableness in every possible variety and aspect', and it
was presumed that they represented the typical official life of
the colony. In accepting Anstey's dismissal, Bulwer-Lytton
referred to the unfortunate condition of the Public Service in
Hong Kong and determined that it should be investigated by
the new Governor. In 1859, the new British Minister to Peking
arrived, to take over control of British relations with China.
The loss of this important part of his functions clearly made
Bowring's position untenable and he was allowed by the
Colonial Office to resign.

Bowring had ability and ideas, he had that humane and
liberal outlook which would have enabled him to lead the
communities of the island into a partnership. He cared for
cultural things; he set up a museum in one of the rooms of

the Supreme Court to the annoyance of the court officials, and he was the leader of the local branch of the Royal Asiatic Society. Yet he seemed to lack the temperament for high office, and made himself intensely disliked by the foreign community. His was the first and only political appointment to the Governorship in Hong Kong, and the experiment was unsuccessful. As a reformer he upset the propertied classes, as a radical in politics and a Unitarian in religion he was out of touch with prevailing sentiment. His character and policy involved too many contradictions. He had brought war to China, though he stood for peace. He had set out to reform the abuses of Hong Kong and had succeeded in bringing his administration to a state of confusion. Undoubtedly there were abuses, but a less liberal man was needed to put them right. He left the colony in May 1859; the Europeans ignored him, but the Chinese presented gifts to show their appreciation of the work he had done for them.

Before turning to economic and social development under Bowring, it will be convenient to follow up the changes made by Bowring's successor, Sir Hercules Robinson.

CHAPTER XI

SIR HERCULES ROBINSON, 1859–65

'*Indeed Hong Kong is totally unlike any other British dependency and its position is in many respects so grotesquely anomalous. . . .*'

Sir Hercules Robinson to Duke of Newcastle, 3 July 1860.

SIR JOHN BOWRING left in March 1859, and it has already been shown that his administration had almost broken down through his inability either to control his officials or to implement his commendable proposals by effective administrative action. This administrative breakdown was made all the more public by the number of libel actions in which many officials were implicated. The choice of his successor was an important matter. Sir Hercules Robinson, a young man of thirty-five, was chosen; after service in the army, he had secured a governorship in the West Indies and appeared to have the necessary character to restore administrative order. He was hurried out with only a few days' break in England on the way, and arrived in September 1859. Caine, the Lieutenant-Governor, assumed control of the colony until Robinson arrived, and then retired on pension. The new Governor was less than four years in the colony; in July 1862, he went home on leave and returned in February 1864 for a further twelve months before being transferred in March 1865 to the governorship of Ceylon. His governorship, though short, marked a new era in the history of the colony. There was a clearing out of old officials. Caine retired in 1859; a specially augmented pension left him dissatisfied, and for some years he pursued the fruitless quest of an honour or title which he thought was his due. Chief Justice Hulme retired on pension in 1859. The suspension of the awkward Anstey had been upheld, and he never returned to the colony. Tudor Davies, the Chief Magistrate, accepted a senior post in the Chinese Imperial Maritime Customs in 1859, and W. H. Mitchell retired a few months after Robinson's arrival; both had given Bowring trouble. Dr. Bridges discreetly left the colony when the Caldwell case was about to be reopened. Rennie and Forth had only very recently arrived in the colony as Auditor-General and Treasurer respectively. A new Colonial Surgeon, Dr. I. Murray arrived in 1859; Inglis, the Harbour-master, soon retired and was replaced by Thomsett, a naval man. In brief, and partly by accident, Robinson had the advantage of working with a new team of officials, and conditions were ideal for the new broom. There remained Mercer, Colonial Secretary, who had been in the colony for seventeen years; he was still under forty, and had contrived to keep aloof from all the scandal of the previous administration. There were also Caldwell and May, both under a cloud.

The immediate task was to conduct the enquiry into the Hong Kong government service which had become necessary because of the Caldwell affair. Caldwell had been largely but not completely exonerated from serious charges by a Commission of Enquiry set up by Bowring. In a subsequent libel action brought by Dr. Bridges, against a newspaper editor called

Tarrant, there appeared evidence that Anstey had been justified in bringing his charges against Caldwell, and this incriminating evidence had been burned. Anstey had campaigned in England against the decision to suspend him, and protests against the state of affairs in the colony were made by various organizations throughout England. The affair had dragged on because of the mass of papers involved, and Robinson had been in the colony some time before he was instructed to make the enquiry, the object of which was to see if May and Caldwell could properly be retained in their offices. Robinson decided that the enquiry should be held in public before the Executive Council, and the Civil Service Abuses Enquiry commenced on 13 August 1860. It sat on thirty full days over the next thirteen months; the delay was due to leave, to sickness, to the complicated nature of the case and difficulty in getting Chinese to come forward and testify, but mainly to Caldwell himself. There had earlier been defalcations in his office involving the loss of £418 and he, as the responsible head, had been called upon to make the amount good by deductions from his salary. In February 1861 Caldwell complained that he could not live on the reduced salary; he resigned his post, and refused to continue his defence before the Executive Council. His resignation was not accepted and Robinson refused to allow the investigation to be stopped. Only Y. J. Murrow, editor of the *Daily Press*, and a bitter enemy of Caldwell, came forward in response to Robinson's invitation to the general public to give information. Robinson had indeed a difficult task, and complained that there was no specific charge, and that therefore everything relating to Caldwell and May had to be enquired into. Difficulties were created by the unreliability of Chinese witnesses, by the impossibility of substantiating much of the evidence; records had been destroyed or lost, witnesses could not be produced, the accuracy of translations was challenged, and generally the enquiry was confronted with every form of evasion and equivocation.

The verdict was that '. . . Mr. Caldwell's long and intimate connection with the pirate Ma Chow Wong was of such a character as to render him unfit to be continued in the public service . . .', and Robinson, in reporting this, also stated that if the verdict had been different, he would have been forced to recommend his dismissal because of his treatment of May, and of his abandonment of office in the middle of the enquiry. Caldwell was not of pure European descent, he had married a Chinese, and he was made to feel that these were disadvantages. He was never again employed by the government and yet his fluency in the vernacular continued to make him almost indispensable in the detection of crime. Charles May whose conduct was enquired into at the same time, was absolved from all charges of misconduct. Caldwell's evidence against him was proved to be inaccurate and 'May's long and meritorious public services' were acknowledged by the Executive Council with the added opinion 'that his removal from government employment would be a great loss to the colony'.

There were other influences besides the Civil Service Abuses Enquiry which led to improvement in the civil service. Bowring had introduced a cadet scheme for supplying consular staffs in China with the necessary Chinese language training, and he suggested a similar scheme for the colonial government. Robinson brought it forward again and in 1861 it was accepted. Three young men recruited by examination in England were to be given two years' full-time study of Chinese and then become interpreters, afterwards being eligible for the highest posts. The first three cadets, W. M. Dean, C. C. Smith and M. S. Tonnochy, arrived in September 1862; officials who could deal with the Chinese were so urgently needed that they all received acting posts before their period of study was up. Robinson's complaints that not a single senior administrative officer was familiar with the Chinese language, gradually ceased to be true. Robinson also took the necessary step of making a general increase in salaries. The commercial world offered much higher rewards and the colonial government could not retain the services of the officials it needed, particularly in the lower grades. The recently established Chinese Imperial Maritime Customs service began to attract the more senior officials. The cost of living was extremely high compared to other colonies. Bowring had made piecemeal improvements, but it was left to Robinson to set out an all-round upward revision, which the unofficial members of the Legislative Council supported; at the same time the salaries were placed in a civil list and not voted each year with the financial estimates. A pensions scheme was introduced; Robinson wanted the officials to make some contribution, but since other colonies had introduced non-contributory pensions he accepted that principle for Hong Kong. The old type of colonial official disappeared; and the government no longer looked to the army, Australian adventurers, and ships' officers for the supply of personnel.

One result of the recent hostilities against China was the severance of the colonial from the diplomatic and consular duties in China; Robinson was the first Governor under the new conditions. The colony authorities were no longer able to take immediate action in its interests, and the island gradually ceased to be regarded as the headquarters of British trade and influence in the Far East. Another important result was the extension of the colony by the acquisition of Kowloon Peninsula on the mainland, a little more than a mile away from the island. In the early days some British and Americans had attempted to build residences there and were stopped by Davis, but the cricket club advertised regular practices on that side. Davis reported in 1845 that Kowloon 'has long been considered as a sort of neutral ground'.

During the hostilities leading to the Treaty of Tientsin in 1858, the military commander, General Straubenzee, suggested to the War Office the cession of Kowloon for military purposes. Bowring, who had not been consulted, but who saw the letters, urged the cession on the Colonial Office in August 1858, on the ground that the land was worthless to the Chinese, but valuable to the British for military, commercial, sanitary and police purposes. Since the treaty had already been drawn up, Bowring suggested that the cession should be arranged locally with the Viceroy at Canton.

The renewal of hostilities against China, brought about by the attempt of the British minister to force his way up the Peiho River in face of Chinese opposition, revived the Kowloon question, and the troops assembling for the 1860 campaign used the peninsula as a camping ground. In 1859, Caine had reported a riot at Tsim Sha Tsui as showing the lawless character of the inhabitants and the lack of control by the Chinese officials at Kowloon City, and it was largely on that ground that the Colonial Office agreed to recommend the retention of Kowloon in any settlement. Bruce, the British minister, agreed that Kowloon might be kept as part of the

indemnity which would be demanded from China at the end
of the war. Parkes, the consul at Canton, wrote in March 1860
to say that the Viceroy had no objection to the military encamp-
ment, and that the Viceroy had been informed that Kowloon
would probably be held in part payment of the indemnity.
Parkes was ordered to proceed with the negotiation of a lease;
the Viceroy raised no difficulty, and on 26 March 1860 Kowloon from Kowloon Fort to the point opposite Stonecutters
Island was leased in perpetuity to the British. Lord Elgin was
instructed by the Foreign Office not to lose any opportunity
of acquiring Kowloon, but when he suggested that it should be
accepted as part payment of the indemnity, Lord John Russell
replied that the British Government 'would gladly acquire
Kowloon Peninsula', but must leave it to Elgin as to the best
means of doing it 'or even abstaining altogether from attempting to do so if it is likely to lead to other demands injurious to
China and unfavourable to British interests.' The military refused to assume responsibility for its administration, and the
peninsula was handed over to the colony and temporarily
administered by Charles May as special commissioner, using
as far as possible Chinese law and custom. By the Convention
of Peking, October 1860, the lease of the peninsula was cancelled, and it was ceded outright as a dependency of the Colony
of Hong Kong, 'with a view to maintaining law and order in
and about the Harbour of Hong Kong'. A mixed commission
of British and Chinese was to determine the compensation to
be paid to any Chinese evicted as a result of the British occupation. This proved most difficult because there was no official
record of owners or tenants of land, and deeds were incorrect
and did not show any boundaries. Many conflicting claimants
appeared and there was evidence of a considerable manufacture
of spurious deeds with which to claim compensation. Proprietors were to get 999 year leases and pay the same rent as
they had paid before. Rough-and-ready methods of giving the
compensation were adopted; land was sold where doubt existed
and the money shared among claimants under the supervision
of Chinese officials. In fact few had legal title to land, as a considerable Chinese settlement had only recently sprung up.

The dispute between the colonial government and the
military over the disposal of the newly ceded territory was even

more difficult to resolve and dragged on for four years, delaying the organization of the new acquisition. The military claimed the whole of Kowloon for a cantonment to which all the troops in Hong Kong should be moved, and twenty-seven sites for forts were marked out. Robinson wanted to lay out Kowloon in plots for building and recreation, to ease the pressure on the island. He wanted the south-west portion for commercial purposes and wharves, because it was adjacent to deep water. Navy, army and Governor appointed a joint commission to try to reach agreement, but three different reports were submitted and the matter had to be referred home. The service departments were supported by the home government and Robinson was told to make no private grants of land until Imperial needs were met. The army was forced to moderate its demands by the threat that the colony might not be willing to assume the cost of administration, but it still retained the most eligible sites, though Robinson was able to save land adjoining deep water for commercial purposes. But the proposed praya from Tsim Sha Tsui to the boundary opposite Stonecutters Island had to be abandoned and has never been constructed. The payment of compensation to dispossessed Chinese was delayed until 1864, when a sum of $29,291 was paid. Chinese not dispossessed were to have leases of 999 years, but others were to have leases only of a length sufficient to induce them to build substantial buildings. At the end of it all the Colonial Office commented that the 'Colony is much indebted to Robinson for the warm and intelligent advocacy of its interests'. The new Secretary of State for War, Sir George Cornewall Lewis, reopened the controversy, and it was not until 1864 that the plots were marked out for sale after some reclamation had been made and a sea wall begun.

Robinson carried out further administrative reforms, many of which had originated under Bowring. The composition of the Legislative Council had been fixed at six official and three unofficial members with the Governor as chairman, and Bowring had added two more officials, creating a disproportion that had given offence to the unofficial members. In 1858, the Legislative Council began to vote the annual budget. Until then the practice was for the Governor to submit the financial proposals to it merely for suggestion and comment, but not to be voted upon. The Secretary of State pointed out that colonial regulations demanded that the legislature in all colonies, however constituted, should vote the budget, and he ruled that 'every item of expenditure and taxation must pass a majority of the Legislative Council, and is to be passed in the form of an ordinance'. He also drew attention to the principle of a civil list by which the salaries of officials were put into a separate ordinance, and not passed annually; this practice was also adopted.

In 1860, the colony assumed control of the local post office which up to that time had been directly subject to the imperial postal authorities in England. There was some demur on the ground that the colony would incur additional expense through taking charge of the outlying post-offices in the Treaty Ports. It was suggested that British stamps might be used, but the home government decided that Hong Kong must have its own 'stamp labels' and stamps of the denominations of 2, 8, 12, 18, 24, 48 and 96 cents were ordered, the colours being left to be decided by the Postmaster-General. The stamps were issued, without any local enthusiasm, on 8 December 1862, and additional denominations of 6 cents and 30 cents were ordered to meet the Marseilles postage rates.

The judicial arrangements had to be revised, as the existing courts were overburdened because of the greatly increased population and cases remitted to the colony from the Treaty Ports and Japan. Cases heard before the magistrates rose from 1,922 in 1851 to 7,352 in 1860. Robinson suggested a puisne judge to take debt and smaller civil cases and summary cases; eventually a summary court with a judge was set up to relieve both High Court and Magistrates' Courts, and at the same time, the posts of Chief and Assistant Magistrate were abolished and replaced by two Police Magistrates, and for these posts a knowledge of Chinese came to be regarded as more important than the possession of legal qualifications.

Robinson was anxious that the Chinese should understand the government's policy; few of them could read English or understand British institutions, with the result that incredible rumours were believed and acted upon, and the unscrupulous exploited this ignorance. For example, when the salt monopoly was abolished in 1858, some men fraudulently continued to levy the charge, and many Chinese paid because they did not know any change had occurred. Murrow of the *Daily Press* began a Chinese edition of his paper in 1860, but this was unsatisfactory because his attacks on the government misled the Chinese. Robinson established a Chinese edition of the Government Gazette to give official information and explanations, reports of legal cases of interest and a summary of European news. He paid officials $10 a month to learn Chinese, but only three offered themselves as candidates.

Robinson was faced with the problem of police inefficiency, and when May was promoted to be Police Magistrate, he brought Capt. W. Quin from the West Indies as his successor. The increased population and additional area of Kowloon made some reorganization necessary. Robinson thought, as others did, that the recruitment of Chinese as police was impossible because of 'squeeze'; the Indians were unsatisfactory as they were often Lascar seamen and inferior to the Chinese in strength and intelligence. The Europeans were chiefly discharged seamen and soldiers of a roving type, and their average length of service was three months. Dismissals for drunkenness were frequent, and many quitted voluntarily. Robinson tried Indians from the Bombay Native Infantry who had served in the campaign, and recruited 150 additional men direct from Bombay. After some tentative reforms, he introduced a Police Ordinance in 1862; this reorganized the force, allowed more promotions by grades, and raised the pay in each grade to encourage efficiency; all men had to serve for five years and could retire on pension after ten. The water police was increased and the harbour continuously patrolled. The annual cost of the police was now £25,000; yet crime continued.

The reconstruction of the jail, begun by Bowring, was completed in 1862, but immediately proved inadequate because the number of prisoners had almost doubled since 1858 when the scheme had been adopted. Robinson proposed a new jail on Stonecutters Island, but the pressure was so great that in 1863 a convict hulk, *The Royal Saxon*, was bought, and moored off that island until the new prison was ready, and 280 men were transferred to her. Chinese squatters on Stonecutters Island were obliged to leave, and given $3,211 as compensation. A month later, thirty-eight convicts were drowned by the capsizing of a boat alongside the hulk; the jury brought in a verdict of accidental death, but added that there was a lack of discipline, and that the boat used was quite unsuitable. The superintendent of the hulk was dismissed, and it was drawn nearer the island, so that convicts could proceed ashore by a gangway. There resulted, in the following year, a mass escape by 100 convicts. An enquiry into the incident concluded that the escape was due to inefficiency amongst the turnkeys; the police guard was found to be inadequate and the police arms defective. The Chinese government promised assistance in the recapture of the men, but none were caught. Robinson introduced the system by which prisoners could earn remission of a portion of their sentence by good behaviour, and could receive a gratuity on leaving the prison.

The new Colonial Surgeon asked for by Bowring, Dr. I. Murray, arrived in 1859, just in time to take over the new civil hospital. Robinson allowed him to have a private practice, with a reduced official salary, and the principle introduced by Bowring that officials were to devote their whole time to their duties was allowed to drop. In his annual report for 1860 Murray made such sweeping criticisms of the medical arrangements and of the colony's sanitation that the report was suppressed by the Governor, as he did not consider the annual report was the proper place for such criticism. The following year, Murray again renewed his charges, and his report was returned to him for revision. His criticisms were severe, drainage and sewage in Hong Kong 'had never yet received adequate attention, nor been carried out on any comprehensive plan'; there was only one inspector of nuisances and the police were lax in their duty to report cases for his attention; the police were inefficient and monthly medical inspections were neglected. He roundly condemned the collection of refuse and nightsoil and suggested that carts should come around at daybreak. The hospital was inadequate, there were no wards for infectious cases and no provision for the treatment of Chinese, there were no baths or means of ordinary cleanliness, 'often most useful aids to medical treatment', as he sarcastically observed. He was allowed to send his own paying patients to the hospital, but the seamen's hospital then complained that they lost money and asked to be taken over. The prison came in for his strictures;

there was stench, overcrowding and lack of ventilation 'beyond description'. Continued changes of staff occurred so that he found it difficult to get his instructions carried out. The floggings inflicted were so severe that he had to take this question up with the authorities, and he complained that the fettering of prisoners left permanent marks and deformity. Yet he had reported in 1859 that 'the Chinese thrive amazingly in confinement and after a few months' incarceration are sent out fat and healthy', and by 1864 he reported that the 'sanitary measures were eminently successful'. Some reforms were achieved. The hospital was enlarged and for the first time destitute Chinese were admitted as patients. The post of medical superintendent of the hospital was created, but the first holder of that office had to be dismissed for neglect of duty, as he used to lock his door at night to prevent the Chinese attendant from waking him to attend to accident cases. A Sanitary Committee was appointed in December 1862, primarily to take precautions against the spread of cholera, which was prevalent on the mainland and in Japan, and had appeared among the convicts on Stonecutters Island, causing a ten per cent mortality there. The Committee reported in December 1863 and gave a depressing picture of sanitary conditions in the colony. It suggested that a complete reorganization of the drainage system was essential, and offered a prize of $500 for the best plans to be submitted from suitably qualified persons. This produced only one vague scheme which was found to be impracticable. Refuse bins needed washing and draining, since the Chinese used them as lavatories. Chinese graves should be licensed, depots for receiving night-soil should be removed from the most populous parts of the city; and the police should be more watchful as 'it is notorious that all manner of abuses are committed with impunity'. The committee did not give any detailed scheme, or examine costs, and it is not surprising that little was done. The fact was, as the Surveyor-General said, that the settlement had grown too fast, and in the early days it was never realized that the town would grow as it had done. An estimate was prepared giving the cost of effecting the desired improvements, but the home government decided that the work must not be undertaken without clear proof that the revenue was able to bear it. There the matter was left. The

I

surprising thing is that the health of the colony remained good, and it gradually lost its bad reputation. But the problem remained.

One great achievement was the carrying out of a water-supply scheme, without which no advance in sanitation was possible. It had been mooted under Bowring, but nothing had been done. Robinson considered it urgent, for 1859 had been drier than usual and his arrival coincided with a period of water shortage. He acted with decision, offered $1,000 for the best scheme produced, and set up a committee to judge the competitors. A civilian clerk of works, S. B. Rawling, employed by the Royal Engineers, was awarded the prize, and his scheme to bring water to the city by a conduit from a reservoir at Pokfulham was, with some modifications, adopted, and Rawling was seconded to supervise the work. It was estimated to cost £25,000; provision was made for future needs by voting an extra £5,000 to carry water 'to the parts not yet built on', and an ordinance was passed allowing the imposition of a two per cent rate on property to cover any part of the cost not met out of revenue. It was hoped to complete the work in two years, but the supply was not ready before 1864, and the amount was sadly under-estimated. The whole of the eastern part of the town could not be reached by the scheme, and in the first year $10,000 had to be voted for extension work. The history of this first water scheme was to be repeated many times, and the supply of water was to wage a losing battle against growth of population.

Rapid growth of the colony's population continued. In 1859 there were 86,941 people living in the colony, of whom 85,330 were Chinese. By 1865 the total was 125,504, roughly a fifty per cent increase in six years, of which Europeans numbered 2,034, 'coloured' people 1,645, and the remainder were Chinese.

This enormous influx of Chinese was due to disturbed conditions caused by the Taipings, to better economic opportunities offered in the colony, and to the acquisition of Kowloon. The influx may have reflected the growing commercial prosperity of the island, but it also contributed to it. The period was one of prosperity. Colonial revenue improved because of the demand for land for building, and the revenue from land leases expanded from £17,878 in 1860 to £30,866 in 1865;

premiums from auction sales produced £18,182 in 1860, £36,374 in 1861 and £29,710 in 1862, and were the result of acute competition for land, mainly from Chinese newcomers. Rates for police and lighting levied on property increased from £16,573 in 1860 to £37,624 in 1865, the latter included a water rate. Government revenue increased from £65,225 in 1859 to £175,717 in 1865, and expenditure from £66,109 to £195,776 over the same period. The home government decided that the colony was now able to contribute towards the cost of its defence, and in 1863 an annual military contribution of £20,000 was imposed over the protests of Robinson and of the Legislative Council; the payments commenced at the beginning of 1865.

The growth of trade and population brought about the virtual elimination of English and Indian coins, in favour of silver dollars, which the Chinese used exclusively. The old currency proclamation of 1844 giving equal legal tender to dollars and English and Indian gold and silver coins was therefore a dead letter. Bowring had seen and understood the problem, but his proposals had little chance of being adopted in a period of war. Robinson was asked to report. He said that the 1844 currency proclamation was dead, that all commercial accounts were kept in dollars and the government received practically all its revenue in dollars. Out of £94,000 revenue collected in 1860, only £1,600 had been paid in actual sterling, the rest had been received in dollars at 4s. 2d. to the dollar. The Chinese had no coin between copper cash at 1,200 to the dollar and the silver dollar itself, and they usually accepted whole and broken dollars by weight. Robinson suggested that the accounts of the colony should be kept in dollars on grounds of obvious convenience. He also proposed that because so much bad cash, produced by forgers in Kowloon, was circulating, the British government should coin copper cash at 1,000 to the dollar, and suggested two new coins, a bronze cent piece and a silver ten cent piece. He advised that the silver dollar of Spain, Mexico or the South American states should be declared legal tender in addition to the coins to be minted in England. The home government agreed to the accounts being kept in dollars and this reform was introduced on 1 July 1862. The mint officials pointed out the high relative cost of minting and transporting coins of such low value as cash, and raised other difficulties; they suggested making the Mexican dollar legal tender and coining a bronze one cent piece. While home on leave Robinson suggested the colony should have its own mint to coin its own dollar as well as the cash, the cent, and the ten cent pieces. This was accepted, not without some misgiving by the Treasury; the coins were to be temporarily supplied by the London Mint, and were put into circulation in January 1864. Robinson pressed on with his plans for the mint, but he left the colony shortly after, and this costly and unsuccessful project was left to his successor.

There were other commercial developments during these years. Currency reform stimulated banking. The first bank in Hong Kong was a branch of the Oriental Bank established in 1845, soon after the colony had been founded, but it was not until twelve years later that the home government permitted its notes to be received by the local treasury; the bank had to provide a monthly return of its note circulation and to allow its reserves of specie to be inspected. Its note circulation increased from $54,310 in January 1853 to $342,965 in December 1857, by which time its first competitor appeared; the Chartered Mercantile Bank of India, London and China opened a branch on 1 August 1857; in 1863 the Bank of India, Australia and China and the Agra and United Service Bank appeared, by which time the Colonial Office had laid down regulations regarding the question of official recognition.

In the summer of 1864, the Hongkong and Shanghai Banking Corporation was established with a capital of five million dollars. This was a new venture by the merchants of the colony. A notice issued by Dent & Co. explained that the formation of a local bank had long been contemplated because of greatly increased trade with China and Japan; that existing banks were primarily interested in exchange operations, and a local bank was necessary to be of more direct assistance to the colony's trade. In addition, the view was expressed that the new mint and currency would do away with the compradore system of making payments, and the bank would assist in this. A temporary committee under Francis Chomley was appointed and it secured a local ordinance of incorporation, and opened its doors on 3 March 1865.

Other reforms of great value to the commercial world were

also brought in by Robinson. In 1861 imprisonment for debt was abolished in England, and a corresponding bankruptcy ordinance brought the colony law into line with the more humane spirit of the time. The judicial reforms and the court of summary jurisdiction had provided greater facilities for debt recovery and so made this reform more practicable. A companies' ordinance was also passed, giving the protection of limited liability following legislation in England of 1855–56. This ordinance was strongly opposed by some of the leading merchant houses. In all these questions relating to trade and finance, the Hong Kong Chamber of Commerce, which had been founded on 29 May 1861, played a notable part as a forum of merchant opinion. The Chamber came into existence as a result of the need to protect the colony's commercial interests following the hostilities against China as a result of which the superintendency of trade and diplomatic headquarters were moved to the north.

In 1862 the Volunteer Corps was founded. A Volunteer Corps had been raised in 1854 during the Crimean War scare, but did not long survive the removal of the tension of that year. It was a government inspired and improvised body, and was not a movement. In 1857, when the garrison was weakened by the hostilities against Canton, Bowring was anxious to revive the Volunteers, but reported 'every attempt to effect this object has proved an utter failure'. In July 1859, when the news arrived of the disastrous repulse at the mouth of the Peiho River, the commander of the forces suggested the raising of a Volunteer Corps in the colony, but Caine, who was temporarily in charge of the government, replied that he had increased the police, and if that did not provide the desired security he would then raise volunteers. No disturbance came, and hence the corps was not formed.

The Volunteer movement of 1862 was inspired by the Volunteer movement of 1859 in England which spread to all the colonies with the blessing of the Colonial Office. The subject was mooted in the press in 1860, but the prime mover was an enthusiast, Captain Frederick Brine of the Royal Engineers. He formed the Shanghai Volunteers in 1861 and his arrival in Hong Kong in January 1862 led to the Hong Kong Volunteer Corps being formed on 7 April 1862, as 'an artillery corps',

with Brine, a regular soldier, as the first commandant. Later
in the year he went to Hankow and Yokohama to form Volunteer Corps there. There was trouble with the military over the
supply of equipment for which the local brigadier was reprimanded. In 1865 the Volunteer Headquarters building was
begun.

Robinson's governorship was a period of development and
the colony seemed suddenly to become modern. The acquisition
of the Kowloon Peninsula, changes in currency, postage stamps,
street lighting by gas on 1 January 1865, the first attempts to
use the Peak as a residence, the departure of old officials, the
cadet scheme, the development of banking, the chamber of
commerce, the water scheme, were all striking changes in
themselves. Public works showed remarkable expansion with
a new hospital, central school, central police station, and jail;
Bowring's praya scheme was continued, though the navy
refused to allow the road to be extended in front of the naval
area. Other efforts were made to embellish the city; trees were
planted along the streets, a clock tower was erected at the
junction of Queen's Road and Pedder Street, and plans for a
City Hall were actively canvassed.

Robinson left in March 1865 to take up the post of Governor
of Ceylon; he had proved an efficient, zealous Governor. He
had the necessary strength of character to rescue the administration from the bad name it had acquired, and complete the
reforms conceived, but not carried out, by Bowring. He had
a great colonial career in Ceylon, Australia, New Zealand and
South Africa and was eventually raised to the peerage for his
services.

CHAPTER XII

SOCIAL AND ECONOMIC CONDITIONS, 1848–65

'Therefore in a British Colony, British authorities will not allow themselves to be governed by Eastern standards, or influenced by the insensibility to the claims of justice which may prevail around.'

Duke of Newcastle to Sir Hercules Robinson, 18 September 1860.

SIR HERCULES ROBINSON'S governorship was a formative period in the development of Hong Kong, and is a convenient point at which to pause to examine the social and economic progress made and to see some of the effects of British rule upon the Chinese. The Colonial Office and many local administrators referred to the colony as peculiar, and different in character from other colonies. It was a trading post, in which the vast majority, Chinese and foreign alike, were temporarily resident traders or artisans and not settlers. Both Europeans and Chinese were content to be governed provided there was a minimum of government consistent with security of life and property and opportunity for commercial enterprise. Benthamite *laissez-faire* suited the Chinese as well as the free-trade western merchants.

Hong Kong may have been unique in one sense, but its acquisition and administration, and those of the British settlements in the Treaty Ports, were truly representative of the forces that underlay British overseas expansion in that period. In that sense, Hong Kong was not only not unique but typical. The only surprising thing was the phenomenal influx of the Chinese and their willingness to live under the British flag, for which event British administration was quite unprepared. The Chinese clung to their own way of life and were generally intractable, and yet the British liberal régime enabled them to thrive, and soon the more respectable traders came. By 1866 foreign and Chinese communities in the island were flourishing; each found the other economically useful; economic co-operation for mutual advantage was the essence of the unwritten compact. Each maintained a good-natured contempt for the other, and Bowring noted in September 1858 that 'the separation of the native population from the European is nearly absolute; social intercourse between the races wholly unknown.' But whereas the liberal Bowring was appalled by this segregation, Robinson accepted it as desirable, and in this he reflected the usual attitude of the foreign community. Writing to the Duke of Newcastle in February 1861 on the subject of Kowloon, he said, 'My constant thought has been how best to prevent a large Chinese population establishing themselves at Kowloon, and as some native population is indispensable, how best to keep them to themselves and preserve the European and American community from the injury and inconvenience of intermixture with them.'

British representative institutions were not brought to the colony but the British conception of government was. The Chinese might not understand that the Executive could not act arbitrarily, but only in accordance with law, and that any government official attempting to act outside the law was liable to be sued in the courts, but they benefited from these principles. Secondly, over the island's government was the Secretary of State in England, ready to take an impartial, almost judicial view, and answerable to a British parliament in which injustice did not pass unchallenged and absolute honesty of administration was demanded.

In practice some injustice did occur. Officials made money by property speculations. Caine and A. R. Johnston have already been mentioned. Charles May, Police Superintendent, and Masson, Assistant Registrar of the Supreme Court, were reported by Mercer, acting Governor in 1862, as successful speculators, with the revealing remark 'but I have so frequently seen the bad effects of government officers occupying themselves with trade matters.' D. L. Caldwell was implicated in extortion and piracy through his friend Ma Chow Wong and dismissed the service in 1861. A prominent local barrister, Dr. W. T. Bridges, who acted as Attorney-General and then as Colonial Secretary under Bonham and Bowring, was found guilty of collusion with the opium farmer in 1858, and was also associated with the discreditable Caldwell affair. The influx of Chinese led to high rents and to the evil of building as many houses in as small a space and as cheaply as possible. The

Building and Nuisances Ordinance of 1856 has already been referred to (see p. 97). It laid down minimum standards and created alarm and opposition among property owners, including many J.P.'s. The Assistant Magistrate, W. H. Mitchell, himself a property owner, hit on the device of inviting the unofficial J.P.'s to sit with him on the bench when cases under this ordinance were being taken, knowing that they would dismiss prosecutions under the ordinance. Bowring protested in vain against such a travesty of the law. The treatment of suspects in 1857 after the poisoning case was harsh, but excusable in view of the indignation aroused. In defence it must be remembered that crime, violence, robbery and lawlessness of every kind existed on such a scale that it would have been remarkable if no abuse of power had occurred. Chinese preyed on each other and blackmailed new-comers under the threat of proceedings for some alleged breach of British law.

After a riot in November 1856, the Chinese were asked to state their grievances, and they made the following complaints, which throw some light on conditions at that time: heavy fines under the Nuisances Ordinance should cease; the police should strike only if they actually saw someone robbing and stealing and should not strike everyone in custody; time should be given to allow goods landed from boats to be moved into the shops; hawkers were poor people and should be ordered away, but not have their goods confiscated; when Chinese falsely claimed goods in shops as having been stolen from them, the matter should be referred to Chinese shopkeepers for enquiry; and Chinese rebels should not be allowed to seize boats or plunder vessels in the harbour.

There is much to be said on the other side, and in general, Hong Kong was governed efficiently and with care for Chinese interests. The appointment of Chinese to responsible positions was agreed to in principle as early as 1855, and municipal self-government for the British was refused on the main ground that they ought not to be entrusted with control over the Chinese majority. In 1857 the home government upheld a clause in a local bill against the opposition of the Attorney-General and other local British lawyers, allowing Chinese to qualify as lawyers. In 1857 a European, Murrow, and five Chinese were found guilty of keeping 240 coolie emigrants in confinement against their will while awaiting a ship; the Chinese were sentenced to six months' imprisonment, but Murrow got off with a $5 fine. This discrimination drew from home the comment that 'the case is not one to do credit to British authority or increase respect for British administration.'

The Colonial Secretary of State sometimes erred on the side of strict justice. In 1857 seventy-three pirates brought in by the navy were found to have a case to answer; Bowring pardonably shrank from the possible mass execution of seventy-three men and handed them over to the Kowloon magistrate. He was reprimanded and told that the Supreme Court had been set up in Hong Kong for the very purpose of dealing with such criminals.

In 1858 the law regarding the sale of wines and spirits was amended and a distinction drawn between Chinese and foreign spirits. This drew from Labouchere a statement of principle 'as far as possible, to be followed, viz., uniformity of legislation for the several races inhabiting the colonial possessions of the Crown' which was 'so necessary for the maintenance of that extended empire which is not to be preserved by forcibly creating and maintaining a dominant race or class.'

This policy of non-discrimination involved the abandonment of the earlier principle, expressed in Elliot's first proclamation, of having dual Chinese and British law and administration side by side in the colony. This experiment of indirect rule by which the Chinese were to be governed by their own officers in accordance with Chinese law and custom, had already broken down. It had never had a fair trial because the prevalence of crime militated against a devolution of authority. The maintenance of law and order remained firmly in British hands, and the Chinese *tepos* had little real authority. They were badly paid by a levy which made them unpopular; in any case the Chinese society in Hong Kong did not conform to the normal Chinese pattern of society since there was little family life and it contained a large lawless element which was against all authority of any kind. There was no fundamental change in British policy towards colonial peoples; it was now felt that native interests would be better protected by the policy of non-discrimination than by that of maintaining a separate administration of native law and custom administered by native officials. Native law and custom were still to be respected as far as possible. Significant of the new attitude was the emendation in the Governor's instructions[1] handed to Sir Richard Graves Macdonnell when he came out in 1866. He was forbidden to agree to any ordinance 'whereby persons of African or Asiatic birth may be subjected to any disabilities or restrictions to which persons of European birth or descent are not also subjected.'

The new policy implied that the Chinese were to be increasingly brought within the scope of the administration. While the Chinese were few they could be left to themselves, now that they were more numerous, greater regulation and control were inevitable. Chinese custom and prejudice presented great difficulty in this process, but it was the first essential step towards a more fruitful partnership between the races.

Certainly the Chinese throve under British rule. Their number increased from 20,338 in 1848 to 121,825 in 1865; the latter figure included Kowloon, but even so, the increase is astonishing. In 1855 those rated for police rates at or above £10 numbered 1,999, of which 1,637 were Chinese, 186 British and 176 other foreign nationals, and those rated at or above £40 numbered 772, of which 410 were Chinese. 'This shows a remarkable amount of wealth among the Chinese', as one official at the Colonial Office commented. The small number of English and other non-Chinese would be partly accounted for by the fact that it was the custom of merchant houses to provide free accommodation for their staffs. Population figures do not show the turn-over, nor the number who settled in the colony; all Chinese tended to return to China; the change was that many remained longer and returned to China only to spend their declining years.

The period from Bonham to Robinson is one of great commercial development. The main factors in this were (1) the mood of despondency passed, (2) the growth of Chinese population increased native trade, and increasing prosperity brought more Chinese into the colony, (3) Chinese emigration to North America, Australia, the Straits and elsewhere, (4) the opening of more ports to trade in China, Japan and Siam, (5) the legalization of the opium trade, (6) the growth of entrepôt trade based on the need to supply Chinese communities abroad.

[1] Dated 14 October 1865.

Hong Kong's anticipated function of being the centre for the supply of British manufactures to China began to materialize; its prosperity was linked with that of China and of the Chinese communities abroad.

Shipping using the harbour showed continuous increase. In 1848, the year in which Bonham assumed office, the number of ocean-going ships entering and clearing was 700 of 228,818 tons; in 1854, the year in which Bowring came, there were 1,100 such ships and the tonnage at 443,354 was nearly doubled; in 1859 when Robinson arrived, there were 2,179 ships of 1,164,640 tons. In 1864, the last complete year of Robinson's governorship, the tonnage passed the two million mark for the first time, and the number of ships was 4,558. It is difficult to get a reliable account of the colony's trade, but these shipping figures at least provide evidence of phenominal growth. Many ships would call for orders or stores and in 1848 about half of those calling were reported as having some cargo for discharge; ten years later, 855 ships out of 1,007 calling had some cargo for the colony. W. H. Mitchell, who in 1852 reported on the China trade, made a private report to Bonham in 1850 on the colony's trade. He said that under Pottinger and Davis the great change in the conditions of trade in the Canton area made by the opening of the Treaty Ports had been quite overlooked, and in addition Hong Kong had not displaced Canton as the great southern Chinese trading centre because the Americans maintained their business houses in Canton and forced the British to do the same. He thought that the colony would never have any legitimate junk trade until the restrictive clauses of the Treaty of the Bogue were abolished, but in any case Hong Kong's junk trade was too insignificant to awaken the jealousy of the Chinese.

American trade and shipping certainly were active, and in 1850 no less than 90 American ships of 37,807 tons arrived in harbour compared to 65 British ships of 31,213 tons. American whalers using the island for refitting and selling their oil helped to swell the total until 1854, but thereafter American shipping declined in relative importance.

Much of the colony's growing prosperity was due to Chinese emigration to the Straits, to Australia and across the Pacific. These new overseas Chinese communities clung to their own way of life and retained close ties with China, and Hong Kong became the centre of a trade to cater for their needs. Tea exports in 1849 were given as 5,570 chests and 910 boxes to the United Kingdom, 1,668 chests to Australia, and 1,869 chests to San Francisco. In 1853 exports of tea were: to the United Kingdom, none reported; to Australia, 13,730 'packages' and 2,850 chests, and to North America, 3,614 packages and 3,304 boxes. Rice and sugar were shipped in similarly increasing quantities. The colony supplied the Treaty Ports chiefly with rattan and other East Indies products, rice and sugar. The figures given were admittedly unreliable, and after 1855 official estimates of the colony's imports and exports ceased altogether. Once the colony's economic recovery got under way it proceeded steadily, and attracted increasing numbers of Chinese, who in turn brought increasing trade. The Taiping movement in China accelerated the process and emphasized the relative security which the colony offered.

The 1849 gold-rush to California and that of 1851 to Australia brought a wave of Chinese emigration abroad. Chinese emigration was composed both of free emigrants and contract coolie labour. All Chinese emigration was nominally illegal, but had gone on for centuries. Gutzlaff, in his report on the junk trade for the year 1844, mentioned junks from the north carrying Chinese emigrants to the Straits. In 1843 there was much discussion over the demand for coolies by the British West Indian Colonies, which had been refused by Lord Stanley because no safeguards against abuse existed. The demand continued, and in 1849 Bonham was asked by Earl Grey to advise on the necessary conditions to guard the coolie traffic against abuse. In this interval the shipment had begun of coolies, chiefly Fukienese from Amoy to Havana, to the islands in the Indian Ocean and to Australia.

By a series of Passengers' Acts, the British government had attempted to lay down minimum standards in ship accommodation for emigrants generally, but the minimum of 15 cubic feet per person was criticized as too expensive for the shipment of coolies which the government were now prepared to encourage, and in 1853 the Passengers' Act was amended to allow 12 cubic feet per person, while retaining other restricting conditions. The Governor was advised to adopt the act by proclamation, but Bonham took no action because he thought that restrictions would drive the trade from Hong Kong, and that they could in any case be easily evaded. The shipment of coolies on contract, particularly to Latin-American countries, was full of abuse. The coolies were treated like slaves, deluded with false promises, herded in barracoons and ill-treated, and they on their part often accepted engagement money and then attempted to escape; and at sea many attempts were made to murder the officers and seize the ship. British shippers used Chinese crimps to procure coolies on a commission basis and they were interested only in getting numbers.

In May 1854, Caine reported that ships were leaving the port under no control and crowded with human beings; since 1 January, 5,500 had gone to San Francisco, and 2,100 to Melbourne, and he said that in Hong Kong and Canton 12,000 were waiting to go. The Passengers' Act was now applied and Hillier, the Chief Magistrate, was appointed Emigration Officer. Bowring was also anxious to check abuses and proposed an ordinance, but the difficulty was that an ordinance had no force outside the colony. In 1855 nine Hong Kong merchant houses protested against the new restrictions of the Passengers' Act, which they condemned as 'proverbially inapplicable' and said it would interfere with the emigration trade, 'to which branch of commerce the growing importance of the place is mainly to be attributed', and they raised many objections to the method of measuring accommodation and of medical facilities demanded. As a result Hillier was instructed to ease the regulations pending a reference home. There, it was decided to deal with the abuses by parliamentary legislation, and in 1855 a Chinese Passengers' Act was passed. The effect was to drive the trade to Macao and elsewhere, and to increase the use of ships under other flags. Emigrant ships were usually fitted out and provisioned in Hong Kong and then sailed to pick up their human cargo elsewhere. In July 1856, Bowring reported that only one emigrant ship had used the colony since the act came into force on 1 January 1856. The Admiralty had not been consulted about the act, and refused to instruct the Pacific squadron to seize ships found infringing it. One difficulty was that the act made no distinction between contract coolie trade and free Chinese emigrants. Two bad cases occurred in 1857,

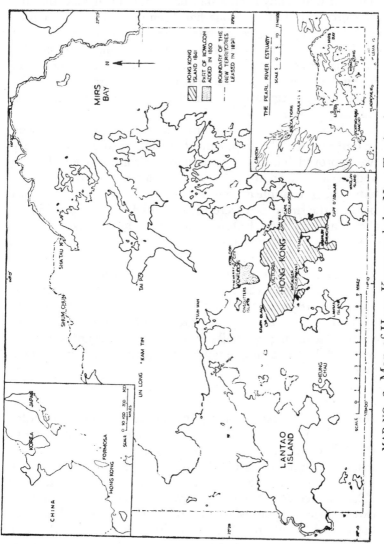

MAP NO. 2. Map of Hong Kong and the New Territories.
Insets: Hong Kong and the Far East *and* Hong Kong and the Canton Delta.

when two ships were allowed to sail from the harbour for Havana with contract coolies; excessive mortality led to enquiry, which revealed that many coolies had been kidnapped, that the ship measurement at Hong Kong had been inaccurate, and Hillier and the Hong Kong government were censured.

Mortality on British ships continued to be high, and in 1858 Bowring was told to bring in another ordinance arranging for hospital accommodation on board British emigrant ships. The Hong Kong Legislative Council passed the ordinance, but wanted to exempt Chinese fare-paying passengers and those travelling on business trips from its operation, but Bulwer-Lytton refused. The employment of Chinese surgeons on board was approved. The colony ceased to ship contract coolie labour, and became a great centre of free emigration. Bad cases of kidnapping continued, but the colony was implicated only because the ships used were usually fitted out and provisioned there, and in 1862 Robinson arranged for all ships leaving harbour to be boarded and inspected, but shippers evaded this precaution by completing outside Hong Kong territorial waters any arrangements they did not want to be seen.

In 1855, 14,683 Chinese passengers left the port; in 1857, 26,213; in 1859, 10,217; in 1861, 12,840; in 1863, 7,809 (and 7,193 returned). In 1865 emigration to San Francisco was reported as having virtually ceased. The outward flow was matched by returning immigrants, many of whom brought gold.

The contraband trade in salt and opium remained a source of prosperity. Mitchell in his report stated that for the period 1845–49 three-quarters of the Indian opium crop was handled in the harbour, and that on the average over 40,000 chests worth $16 million were in store in the colony. Most of this was sent in bulk up the coast and abroad. The retail trade in opium was estimated at 250 chests a month and went to the coast chiefly in return for sugar and sycee. Mitchell stated that the two big firms, Jardine Matheson and Dent, co-operated to check the growth of the retail trade in Hong Kong. The P. & O. steamers were used from 1845 onwards for the conveyance of opium and treasure; in 1848 they imported 10,613 chests out of a total import of 45,479 chests and exported $5,625,827 worth of treasure. In 1854 they imported 46,765 chests and

$20,770,463 of treasure, and in 1859, 27,577 chests and $18,633,522 of treasure; Hong Kong was clearly the head-quarters of a valuable trade in opium. Under Robinson, opium figures disappeared from the annual reports, presumably because the trade was legalized.

Piracy continued seriously to affect British trade; Bonham made repeated complaints and abuses connected with the unofficial convoying system came to light. The captured pirate vessel used by Davis for anti-piracy work was wrecked in the 1848 typhoon; Palmerston urged stronger action, and in November 1848 the Admiralty agreed that the fleet should, in co-operation with the Chinese Government, take a more active part in the suppression of piracy. The result was that vigorous naval action led in 1849 to the destruction of a pirate fleet under Chiu A Po at Bias Bay, forty miles north of the colony, and of another under a famous pirate leader, Shap Ng Tsai, to the west. D. R. Caldwell, Hong Kong police assistant super-intendent, supplied the necessary information; but these successes only temporarily checked the evil.

In August 1851, Rear-Admiral C. J. Austin made the direct accusation that petty piracy in the neighbourhood of Hong Kong arose from collusion with the Chinese living on the island. Bonham agreed, and said that a Jardine Matheson employee had been sentenced to fifteen years' transportation in 1851, but he pointed out it was almost impossible to secure evidence be-cause the Chinese witnesses feared retaliation. The arrival of Rear-Admiral Sir James Stirling on the station in 1854 led to greater vigour in the attack on piracy. He asked for shallow-draft steamers to pursue pirates inshore, and eight small gun-boats were sent out in 1856; he also began to organize naval convoys. Bonham and Bowring had wanted the steamers for anti-piracy work to be under the local government, but the Admiralty always preferred to retain control. Further naval operations against pirates in 1857 and 1858 checked the evil, again only temporarily.

Under Robinson, the character of piracy changed, and instead of marauding fleets there were carefully planned attacks on selected vessels, and in 1864 he reported the attacks on European vessels with great atrocities 'within sight almost of this harbour'. The Taiping Rebellion made it almost impossible

K

to eradicate piracy; the Governor urged that all pirates should be handed over to the Chinese because he thought British judicial procedure too cumbrous in view of the difficulty of obtaining evidence. In the five years he had been in the colony, he said in August 1864, out of 244 persons charged with piracy only 157 had been convicted. The policy of rendition was agreed to, subject to safeguards. The admiral, A. L. Kuper, was instructed to make four gunboats available for anti-piracy work around Hong Kong. Kuper was very critical and charged the colony's government with failure to control native shipping in the harbour and to control Chinese living in the colony; he alleged that pirates were able to purchase all the arms they needed, and he returned to the old argument that the navy was being asked to do what an efficient colonial police ought to be doing. It was left to the next governor, Macdonnell, to take the necessary action on these points.

Local industry developed around shipping; ship refitting, repairing and building developed. There were 240 ships' chandlers in 1853 and twelve rope manufactories and two cannon foundries. By 1865 there were 427 chandlers, ninety-three boat builders, twenty rope works, and one dry dock.

CHAPTER XIII

THE GROWTH OF A PUBLIC SYSTEM OF EDUCATION, 1841–65

'*The Chinese have no education in the real sense of word.*'
Frederick Stewart, Education Report for 1865.

NEITHER British nor Chinese had any tradition of state education, and in the early years of the colony neither demanded it. Chinese teachers were paid fees from their pupils, whose education was largely confined to learning the classics by heart; class teaching hardly existed. In England, education was left to private arrangement or public generosity, and in the early nineteenth century the churches began to build schools for the poorer children as a work of charity and to teach their own dogmas. In 1833 the State assisted with a grant of £20,000 to the Anglican and Nonconformist education societies for school buildings. From this modest beginning sprang the modern English system of public education owing much to local and voluntary effort, assisted by State grants. Acceptance by the State of reponsibility for education only slowly emerged towards the end of the century. Hong Kong education owed something to the Chinese tradition, but much more to the British tradition of voluntary effort. Yet, curiously, the first public grants were made to the Chinese schools and not to those of the religious bodies. It is a tribute to the Christian churches that they embarked on the work of education almost immediately on the occupation of the island, before its formal cession and in face of difficulties; children of the boat people and from the scattered seaside villages made unpromising material; the settlement of Victoria attracted few respectable Chinese, and those who came usually left their families in China. Undoubtedly propagation of the faith was the main aim, and this led to the setting up of colleges or seminaries for the training of Chinese candidates for the ministry, with attached schools to produce the candidates. Yet there is no reason to doubt that the churches were interested in education for its own sake.

The Morrison Education Society under the presidency of the American missionary Dr. E. C Bridgman was first in the field in Hong Kong. It had been formed at Canton by public subscription in 1835 as a memorial to Robert Morrison, the first Protestant missionary in China, to promote education in China and amongst Chinese overseas by schools and other means, to enquire into the state of education in China, and to open that country to western ideas. All teachers employed were to be proficient in Chinese, but English was also to be taught and the Bible was to be placed in the hands of all pupils, but no religious tests were to be imposed. It assisted a school in Macao which had been founded by Mrs. Gutzlaff, and in 1842 it decided to move this school to the island. Sir Henry Pottinger became a patron of the Society and encouraged it with a grant of land on Morrison Hill in the spring of 1842, and the school was opened in November 1843. The London Missionary Society also applied for a plot of land for an Anglo-Chinese College similar to that at Malacca. Pottinger refused this request on the ground that two similar educational institutions in a small island were superfluous; he criticized the 'early and ill-digested measures' of the London Missionary Society and thought schools and colleges would not be needed 'for many years to come'. He considered it wiser to wait to see what success the Morrison Education Society had and suggested that the two bodies might link up and that the financial aid granted to the college at Malacca for the purpose of encouraging the production of interpreters should now be transferred to the new Morrison Society Institution. In December 1843 the latter was pressed for funds and appealed to Pottinger, who gave it $1,200, being one year's subsidy due to the Anglo-Chinese college at Malacca.

The Morrison Education Society lost its chief supporter when Pottinger left in 1844. The London Missionary Society had appealed to Lord Stanley who instructed the new Governor, Sir John Davis, to enquire if its request for a free gift of land could not be granted. Davis was unsympathetic to the Morrison Education Society, and in 1845 reported that it had fallen entirely under American missionary influence; he advised against giving it further support on the ground that it refused to link up with the London Missionary Society and refused to take any children other than Chinese. Its school on Morrison Hill lasted six years and was closed in 1849. The Society continued to exist and to make grants for the education of Chinese children until the failure of Dent & Co. in 1867 deprived it of most of its funds; its library became merged in the City Hall scheme in 1869. In 1873 it offered money to the government to found a scholarship, but the conditions were not acceptable, and it soon after became defunct. The Morrison Education Society failed because its scheme was too ambitious and because it was an undenominational society relying on a few merchant houses for its funds, which were insufficient to form a permanent endowment; the various churches from whom support might have been expected were anxious to have their own denominational schools as part of their mission work.

The London Missionary Society secured its grant of land, and its representative, Dr. James Legge, established an Anglo-Chinese College in 1843 as a seminary for training ministers, with a preparatory school attached. The Catholics organized a seminary in connection with the Catholic church in Wellington Street in 1843. The Colonial Chaplain, Rev. Vincent Stanton, began to organize St. Paul's College as a similar training college for Anglicans; it was an ambitious scheme and the building was not completed until 1851. In 1845 he founded a school for English children.

The Chinese on their part began to set up schools on traditional Chinese lines. In 1845 Charles Gutzlaff, Chinese Secretary, stated that there were eight Chinese schools, two of which were 'supported by foreigners', and all badly housed in hovels; he proposed each school should be given financial assistance at the rate of $10 per month, on the ground that such a gesture would be greatly appreciated by the Chinese. Stanton shortly after asked for a grant for his school for English children which he was financing from his own resources supplemented by gifts. Dr. Legge also suggested that the government should establish a free school for Chinese as had been done at Penang and Singapore. Davis accepted the principle of financial grants to existing schools and referred the matter home. The Colonial Office was sympathetic, but wanted to know more about the schools, and their curriculum, teaching methods, staffs, and mode of appointments; Sir James Stephen regarded the missionary societies as the 'most effective, almost indispensable auxiliaries' in education in the colonies and the missionary bodies at home were accordingly asked regarding their plans for education in Hong Kong.

In England at this time the development of a national system of education was being delayed by religious differences and sectarian jealousies over the distribution of state grants to assist the denominational schools; Lord Grey had therefore to be particularly careful to guard against the possible use of public funds in Hong Kong to support sectarian education. For that reason, and also because he thought English parents could afford to pay, he refused to allow any grant to Stanton's school for English children. He found that the Missionary Societies had not, by 1846, made definite plans for education in the colony, and he agreed that some public assistance was necessary. In the case of the Chinese schools 'where the contribution required is moderate' and 'no religious differences can arise', and being

assured by Davis that these schools had 'no idolatrous prejudices whatever', he decided, in August 1847, that $10 a month
should be granted to each of the three Chinese schools at
Victoria, Stanley and Aberdeen. In December 1847 the grants
were announced and a committee consisting of the Colonial
Chaplain, the Chief Magistrate, and the Registrar-General,
was appointed to supervise the three schools and administer
the grant. This was the beginning of the colony's public system
of education which originated with Gutzlaff's almost haphazard proposal of 1845. It will be convenient to deal with this
public system first and then return to describe the work of the
missionary and other voluntary bodies.

The first annual report of the Education Committee, that
for 1848, showed a total of 95 boys attending, 40 at Victoria,
24 at Stanley and 30 at Aberdeen; the first had been visited
once a month, but there had been no effective supervision over
the other two. It agreed that the assistance was properly
appreciated and 'of substantial benefit'. In 1849 the Chinese
at Wong Nei Chong petitioned for and secured a similar grant,
and in 1851 the Chinese school at Little Hong Kong, near
Aberdeen, was put on the list, making a total of five schools in
receipt of government assistance. Control was exercised directly
through the teacher who received the grant, provided the room
and met all incidental expenses, so that the pupil paid no
fees at all in these schools. The policy pursued by the
committee was not to interfere with the traditional Chinese
curriculum and method except to introduce some Christian
teaching on a voluntary basis. The teachers were found to be
unsatisfactory, and when the Stanley teacher resigned in 1849
he was replaced by a Chinese Christian with the hope that he
would have 'sounder principles than that on which his predecessor acted'. Next year the teacher at Aberdeen was dismissed for gross misconduct, and the one at Victoria proved
unsatisfactory and was removed. By the end of that year all
the teachers were nominees of the committee and all were
Christian converts. In 1850 the committee recommended that
the Anglican Bishop, George Smith, should have the superintendence of the schools, and in 1852 the committee was
reorganized. The Bishop became chairman, with Hillier and
a London Missionary Society representative as members, and

añ additional Anglican clergyman was added a little later; such a committee was bound to be interested in spreading Christianity. The Bishop's advent implied an official policy of increasing Christian and Anglican influence in the government schools, and by 1853 half the day was devoted to the scriptures 'and to books composed under the superintendence of foreigners' and the other half to the Chinese classics. Bishop Smith wanted the government schools to act as feeders for his St. Paul's College, and inducements were held out to the pupils to take its examination for admission. This college, founded by Stanton and Bishop Smith, was designed to prepare Chinese candidates for the Anglican ministry, but it also provided some form of general higher education and received financial help from the Foreign Office to produce interpreters for the consular service, though in fact it never produced any. Many pupils were eager to attend St. Paul's purely for the economic advantage of learning English.

The committee was strengthened in 1853 by the addition of Dr. Legge and the Rev. M. C. Odell, an Anglican clergyman, and its policy was to encourage the study of English not only for the value of its literature but 'to prevent misunderstanding' and act as 'a bond of union between the many thousands of Chinese who have made this place their residence and the handful of Europeans by whom they are governed.' Two Chinese pupil teachers from St. Paul's were sent to the village schools 'once or twice a week' to teach English. Progress in the state-aided schools was slow and supervision was quite inadequate. The committee wanted new school buildings 'in lieu of the apartments now used as school rooms which are confined, miserably dirty and altogether unsuitable.' Two new schools were built in 1853 at Victoria and Wong Nei Chong, but unfortunately the former had to be pulled down the following year when the hillside from which the site was cut, slipped following heavy rain. Attendance was irregular; children at Aberdeen and Stanley were taken away fishing and all children were withdrawn early to seek employment. The 1850 education report observed sadly that though the Chinese parent was attached to education 'this was secondary to his attachment to gain'.

Numbers in the aided schools slowly increased from ninety-five for three schools in 1848, to 134 for five schools in 1852. In this year the committee decided to stimulate the teacher to maintain the school numbers by reducing the grant if the school numbers fell below thirty, but it was subsequently discovered that this merely resulted in inducing the teacher to claim more attendances than was actually the case.

Bowring's governorship was marked by a great development in government-sponsored schools. He was a man of liberal ideas and very keen to develop the educational system. He wrote home in 1854: 'It is quite monstrous to see a charge of £8,620 for police . . . contrasted with an expenditure of £120 for the instruction of the people.' He was not an Anglican and was opposed to any attempt 'to wean the natives from their religious opinions or practices'; he was a secularist and thought the schools should be run by laymen.

The Education Committee in its 1854 report reacted to the views of the new Governor by strong criticism of the existing system. It pointed out that the five schools had accommodation for only 150 and put the number of Hong Kong children at over 8,800. Government education was 'at almost its lowest ebb; it has neither suitable buildings, suitable masters, nor suitable supervision.' Four proposals were made for its improvement; suitable school buildings should be provided, a system of apprentice teachers should be introduced, all schools capable of enlargement should have assistant masters capable of teaching English, and an Inspector of Schools should be appointed to conduct weekly inspections of all government schools. In May 1856 a German missionary, the Rev. W. Lobscheid, was appointed Inspector of Schools and at once began a system of inspections in which he was often accompanied by members of the committee. At the same time a programme of expansion was carried out. From 1854–59, the period of Bowring's governorship, the number of schools in receipt of government money increased from five to nineteen, the number of children attending, from 102 to 873 boys and 64 girls, and the annual cost of education went up from £125 to £1,200. There were now three schools for Hakka children and Victoria had five schools, but most of the additional schools were in the villages; and they were small, generally backward, and added seriously to the problem of supervision. Girls began

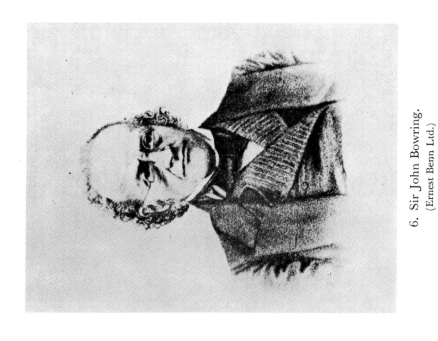

6. Sir John Bowring.
(Ernest Benn Ltd.)

5. Sir John Francis Davis, Bart.
(British Museum.)

7. Government House in 1869.
(Public Record Office C.O. 129/143)

8. View of Hong Kong in 1869.
(Public Record Office C.O. 129/143)

attending the Victoria Government Schools in 1858 and had their own school soon after. An assistant was appointed in one large school at Victoria, where the numbers increased to eighty, and some additional English teaching was undertaken in the larger schools. There was no system of teacher training, and the committee still complained in the 1858 report that the moral and intellectual tone of the Chinese teachers was low.

In 1856, Bowring announced his intention to examine the whole question of education and he appointed a commission of enquiry under Hillier the Chief Magistrate, to enquire and report on the subject. However, two members left the colony, the *Arrow* dispute came on, and the commission never got to work. Bowring met other difficulties in his plan to reform education on a secular basis and in the end no change in the curriculum was made. He complained, 'the missionaries alone give active assistance, yet they have special objects that unfit them for general and popular Education.' He was baulked too by finance and by his inability to control the bickerings of his officials. The Bishop remained firmly in control, but Bowring had brought the question of education to the front and there could be no looking back.

His successor, Sir Hercules Robinson, took the first steps in the reform which Bowring had planned. In 1860 the Education Committee was reconstituted as the Board of Education still under the chairmanship of Bishop Smith. This was part of a new scheme proposed by Dr. Legge in 1860. The number of schools for which government accepted responsibility had risen to twenty, and Legge argued that the travel involved was so great that one full-time inspector could give no more than two or three hours per month to each school and that under such circumstances progress was hardly possible. He suggested that the various government schools in Victoria should be closed and the pupils concentrated in a new Central School under a European headmaster. Legge hoped to improve standards by having a large, specially designed building instead of the single-room hovels which had been so often condemned, with a trained schoolmaster actually engaging in the work of education. He thought the new Central School would give English teaching the more prominent place it ought to have, and that the wide demand for English would permit of a fee being charged for it, leaving the normal Chinese education free as before. In addition the headmaster was to be responsible under the Board for inspecting the outlying schools. In effect, the scheme sacrificed the village schools in the hope of getting an efficient school in Victoria, and perhaps that was all that could be achieved at that time. The Board recommended Legge's scheme to the Governor and it was accepted at home. The American Baptist Society's premises in Gough Street were secured; a headmaster, Frederick Stewart, was recruited from home, and the Central School was opened on the 1st January 1862. The Rev. W. Lobscheid had resigned in the summer of 1860, and many believed that this had been engineered by Dr. Legge in furtherance of his scheme, which he was then putting before the authorities.

In 1864, the Central School had 140 pupils and a new wing with accommodation for ninety had to be built. The curriculum was maintained unchanged, viz., Chinese classics, Scripture and some English. The difficulty of supervising the outlying schools remained; Stewart made surprise visits and discovered such poor attendance, in contrast to what the school registers entitled him to expect, that the worst schools were abandoned. By 1865 the number of government schools had dropped from twenty-one to twelve, and the number of pupils to 597, but government education was on a firmer basis. Stewart believed in secular education, but could do little until the Bishop left the colony on retirement in 1864, and next year, before his successor could arrive, the Board of Education was abolished and the decisive step was taken to free the government schools from church influence. Stewart was thus enabled to introduce a more systematic reform which opened a new chapter in Hong Kong education.

The Education Committee and its successor the Board had been faced with an almost impossible task and they fully realized the weaknesses of the government schools. Buildings, teachers, supervision and finance were all inadequate; the Chinese were keen to get the schools and the grants, but removed their children from school to suit their convenience. The teaching of Christianity in the schools was not surprising; many held the view that education should not be separated from religion, and by having the Bishop as chairman and church leaders as members of the committee, the policy of teaching religion in the schools received official encouragement. The Committee claimed, and to their credit, that the teaching of the scriptures was never made compulsory, but it is clear that it was strongly encouraged. Frederick Stewart was to find that the abolition of the Board and the discouragement of Christian influence did not solve his difficulties.

The Chinese private schools flourished, and the hope that the government schools for Chinese would supersede them by virtue of being free and of attaining higher standards proved wide of the mark. The government schools attracted only children of the poorer class, at least until the founding of the Central School. Those who could afford it preferred the traditional Chinese education, free from government interference, and from western influence. Class teaching was disliked, and the more traditional system favoured by which the teacher was available from six o'clock in the morning to four o'clock in the afternoon, to receive pupils as they were sent along. The teaching of Christianity was not a great objection, for the Committee once reported that at Stanley a government school where Christian teaching was voluntary had a roll of twelve while a neighbouring mission school, where it was obligatory, had a roll of forty, and generally more Chinese attended the mission schools than the private Chinese schools. Many Chinese distrusted the government and asked for nothing more than to be left alone.

The missionary bodies were left to their own resources during the whole of these years largely because no Secretary of State dared risk censure in parliament by sanctioning the use of public funds to support sectarian education. They were interested in all children, not only Chinese, aimed at free education, and introduced the teaching of Christianity while retaining the Chinese classics. Their policy was similar to that of the Education Committee, which in fact was controlled by Protestant missionaries. The only difference was that the mission schools were free from government control with the advantage of freedom to experiment.

In 1844, the first year for which there are official figures, the London Missionary Society provided two free schools, teaching Chinese classics, the New Testament and English;

the Roman Catholics had one school, teaching Chinese language, reading and writing; the American Board of Foreign Missions had a free school teaching Chinese, English, history and geography and had some boarders at $1.50 per child per month. Seven Chinese schools of the traditional type were mentioned, and there was the Morrison Education Society's school which was the biggest with thirty-two children. Next year, Stanton, the Colonial Chaplain, set up a school for English children and the Catholic Church did the same. By 1848, the first year of the government schools, Stanton's School for English children and the Morrison Society's school still existed, the London Missionary Society had only one school for Chinese, and the American school had disappeared. The Catholics had three schools, one for European boys with teaching in English and Portuguese, one for European girls under the Sisters of Charity and one for Chinese. There were ten traditional Chinese schools, of which three were aided and supervised by the government. Clearly the mission schools had not yet begun to attract Chinese in any great numbers. The Anglicans set up their first school for Chinese in 1849 as St. Paul's College, and Stanton's English school soon died.

In 1850 Legge experimented with boarders; and a Catholic seminary, teaching Latin and Chinese, was reported as being in Queen's Road; two Catholic schools for Portuguese were also mentioned as being 'supported by the scholars'. The Catholic Church was the most active; it had five schools in 1853, but only two of them were for Chinese, and one was the seminary; the only other Chinese schools mentioned in the annual report of that year were the five schools for Chinese in receipt of government grants. All schools were described as free schools. Few of the schools were deeply-rooted and the numbers attending were small. Under Bowring the chief development was in government-assisted Chinese schools.

The missionary bodies did not flourish until after the Treaty of Tientsin of 1858, as a result of which missionary work was given a great fillip by being admitted to the Chinese field. By that time the Chinese population in Hong Kong had increased and the Taiping movement had resulted in more families being in the colony. By 1865 the London Missionary Society had two free schools for Chinese, giving a Chinese education with some religious teaching. The Catholics had two seminaries, their Portuguese schools had become St. Saviour's College with 152 boys; and they had three Chinese schools, one of them for girls, giving a purely Chinese education. They had also established a Reformatory for boys at West Point; the Italian Daughters of Charity had a school in Caine Road with 192 girls of all nationalities, and the French Sisters of Charity had a school at the Asile d'Enfance. St. Paul's had become partly a boarding school, and the Church Missionary Society made its belated appearance; it set up a free boarding school for girls in Bonham Road, and Miss Jane Baxter, a great pioneer of education for girls, founded the Diocesan Native Female School. But the experiment of educating Chinese girls in English proved to be a blunder and had to be dropped, since most of them became mistresses of Europeans, and the Diocesan Boarding School experimented with boys and mixed classes and tended to cater for Eurasian children.

In 1865 it was estimated that out of 22,301 children in the colony, 14,000 were of school age, and of these about 1,870 attended school. These were years of preparation, experiment and struggle; the main result was that schools were now beginning to emerge.

CHAPTER XIV

SIR RICHARD GRAVES MACDONNELL, 1866–72

'There is however no parallel between this and any other British settlement. It is a mere depot. . . .'
Sir Richard Macdonnell to Duke of Buckingham,
29 October 1867.

ROBINSON'S successor, Sir Richard Graves Macdonnell, had nearly twenty years' experience as a colonial governor, first in the Gambia in 1847, and then successively in the West Indies, South Australia and Nova Scotia. He had great energy and his governorship was marked by an intense activity which brought the Chinese much more within the scope of colonial legislation and control. This impact on Chinese habit and custom was not based on any conscious attempt to create one community in Hong Kong, but it was the necessary prelude to the integration in it of the Chinese. In spite of an economic recession which gave him a financial problem, Macdonnell embarked with energy and zest on a series of reforms in the Hong Kong administration. He handled all government business personally, was a skilled debater and had little difficulty in silencing his many critics.

Macdonnell arrived in the colony in March 1866, twelve months after Robinson had left, during which interval Mercer, the Colonial Secretary, again administered the government. Relations with the Chinese government created a problem upon which a decision could not be delayed until the new Governor arrived. The Viceroy at Canton demanded the rendition of a Chinese resident of Hong Kong who had been accused of piracy. The British government had agreed that those charged with piracy outside colonial waters should be handed over to the Chinese authorities, provided no torture was used in the subsequent proceedings, and Mercer was ordered to pass the necessary ordinance. The Treaty of Tientsin had made the rendition of criminals to China obligatory on the British without condition, and when the Viceroy pointed this out, the 'no torture' clause was dropped from the ordinance, and it was some time before the Chinese reluctance to give such an undertaking was overcome. At the same time, these negotiations had been carried on directly between the Viceroy and Mercer, it was now laid down that all communication between the Hong Kong government and the Chinese officials should be made through the British Minister in Peking or the consular officials.

Mercer had applied for a colonial governorship and was bitterly disappointed at being passed over in Hong Kong. He allowed Macdonnell to arrive to find Government House unprovided with the commonest domestic necessaries, and he found it impossible to work with the strong-willed Governor, who soon showed his intention of making sweeping changes. Macdonnell by-passed him in conducting official business; 'I myself transact nearly all the daily business,' he wrote two months after his arrival. A little more than a year later, in May

1867, Mercer went home on sick leave, and the Colonial Office reluctantly acquiesced in a pension for him at the early age of forty-five. He was the last of that band of officials sent out from England to organize the colony in 1844. J. Gardiner Austin, who had spent some years in the colony as Agent for British Guiana for coolie contract labour, succeeded him as Colonial Secretary in May 1868.

Before leaving England, Macdonnell had been instructed to enquire into the related problems of piracy and police efficiency over which the colony had been accused by the Admiral of culpable neglect. He was to enquire into the possibility of registering all boats and of controlling the sales of arms to help the navy in its task of suppressing piracy, and into the allegation that piracy had been encouraged in Hong Kong by the difficulty of securing convictions. Macdonnell, perhaps impelled by the evil reputation from which the colony was only beginning to emerge, acted as if faced with a crisis, made a searching enquiry into every department and found much to criticize. He found that the police were 'the most ineffective . . . that I ever came in contact with,' and that 'literally nothing is known of the haunts of pirates who frequent Hong Kong.' The prison system, sanitation, and water-supply all came in for severe criticism. Finally he considered the colony was heading for bankruptcy. He acted with determination, and by July 1866, only four months after his arrival, he had sketched out a series of reforms that were to embrace almost every aspect of colonial life, and bring him to grips with the Chinese. Ordinances were proposed dealing with increased taxation, control of native craft, registration of houses and servants, prevention of piracy, order and cleanliness, and the branding and deportation of criminals. These ordinances formed a single policy in which each part dovetailed, and were meant to be judged as a whole. Reform was needed, but this wholesale programme was a product of the Governor's own dominating personality and dictatorial outlook. The Colonial Office in London might grumble at 'his entire preoccupation with his own views', but the Governor went his own way with sincerity and determination which went far to disarm criticism coming from Chinese and foreigners alike.

First there was the problem of finance. A commercial recession had now set in, at home as well as in the Far East. The Agra and Masterman's Bank failed in 1866, and by February 1867, of eleven banks operating in the colony, only five remained. The great house of Dent & Co. failed in 1867. The influx of Chinese into the colony was halted and revenue suffered because sales of land practically ceased. The mint was a great drain on the colony's resources, though it was hoped eventually to produce large profits. Macdonnell took a pessimistic view. Premiums on the sale of land had been treated as revenue, yet they were capital assets steadily diminishing as more land was sold. The colony had a balance of $475,000 on 1 January 1863; three years later it was only $55,000, and the accounts for 1865 showed a deficit of $94,000. As a temporary measure he delayed the payment of the military contribution, stopped all but the most urgent public works, and to meet immediate needs borrowed $80,000 from The Hongkong and Shanghai Banking Corporation at a modest eight per cent interest, the normal rate being twelve per cent. But Macdonnell saw the situation must be met by increased taxation rather than by the curtailment of expenditure. Hong Kong was a centre of commerce; 'it is here that those reside who direct the principal transactions' of the China trade; it should therefore be made 'habitable and suitable' and 'a healthy place of residence' to fulfil its proper role. He introduced a Stamp Ordinance by which all official documents, including bank notes, were to pay stamp duties, fixed so as to make up the estimated annual deficit of $120,000. This met with great opposition. The three unofficial members of the Legislative Council protested, and a public meeting of the foreign community equally condemned it. The merchants dreaded its extension and its interference with commercial practice, and feared that the Chinese would avoid payment. The argument was also used that certain items of expenditure, $50,000 for the extension of the Pokfulam Water Scheme and $26,000 for half the cost of a gunboat to be used for the suppression of piracy, should either be dropped or else paid for out of the rates; this was a device to shift the financial burden on to the Chinese who were the chief ratepayers. Macdonnell replied that more water was needed for cleansing and the prevention of disease and was to the advantage of the whole colony. The Chinese also presented a memorial against

Macdonnell's proposals. The Secretary of State upheld the Governor and the ordinance came into operation in October 1867, with certain concessions, for example, the stamp duty on bank notes was reduced from one per cent to $\frac{2}{3}$ per cent.

One big financial problem was the mint. On Macdonnell's arrival in March 1866 the mint had already cost $310,000, and an additional $20,000 was being spent on barracks for the military guard upon which the Governor insisted. After some delay through the non-arrival of the dies, the mint was officially opened for minting on 7 May 1866. It proved to be a complete failure. Accidents to the machinery delayed operations for a week and faults in organization showed up, which Macdonnell rightly said should have been foreseen. To cover expenses it had to coin 27,000 dollars a day, but the daily output never exceeded 15,000, and was usually much less. Macdonnell estimated that at the rate achieved it would take two and a half years to coin the amount of silver deposited; the banks began to withdraw their silver from the mint, since delay meant considerable loss. An official enquiry set up in October 1866 found that the machinery was quite inadequate, the flow of silver to the mint had ceased, and that it was impossible then to buy bullion and coin it at a profit. By the late summer of 1867 the mint came to a complete standstill, though its expenses were still between $50,000 and $60,000 a year, and in February 1868 Macdonnell was authorized to close it if the Executive Council and the community at large raised no objection. The banks were approached for assistance; the Comptoir d'Escompte offered $3,000 a year towards its expenses, The Hongkong and Shanghai Banking Corporation offered to take over responsibility for the mint for five years in return for certain privileges which the Governor could not grant. The mint was closed in April 1868 and the machinery sold to the Japanese government for $60,000. Macdonnell put his finger on the cause of the failure when he said that the Hong Kong currency could not be regulated apart from that of China, and the Chinese were quite satisfied to handle silver by weight and touch without incurring a two per cent charge for coining.

Piracy was recognized by all to be a burning problem. Macdonnell thought there was justification in the charge frequently made that Hong Kong was not free from censure;

L

'literally nothing is known of the haunts of pirates who frequent Hong Kong, nor of the parties who fit them out,' he said. His remedies were, increased police efficiency; much closer super-vision of the Chinese, ashore and afloat; the setting up of a special piracy court; the prohibition of arms and munitions on Chinese junks; and close co-operation with Chinese local officials. Ordinances were passed for the better registration of houses and servants, and the Registrar-General was given power to summon Chinese inhabitants for the purpose of conducting enquiries. Householders were made responsible for all occupants of their houses in regard to certain crimes and the payment of court fines. The control of the Registrar-General was strength-ened by the enrolment of Chinese watchmen under district chief watchmen who reported direct to him. These *lokongs* who were to carry out their police duties only among the Chinese and in the Chinese portions of the city, had been proposed by the Chinese merchants themselves and were paid by them, with small financial aid from the government. This private Chinese police force was disliked, but for the moment it strengthened the hand of the Registrar-General and furthered the policy of the Governor. Money-changers were also brought under close supervision.

Another ordinance set up a rigid system of registration and control of the movement and anchoring of all junks, and ensured that no junk could enter or leave colonial waters with-out being inspected and given a clearance. An ordinance also set up a new piracy court to simplify procedure against pirates and their confederates. The main objective of all this legislation was a vigorous attack on piracy through effective police action against its roots in the colony itself.

The ordinances came into effect on 1 January 1867, though some time was to elapse before they assumed their final form. This legislation being directed specifically against the Chinese, the prior assent of the home government was necessary and was given on the ground that the suppression of piracy was essential, and Chinese protests were not upheld. The immediate effect was the disappearance of all junks from the harbour and about two thousand Chinese left the colony; but after the initial scare the Chinese merchants were reassured, and by 15 January 344 junk licences and permits had been applied for, and the number increased to over 2,000 in the next twelve months. Macdonnell strengthened the water police to inspect all the anchorages in the island, and, pending the building of a colonial steamer and to the great amusement of the community, he fitted out a junk named the *Preposterous*. The new piracy court had to be given up because the Admiralty made difficulties about the status and precedence of its naval members, and instead the Supreme Court was strengthened in piracy cases.

Macdonnell was very keen that there should be a general disarming of all Chinese junks and fishing vessels, but in this the co-operation of the Chinese was essential. In July 1868 fishing vessels were disarmed by proclamations in Canton and Hong Kong, but as the Viceroy took no action to implement them Macdonnell cancelled the proclamation in the colony and refused to co-operate in the proposed next step of disarming all junks; for this action he was reprimanded by Earl Granville, the Colonial Secretary. The new policy did effectively reduce piracy around Hong Kong. There was a recrudescence in 1872, attributed by the Governor to the change in Admiralty instructions by which British warships were stopped from taking action against pirates without the concurrence of the Chinese authorities; this was a part of the new Clarendon policy of supporting the authority of the Chinese government. Macdonnell again took determined action. He armed two junks with police, took a Chinese official from Kowloon City on board, and attacked the pirates, many of whom were captured. But they were acquitted by the Supreme Court as being beyond colonial jurisdiction. The home government disapproved of these proceedings, as action outside colonial waters ought to have been left to the navy. But whatever criticism is made against Macdonnell, it has to be admitted that piracy in local waters ceased to be the chronic problem it had been.

The attack on piracy by legislative control over Chinese activities ashore and afloat necessitated an efficient police, and the Governor, following his instructions, dealt with police and crime. He early discovered that police corruption centred around the illegal gambling houses. He was led therefore to take up the problem of gambling, and no part of his reforms created more difficulty or aroused more controversy than that concerning gambling.

The Chinese were addicted to games of chance, lotteries and the lesser forms of street gambling. Besides being offensive to the conscience of evangelical opinion in Victorian Britain, gambling was a social evil, since gambling houses tended to be centres of crime and vice, and its prohibition had become a dead letter because of police bribery. 'More than half the inspectors were in receipt of monthly allowances,' the Governor reported. The illicit gaming houses were fitted with strong doors to resist a sudden sally by the police and allow the inmates to get away. Macdonnell concluded that police reform was impossible as long as this dangerous source of corruption remained. Early in 1867 a police constable was accused of having accepted a bribe, but was acquitted on the ground that there was no ordinance under which he could properly be charged. The result was that bribery became rampant. The gambling houses controlled and bribed all those likely to give evidence against them. Macdonnell accepted the logic of this situation; if gambling could not be suppressed, it was better licensed and controlled, and a source of police corruption cut off. He determined to license a limited number of gaming houses, leaving lotteries and street gambling for later action. So in the 1867 ordinance 'for Order and Cleanliness', a clause, No. 17, was inserted allowing the Governor 'to pass such rules regulations and conditions as may be deemed expedient for the total suppression or in the meanwhile for the better limitation and control of gambling in this colony.' This innocent phrasing masked the decision already taken to license gambling, and perhaps hoodwinked the home authorities who had already refused the applications of his two predecessors, Bowring and Robinson, to do just what he was now proposing to do. In defence of Macdonnell, it is clear that his aim was to create an efficient police force, not to reform or regenerate the Chinese character. He undoubtedly shared the prevailing British opinion that gambling was evil, but this did not solve his very practical and immediate problem of police corruption. He defended his proposal both in dispatches to the Secretary of State and in the Legislative Council with conspicuous energy and conviction, and in July 1867 the licensing system, based partly on that already operating in the Portuguese colony of Macao, was introduced; eleven houses were opened under the control of the Registrar-General. The only protest came from six Protestant clergymen, who sent a memorial to the Secretary of State. They accused the Governor of acting in 'an underhand, unenglish way', declared that it was 'barefaced hypocrisy' to say that licensing would lead to suppression.

The Duke of Buckingham, once he had fully grasped the nature of the Governor's policy, ruled that 'general control and ultimate suppression must be kept steadily in view', and asked how the revenue from the gambling licences was being used. The Governor's aim was not revenue, but to improve the police system, by better pay, status, and improved accommodation, and in getting additional vessels for harbour police duties. Macdonnell made a check of gamblers and found the daily total 14,631 Chinese (he estimated that about half this total represented individual gamblers), and 204 Europeans. Suppression was a long way off.

Abuses crept in. In September 1868 Macdonnell admitted that some licensees were selling their licences at a premium, and then he casually discovered that, despite the rule that they should deal with the Registrar-General direct, the licensees, acting together, 'had agreed to pay and were paying Mr. Caldwell as their managing agent the monstrous salary of $20,000 per annum'. The irate Duke of Buckingham expressed his 'entire disapproval of those proceedings which your dispatch discloses', and demanded a complete change in the mode of granting licences, which should be sold by auction to the highest bidder or allocated by lot.

In December 1868, the Liberal government with its strong nonconformist backing, came into power, and Lord Granville, the Colonial Secretary, took a firmer line. The whole experiment was, he said, intended to facilitate the total suppression of gambling. The revenue from it must be kept quite separate and not used to relieve the colony from ordinary taxation, but for the special purposes concerned with furthering the suppression of gambling. Macdonnell defended himself and claimed that licensing had helped detect crime; fifty criminals had been arrested on the information of licensees and eighteen of them were found to be branded deportees. He denied that Caldwell had any undue influence and his salary was now only $4,800. The whole experiment was intended to deal with crime and corruption.

Granville complained of the tone of Macdonnell's reply and laid down specifically the objects upon which the special fund derived from gambling licences might be expended. He agreed to charging the cost of the police vessels against it, also to a grant of $13,000 towards a Chinese hospital. On ordinary police expenditure, Granville sanctioned a general grant of $30,000 a year from the special fund, 'which I consider a handsome but arbitrary contribution', and extra sums spent on the police must be repaid. The Governor still clung to his view as to how the special fund should be spent and when the estimates for 1870 arrived in the Colonial Office, it was found that he had proposed to appropriate more for police purposes than had been sanctioned. His tenacity was rewarded by an increase of the police grant from the special fund from $30,000 to $50,000; he was bluntly told, 'you will take these instructions for your guidance', and new estimates were demanded. Granville was fighting for the essential principle on which alone he could face parliamentary criticism, that the colony must not benefit financially from vice. The Governor was driven to farming out the gambling licences, as it would then be to the interest of the licensees themselves, and not of the police, to suppress all unlicensed gambling; since the Chinese were willing to pay large sums he could not help gaining a large revenue. He defended his actions with strong phrases, but he was in financial difficulty, for Buckingham had appeared to give him more freedom in using the proceeds of the special fund for police reform and to benefit the Chinese, than Granville was now disposed to allow.

The stubborn Governor made a final appeal in March 1870, but Granville was adamant, and the Governor was forced to repay $129,701 to the special fund, and to give up the steamer *Victoria* which had been commissioned for police work, and which was now sold to the Chinese government. When the Governor went home on leave, after four years of 'unremitting toil', opinion in the colony hardened against the system of licensed gambling. Major-General Whitfield, the Acting Governor, brought the question before the Executive Council, and it was decided to close the houses and withdraw the licences on 1 January 1871, and a proclamation was issued to the effect.

Granville refused to allow any change in the absence of the

Governor, and the licences were again put up to auction and sold for $15,800 per month. The Chinese now sent a widely signed petition against gambling, which had led to an increase in the evil of selling children, and they asked why foreigners were prohibited but the Chinese were allowed to 'engulf themselves'. At home the Governor had had to admit that a turnover of population at the rate of 1,500 a day made a regeneration of the Chinese impossible. On his return from leave in December 1871 he announced that he had been instructed to end the system of licensed gambling as soon as was convenient. A proclamation was issued by which the gambling licences were cancelled from 20 January 1872. Two officials, the Registrar-General and Captain Superintendent of Police, were now made personally responsible for the suppression of gambling; to the end Macdonnell refused to allow it to be a police matter. He stubbornly held his ground that Hong Kong was an exceptional place and that policy towards gambling should not be judged through a 'special and narrow English medium'. His trouble was less with the Chinese than with the Anglo-Saxon conscience, but it was tragic that this able man should have allowed himself to become entangled in so intractable a problem.

The Governor aimed at an efficient police force free from corruption, and had hoped to use the revenue from gambling to meet the cost of reforms. He reported Quin, the Captain Superintendent, as quite incompetent; he was pensioned off and replaced by Deane, a cadet officer. The Bombay police brought in by Robinson were not retained, and Macdonnell recruited in their place a hundred Sikhs chosen by C. V. Creagh, a police officer from Sind who was made Deputy Superintendent of Police. They arrived in June 1867 and Macdonnell thought so highly of them that another hundred were secured. Eight British inspectors were dismissed or allowed to resign. Unfortunately much of his programme had to be modified because of the ruling of the Colonial Secretary that only $50,000 a year could be charged to the special fund for police purposes.

The police continued to be criticized, and when Macdonnell went on leave there was trouble. Major-General Whitfield, the Lieutenant-Governor, inspected the police and found their arms filthy and uncared for, and the police stations and barracks dirty. Deane, the Captain-Superintendent, was on leave, and

Creagh, his deputy, fell foul of the General and was sent home on leave under a threat of suspension. Whitfield used Rice, the Assistant Superintendent, to carry out police reform on his own lines, but the Colonial Secretary countermanded his extraordinary proceedings and Creagh was ordered back to Hong Kong. Whitfield thought the Sikhs a failure and wanted to recruit West Indians. Smale, the Chief Justice, severely criticized the methods of the police in making enquiries, by which innocent men were wrongfully detained for days. On his return Macdonnell agreed to a commission of enquiry into the police, four of the seven members being the unofficial members of the Legislative Council. Crime had increased owing to the suspension of the Governor's deterrent policy, though Macdonnell attributed it to 'administrative weakness and incapacity'. The Governor left in April 1872, with the police problem still unresolved. He was able to do one thing; finances had so far improved as to allow him to recruit more police from home, and in January 1872 twenty Scottish police arrived and began the necessary strengthening of the British element.

Closely associated with the problem of the police was that of crime. The prison population had increased with the civil population, and Robinson had found a new jail on Stonecutters Island necessary. Macdonnell thought the penal system was not sufficiently deterrent and set himself to reverse this trend. Hong Kong was the centre of British commerce in the Far East, and his aim was to make the island 'more habitable'. He regarded crime in Hong Kong as exceptional in character, and disturbed conditions in China brought 'a living wave of crime' into the colony; it was impossible, he said, to reform 'the moral refuse of Canton', and besides, the population was changing round at the rate of 1,500 a day, and the only policy was to be deterrent. He removed all the convicts from Stonecutters Jail to the island and hoped by deterrent methods to reduce the number of criminals. He approved of flogging and hard labour, and in October 1866, only six months after his arrival, he was able to report that the number of convicts had decreased from 876 to 714. At the same time he reported that many convicts had petitioned to be liberated on condition of agreeing to be deported and branded 'with a small broad arrow on the lobe of the left ear', the branding having the purpose of making return more difficult. Macdonnell adopted this procedure as an experiment. Lord Carnarvon objected to the revival of the deportation and branding; the Governor defended it with vigour on the ground that it applied only to those convicts who voluntarily chose it rather than serve their sentences.

The new deterrent policy reduced the number of prisoners by September 1867 to 363, but the home government regarded his policy with suspicion, as it was in direct contrast with the more humane methods being adopted in England. His great aim was to decrease crime by keeping the criminal class away from the colony, by removing police corruption, and by cleaning up piracy. His measures were popular with Europeans and crime decreased.

Deported and branded criminals who were found in the colony were jailed to complete their sentences and flogged. There was some doubt about the legality of this and the system was dropped in May 1870, when Macdonnell was home on leave. Soon after, the home government decided that deportation should be abolished and the law was amended so that persons who were not British subjects could be banished by order of the Governor-in-Council or by the Supreme Court if they were dangerous to the peace and good order of the colony. There followed a serious recrudescence of crime, and gangs operated with much violence. Official J.P.'s demanded an enquiry, and declared that life and property had never been so insecure. On his return, Macdonnell agreed to set up an independent commission of enquiry into the police and crime, and passed an ordinance allowing a criminal to opt for branding and banishment, with flogging for subsequent return, to the great satisfaction of the community, but to the great reluctance of Lord Kimberley at home.

The attempt to control gambling indirectly resulted in the founding of a great charitable institution, the Tung Wah Hospital, which arose out of the Secretary of State's ruling that part of the gambling revenue might be devoted to the welfare of the Chinese. The need of a Chinese hospital for destitutes had long been acknowledged and the Chinese prejudice against allowing a person to die at home demanded an institution to which moribund Chinese could be sent. Chinese usually wanted to be buried in their native villages, but bodies

could be removed only when certain obscure geomantic conditions (*fung shui*) were considered favourable, and so there was
a demand for storing coffins during the waiting period.

A temple, the *I Ts'z*, the site of which had been given to the
Chinese community in 1851, gradually came to serve these
purposes, though the fact was not discovered until soon after
Macdonnell's arrival, when the Surveyor-General reported that
coffins were being stowed in rooms adjoining the temple. The
Colonial Surgeon thought this was not objectionable; much
worse was 'the practice of the keeper to let out a few small
contiguous rooms to the friends of poor people sent there to
die.' In April 1869, Lister, the acting Registrar-General, visited
the *I Ts'z* and found the 'dead and dying huddled together
indiscriminately in small filthy rooms.' An inquest held on one of
the bodies revealed that no case was sent to the *I Ts'z* unless it
was regarded as hopeless. There was much press comment on
Chinese inhumanity and the better-class Chinese were shamed
by the revelations into taking some action. The *I Ts'z* was
renovated as a temporary hospital and relief centre for the
poorest class of Chinese, providing food, clothing, shelter and
medical treatment.

The Governor encouraged the project of a Chinese hospital
and offered financial assistance from the gambling fund. The
Chinese subscribed liberally, and in April 1870 an ordinance
was passed by which the Tung Wah Hospital providing for
destitute and dying Chinese was set up. Annual subscribers of
$10 or over were empowered to elect the Board of Direc-
tors, who were to appoint the Board of Management to
look after the hospital itself, subject to general government
control. The Chinese gave more than $40,000 towards the cost
and government gave $15,000. The site, described as 'a gift
from the Queen to the Chinese Community', was provided, and
Lord Kimberley also authorized a grant of $100,000 from the
gambling fund as a capital fund. The Governor performed the
opening ceremony on 14 February 1872 and publicly handed
the sum of $96,760 to the Registrar-General as Protector of the
Chinese, being the residue of the sums voted. Of this, $90,000
were invested in The Hongkong and Shanghai Banking Corporation and the rest allocated to the purchase of furniture.
It was hoped that the interest on the sum invested and annual

subscriptions promised by the Chinese would provide the organization with an adequate annual income. The fear that the Tung Wah would be crowded out with all the undesirables and incurables of Canton did not materialize. The directors were men prominent and influential in the Chinese community and soon became its acknowledged spokesmen.

Financial stringency persisted because of the commercial recession; and revenue remained stationary in spite of increased taxation—$843,440 in 1865 and $844,418 in 1871, the expenditure being $936,955 and $894,209 for these years. The loss on the mint was met out of the colony's capital assets. Macdonnell wanted to make Hong Kong more habitable, but was able to undertake only few improvements. The extension of the Pokfulam water scheme he considered essential and the reservoir was completed in 1871; it cost double the estimated $100,000. He found the Chinese area insanitary, but there was no money for the street drainage and paving he desired, nor for the badly needed new civil hospital. Two typhoons in 1867 destroyed part of the praya; it was found to have been badly constructed and the Governor decided to rebuild it completely, and as the marine lot holders again raised great opposition to bearing any part of the cost he had to take legal proceedings against them. The decision went against him, however, and the result was to make the praya a public responsibility, although it was difficult to find funds for repair much less for the reconstruction.

Kowloon showed no expansion. Land values were depressed and the reclamation of marine lots was commenced only when rents were reduced to one quarter for five years in order to discourage the holders from throwing up their lots.

The Governor had harried the Chinese by strong action to suppress piracy and crime, but this was in the common interest, and he was prepared to take equally strong action to defend the interest of Chinese and foreigner alike in the colony. When the Chinese government seized a steamer belonging to a well-known Chinese resident in the colony, Kwok A. Cheung, because it was found in a non-Treaty Port where it had been sent to tow a junk to the colony, he made the strongest representations and criticized Robertson, the Consul at Canton, for his failure to protect the interests of the colony. The Chinese eventually allowed the owner to buy his ship back. Macdonnell took an equally strong line in 1867 when the cotton hongs in Canton attempted concerted price action against the Hong Kong cotton goods merchants, and he demanded and secured from the Viceroy a proclamation against forming combinations of merchants directed against the colony. He also took strong action against the so-called Hong Kong blockade.

Regarding constitutional development, Macdonnell's instructions, dated 14 October 1865, fixed the constitution of the Legislative Council more precisely. The Chief Justice, Colonial Secretary, Attorney-General, Treasurer and Auditor-General were to be official members *ex officio*, and four others, one government official and three private individuals, were nominated as unofficial members; the former were to have precedence. The old balance of six government to three non-government members was maintained. The right of official members to vote as they saw fit was now stopped. In 1866 Lord Carnarvon ruled that 'H.M. Government have the right to consider opposition by official members of the Legislative Council to its settled policy as incompatible with retention of office, and I am equally of opinion that they are bound, if required to do so, to support by their vote and not to oppose by any public act, a policy which may originate with the governor.' Agitation over the Stamp Ordinance, and the passing of the Reform Act of 1867 at home, renewed the local demand for reform of the Legislative Council. A Reform Association was formed in 1867, but Macdonnell reported in 1869 that it had 'died out through sheer inanition', and that the best opinion in the colony did not regard such reform as practicable or desirable.

In March 1868 the establishment of a fire brigade, with Charles May as superintendent, and paid for by a ¾ per cent rate on property, helped to meet the menace of recurring fires; Europeans and insurance companies had little faith in it and for some time continued to make their own arrangements. The first telegraph was introduced in 1866 by Jardine, Matheson & Co., linking their establishments, and soon all police stations were in telegraphic contact. In 1870 direct telegraphic communication with Europe was established by submarine cable to Shanghai and thence by the Danish trans-Siberian land line.

Macdonnell was the first Governor whose actions could be immediately called to account.

A magnificent City Hall was a tribute alike to the wealth and public spirit of the colony. It was designed by Hermitte, a Frenchman, in open competition, and comprised a library, museum, assembly hall, ballroom, supper room and theatre. It was due to a generous contribution from Jardine, Matheson & Co. that the required funds were found, and the government gave $10,000 and the site. The building was opened by the Duke of Edinburgh in 1869. The Duke also laid the foundation stone of the new chancel of St. John's Cathedral. When Bishop Alford, 1867–69, resigned because of disagreement over the proposal to set up another Anglican bishopric in China, opportunity was taken to disestablish the Anglican bishopric in Hong Kong; appointment by Letters Patent, by which the bishop was assigned a territorial designation and sphere of jurisdiction, ceased and Bishop Burdon (1871) and his successors were appointed by the Anglican Church alone and not by the state.

In one respect, perhaps, public spirit fell away. The Hong Kong Volunteer Corps was disbanded on 31 May 1866, owing to lack of public interest; it was without a commandant for twelve months, and the strength fell to forty, with only half that attendance at drills.

Sir Richard Macdonnell left the colony on retirement in April 1872, having won the respect and esteem of all sections of the community. He had combined sincerity and earnestness with great ability and determination, and it was his misfortune that his rule coincided with economic difficulties and restrictions, and that his eagerness for reform led him to become embroiled in the problem of gambling. It was regrettable too that his very qualities led him to defend his views with excessive vigour. His governorship marked an epoch in the development of the colony, and relations with the Chinese could never go back to the old footing of leaving them largely to their own devices.

CHAPTER XV

SIR ARTHUR KENNEDY, 1872–77

*'Sir Arthur Kennedy indeed was . . . one of those few men
who deserve a statue because they do not need one.'*

E. J. Eitel, *Europe in China*, 1895.

THE new Governor, Sir Arthur Kennedy, who arrived five days
after his predecessor had left, was a very different man; he was
genial, and possessed a great sense of humour, much common
sense and a strong Irish accent. He embarked on no crusade,
launched no new policy, but was content with the practical
task of administering the colony as he found it.

He had had an army career until 1846, when he accepted a
civil appointment in Ireland following the famine. He became
a colonial governor in West Africa in 1852 and then in Western
Australia, Vancouver, and again in West Africa, and so brought
great experience to his new post in Hong Kong. He was in no
hurry to make up his mind about the colony and its problems,
preferring to wait until he was more familiar with them.

His first problem was that of police. The Police Commission
set up by Macdonnell reported in July 1872, but was not
unanimous; broadly it agreed to recommend an Anglo-Chinese
police force with more men and better pay and conditions. The
recruitment of Chinese police had been strongly advocated by
Dr. Legge, as most likely to bring about good understanding
between the government and the respectable Chinese, and the
commission was influenced by evidence of the efficiency of the
Chinese police in Shanghai. Charles May, who had been
associated with the Hong Kong police as Superintendent and
Magistrate for nearly thirty years (since 1844), took the opposite
view; 'they are useless, physically and morally' was his verdict.
Kennedy did not officially comment on the report for a year,
but began to adopt Legge's idea of a Chinese police force for a
predominantly Chinese community. 'We shall learn to rely on
them more than at present,' he said of the Chinese, and secured
better results by placing them under a Cantonese-speaking
cadet officer. He agreed to pay increases, though less than those

proposed by the commission because of opposition in the Legislative Council to the increased financial estimate for police. Lord Kimberley protested against the new police vote amounting 'to more than one-fourth of the whole estimated revenue of the colony', and hoped it might be cut down. Forty-five men were brought from Scotland during 1872, and the process of weeding out unsatisfactory Europeans was continued. Kennedy kept the Sikhs as jail guards, but he condemned Whitfield's proposed recruitment of four hundred West Indians 'as little short of insanity', and an affront to the well-disposed Chinese community. The creation of a Chinese police force necessitated Cantonese-speaking officers, but for some time this remained voluntary and was encouraged only by the payment of a small allowance. Police efficiency did not come overnight, but Kennedy's acceptance of a Chinese police force proved to be the solution of what had been a chronic problem.

Kennedy upheld Macdonnell's views on the necessity of making conditions sufficiently deterrent for the criminal in Hong Kong. In 1872, just before Macdonnell had left, branding and deportation had been reintroduced, much to the satisfaction of the community. Conditions were not made easier by the practice of the police of the International Settlement at Shanghai of shipping their destitute and undesirable Chinese to Hong Kong. Kennedy reported in July 1873, 'the miscalled system of branding which is merely tattooing with indian ink, is seldom resorted to, but works well.' By that date the jail population had fallen to 331, and the empty and useless jail building on Stonecutters Island was allowed to decay, except for the jail chapel which was used as a smallpox hospital. Gambling had been suppressed in the colony, but had now arisen just over the border at Kowloon City, and Robertson at Canton was asked to approach the Viceroy to suppress it.

There was a great increase in crime in 1876, attributed by Kennedy to competing river steamer lines cutting their fares from Canton to ten cents. The result was a considerable influx of vagabonds, which within three weeks had sent the gaol population from 386 to 519. In December 1876, Kennedy brought in a Consolidation Ordinance dealing with criminal legislation and procedure, in which the law regarding deportation was retained. Lord Carnarvon was very critical of this in his reply addressed to Sir John Pope Hennessy, Kennedy's successor, and thus prepared the way for Hennessy's complete reversal of the deterrent policy. Just before he left, Kennedy dealt with the question of jail discipline and appointed a commission of enquiry. Jail regulations dated from 1857 and were now revised. Extra diet was to be ordered by the Medical Officer more sparingly, and the power of flogging was taken out of the hands of the Superintendent acting alone.

The Governor's administrative bent found scope in a programme of public works which had been severely curtailed by the financial and business recession. In addition, Cleverly, the Surveyor-General since 1846 and in the colony since 1843, retired on pension in 1865; his inefficient successor, Moorsom, resigned in 1872, and Kennedy had the advantage of having a most able successor in J. M. Price. The Governor was anxious to increase the water-supply, which was still unsatisfactory, despite Macdonnell's efforts; there had been gross miscalculation regarding the Pokfulam extensions and the daily supply was only one-third of that estimated because the piping system was inadequate. A large conduit was now constructed along the 500 foot contour to supply the central and western districts and was completed in 1877. To supply the eastern areas of the city, Price proposed to bring water from Tai Tam by a tunnel through the hills; his scheme was efficient and farsighted, but the Governor and Legislative Council were shocked to discover that it would cost £350,000, and he was asked to modify it. The Tai Tam water scheme was referred to a prominent consulting water engineer at home, and a modified version was proposed at a cost of £136,400. This was again very much whittled down, and a scheme finally adopted was to cost only £50,000, but was such that it could be added to as necessary.

The Chamber of Commerce through its chairman, J. Whittall, suggested lighthouses in the approaches to the colony, and the Governor and the Legislative Council supported the proposal. The sites thought best were all on Chinese territory, Waglan Island, Lemma Island, and Gap Rock which was twenty-six miles to the south of the colony, but the Chinese government refused to provide any sites, and Wade, British Minister at Peking, suggested the lights should be on the colony's own soil.

Cape D'Aguilar, Green Island and Cape Collinson were then suggested as suitable, and the work was put in hand without delay. The Cape D'Aguilar light was first shown on 16 April 1875 and that at Green Island on 1 July of the same year. Light dues of one per cent per ton were charged on shipping entering the harbour except junks and river steamers, and it was estimated that the cost of the lights would be liquidated in thirteen years.

The problem of public works was affected by 'the most destructive typhoon in the history of the Colony', that of 24 September 1874. The civil hospital was damaged and abandoned, three miles of the praya were badly damaged and two hundred houses were destroyed. The construction of the praya and sea wall had been faulty, and Kennedy was anxious that any work done should be solid and permanent. Before this could be done the question of further reclamation had to be decided. The Chinese holders of the western marine lots were anxious to reclaim and add to their own holdings, but a Board of Enquiry in 1875 decided against reclamation in the Sai Ying Pun and Sheung Wan areas. In the central area, where Kennedy thought 'no reclamations were likely ever to be made' because of the very valuable property there, he decided to rebuild the sea wall so effectively that damage from typhoons was unlikely, and to widen the praya to sixty feet. At the same time there was an important proposal to extend the praya to the east, in front of the naval and military areas. The local naval authorities to whom access to the harbour was vital were prepared to agree.

The military cantonment and naval yard together occupied most of the slope down to the water's edge, just east of the central district. Queen's Road ran parallel to the sea through this area, and was the only link with Wanchai, the growing suburb to the east. The naval and military area therefore effectively cut the settlement in two or, in the graphic phrase of J. M. Price, Victoria was 'strangled at its waist'.

The harbour was silting up in front of the naval yard, so that the small naval pier was practically high and dry at low tide, and stores being landed had often to be dragged over the mud. Price's scheme was to extend the praya to link up the eastern district, which would 'ease the unceasing native and foreign traffic through Queen's Road Central'. The new sea wall would

M

adjoin deep water, and it was intended to curve it so as to keep it clear of silt by a natural scouring. Entrances to the naval yard for small boats were to be provided under the praya, and there was to be a swing bridge so that large ships could enter to refit. The military in Hong Kong was against the proposal on ground of expense, but Kennedy pressed the scheme hoping that the Admiralty and War Office would contribute to the cost. The moment seemed propitious for the removal of this constricting naval and military area, but it was allowed to pass. The Admiralty proved to be less accommodating, and the scheme fell through largely because the Service departments at home wanted the colony to bear the whole cost. Kennedy consulted his Executive Council and unofficial members of the Legislative Council; the latter wanted the full praya scheme, but as the Service departments would not assist with the cost it agreed to abandon the scheme, and to repair the existing central praya to ensure the maximum permanence. The home government wanted delay because these works were of such magnitude as to warrant special reports by consulting engineers, but Kennedy had already started work, observing that the bigger scheme would have to be taken in hand sometime.

This important praya scheme failed partly because of the accident of the temporary fall in the value of land in the eastern part of Victoria. The telegraph and the Suez Canal had brought changes in commercial practice; large stocks used to be kept by the European firms to meet any advantageous price changes; but now shipments could be arranged far more quickly. The result was that large godowns in the eastern district were no longer necessary, and coolies moved to the western part of the city in search of employment. To meet this change a new Chinese area was laid out on partly reclaimed land, and named Kennedy Town after the Governor. Rents in the eastern district fell by forty to fifty per cent: and the lot-holders there asked for a reduction of Crown rents, but Kennedy did not agree. An alternative road to the eastern district following the southern boundary of the military area which Macdonnell had proposed, was now again proposed by Kennedy, as the failure of the praya extension scheme made an alternative road all the more necessary, and after further disputes over the boundary, Kennedy Road came into being. Kennedy also encouraged the development of the Peak. He repaired and renovated 'Mountain Lodge', built by Macdonnell as a summer house for the Governor and government officials, but it was destroyed in the 1874 typhoon. Building on the Peak followed this official encouragement, and roads were now begun there and wells dug to assist in its development. Kowloon began to grow slowly too, and the Yaumati area on the British side of the border was laid out and a wharf built at Tsim Sha Tsui for ferry passengers to and from the island.

A new civil hospital was a recognized need, and soon after his arrival Kennedy appointed a committee to fix the site and prepare the plans. A new Colonial Surgeon, Dr. Phineas Ayres, arrived in 1873, and pressed for a new hospital. The 1874 typhoon destroyed the old building and made the provision of a new hospital an urgent matter. The Secretary of State insisted on having the plans prepared at home; this caused delay and when the plans arrived, they were found unsatisfactory. In 1876 Kennedy proposed to start building at once, but was told by telegram to incur no avoidable expense; meanwhile makeshift arrangements had to be made. There was similar delay over the new Central School; a site was recommended and plans prepared for a building to cost $52,000 and money voted, but doubts were raised and the building was left to Kennedy's successor. His great contribution to education in the colony was the introduction of the grant-in-aid scheme by which the voluntary schools were financially assisted.

The process of evolving the colony's constitution was continued when the Hong Kong Charter was amended, 8 June 1875. It was now laid down that if the Governor died or were absent or incapacitated, the office was to be exercised by the Lieutenant-Governor, or if no one were commissioned as such, by the Colonial Secretary, subject to such instructions as the Governor might have received.

In the early days of the colony the Major-General commanding the troops was regularly commissioned as Lieutenant-Governor. In 1854 Caine had been appointed to this office which was intended to be the chief executive post of the colony, though this scheme miscarried. After Caine left in 1859, Mercer as Colonial Secretary deputized for the Governor as required, until the appointment of Macdonnell, when the system of commissioning the Major-General commanding the troops in the colony as Lieutenant-Governor was revived. When Kennedy was appointed it was decided to change back and make the Colonial Secretary responsible for the administration in the absence of the Governor. The Colonial Office argued that the senior officials should be able to look forward to the exercise of the chief responsibility, and that they were more experienced and familiar with the problems likely to come up for decision. In addition, when Macdonnell had gone on leave, General Whitfield had made many errors; he had attempted to reverse the policy of the Governor in regard to gambling, and had had to be stopped making extensive changes in the police system. He, as General, used to address letters to himself as acting Governor, 'a whimsical proceeding' as a colonial official described it; and he had reflected on the policy of the Colonial Office regarding the disposal of the gambling special fund. Whitfield's successor, Major-General Bruncher, was made Lieutenant-Governor, but he died soon after his arrival. The change was then made, and the next General, Colborne, did not receive this commission, the War Office being told that the practice of making the General Officer commanding the troops in the colony the Lieutenant-Governor was now to be discontinued. In October 1874, Kennedy was invited home for consultations because his wife was seriously ill in England, and he was told that J. Gardiner Austin, Colonial Secretary, would administer the government. Kennedy reported that this '. . . has nearly caused General Colborne a fit. He has fairly exploded, and judging from the effect . . . he must have had an enormous stock of explosive matter stored up.' Kennedy in fact shortly returned to the colony, having at Singapore received news of the death of Lady Kennedy. Colborne protested strongly to the War Office, and refused to attend meetings of the Executive Council. This, as Kennedy remarked, 'was not attended by any ill-effects for the Colony', until, because of the amalgamation of various offices and absence on leave, he could not get a quorum for the Executive Council. Price was then appointed a member. Colborne remained sullen and unco-operative, though when he was absent from the colony he had no objection to his military secretary attending in his place. This meant that the relations between the civil and military powers were rather strained. 'There is always a row between the Government and the General at Hong Kong . . . and I conclude it is one of the local occupations,' commented one Colonial Office official.

Kennedy suggested that the military areas at Sai Wan and Stanley should be given up. They had been abandoned for many years except that the seventy acres at Stanley had been used for artillery practice once a year, but the General refused. The military also claimed the right granted by Earl Grey in 1851 to drill on the cricket ground, though Kennedy reported 'soldiers have not been paraded on the ground more than a dozen times in the last quarter of a century'. Colborne wanted to join it to the Murray Parade ground on the other side of Queen's Road, and even claimed the road until he was told this was inadmissible.

The Governor's instructions were also amended to give the Legislative Council the power to debate any question duly proposed and seconded, and the Governor's right of initiation was retained only in matters of finance. Under Macdonnell the Legislative Council had met more frequently to pass financial votes, so as to avoid the system of having to take supplementary votes the following year. Now in 1872 a Finance Committee of all the members of the council was set up, presided over by the senior member, to which the Governor was to submit financial business for consideration. The unofficial members thus had more opportunity of taking an independent line; they criticized Deane, Superintendent of Police, because he kept the police in barracks during the 1874 typhoon, and proposed to reduce his salary, and they wanted to reduce the vote for the fire brigade because they were dissatisfied with its organization. The constitution of the Executive Council was amended and its number increased to five: the Officer Commanding the troops, Colonial Secretary, and Attorney-General were to be members ex officio, and two other government officials, C. C. Smith and J. M. Price, were to be members, but not in virtue of their office.

Retrenchment in colonial expenditure was necessary because of the trade recession; on the retirement of Rennie in 1870, Macdonnell had combined the offices of Colonial Secretary and Auditor-General, and when Forth left in the same year the Treasurership was combined with the office of Registrar-

General. To save expense, Kennedy stopped the recruitment of cadets from England, and in 1875 suggested dropping the cadet scheme. By raising the pay of the lower clerkships he thought he could attract local recruits for interpreterships, and he appointed as the first of this new class of officer, J. Dyer Ball, the son of a Canton missionary who had been brought up in China and spoke Cantonese. He also encouraged officials to study the language by an allowance of $10 a month. Lord Carnarvon was critical; he agreed good interpreters might be recruited locally, but not those of sufficient education to act as heads of departments. He renewed the cadet recruitment by examination and arranged that successful candidates spent a year at Oxford under Dr. Legge, who had become professor of Chinese there.

The cadet scheme had worked well. The first three cadets who arrived in 1862 very soon became heads of departments; C. C. Smith became Registrar-General in 1864, Deane, Superintendent of Police in 1867, and Tonnochy, Superintendent of the jail in 1875. J. Russell and A. Lister were recruited in 1865; the latter became Postmaster-General in 1875 and Russell rose to be Chief Justice.

The judiciary was reorganized. Judge Ball, of the Summary Court, who suffered from epileptic fits, retired in 1873; this court was then abolished and J. Pauncefote, who had been Attorney-General since 1866, became Puisne Judge; he left the same year on appointment as Chief Justice in the Leeward Islands, and was succeeded by Snowdon. John Bramston became Attorney-General, 1874–76, and on his appointment to the Colonial Office, he was followed by G. Phillippo.

For some time there had been pressure from the Colonial Office upon all colonies to introduce legislation to secure complete records of births, marriages and deaths. Macdonnell had refused to do this as 'exciting the suspicions and wounding the prejudices' of the Chinese. In 1872 Kennedy made the registration of births compulsory and arranged for the registration of deaths; in 1875 he passed a Marriage Ordinance with a compulsory registration clause and with other clauses providing for preliminary enquiry by the Registrar-General and the previous issue of his certificate. The Catholics under Bishop Raimondi strenuously opposed the ordinance and threatened civil disobedience; it was suspended pending a reference home and was amended to meet some of the objections raised.

The government contributed to the building of St. John's Cathedral chancel and the repair of its roof, to the building of St. Joseph's Catholic church, and to the rebuilding of this and the Italian Convent after their destruction in the 1874 typhoon. The Liberal government at home was anxious that colonial funds should not be used to support one denomination to the exclusion of others, and on the votes to the Anglican cathedral Lord Kimberley expressed the view in 1873, 'The maintenance of the fabric of this and any other Anglican places of worship should fall on the Anglican community', and arrangements were made to hand over the control of the cathedral to a Church Body, the government making a contribution for its use by troops.

The governorship of Kennedy was a period of quiescence and showed how much could be achieved by humane, common-sense administration. He had a balanced, friendly approach; he consulted the community, took pains to treat the Chinese with friendliness, and was the first Governor to invite them to functions at Government House. He developed the Gardens and Afforestation Department, and began systematic tree-planting in the streets of the city. The great blemish on his administration was that in spite of full reports from the Colonial Surgeon and the Surveyor-General on the insanitary condition of the city, he made no attempt at improvement. His departure in March 1877 to become Governor of Queensland was sincerely regretted by Chinese and Europeans alike. On the news of his death in the Red Sea, on his way home from Australia in 1883, a public meeting decided to erect a statue to his memory, in the Botanical Gardens, the only Governor of Hong Kong to be so honoured.

CHAPTER XVI

SIR JOHN POPE HENNESSY, 1877–82

'*Now I believe that the duty of a Governor in dealing with a community such as I find here, is to avoid the encouragement of any body or of any class, but to simply hold the balance evenly between all men.*'

Hennessy, Speech to Legislative Council, 3 June 1881.

'*I am afraid that a watchful eye is necessary over Mr. Hennessy's proceedings.*'

Minute by the Secretary of State, Lord Carnarvon,
17 August 1877.

JOHN POPE HENNESSY, the fourth of five successive Irishmen to act as Governor, had been a member of Parliament for an Irish county. In 1867 he became Governor of Labuan and then served as Governor in West Africa, the Bahamas and the Windward Islands before coming to Hong Kong in April 1877. He was knighted in 1880. He brought a new attitude towards the Chinese which quickly shattered the tranquillity of Kennedy's régime. He treated the Chinese community with marked consideration, and showed respect for its increasing importance in the colony by the appointment for the first time of a Chinese member to the Legislative Council. This offended foreign sentiment; but when he treated Chinese criminals with a more humane sympathy and reversed the deterrent policy of Macdonnell and Kennedy, the indignation of the foreign community was intense. Hennessy was representative of the more enlightened British official opinion which believed in the principle of equal treatment for all peoples as laid down in the Hong Kong Governor's instructions since 1866. The foreign community regarded this as hopeless idealism; equality before the law was an ingrained British habit, but that was as much equality as they were willing to concede.

Unfortunately Hennessy combined this idealism with great polemical skill which masked his administrative inefficiency and lack of practical common sense. The Colonial Office officials who had been dealing with him for ten years, and knew him, were equally irritated by this combination of traits. 'He has muddled the finances of every colony he has governed,' minuted one official; 'we must watch his proceedings very narrowly,' wrote another. On one occasion he was sent a list of thirty-nine dispatches which he had left unanswered, and the Colonial Secretary was driven to adopt the expedient of having those dispatches on which he required some action, printed and published in the colony for all to see.

The abolition of transportation of convicts in 1857 had stimulated interest in the humane treatment of criminals and the adoption of more remedial aims in punishment, particularly after the parliamentary legislation of 1865. These ideas spread to the colonies by way of the Colonial Office, and Hennessy, in wanting to change the harsh deterrent system in Hong Kong, was only acting in accordance with enlightened opinion of his time. In a series of dispatches written soon after his arrival, he condemned the whole penal system of the colony, and criticized Kennedy's explanation that the increase in crime was due to cheap fares from Canton. Much of the crime was petty mendi-·cancy, unlicensed hawking, or being out at night without a pass or light; and in any case, since October 1876 only two offenders in five were not first offenders. The jail system was bad because no effort was made to separate young offenders from hardened criminals and there was no moral or industrial training. He criticized the education system which had only 4,640 in school and more than 12,000 children unprovided for. He opposed the system of voluntary branding and deportation in return for full or partial remission of sentence, because good, bad, long-term, and short-term prisoners were all treated alike, and the petition for branding, being in English, was not understood. There was much other deportation, and he instanced two Chinese women, resident many years, now aged seventy-two and eighty and too old to work, whom he deported 'with pain and reluctance' for mendicancy. Against the unanimous advice of the Executive Council he soon began to refuse to deport where he felt there was a doubt about the convictions. The practice of forcing all Chinese convicts at the end of their sentences to find two securities or be deported was found to be technically illegal and was stopped, and he called for reports with a view to the abolition of public flogging. In the jail, he found the foreign turnkeys of a low type, brutalized by having to administer excessive floggings, often fined for drunkenness or beating prisoners, and yet retained in the service. He got rid of the worst and began the recruitment of trained prison warders from England, and refused to liberate any convict unless he had served two-thirds of his sentence. He aimed at abolishing branding, now apparently done on the neck, as it prevented a man from gaining an honest living.

The Governor's policy was held to be too lenient to the criminal, and 1878 saw a big increase in serious crime, such as robberies and burglaries by armed gangs, and much crime was accompanied by violence. In October 1878 a great indignation meeting was held on the cricket ground to protest against the policy of the Governor and to demand public flogging and deportation by which alone, it was believed, public security could be achieved. It memorialized the Secretary of State and asked for an enquiry into the criminal law administration in the colony, and also into the relations between the Governor and his officials. The opposition to the Governor was led by William Keswick, an unofficial member of the Legislative Council. The Chinese soon after presented a widely signed address to the Governor in support of his policy. The Secretary of State broadly upheld the Governor, not without some criticism and fear of the effect of his policy, and he was asked to prepare full and complete plans for the reform of penal legislation and jail discipline and methods.

Hennessy proposed a new jail on Stonecutters Island with sufficient accommodation to allow the segregation of convicts into classes, but the home government preferred a site on the Hong Kong island. He converted two basements of the Victoria jail into forty cells as a beginning of prison reform. In 1881, ordinances were passed to abolish partial remission of sentences on condition of voluntary branding and deportation; and against public flogging and flogging on the back. Flogging was retained only for crimes of violence, and the cat was replaced by the rattan. Most significantly, penal laws directed specifically against the Chinese and dating from the panic legislation of 1857 were dropped.

The Banishment Ordinance of 1882 replaced all the deportation clauses of previous enactments. Deportation was objected to because the colonial legislature, having no power outside the colony, had no power to deport, and trouble had arisen when the police allowed deportees to board ships for Australia, a practice which Kennedy stopped when he became Governor of Queensland. Banishment was retained as a discretionary power in the hands of the Governor; it was to be for not more than five years, the reason had to be given, and it was not to apply to Chinese alone, but to any person not being a natural born or nationalized subject. Hennessy was accused of encouraging crime and of wanting to abolish flogging and deportation altogether. His enlightened attitude was mistaken for excessive leniency. In fact he urged heavier punishment for the hardened criminal and cut down the jail diet and introduced the treadmill. He wanted transportation of the worst criminals and even suggested that Labuan should become a dependency of Hong Kong for the purpose of receiving Hong Kong criminals.

One species of crime, the kidnapping of women and girls, raised in an acute form the conflict between British law and Chinese custom that arose over the policy of bringing the Chinese more closely under British administration. The number of cases that came before the courts increased from fifty in 1874 to 107 in 1880, and arose from the fact that woman and girls were bought and sent overseas, where the price might be as high as $350, or disposed of in the colony at prices up to $45. Women were lured to Hong Kong on completely false promises. Unfortunately this traffic in human beings had some basis in the deeply rooted Chinese custom of the purchase of children for adoption, and particularly of girls for domestic servitude, called *mui tsai*. The abuse of this custom brought discredit upon the Chinese, and in 1878 a group of Chinese merchants requested and secured permission to form an anti-kidnapping association to combat the evil. At the same time the Chief Justice, Sir John Smale, in dealing with certain cases of kidnapping, went so far as to describe the whole system of purchase for whatever purpose as a form of slavery, contrary to English law, and a disgrace to the colony. Phillippo, the Attorney-General, argued that the judge should have confined his remarks to the kidnapping cases before the court, and he refused to institute proceedings against the practice of selling children when requested to by Smale, on the ground that there was no law against adoption, whether accompanied by a financial agreement or not. Dr. E. J. Eitel, who had become Chinese Secretary to the government, produced a long memorandum to say that slavery did exist in China, but was quite distinct from the purchase of children for adoption or for domestic servitude.

Sir John Pope Hennessy was in a dilemma. On the one hand he was against any trafficking in human beings; on the other, he was anxious to respect Chinese custom and usage. He eventually refused to allow any proceedings against the practice of adoption and *mui tsai*, hoping that the Chinese themselves would eliminate abuse. The Chinese, in petitioning to form their anti-kidnapping association, made a clear distinction between the practice of disposing of children and the abuses that had crept in, and appealed to the 1841 proclamation of Elliot guaranteeing to all Chinese the free enjoyment of their customs. Hennessy appointed a committee to go into the question of the rules of the suggested association. In 1880 Lord Kimberley took the matter up more strongly and urged that the proposed society should be formed without delay, and the anti-kidnapping society became the Society for the Protection of Virtue, or the Po Leung Kuk, and was officially recognized in June 1880. In a final dispatch, 18 March 1882, the Earl of Kimberley had to agree that 'the question arising out of the condition of adopted children or of children employed in domestic service are more perplexing,' and felt that though this practice might sometimes be to the child's advantage, no question of a money payment should affect the right of a parent to his child, and that safeguards in the nature of registration or the imposition of conditions on the purchaser might be necessary. 'I cannot avoid the conviction that the position of the children now under consideration is one of peril,' he said, and asked for a full enquiry into the whole subject.

Hennessy angered the foreign merchant community by taking a pro-Chinese attitude over the so-called customs 'blockade', and over extending the areas in which Chinese were allowed to live.

A census held in 1876 showed that compared to the previous estimate of 1872, the population had increased from 121,985 to

139,144; the increase of 17,159 was predominantly Chinese, for British adult males fell by eighty-six, and only the Portuguese influx after the 1874 typhoon kept the number of Europeans from falling. Chinese business firms were increasing and prospering and European firms were cutting down because Chinese could market European goods and supply Chinese produce to Europe more cheaply. 'One sees warehouses that a few years ago were in the midst of a European district . . . now in the occupation of the Chinese,' Hennessy reported in 1878. Segregation of the communities was accepted in the social life of the colony. A clause in the leases restricted the building of houses to those in keeping in the neighbourhood; no difficulty had arisen because the Chinese built to the east and west, leaving the central district to the Europeans; but the taking over of European property meant that the Chinese could no longer be confined to their own areas. Hennessy supported them and in 1877 it was agreed, 'there being no legal impediment in the way, and it being a matter of principal importance that no obstruction should be put in the way of the natural course of trade', that 'permits be freely granted for native structures along any part of Queen's Road, and business streets immediately adjoining' to a line joining Upper Wyndham Street, Hollywood Road and Aberdeen Street. C. C. Smith, the Registrar-General and Protector of the Chinese, strongly opposed this concession; the Governor on the other hand criticized the new demarcation line as not doing enough justice to the Chinese, but Lord Carnarvon upheld it as the limit of the concession to be made without further consultation. Objection came from another quarter; the General, who was on bad terms with the Governor, protested against the insanitary condition of Chinese housing and complained that the health of the central cantonment was threatened by the new concession and by the proposed building along Kennedy Road above the cantonment. This led to the sending out of Osbert Chadwick to enquire into the sanitary condition of Hong Kong and to his important report of 1882. (See page 187.)

There was one other result of the concession, equally unforeseen, a vast speculation in land by the Chinese. A new census was ordered in 1881, and showed that the population had risen to 160,402; the European increase was 273, and the Chinese nearly 21,000. From January 1880 to May 1881, Chinese bought land and property worth $1,710,000 from foreigners and $17,705 from the government. The census revealed all-round increase in Chinese trades and professions, and explains the pressure on land and accommodation and the consequent land speculation, confined primarily to Chinese, of 1881. The crash came next year; many prominent Chinese were in financial difficulty, and a meeting was held to discuss an appeal to the government to arrange mortgages. There was a rapid recovery, and the normal course of trade was hardly affected.

Increased prosperity brought up once more the question of currency, and in 1877 the Chamber of Commerce asked that the American trade dollar should be made legal tender until British dollars could be coined in England or in a revived mint in Hong Kong. This was supported by a memorial from the inhabitants, and for some time the agitation for a local mint continued. Hennessy suggested making the Japanese yen legal tender, especially as Japanese trade had grown since the Mitsubishi Line steamers began to call, but the home government would not agree.

The greater regard for Chinese custom and opinion shown by the Governor was inevitably reflected in his proposals for constitutional and administrative change. In January 1880, on the retirement of H. B. Gibb from the Legislative Council, Hennessy suggested and provisonally appointed a Chinese, Ng Choy, as a member. He was a British subject, born in Singapore and educated in England, and was the first Chinese to be called to the English bar and to practise at the Hong Kong bar. The Governor thought the time had come when the interests of the Chinese community should find representation in the Legislative Council. 'The wealthy and better Chinese' whom the Governor said he had consulted, had agreed that Ng Choy was well able to represent them. The Chinese had begun to demand such representation, and in a memorial sent to London in January 1879, they had claimed that, being ten times the foreigners in number, 'it would be but fair to allow the Chinese community a share in the management of the affairs of the colony.' Singapore had had a Chinese on the Legislative Council since 1869, and Hennessy had made such an appointment in Labuan. Hennessy proposed a reorganization of the Legislative

Council to contain six official members, all holders of six named offices, and five unofficials, of whom four were to be British and one Chinese; but Sir Michael Hicks Beach, Colonial Secretary, was against any change and agreed to Ng Choy only temporarily, until the return of Gibb, or for three years. He argued that if in a period of strained relations with China, the Governor wished to consult the Legislative Council, the presence there of a Chinese would be difficult, and he also thought a Chinese merchant might have been preferable. Shortly after, Ng Choy was appointed an acting Magistrate, the first Chinese to hold the post in Hong Kong. In July 1880 Gibb resigned from the Legislative Council, and Hennessy strongly advocated the appointment of a permanent Chinese member as the Chinese were the largest owners of property, paid ninety per cent of the colonial revenue and made a great contribution to colonial prosperity, but Hicks Beach refused to alter his decision that Ng Choy's appointment was to be for no longer than the three years originally stated. A Colonial Office minute to the effect that Hennessy's successor was to be told to appoint a Chinese member of the Legislative Council, showed that it was not opposed to the principle, but rather suspicious of Hennessy's general policy. In August 1881, Hennessy nominated Belilios, an Indian and Chairman of The Hongkong and Shanghai Banking Corporation, as a member of the Legislative Council.

Soon after his arrival Hennessy suggested the reintroduction of the cadet scheme, which had already been decided on in England, and an improvement of interpretation. The discovery that a Chinese woman had had to sell her son to pay a fine imposed by the Registrar-General led to the appointment of a commission of enquiry into the Registrar-General's department, and Hennessy accused C. C. Smith of illegal and immoral practices. He stopped the system of informers used to incriminate prostitutes, and wanted to take away the judicial powers of the Registrar-General over brothels, where he was accuser, judge and jury. The two men disagreed completely over Chinese policy, and it was essential to the Governor to have as Registrar-General and Protector of the Chinese, a man in sympathy with his general policy of consulting Chinese opinion. The result was that when the Colonial Secretary, J. Gardiner Austin, retired in 1878, Hennessy refused to recommend C. C. Smith, who

had been marked out to succeed him; Smith secured his promotion as Colonial Secretary of the Straits Settlements and a
new man, W. H. Marsh, was brought in from Mauritius.

The Governor now attempted to reorganize all the administrative arrangements for dealing with the Chinese. The
Registrar-General's department was to lose a great part of its
duties, a new interpreters' department was suggested under a
senior official who would not only be responsible for interpreting in the courts, but would act as Chinese secretary to the
Governor, and receive all Chinese petitions and communications and have them translated. The Governor hoped in this
way to be in more direct touch with Chinese affairs. Dr. E. J.
Eitel was suggested for the post at a salary of £1,000 per year.
Lord Kimberley refused to accept the scheme. He thought the
relations between the colonial secretariat, the Registrar-
General's department and the new interpreters' department
were not clear, and he reminded the Governor that it was the
purpose of the cadet scheme to supply men able to occupy the
highest posts without the aid of interpreters, and that the
Registrar-General should be as he had always been, the official
channel of communication between the government and the
Chinese community.

Hennessy was a difficult man to work with and quarrelled
with all his officials. Marsh, the Colonial Secretary, asked to
be transferred to another colony because Hennessy handled all
government business personally; Stewart, headmaster of the
Central School, and promoted on one occasion to be acting
Colonial Secretary, refused the offer of the post of Registrar-
General under Hennessy and accepted a post as Police Magistrate, which gave him more freedom from interference; the
Harbour-master was charged with being remiss in the examination of emigrant ships, and C. C. Smith went off to Singapore.

Hennessy also quarrelled with the military. General Donovan
refused to sit on the Executive Council, and when absent refused
to allow his deputy to sit. On the occasion of the Queen's birth-
day, 24 May 1880, Governor and General organized rival
dinner parties, with the one military band being ordered to
attend on the General; on appeal by Hennessy, the War Office
ordered by telegram that the General's preparations should
cease. The General wanted to take more land in Kowloon

for military purposes, and began a series of complaints against Chinese lack of sanitation, out of which unhappy bickering came the first great enquiry into the condition of Hong Kong, the Chadwick Report of 1882.

The danger of war with Russia in 1877 led, in May 1878, to the formation of the Hong Kong Artillery and Rifle Volunteer Corps, the third volunteer corps to be formed in the colony. It numbered 150 by the end of the year, but when the crisis passed interest waned; there were quarrels, and all equipment borrowed from the military had to be returned. Numbers fell, and by 1881 it practically ceased to exist. After Hennessy left, an appeal was made for government assistance, and Marsh, the administrator, agreed. The Volunteer Corps was disbanded, and a new Volunteer Corps consisting of two companies of Artillery was formed in November 1882, on a new basis which gave the volunteers more official standing.

The war scare of 1877–78 and the wars in South Africa and Afghanistan drew attention to the whole problem of Imperial defence and the extent to which it could be assisted from local resources, and local committees of defence were set up in all colonies. In Hong Kong battery sites and fortifications were prepared, an ironclad turret ship, the *Wyvern*, built for the American Confederates, was stationed in the harbour for defence, and the question of a local defence force was discussed. The widest diversity of views was expressed regarding the composition of such a force. Hennessy, as might be expected, urged that the Chinese would furnish good material for such a force, but his idea was not adopted. An interesting suggestion was made by Colonel Crossman, who had been sent out specially from the War Office, that Causeway Bay should be reclaimed to serve as the naval and military area. The scheme, unfortunately, was never adopted.

Finances became much more healthy during Hennessy's governorship, largely due to the great influx of Chinese and the continued expansion of trade. The Governor set up a Chinese stamp-selling agency on a commission basis, and so secured much greater stamp revenue. He broke the opium licence ring and increased the revenue from opium from $132,000 to $205,000. Without any additional taxation, revenue increased from $947,637 in 1878 to $1,209,517 in 1882.

N

Hennessy wanted to reduce the incidence of taxation on the Chinese, particularly junk-owners, but the Legislative Council suggested a reduction of municipal rates, and they were reduced by two per cent. The Secretary of State refused this reduction and urged greater expenditure on the urgently needed public works.

Under Hennessy, public works were subject to such prolonged delay that practically nothing was done. The strengthening and rebuilding of the praya, begun by Kennedy, was continued, but other essential projects were just left. The Central School, urgently needed in 1876, was held up because the Governor was critical of its inadequate English teaching. A new civil hospital was sorely needed to replace the one destroyed in the 1874 typhoon; it had been forced into temporary premises which were destroyed by fire in 1878, since when it had temporarily taken over the Lock Hospital, and a new school building at Sai Ying Pun. Kennedy had suggested converting the Lock Hospital into the general hospital, and when this move was made, Hennessy reported that the new hospital had been completed; in fact, the intended conversion had not even been started. The new jail was equally delayed. The Tai Tam water scheme was held up because Hennessy thought that the provision of water-tanks for fire-fighting would go far to meet the water problem, and he held strong views about the Chinese 'dry earth' sanitation system which he thought would make additional water supplies unnecessary.

The observatory was similarly delayed. Kennedy had suggested a time ball for the convenience of shipping in the harbour, and the Colonial Office had replied suggesting the possibility of an observatory. Hennessy had plans for an observatory on Mount Elgin, Kowloon, but was dissatisfied, and a much more elaborate scheme was drawn up by a Major Palmer, R.E., in 1881, which Hennessy proposed to call the K'ang-hsi Observatory after the Emperor who built that at Peking. Again, at the first Executive Council meeting he held in the colony, Hennessy proposed the building of a breakwater at Causeway Bay to form a junk refuge to avoid the heavy loss which the typhoon of 1874 had caused among the boat population. Lord Carnarvon insisted that the plans should be seen by the specialist engineering consultant, Sir John Goode, and agreed to the cost being met from the special gambling fund. Nothing was done, and in December 1881 Lord Kimberley asked why no plans for the breakwater had been sent, and asked about the progress of the other public works. Hennessy blamed Price for the delays, but in fact they were due to his own preoccupation with the problem of crime, his quarrels with his officials, his insistence on handling all business personally, and to the difficulties caused by his new policies. In fact, for excellent reasons convincingly expressed, the programme of urgently needed public works was held up during the whole of his governorship.

The Governor was accused of encouraging the Chinese too much. He pursued a policy of humane treatment towards the criminal, of consideration for the customs and usages of the Chinese, for their commercial interests, and for their representation on the Legislative Council. The Chinese were no longer to be treated as aliens in Hong Kong, as he put it, and he pursued this policy consistently. When referring to the buoyancy of the colonial revenue, in 1880 and 1881, he said it seemed to be 'not uninfluenced by the policy of treating H.M.'s Chinese subjects . . . on terms of perfect equality with the other residents in the colony.' He wanted baths and wash-houses for poor Chinese; he opened the lower government posts to competition; and he objected to the practice which had grown up of giving Chinese government employees gratuities instead of pensions on the same basis as the others. He suggested a general naturalization ordinance for Chinese, but this was not possible without special legislation, and all he could do was to pass local private naturalization ordinances by which a number of local residents were individually made British Subjects in Hong Kong. The Chamber of Commerce wanted legislation to compel Chinese to disclose the names of all the partners in Chinese business hongs, but having consulted the Chinese, Hennessy refused.

He caused great annoyance to the foreign community by opposing race discrimination in the use of the City Hall, the committee of which had decided, some few years after the opening in 1869, to restrict the use of the museum and library to Europeans on Sundays and at certain hours on week days, and to Chinese women on one morning per week. Hennessy threatened to withdraw the government grant, which provided the curator's salary, if this rule was not withdrawn. The Liberal Lord Kimberley agreed that public money should not in principle be granted to an institution where any distinction of class or race was made in the rules of admission. The Governor, perhaps unnecessarily, also stopped the sale of 'spirituous liquors' in the building on the occasion of theatrical performances and other functions, on the ground that the City Hall was not licensed, though the practice had gone on for years.

The Governor was keen on education for the Chinese, and yet surprisingly enough his view was that English should be the basis of the public education system. This was quite inconsistent with his respect for Chinese custom and usage, and it led him into wholesale condemnation of what had already been achieved in the way of vernacular education, but it secured the wider extension of the grant-in-aid scheme to schools of the religious bodies.

In 1881, partly as a result of an application by Bishop Raimondi for financial assistance for the religious work of the Roman Catholics, the Liberal government finally decided to end grants to all religious bodies. It was arranged that when the Colonial Chaplain retired the appointment was not to be renewed, and the Anglican church was thus to be disendowed.

Sir John Pope Hennessy was the first Governor to be shocked by the unequal treatment of the Chinese which was a relic of the early days when respectable Chinese avoided the colony. He took the first steps to translate into reality the sentiment of non-discrimination between races which had appeared in the Governor's instructions in 1866 and in British colonial policy even earlier. He treated the Chinese as partners, and largely because of this he was hated by the Europeans. In his enlightened policy he was in advance of his time.

On the other hand, he proved to be a poor administrator, and his record of actual achievement was small. He was an impossible man to work with, he quarrelled with all his officials and was distrusted by the Colonial Office. He was able, and capable of laying down principles. Yet he was not open in character; his dispatches were too frequently polemical efforts to prove his own case, in which he could be quite unprincipled. The enlightened policy of partnership with the Chinese did not benefit from being associated with a man who excited so much hostility and distrust.

He left in March 1882 for the governorship of Mauritius, where he aroused intense hostility as he had done in Hong Kong, and a former Governor, Sir Hercules Robinson, had to be sent from Ceylon on a special mission to restore tranquillity.

CHAPTER XVII

SOCIAL AND ECONOMIC CONDITIONS, 1866–82

'My report will show the necessity for strong and complete measures of sanitation . . . without waiting for the necessity to be demonstrated by the irresistable logic of a severe epidemic.'
The Chadwick Report, 1882.

PUBLIC health emerged as one of the main problems of these years. In Britain itself opinion was only slowly moving towards organized health measures; a return of cholera in 1865–66 led to the Public Health Act of 1866 dealing with nuisances, water supply and sewers, and in 1869 a Public Health Commission laid down the main conditions necessary for public health. In the 1874 general election Disraeli focussed public attention on the subject. In Hong Kong, successive colonial surgeons, particularly Murray, had severely criticized sanitary conditions, and the Sanitary Committee of 1863 had underlined the accusations, but it must cause no surprise that little was done. As long as the Chinese community lived apart, few realized the serious nature of the problem; in addition little could be done in this sphere without impinging on Chinese custom and prejudice. Public health measures presented the policy of integrating the Chinese into the colonial administration with its greatest challenge.

After the recession of the 1860's, population steadily increased and the colony was subject to serious overcrowding. In 1865 the population totalled 125,504, of which 121,497 were Chinese and 4,007 non-Chinese; next year it was 10,000 less because of Macdonnell's legislation. The census of 1876 gave the total as 139,144, of which 130,168 were Chinese and in 1881, the next year in which a census was held, the total was 160,402, of which 150,690 were Chinese. In the fifteen years 1866–81 the number of Chinese residents increased by 39,208, or 32.2 per cent and it was difficult for housing to keep pace.

Dr. Murray continued to criticize the insanitary state of Hong Kong. His annual report for 1870, a year during which there had been much fever, complained of the drains, saying that it was 'not creditable to this colony, that after their unhealthy condition had been pointed out both by myself and the Sanitary Commission, they should remain as they are, a source of disease and death'. He said that the owners of the marine lots had approached the government through him regarding the drains opening into the sea and fouling the shore, and that 'lack of funds is the excuse offered for the unavoidable continuation of this most dangerous nuisance.' He wanted better hospital accommodation and the registration of deaths. His disclosures of treatment of moribund Chinese led to the founding of the Tung Wah Hospital. He urged more tree-planting and the use of carbolic acid as palliatives.

Sir Richard Macdonnell, with his usual energy and conscientiousness made plans to improve the Chinese district of Tai Ping Shan by street paving, more surface draining, and linking up the houses with the main drainage, and introduced an Order and Cleanliness Ordinance in 1866, which prohibited the keeping of pigs and similar animals in dwelling houses without a licence. The Governor undoubtedly saw the problem, but he was soon engrossed in tasks concerning police, gambling and piracy, and could do little. He was in any case unwilling to disturb the Chinese more than was necessary, and thought he could reform them without first having to change their environment. He was very keen on the virtues of carbolic acid, and when the P. and O. Steamship Company refused to carry more than two pounds at a time, he secured a supply from France.

Dr. Murray retired in 1872 after fourteen years' service; his successor, McCoy, died soon after, and in November 1873, Dr. Phineas Ayres arrived as Colonial Surgeon. He and J. M. Price, who had come as Surveyor-General in July of that year, were for many years the chief officials connected with public health. Almost immediately Ayres condemned the sanitary conditions that he found. In January 1874 he reported the brothels were producing cases of typhoid; they were filthy, with rooms built within rooms, and many were completely lacking in any form of sanitation. In April he reported on the city, and again thoroughly condemned what he found; houses were occupied by five to ten families which 'would not be considered fit to put pigs in by any decent person'. These houses were owned by Europeans and wealthy Chinese 'who squeeze those who have no power to make their complaints known'. 'The construction of this class of house,' he said, 'was against every sanitary rule,' with no yard and no ventilation; the ground floors were of mud or stone or tiles; the floors of upper stories were so thin that they could not be washed without the water dripping through to the rooms below. He found three to eight families to a room, each paying one and a half or two dollars a month. Pigs were universally kept, in kitchens, or upstairs, and 'a very favourite place for them is under the bed'; often a room was divided into four, each with its pigs. Yet the rents were high, and a house of three rooms of fourteen feet square rented at £55–70 per year. Ayres was surprised that typhus, typhoid and cholera were not more frequent, and he suggested a thorough reform of buildings, drains, and animal keeping. In his report for 1874 he repeated his criticisms, adding two new discoveries; he had found wells inside houses and open to pollution, and had discovered many houses not linked up to any drainage system at all. In the same year, Price reported that the whole system of drains and sewers was defective and that some streets were completely without drainage.

Ayres found no encouragement or support; his two reports remained in the Colonial Secretary's office, with certain marginal contradictions by C. C. Smith the Registrar-General. All the paragraphs on sanitation in his annual report for 1874 were cut out. Naturally Ayres' subsequent annual reports were much less trenchant. In that for 1875, he complained of a great lack of conveniences in theatres, hotels and public places, but agreed that without a new building ordinance little more could be done; the scavenging contractors were often summoned for negligence, and he was able to report that 'pigs, cows and goats were no longer to be kept in dwelling rooms'.

Kennedy had been complacent. He reported Price's remarks about the faulty drainage and placed $5,000 in the estimates for 1875 for repairs, which, as Price said, would go 'a very little way'. Lord Carnarvon's reply was that a complete drainage scheme should be submitted, but that Kennedy should not hold up any work at the risk of serious illness.

Hennessy at first also did nothing, but for very different reasons. He brought a much more sympathetic attitude towards the Chinese, wished to elevate their status in the mixed Hong Kong society, and consulted their leaders on all important issues which affected them. This respect for Chinese customs and interests blinded him to the danger of the sanitary conditions that had so often been revealed. 'The Chinese inhabitants maintain that the attempts now and then made by successive Surveyor-Generals and Colonial Surgeons to force what is called "western sanitary science" upon them, are not based on sound principles,' he wrote in 1877. The Chinese, he thought, had a long civilization and knew what conditions suited them; if they were allowed to build houses in Hong Kong like those in Canton, with the dry earth system of sanitation, the sanitary danger would be minimized. He supported the Chinese therefore in opposing flushing systems and water drainage. He thought that left to themselves, they were naturally clean; but he overlooked the gross overcrowding that made normal habits almost impossible.

The situation might have gone on unchecked but for the fortunate accident of a series of quarrels with General Donovan. Hennessy's temperament was such that no one could work with him and the relations betwen the Governor and General degenerated to the level of personal animosity. An ordinance to extend the area in which Chinese houses could be built was resented by Donovan, and in a 'series of complaints' he made the most outspoken and scathing attack on the filthy and insanitary condition of Chinese houses in the colony. He complained that the Chinese were already crowded near the barracks, 'giving ocular, auricular and nasal demonstration how unfitted they are for the neighbourhood of Europeans', and he called for measures to protect the health of the troops. In these letters he referred to the special reports of the Surveyor-General and Colonial Surgeon of 1874 which had not been sent home and to the Colonial Surgeon's annual report for that same year from which excisions had been made. The Surgeon-General of the army medical department was sent to Hong Kong and his report dated 1 September 1880 condemned not only sanitary conditions, but also the policy of the Governor, accusing him of a complete reversal of the wise policy of his predecessors in sanitary matters '. . . and what is equally to be regretted, he has paralysed the hand of the English functionaries of the government sanitary staff.' Lord Kimberley called for the 1874 sanitary reports, and in 1881 it was decided to make a full-scale enquiry into the sanitary condition of Hong Kong; an engineer, Osbert Chadwick, a former Royal Engineers officer, was chosen to carry out this task.

Meanwhile, Ayres had continued his work under discouraging conditions. The hospital occupied scattered makeshift accommodation. Hennessy strongly criticized him for not doing any vaccinations and praised the Tung Wah, which did nearly 2,000 a year, though to treat the general public had never been part of the Colonial Surgeon's duty. The Tung Wah continued to do good work; in one year, 1879, for example, it admitted 1,614 poor Chinese, treated 82,648, provided 221 burials, and sent 123 destitutes back to China; but Ayres was critical of its low standards and of Chinese medicine. In the government civil hospital, he found a staff of one when he arrived in 1873, and he gradually built up an administrative and nursing staff.

He continued to be critical about sanitation, and called a disastrous fire of 1878 'a sanitary dispensation of Providence'. In his 1880 report he said sanitary conditions were worsening because houses of three and four stories were replacing those of one and two, resulting in more serious overcrowding. Next year he referred to the difficulty created for the inspectors of nuisances by Hennessy's ruling that offences under their cognizance were to be proved in the Magistrate's Court before fines were inflicted. It was inevitable that Ayres could not agree with Hennessy's support of Chinese views on sanitation. Ayres' reports suffered because he had a theory that opium smoking did no harm, and he devoted unnecessary labour each year to attempting to demonstrate this.

Chadwick's report of 1882 marked a turning point in the

history of the colony's health service, and out of it arose the
Sanitary Board, from which has sprung the modern department
of Urban Services with some form of municipal control on an
elective basis. Chadwick gave a comprehensive review of the
whole social problem. He was at particular pains to elicit the
views of the Chinese, and was surprised how well they received
him, and what little obstruction was shown. The main points
made in the report may be briefly summarized. 'The sanitary
condition of Hong Kong is defective, and calls for energetic
remedial measures'; even under Chinese systems, proper drainage was still necessary. Water supply was inadequate, and
neither 'the proposed works, nor works many times larger,
would satisfy the wants of the city', while the water-rate was
unequal and unjust in its incidence. Houses were defective, and
a new building ordinance was necessary. House drainage was
'radically bad', the whole town required re-draining. Scavenging must be more thorough, and separated from night-soil
collection. An organized sanitary staff under a special officer
was necessary. To secure the co-operation of the Chinese, the
duty of enforcing cleanliness should be placed on the district
watchmen, who should be given extra pay; the sanitary officials
should have very close relations with the Registrar-General's
department. He recommended more public conveniences, baths,
new markets, and a proper water-supply for Kowloon. The
voluminous report gave a fairly complete picture of the city
and of its inhabitants, and is clearly the work of an acute and
humane observer; his attention was often called by the Chinese
themselves to various abuses, and he was most anxious, in
his report, to suggest the means by which the necessary reforms
could be made acceptable to them. His answer to Hennessy
was that the houses of Hong Kong were not similar to those he
found in China, and that Chinese ideas on sanitation were not
applicable to Hong Kong. By the time the report was published,
Hennessy had left. He had suggested the creation of a new
sanitary department from which Dr. Ayres and J. M. Price
were to be excluded as incompetent in sanitary matters, but
Lord Kimberley refused to entertain any proposal until Chadwick had reported. The account of the implementation of the
Chadwick report must be left to a later chapter.

An important issue raised during these years was the so-called

Chinese customs 'blockade' of Hong Kong to which Macdonnell with characteristic energy and bluntness, offered intense opposition, making himself the mouthpiece of outraged public opinion. The 'blockade' began in November 1867, when Macdonnell reported the seizure of an opium-carrying junk by Chinese customs revenue cruisers operating off the entrances to the Hong Kong harbour; writing in the strongest terms to Robertson, the Consul at Canton, he demanded and eventually received the junk and the value of its cargo. The Duke of Buckingham passed the dispatch to the Foreign Office, but expressed his 'entire disapproval of the language used' in which the Governor had seemed to question the right of the Chinese government 'to exercise its own jurisdiction over its own subjects in its own waters in a manner which it considers conducive to its own interests.'

Next year the Governor reported that nine marine and land customs stations had been set up around the colony, and that all native vessels were being stopped and searched. The Chinese maintained that they were losing revenue as a result of smuggling from Hong Kong; Alcock, the British Minister to Peking since 1865, supported this contention in a letter to the Foreign Office in May 1868, in which he referred to Hong Kong as 'being little more than an immense smuggling depot'. Opium had been legalized by the Treaty of Tientsin in 1858, but until 1868 it could be carried only in foreign vessels which were confined to treaty ports where opium import duty and likin transit tax were paid, but this prohibition had been disregarded by the Chinese in Hong Kong, whose junks were under no such limitation. The Chinese government therefore lost revenue on junk-carried opium. The Chinese had other grievances against Hong Kong. It gave the protection of the British flag to vessels owned by Chinese Crown lessees of land in the colony, though these were comparatively few in number. There was the whole question of Hong Kong's expanding local coastal trade which was largely in the hands of Chinese merchants in Hong Kong, who acted as local distributors of foreign goods purchased from the European importers and agency houses. Thus the obligation to confine foreign trade to the treaty ports was circumvented. The defence was that Hong Kong was a free port and it was a matter for the Chinese to suppress illicit trade. There was also the claim of the colony to the privilege of Treaty-Port status in respect of the right of transhipment of goods to and from other treaty ports without additional customs duty. The struggle was between Canton and Hong Kong for control of the local distributing trade. The Viceroy was concerned over the loss of opium revenue at Canton, collected by the Imperial Maritime Customs, and particularly over the likin tax of $16 a chest on opium sent inland from a treaty port. The opium import duty of $30 a chest levied outside the treaty ports was a matter for the Hoppo, who controlled the collection of Chinese native customs. These two collecting agencies, operating side by side in the check on all native craft using Hong Kong, constituted the customs 'blockade'. The Chinese had the support of Alcock and Robertson in the purchase of the gunboats used.

Macdonnell took up the Chinese challenge and forcibly argued that the right of searching native vessels would lead to 'endless dissension and bad feeling'; that the Treaty of Tientsin had fixed the import duty on opium at $30 per chest, but made no mention of the likin tax, which was therefore illegal; that the wording of the proclamation instituting the 'blockade' made no distinction between Chinese and foreign vessels, though in practice only Chinese vessels were affected; and that vessels bound for ports outside China were equally affected with those bound for the mainland. Robertson had defended the Chinese action on the ground that it applied only to opium, but Macdonnell replied that there was no guarantee that it would always be so confined. He denied that there was much opium smuggling; he estimated that the total yearly import of opium into Hong Kong averaged 80,000 chests, of which 63,000 went to northern ports and 3,000 to California; he put smuggling at 1,500 chests from Hong Kong and about 4,500 from Macao. The Chinese put smuggling at 30,000 to 40,000 chests annually and asked to be allowed to set up customs stations in the colony. Alcock proposed a Chinese consul for Hong Kong, but Macdonnell, with the support of the Legislative Council, said there was already much improper pressure on local wealthy Chinese, and this would be worse if a Chinese consul were placed in the colony in 'the special and exceptional circumstances of this very peculiar place, its very peculiar inhabitants and most peculiar geographical position'. Finally, the Governor strongly complained of the secrecy with which the Chinese plans were prepared. Robertson and Alcock knew and approved of the 'blockade' measures and yet the Governor was not even consulted on a matter vitally affecting the interests of the colony. The home government objected to Macdonnell's unrestrained language, in which he described the customs cruisers as 'a new species of corsairs', and supported the Chinese government. 'More than one of the claims advanced by you have been exaggerated and untenable . . . the interests of H.M. Service are injured by the tone in which they are advanced. . . . I hold you in no slight degree responsible for the want of co-operation which at present exists,' Lord Granville told him, and the 'blockade' continued. Macdonnell's intemperate opposition had added to the difficulties and delayed a solution.

Kennedy maintained opposition to the 'blockade', but was ready to make concessions. He set up a commission of enquiry in 1874 which reported that the Chinese should be asked to remove the customs stations and revenue cruisers from the vicinity and collect all dues at the Chinese port of entry; failing this, protection of trade should be asked for. Kennedy commented that undoubtedly the colony's trade had been seriously interfered with, and that there was probably much 'squeeze'. Robertson had urged a Chinese customs station in Hong Kong and Kennedy thought this the best solution, though he realized it would be unpopular. Wade, who succeeded Alcock as Minister in Peking in 1871 had even suggested that Hong Kong might be considered a Treaty Port and placed completely under Chinese customs surveillance, even if this involved handing back to China the sovereignty of the island. The Board of Trade at home, to whom the dispute had been referred, asked if the trade between the United Kingdom and non-treaty ports was large. Kennedy believed it was, though there was no accurate information, and often junk-masters themselves did not know whether the goods they carried were British or not.

Complaints against the 'blockade' in the colony continued, and in 1875 Chinese merchants sent a memorial to the Secretary of State condemning it. Cases of seizure and collection of money occurred that were never reported to Canton and were presumed to be irregular. It was impossible to obtain a precise statement of the rules under which the Hoppo's men worked.

There was no complaint against steam revenue cruisers commanded by Europeans acting under the control of the Imperial Maritime Customs foreign staff, and Kennedy's remedy was to place these in sole control to the exclusion of the Hoppo's men, but Lord Carnarvon thought this would involve too much delay, and he invited further proposals for settling the issue. The suggestion to appoint a Chinese consul in Hong Kong, Kennedy said, would be opposed by everyone. By the Chefoo Convention of 1876, a joint Anglo-Chinese Commission was to be established to find some way by which the Chinese could protect their legitimate revenue without detriment to the colony.

Kennedy now suggested, as a basis of settlement, that the Chinese should be allowed to place customs stations and revenue cruisers in the proximity of the colony, and in return, the tariff of duties should be fixed by agreement, and any seizures of junks from the colony should be reported and enquired into jointly, and referred to the Supreme Court of Hong Kong in case of failure to agree. Unfortunately Robertson fell ill, the commission was delayed and the 'blockade' continued.

Hennessy angered the British community by departing further than Kennedy had done from Macdonnell's policy of rigid opposition to the 'blockade'. Just before his arrival, the Chinese customs cruisers had seized an opium junk in colonial waters, and a great outcry followed. Hennessy demanded the return of the full value of the junk and the opium seized, but refused to return his property to the junk owner as he had illegally left port at night without a clearance, and was an obvious smuggler. Colonial opinion viewed this treatment of the junk owner as a clear invitation to the Chinese government to continue the 'blockade'. Hennessy found that specially equipped well-armed vessels were engaged in salt and opium running from the colony to the mainland, and that there was complete defiance of the Harbour Ordinance of 1866. He proposed an ordinance to prohibit opium smuggling from Hong Kong, but Carnarvon thought the law regarding the clearance of junks should first be applied more strictly. In August 1877 Hennessy reported that there was much less complaint against the 'blockade', since strong action against the smugglers was being taken, and submitted what he called simpler and better proposals for settling the 'blockade' question, which Carnarvon acidly rejected, saying they were simpler and better for the Chinese government since they meant that no junk could have used the harbour without Chinese goverment permission.

The Hong Kong officials showed marked reluctance to take any action against smugglers, and Hennessy complained to Carnarvon of 'the official countenance given to smuggling', but the Colonial Secretary retorted that Hong Kong officials had proved worthy of the trust which had been placed in them. In March 1878, Hennessy reported that the junk trade for 1877 had shown an increase of 1,186 vessels of 71,332 tons over that for 1876, and that complaints regarding the 'blockade' 'have mostly ceased', and paid tribute to the good offices of Robertson in Canton. In fact, complaints continued from foreign and Chinese merchants alike. The Attorney-General and the Executive Council were against the use of the Harbour Ordinance to stop smuggling, and the Chamber of Commerce and foreign community generally were against any interference with the freedom of the port. The Chinese merchants who were regularly consulted by Hennessy, complained that their junks had to pay harbour dues and Chinese customs duties, though foreign shipping avoided both; they did not complain of the Chinese government's attempt to check smuggling, but of its interference with cotton piece-goods, and other legitimate trade. Hennessy's solution was to meet the Chinese government in the matter of opium by collecting all opium dues in Hong Kong and giving a clearance; regarding the contraband trade in salt, he suggested licensing the trade to the Chinese government agents, as was done in the case of the munitions trade. In return the Chinese were to give up the customs 'blockade' and collect any dues on goods other than opium at the port of entry. His chief anxiety was for the Chinese merchants in Hong Kong on whom he thought the prosperity of the port largely depended. Strenuous opposition to having any collecting agency in a free port caused the Governor's plan to be rejected and the final solution was delayed some years more.

The customs 'blockade' showed the opium trade to be still important; in 1868, Macdonnell estimated the annual import to be about 80,000 chests; in 1870 it was 83,000 chests, worth $48,742,238. Most was exported to the Treaty Ports and to Chinese abroad, but there was much smuggling which Hennessy found impossible to suppress, because heavy dues made smuggling profitable. Hennessy, as part of the attempted 'blockade' settlement, tried to stop the illicit salt trade, and in 1879 induced the Executive Council to prohibit the export of salt except to the Chinese government. It is not possible to give actual figures for this contraband trade, but Wade clearly thought it important in amount.

The Treaty of Tientsin of 1858 and the Convention of Peking of 1860 opened a new era in China's relations with the West. The newly won right to travel in China for business and other purposes and the opening of additional Treaty Ports gave a great impetus to trade, the effects of which came to be more visible in this period. Hong Kong's trade, which began to grow in the 1850's, now showed greater expansion. Up to 1883 imports to Great Britain from China exceeded British exports to China, and since they consisted largely of tea and silk, could readily be shipped direct from the Treaty Ports. Hong Kong did not serve as a collecting centre for the shipment of Chinese goods to Britain. On the other hand, during this period almost half the British exports to China passed through the colony. According to the Imperial Maritime Customs returns, Hong Kong in 1880 handled twenty-one per cent in value of China's total export trade and thirty-seven per cent of the import trade, and its development as an entrepôt centre proceeded therefore unevenly. Its great economic assets were its security under the British flag, which made it a convenient headquarters for the largest firms by which much of the China trade was managed. The colony's prosperity was largely a product of these managerial services, and of accounting, banking, insurance, and various agency services, together with shipping. The opium trade, of which the colony was the administrative centre, amounted in some years to as much as forty-five per cent of the total value of China's import trade. Hong Kong was also the centre of the China coasting trade; the China Navigation Company was established by Butterfield and Swire in 1872, the Indo-China Steam Navigation Co. by Jardine, Matheson & Co. in 1881, the Douglas Steamship Co. in 1883 and the Canton & Macao Steamship Co. was formed in 1865.

In the absence of figures for imports and exports, those for shipping must suffice to give a picture of economic development.

In 1866, 1,896 ships of 949,856 tons entered, and a total of 3,783 ships of 1,891,281 tons entered and cleared. As a result of Macdonnell's legislation controlling junks, figures for the junk trade became available in 1867, in which year 20,787 junks of 1,353,700 tons entered, all engaged in foreign trade. They carried firewood, cattle, fruit and vegetables and took opium, rice, cotton, lime, granite and salt fish. A total of 67,715 ships of 5,738,793 tons came and went in that year, of which 4,879 of 2,376,320 tons were foreign-going. In 1874, the Harbour-master reported that the junk trade had increased each year from 1867 until May 1872, when a steady decline had set in, from which it must be concluded that the 'blockade' did not at first have the serious adverse effect which had been claimed. In 1879 it was reported that the junk trade had still not recovered, but that more foreign-built ships were now under the Chinese flag. These could go to any port, and Chinese ships of all kinds now carried 42·36 per cent of the whole of the colony's inward trade.

In 1881 foreign-going ships, excluding junks, entering the port numbered 3,214 of 2,853,279 tons, and of these 2,750 of 2,599,461 tons were steamers. Junk arrivals numbered 24,339 of 1,620,025 tons.

The conclusion that the Chinese were enjoying more of the trade of Hong Kong is borne out by evidence of increasing wealth of the Chinese in the colony. Their buying up of European property has already been referred to. One result of the 'blockade' was their increasing use of steamships to avoid the Hoppo's attentions. They began to operate steamers on their own account, for example, Kwok A Cheung had thirteen steamships in 1877. In 1874 the China Merchants Steam Navigation Company was formed and was strongly supported by the Chinese government in the hope that Chinese would capture the coastal trade.

Chinese became the biggest ratepayers in the colony, a tribute to the liberal regime of the colony. Hennessy reported in 1881 that there were eighteen ratepayers having property rated at or over $1,000 per quarter, seventeen were Chinese and the remaining one was the largest British merchant house, Jardine, Matheson. The Chinese opened up new areas and they were able to market British and European produce and buy Chinese

o

goods for the West, more cheaply than the foreign firms in the colony. Great changes were taking place that favoured the rise of small firms. The Suez Canal, opened in 1869, speeded up transport, encouraged steamships which could maintain regular schedules, and eased commercial risks, particularly after the Parsons turbine improved the marine engine. The telegraph was even more important. Manufacturers were less dependent on the judgement of agency houses in the colony; market reports were available at once. The colony merchants continued to act as agency houses, but there was less opportunity of making a vast profit purely because they were on the spot. The old agency houses had gained by handling bullion on a commission basis; bullion was still handled in large amounts, but the rise of banking made this a less essential feature. There was less need of godowns because of less storing of goods to catch the market. Small import and export firms came into existence as enterprising Englishmen attempted to enter the China market, and the old Canton firms lost their privileged position. They still were shippers, distributors on a large scale and agency houses; the new firms dealt in the humble everyday articles of trade, acting as agents for manufacturers in England.

Hong Kong remained the centre of the great Chinese emigration overseas. This flourished, particularly to and from the Straits. Passenger traffic brought trade, and returning immigrants often brought bullion. In 1866, 5,116 left and 9,253 returned. In 1872, 27,721 left and 23,773 returned, in 1881, 70,625 left and 52,983 returned. This was free emigration, for the abuses of coolie emigration under contract had led to its prohibition from Hong Kong in 1869, except to British colonies, where strict control could be exercised. The abuses of the coolie traffic at Macao led to difficulties in Hong Kong. Soon after Kennedy's arrival in 1872 a Chinese deputation made a strong complaint about the treatment of emigrant coolies in Macao, where some eight hundred coolie brokers were alleged to function.

Lord Kimberley replied by asking what truth there was in the allegation that Hong Kong was implicated in these abuses and made large profits by supplying these Macao coolie ships. In reply, Kennedy admitted that the allegation was true; almost all the coolie emigrant ships using Macao were fitted out in Hong Kong, and supplied from the colony. There was nothing in the law to prohibit supplying provisions; the law demanded each passenger ship should be reported and inspected to see that objectionable fittings were not installed, but he admitted that such fittings were made in Hong Kong and carried to sea for installation. From January to September 1872, fifteen Peruvian, ten French, nine Spanish, three Dutch and one Austrian ships had left Hong Kong for Macao for the coolie trade. Kimberley remarked, 'the state of things is most unsatisfactory', and called for fresh legislation and more thorough search of all passenger ships. Since 1860 emigration from China had been permitted, and was further regulated by a Convention between China, France and Britain in 1866. But in 1869, Lord Granville, in order to remove any suspicion of linking Hong Kong with the abuses of the traffic, prohibited the emigration of Chinese from Hong Kong to any place outside the British colonies. This had been interpreted to mean contract coolie emigration, and Chinese free emigration had not been affected.

The outcome was the passing of a stringent ordinance in 1873 imposing severe penalties on restraining women and children with the object of shipping them abroad, and on the fitting and storing of emigrant ships without a licence, and the seven emigrant ships which were fitting out in the harbour when the ordinance was passed, all left. Free emigration increased. Kennedy reported that from 9 January to 10 May 1874, 7,591 coolies had been shipped to San Francisco, and 1,211 were waiting, and he suspected that some of them might be sent on to Peru or Cuba, the places with the worst reputation, and as a precaution all Peruvian and Spanish emigrant ships were forbidden to use the port. On the cognate matter of serious overcrowding on the river steamers to Macao and Canton, Kennedy passed an ordinance restricting the number of passengers to two for each three tons of net registered tonnage.

CHAPTER XVIII

SIR GEORGE BOWEN AND
SIR WILLIAM DES VOEUX, 1883–91

*'The ordinary work of a civil governor at Hong Kong . . .
is not materially different from the ordinary work of the Mayor
of Portsmouth.'*

Bowen to Lord Derby, 23 May 1883.

THE period following the departure of Sir John Pope Hennessy
was marked by two comparatively short governorships, those
of Sir George Bowen, March 1883 to December 1885, and
Sir William Des Voeux, October 1887 to May 1891. For considerable intervals an acting Governor administered the
government; Marsh assumed the administration from April
1882 to March 1883 and again from December 1885 to April
1887, when he retired with a knighthood. He was followed by
Major-General Cameron until Des Voeux arrived in October
1887. During most of the year 1890, Fleming, the Colonial
Secretary, deputized for Des Voeux, who was on leave, and in
the interval between the departure of Des Voeux and the
arrival of his successor, Sir William Robinson, May to December 1891, Major-General Digby Barker deputized. This continual change was unfortunate, because the Chadwick report
had shown the need for a thorough-going scheme of sanitary
reform, and the colony was faced with a large programme of
public works, the neglect of which had been made more glaring
by the findings of Chadwick. Continuity of policy depended
on the Colonial Office in England. There were other factors
which made for strengthening of Colonial Office control. The
telegraph made it easy to refer questions of policy home, and
colonial Governors were no longer thrown on their own resources. In addition, the colonial service, now recruited by
examination, became more professionalized, more dependent
on the service for promotion, and less inclined to take an
independent line. Bowen was perhaps the last of the old type
of Governor. He had had a good Oxford career, and left a
Fellowship at Brasenose to become President of the University

of Corfu in the Ionian Islands, and he became Chief Secretary there in 1854. He then held governorships in Australia, New Zealand and Mauritius. He adopted in Hong Kong the attitude of an elder statesman and resented the guidance of the Colonial Office partly because two senior officials there had served under him in Queensland. Bowen once strongly criticized 'some permanent gentlemen of the Colonial Department' and was reprimanded and told that the Secretary of State was responsible for what was written to him.

Des Voeux, like Bowen, came to Hong Kong as the climax of his colonial career, which began in British Guiana as stipendiary magistrate, following his qualifying for the Bar in Canada; he served fifteen years in the West Indies, became acting Governor, then Governor of Fiji, and then of Newfoundland. Des Voeux was unwell most of the time; his applications for leave were frequent, and shooting on the Yangtze was his favourite recreation. He spent most of the year 1890 away from the colony on home leave, and while at home an accident delayed his recovery, and though he returned in 1890, it hastened his retirement. Yet he lived another eighteen years.

There was much to be done; the Chadwick report pointed the way to social reform and to a vast programme of public works. A great influx of Chinese during Hennessy's term of office, and the new policy of integrating the Chinese into the community called for vigorous informed leadership. The customs 'blockade' was still unresolved, and fear of French and Russian ambitions in the Far East created a new problem of defence.

Marsh's immediate task was to bring order out of the administrative chaos left by Hennessy. The new hospital, Central School, and junk refuge at Causeway Bay were put in hand. The Registrar-General's office was restored to its former importance and placed under Russell, a cadet, though Ng Choy opposed this on the ground that it was race discrimination to force Chinese and Europeans to deal with the government through different departments. The next urgent task was to implement the Chadwick Report. The home government insisted on the immediate appointment of a Sanitary Inspector, and H. Macallum, apothecary at the civil hospital, was appointed. Marsh set up a Sanitary Board of the three officials most concerned, Surveyor-General, Registrar-General and Colonial Surgeon, but left the details to Bowen. This Sanitary Board had a chequered career.

In May 1883 Bowen introduced a draft Order and Health Amendment Ordinance officially constituting the Board. The three officials were to be members *ex officio*, under the chairmanship of the Surveyor-General and there were to be not less than two other members nominated by the Governor. The wide powers proposed in the ordinance to deal with insanitary houses, inspection of premises, compulsory disinfection and removal of persons who were sources of disease, met with the most determined opposition and the ordinance had to be withdrawn. The Board remained in being, with the Sanitary Inspector and Captain Superintendent of Police as the two additional members. So when Bowen left in 1885, practically nothing had been done.

In 1886, Marsh made the Board stronger by adding four unofficial members as representative ratepayers, and Dr. Patrick Manson, Dr. Ho Kai, A. P. MacEwen and N. T. Ede were accordingly added. The disputed sanitary proposals were referred to the strengthened Board, which in December 1886 brought forward a draft ordinance giving far-reaching powers to be exercised by a partly elected municipal Board of Health. Great opposition came from the property owners, who feared losses on their insanitary property if decent standards of space, drainage, ventilation and light were to be enforced. They demanded compensation, which neither the local government nor the Sanitary Board opposed in principle, but this was refused by the British government. The Chinese in addition, and particularly Dr. Ho Kai their representative on the Legislative Council, strongly opposed the ordinance. He thought it made the 'mistake of treating Chinese as if they were Europeans', and argued that improved standards would cut down the available building space, and so drive up rents. The acting Governor, Major-General Cameron, decided to leave all the contentious clauses affecting property, for example, the demand for a minimum of 300 cubic feet of air space, compulsory backyard space and ventilation, to a future ordinance. Thus in September 1887, five years after Chadwick had condemned the sanitary condition of Hong Kong, an emasculated ordinance was passed. Cameron justifiably questioned whether the 'rights of property . . . should very heavily handicap every effort of government at sanitation.'

The modest proposal of a municipal Board of Health was not accepted, and the 1887 Public Health Ordinance established the constitution of the Sanitary Board, to consist of four officials, the Surveyor-General, Registrar-General, Captain-Superintendent of Police and Colonial Surgeon, and not more than six additional members, four of whom (two being Chinese) were to be appointed by the Governor, and two elected by such ratepayers whose names appeared on the jury lists. The franchise was limited, but even so, this newly constituted Sanitary Board was important, since it was a first step towards local government institutions for municipal affairs and it was the first introduction in the history of the colony of popular elections not confined to British nationals.

Though the 1887 ordinance was weakened by the removal of most of its vital clauses, when the new Governor, Des Voeux, arrived in October 1887, he was faced with a petition signed by 47,000 Chinese against it. The Chinese argued there had been no plague and no epidemics and they did not want any change; they feared increased rents and objected to the inspection of houses; nevertheless the Secretary of State accepted the Public Health Ordinance. Houses were being rushed up to escape the restrictions of the projected legislation regarding buildings left over from 1887, yet it was not until May 1889 that Des Voeux passed the Buildings Ordinance, and even then, the more vital and therefore the more contentious clauses, dealing with ventilation and space for backyards were omitted and left to be dealt with in yet another ordinance. These clauses were put into a Crown Lands Resumption Ordinance of July 1889, as Des Voeux thought the best way to avoid dissension was to use the power of resumption to effect sanitary improvement, compensation being settled by a board of arbitrators. It had taken five years of bitter opposition, but in the end the property owners had got what they wanted. The intention was to resume and rebuild the Chinese area over twenty years. The Secretary of State agreed, only stipulating that leases should in future be so worded as to give rise to no further claims to compensation. The Sanitary Board came in for criticism, partly because it met and deliberated in private, but it is clear that the blame for the failure to deal with the problems of overcrowding, insanitary dwellings, lack of air and light, and the evils of cubicles and basements must rest with the failure of Des Voeux to carry out the Sanitary Board's policy against the combined opposition of Chinese prejudice and the property owners' interest.

Conditions were notoriously unsatisfactory and the Sanitary Board appointed a committee of enquiry into overcrowding. The committee, consisting of Mitchell Innes and N. J. Ede, conducted a detailed enquiry over two years, and their report, issued in October 1890, showed serious overcrowding. They found rooms divided by partitions to form four, six and even eight small rooms, so that the partitions, with furniture, were estimated to take up twenty-nine per cent of the air space. Many blocks of buildings were found to have 1,500 people to the acre, and one even 3,235, and 745 houses were reported to have serious overcrowding. Des Voeux agreed to the recommendation to apply the clauses of the Public Health Ordinance regarding overcrowding, and an amending act was passed to deal with tenants of overcrowded houses. In fact nothing very effective was done to improve sanitary conditions until the plague of 1894 exposed the utter inadequacy of the sanitary arrangements.

In contrast to this policy of vacillation, other parts of the Chadwick Report dealing with drainage, water-supply and similar large public works were carried out boldly and at great cost. Chadwick had strongly recommended the Tai Tam Water scheme as essential to the health of the colony, and this was now put in hand at an estimated cost of $600,000, destined to be largely exceeded. Other public works recommended by Chadwick that were commenced included a new central market to improve the handling of food, new main drains and sewers, dust bins, the reorganization of scavenging, and the reclamation of pestilent swamps at Causeway Bay and Yaumati. The scheme to link up the east and west prayas by a road on the seaward side of the admiralty and military lands was revived. Among other sanitary measures adopted were the employment of more inspectors of nuisances, and the appointment of a veterinary surgeon to superintend the pig and sheep depôt. A new central reclamation scheme, suggested by Sir Paul Chater, also arose out of the desire to relieve overcrowding by providing additional building ground.

Bowen was very soon faced with a demand for constitutional reform, there were various reasons for this. There was great interest in Britain in colonial questions as a result of the Imperial Federation Movement; Hennessy had appointed a Chinese to the Legislative Council; the successful Shanghai Municipal Council was contrasted with the lack of municipal government in Hong Kong, yet the numbers of Chinese and foreigners respectively in each city were approximately the same; and the Sanitary Board had demanded a municipal council.

Ng Choy had been involved in the speculation mania of 1881 and in April 1883 resigned from the Legislative Council. Lord Derby wanted the Chinese community to be represented, and Bowen agreed, but thought the difficulty was that the Chinese who combined 'the proper social position, independent means and education' were not generally British subjects. Within a few weeks, Bowen put forward a scheme of constitutional reform.

He did not favour a municipal council for Hong Kong because it would be difficult to prevent the Chinese from outvoting the Europeans, and the Legislative Council performed all the usual municipal functions. He criticized the Legislative Council because the General was not a member, and because official members filled two of the four places allotted to unofficials, to the annoyance of the community.

Bowen wanted to increase the Legislative Council by three official members, namely, the General Officer commanding the troops, the Registrar-General and Surveyor-General, and two additional unofficial members, making eight official and six unofficial members in all. Of the latter he proposed the Chamber of Commerce should nominate two, and the Magistrates one, leaving three to be nominated by the Governor, one of whom should be Chinese, following a principle adopted in India, New Zealand, Ceylon and the Straits Settlements. He thought two Chinese might be nominated, since the 'Governor as representative of the Queen, is bound to protect impartially the interests of all H.M.'s subjects of every race.' He proposed that members should hold office for six years and not for life, and that the Legislative Council should have a fixed annual session so that a legislative programme could be outlined and submitted for public debate. Bowen also proposed that the Executive Council should be increased by the addition of the Treasurer and Registrar-General, since officials were often absent on leave, and it was difficult to form a quorum. He argued that the chief departmental heads should be on the Executive Council since they had to support government policy in the Legislative Council, and he organized weekly meetings.

Lord Derby accepted these constitutional reforms, with minor changes. The Surveyor-General and Registrar-General were made official members of the Legislative Council, who were now six in number. Unofficial members were increased to five; the Chamber of Commerce and Bench of Magistrates were to nominate one each, and the Governor was to nominate three, one of whom was to be Chinese. Derby thought it undesirable for the Chief Justice to be a member of the legislature, also the General, since he could not be called upon to support the government by his vote, and his opposition might create an awkward problem.

Bowen wanted the General to be Governor, as at Gibraltar and Bermuda; 'Hong Kong is the Gibraltar of the East,' he repeatedly asserted. In any case the General should assume the government when the Governor was away. But Derby would not agree, since the Colonial Secretary should be given the chance to show his ability and readiness for promotion.

The Chamber of Commerce nominated Thomas Jackson, Chief Manager of The Hongkong and Shanghai Bank. That chamber consisted of 34 members, comprised of 20 English, 1 American, 6 of European nationalities, 2 Chinese, 3 Jews, 1 Parsee and 1 Armenian, and Bowen claimed that their nominee represented all races and creeds. The Bench of Justices of the Peace, of whom 62 were English, 7 Chinese, 7 Parsee and 3 Armenian, totalling 79, were all British subjects, yet could be regarded as fairly representative. Nineteen official justices did not vote; the remaining unofficial justices felt that the English element in the Legislative Council was sufficient and they nominated Frederick Sassoon, of an Indian Jewish family, educated in England.

Bowen nominated Wong Shing as the Chinese representative. He had been educated at the Morrison Society School, and in

America, and had served with Li Hung-chang in China and in the Chinese Legation in Washington, and was 'fully qualified to look at Chinese affairs with English eyes and at English affairs with Chinese eyes', and he became naturalized in December 1883. There was some doubt whether the Governor could, without awaiting instructions, immediately appoint a fifth unofficial member, though the home law officers did not uphold this interpretation, and to avoid any humiliation to the Chinese, Jackson stood down to allow Wong Shing to occupy the seat. The newly constituted Legislative Council met for the first time on 28 February 1884. The Governor made his opening speech, and the Council's reply gave 'a constitutional opportunity of expressing their opinion of the conduct and proposals of the Government'. But the request of the Chamber of Commerce at the time of their nomination that the Legislative Council should have the same powers as the Shanghai Municipal Council, was not agreed to by Lord Derby. Bowen set up committees of the Legislative Council for Law and Public Works.

The demand for a municipal council continued, particularly when the rates were increased by one per cent in 1885, but the proposal was resisted by Bowen on the ground that as there were only eighty-three English ratepayers, against 647 Chinese and ninety-eight other nationalities, chiefly Portuguese, it was difficult to imagine that any English would be elected; and since Chinese views on 'water supply, sanitation, police, harbour regulations . . . differed widely from those in Europe', it was impossible to place a large garrison town, with great trading activity, under the Chinese. Bowen thought the Legislative Council was largely a municipal council, and did now represent the community. He made two further reforms. Municipal rating was now placed before the Legislative Council, up to then it had been decided in the Executive Council. Bowen also urged that it should be generally accepted as a constitutional principle that the official majority 'should not be used to control an absolutely united unofficial minority, especially on financial questions'. His contribution to constitutional advance in Hong Kong was therefore considerable.

Bowen's second big problem was that of defence. Russian designs in the Far East and the war between China and France,

1884–85, created tension. The 1878 war scare over the Balkans, in which Indian troops were brought to Malta, revealed the weakness of the arrangements for Imperial defence, and a Colonial Defence Committee was set up in London, assisted by a defence committee in each colony, to co-ordinate the Empire's defence effort and use colonial resources more extensively than hitherto.

It was a leisurely process and led to years of discussion. The colony normally paid a military contribution, the cost of fortifications and defence works, and provided the land necessary. More land was now to be reserved for future military contingency, building being allowed on condition that it could be taken over or torn down in an emergency without compensation. In Hong Kong this was serious because its finances depended largely on revenue from land, which was severely limited in extent. Plans were made to increase the strength of the garrison and erect fortifications with heavy guns at the eastern and western ends of the island, and the whole of the northern part of Kowloon was to be reserved for military defence. The western entrance to the harbour was to be protected by piles on Kellett Bank between Green Island and Stonecutters Island. Linked with these defence proposals was the scheme to move the naval and military areas out of the centre of the city, and to extend the praya along the whole front to Wanchai.

In fact, very little was done, and when the hostilities between France and China came in 1884, Bowen complained that the colony was defenceless. Heavy defence works were begun at Lyemun and High West, but there was no agreed over-all scheme. The garrison was strengthened by the recruitment locally of the Hong Kong Regiment (not to be confused with the later Volunteers) chiefly from Indians with British and Indian officers. But Bowen complained shortly after his arrival in 1883 that the chief need was that the War Office should prepare a final scheme of defence, which the colony would then do its best to carry out, and his complaints continued for the rest of his period of office. In 1885 danger came not only from French operations against China, but also from Russian threats against Korea; this led in May 1885 to the two-year occupation of Port Hamilton in South Korea, which Bowen criticized. He asked for four additional torpedo boats to be sent out immediately. Lord Derby assured him that the Admiralty were 'thoroughly aware of what is necessary for the defence of the colony', but Bowen's complaints continued. The *Wyvern* and *Tweed* were recommissioned as floating batteries. After persistent effort he secured the appointment of an adjutant for the military training of the police. In January 1885, the colony voted £56,000 for defence works on the understanding that the latest weapons would be supplied. The military then proposed further works, and in March 1886 Marsh, following instructions from home, placed an additional vote of £60,375 for military works, which was passed only after much protest, and on the understanding that it was to be the final sum for defence. This total vote of more than £116,000 for colonial defence burdened the colony's finances, already strained by the extensive programme of public works, made a loan necessary, and a sum of £200,000 was raised in 1886. This was again the subject of dispute as the Secretary of State refused to agree to raising the loan locally.

Stonecutters Island became a military reserved area by an ordinance of 1890, although government buildings remained in use on the island for some years longer. The new defences needed an increased garrison, and this led to the demand in 1890 that the colony should pay double the annual military contribution, £40,000 instead of £20,000. This was voted by the Legislative Council, with certain accompanying resolutions: (1) the garrison should be 3,018, of whom 2,525 were to be Europeans, (2) no demand for payment should be made until the garrison had actually been increased, (3) the military already occupied 337 acres of land valued at three million dollars. This led to trouble; the increased military contribution was demanded before the troops arrived, and when the unofficial members all voted against the payment in 1891, Lord Knutsford explained that the additional payment was demanded not on the ground of the increased garrison, but because the colony could afford it, a fact which the unofficials contested. Unfortunately, the new troops, when they did arrive, turned out to be Madras Regiment instead of 'infantry of the line', as originally promised. This led to the demand that the Imperial Government 'should submit the necessary measures in a frank and open manner.'

The French war against China, besides bringing insecurity to the colony, brought difficulties to Bowen. The Imperial Government enjoined a policy of strict neutrality, though no war had been formally declared. Bowen entertained the French admiral and announced he was equally willing to entertain Chinese ministers or officials, while at the same time maintaining British rights. Chinese opinion in Canton and Hong Kong was inflamed against the French. Bowen was away in Japan when the hostilities came, and Marsh, to avoid disturbances in the colony, proceeded against the editors of four Chinese newspapers who had published the edicts of the Canton Viceroy urging all Cantonese to attack French ships and men; but the prosecutions failed and the charges were dropped. In September 1884, cargo boatmen refused to work on French ships, and French owners brought prosecutions against fourteen coolies, who were each fined five dollars. All cargo boatmen went on strike, the work of the harbour was brought to a standstill, and for some ten days in October the situation was tense; actual rioting and violence was directed mainly against Chinese workers, but some Europeans were man-handled. All police were called out, and troops marched the streets. Leading rioters were charged and sentenced to periods of six to twelve months' imprisonment, but this only increased resentment. The offer of the Tung Wah Committee to mediate and organize a return to work was rejected, and a Peace Preservation Ordinance was rushed through the Legislative Council at one sitting. This allowed the detention and banishment of persons, who, though not convicted, 'were dangerous to the peace and good order of the colony', forbade all notices and proclamations in Chinese without the prior consent of the Registrar-General, and forbade the carrying of arms or possession of arms by Chinese. Lord Derby reluctantly accepted the ordinance as a temporary measure, and it was retained on the statute book in an amended form with power to bring it into force in an emergency.

The cargo boatmen had been fined under an ordinance of 1858, which dealt with minimum charges, and the Secretary of State ordered these fines to be remitted on the ground that it was an abuse of the ordinance to apply it in those circumstances. By 14 October 1884, Marsh was able to report that all was normal; thirty-eight orders for banishment were made, but only seven men could be found, including Yau Poot In, a seventy-year-old agent who had been given three thousand dollars to stir up feeling against the French.

One result of the war scares was the placing of the Hong Kong Volunteers on a more satisfactory footing. The movement had been founded by Hennessy in 1878 during the Russian war scare of that year, but all arms supplied by the government had been withdrawn early in 1881, and the corps had languished. Hennessy had been asked to give more definite government assistance, but nothing had been done. When Hennessy left, Marsh was approached, and accepted the new commitments. The corps was disbanded in November 1882, and a new corps, the fourth, was immediately formed. The government undertook to provide winter and summer uniforms, and men were to be passed medically fit for service before being enrolled. It was to consist of two companies of artillery, the commandant being a regular artillery officer from the garrison with a small additonal salary from the government. The Colonial Office was not keen, but the expenditure was approved and Bowen arranged for full equipment, guns and rifles to be supplied. The volunteer movement, no longer left to its own unaided resources, now became part of colonial life. In 1885 Bowen organized the Hong Kong auxiliary flotilla, consisting of volunteers from the water police and yachtsmen, with the assistant Harbour-master as commandant. In 1889, on the initiative of Major-General Edwards, a machine-gun corps, partly mounted, armed with maxim guns presented by leading members of the community, was formed as an addition to the artillery companies.

This period was remarkable for the extended schemes of public works. Arrears caused by Hennessy's neglect had to be made up; there was a heavy programme of defence works, and in addition Chadwick had suggested a special programme of public works in relation to the insanitary condition of the island. At the same time a bold scheme of reclamation was undertaken.

The new Central School which had long been essential because of overcrowding and which had been held up by Hennessy's views on education, was commenced by Bowen in 1884; but the building was delayed for nine months because of a dispute between the headmaster and the Surveyor-General over the needs of the school, and it was not opened until 1889, when it assumed its new name, suggested by Bowen, Victoria College. The Causeway Bay junk refuge was completed, and the Civil Hospital conversions made, together with a lunatic asylum. The Observatory was not quite completed when Dr. Doberck, the government Observer, arrived in August 1883. One crying need, a new jail on modern lines, was delayed, much to the annoyance of the Colonial Office, and eventually a makeshift scheme of altering and enlarging the existing jail was accepted. Public works recommended by Chadwick have already been mentioned.

Reclamation was no new thing in Hong Kong; it had been suggested in the very early days of the colony, and piecemeal reclamations along Bonham Strand, in Bowrington, Kennedy Town, Kowloon, and in the central district had been made; but this central reclamation scheme was the boldest scheme undertaken up to that time. It was suggested in July 1887 by Paul Chater, a wealthy merchant born in Calcutta and member of the Legislative Council, with the object of relieving overcrowding and improving the sanitary condition of the foreshore. A strip 3,400 yards long and 250 feet wide, amounting to over fifty-seven acres was to be reclaimed by the marine lot-holders at their own expense, but under government control; the owners were to get the new land adjoining their existing allotments at $200 per quarter acre. Major-General Cameron, then administering the government, accepted these terms. The cost of the work was estimated at $2,146,228, and the profit at $5,746,593. Des Voeux felt this latter was excessive and that a premium ought to be charged to give the government more than the million dollars it expected as its share, but he pressed the matter halfheartedly. Chater argued his case at the Colonial Office in London and the result was that the original agreement was only slightly amended. A great opportunity was thus lost of reclaiming for the community as a whole. The old praya, now to be well inland, was renamed Des Voeux Road. Private claims were agreed to and the scheme embodied in a Praya Reclamation Ordinance; Sir John Goode, the consultant engineer, suggested an enlarged area of reclamation, but this was rejected by Des Voeux and by the interested lot-holders. The scheme was begun in 1890 and completed in 1904.

The other praya scheme by which the praya was to be extended eastwards on the harbour side of the naval and military areas which had been proposed in Kennedy's time, was now revived by Bowen. It had been strongly supported by Chadwick on sanitary grounds, since the shallow foreshore had become filthy. The original scheme costing £45,000, which was accepted by the Admiralty and War Office in 1875, had been dropped because they refused to pay any share of the cost, though they wanted to secure the additional valuable land which was to be reclaimed. Bowen took up the plan strongly to remove the 'dislocation' by which Queen's Road was the sole communication between eastern and western districts. The tramways now being proposed also needed a decision because of planning their routes.

Bowen suggested that the colony should pay two-thirds of the cost and deduct the remaining one-third from the military contribution over three years. This was refused, and the naval and military in the colony demanded additions to the plan for their own benefit, at an extra cost of £19,000.

The naval authorities were now planning to extend the naval base and claimed the artillery barracks, on the north side of Queen's Road, adjoining the cricket ground. The huge programme of public works put the praya extension scheme beyond the colony's unaided resources, but Bowen in November 1883 urged this scheme as one of 'great and pressing importance'. The War Office again refused to contribute towards the cost. The problem was complicated by the new defence arrangements now under discussion, and the removal of the Services from the north side of Queen's Road was mooted. The local naval authorities were willing to go to Kowloon; and the military asked for additional land on the south side of Queen's Road equivalent to that to be vacated on the north side, but in July 1887 Cameron was informed that the Admiralty was 'unable to come to a decision' on the move to Kowloon, and the plan was held up.

With tragic lack of judgement, Des Voeux opposed the proposed move of the naval yard to Kowloon, because of the expense in removing and re-erecting the buildings, and because of the growing value of land there; and he thought it was essential to keep the navy on the island for defence purposes.

P

This golden opportunity to free the island's 'constriction at the waist' was missed. In January 1889 Des Voeux sent home a revised scheme by which the praya would be built on arches to allow access to the naval basin; additional land was to be reclaimed to help cover the cost and the proportions to be paid by the Admiralty, War Office and colony were fixed at $156,792, $320,000 and $193,208 respectively. The War Office would be the largest gainers since their share of the reclamation was estimated to be worth over a million dollars. The Colonial Office urged the scheme on the Admiralty, but without avail. In October 1890 it was reported that the colonial government and Service chiefs discussed once more the move of the army and navy to Causeway Bay; Major-General Digby Barker supported the move, but the Commodore opposed it. The next Governor, Sir William Robinson, made unavailing efforts to revive the praya scheme, but the extended needs of the naval defence led to the navy taking over the whole area from the military, for a modern naval dockyard.

The enormous programme of public works was not carried through without difficulty. It says much for the resilience of the colony's revenues, that no additional taxation was necessary to meet the service of the loan and the additional expenditure. Revenue increased from $1,209,517 in 1882 to $2,025,302 in 1891 and the new expenditure was absorbed by the continuing growth and prosperity of the colony. The unofficial members of the Legislative Council, who now regarded themselves as 'the lawfully constituted guardians of the public purse', subjected these public works to much scrutiny and demanded to see plans and estimates before they were sent home.

The gradual fall in the price of silver led to the depreciation of the dollar, and made the military contribution and other sterling payments automatically heavier. The salaries of the senior officials were raised by 35 per cent, and of local officials by 20 per cent in 1890 as a result of the recommendation of the unofficial members. The doubling of the military contribution in 1890 led the unofficial members to attempt to postpone the increases of salaries they had already voted, a proceeding which Des Voeux rejected. It did create financial difficulty, with the result that all public works not already started were delayed, and when Des Voeux left in 1891, there was something of a financial crisis, and certainly the liveliest opposition from the unofficial members.

The Chinese customs 'blockade' which had irritated the merchants since 1867, was now ended. The relations between the British diplomatic and colonial authorities which had impeded a settlement had improved. In addition, common sense demanded some concession to the Chinese. In 1883 Russell, the Registrar-General, reported that the local Chinese salt farmer had a collecting agency on the praya which the local Chinese merchants found it convenient to use, and although Bowen protested, this was largely a matter of form. An opium commission had dealt with the question of smuggling opium, and recommended the suppression of the armed bands which were engaged, and this was one of the reasons why Bowen wanted the police trained in the use of arms. In 1885, after two years of negotiation, a new opium agreement between Britain and China raised the duty and likin tax on imported opium to 110 taels per chest, and this had the effect of stimulating smuggling. Bowen sympathized with the Chinese, because the opium revenue at Hong Kong suffered in a similar manner; he took a reasonable view and made many suggestions for a compromise.

In September 1886 the commission provided for under the Chefoo Convention of 1876, to examine the question of the customs 'blockade', finally met and came to agreement. Marsh, in reporting this agreement, admitted that there had been no complaint against the 'blockade' since 1882 and that for some years past, the trade of Hong Kong had not suffered by reason of the 'blockade'. The commission consisted of Shao Yu-lien and Sir Robert Hart for China and James Russell, Registrar-General, and Brenan, British Consul at Canton, on the British side. The agreement, which was signed on 11 September 1886, was largely the work of Russell and dealt primarily with opium. All opium arriving in the harbour was to be reported to the Harbourmaster, and no opium was to be landed, moved, transhipped, stored or exported without his permission and without notice to the opium farmer; all movement of opium was to be accounted for. The night clearance of junks was prohibited; no raw opium was to be imported except by the opium farmer, and there was to be no import or export of amounts under one chest. A branch of the Foreign Inspectorate of the Chinese Imperial Maritime

Customs was to be set up on Chinese territory to sell Chinese opium duty certificates, at 110 taels per chest. The colony undertook to embody the terms in an ordinance. The whole agreement was made conditional on a similar agreement being negotiated with Macao, from the fear that control in Hong Kong would drive the smuggling trade to Macao. A special ordinance was passed against armed bands engaged in smuggling opium by which all Chinese were forbidden to carry arms, except with the permission of the Governor-in-Council, though the home government insisted on changing the word 'Chinese' to 'persons', making it applicable to all.

In March 1887 the Opium Ordinance was introduced in accordance with the agreement, and aroused great opposition, particularly amongst the small traders and junk owners, and some concession had to be made, though the essential controls were maintained. Cameron and Des Voeux reported that the Chinese provincial officials were much against the agreement and would not collaborate. To work the new controls and pass the necessary information to the Chinese a new Imports and Exports Department came into being, under A. Seth, an Armenian; the suggestion that it should be enlarged to cover information on all imports and exports was dropped, and its opium registration functions were placed under the Harbour-master. In 1888, the monopoly for the sale of opium consumed in the colony was once farmed out, but trouble continued for some years because smuggling was so profitable, and collisions on the Kowloon border were frequent. It was found later that the Hong Kong opium farmer was blatantly smuggling opium into China, taking advantage of a loophole in the ordinance by which opium belonging to him was not subject to the provisions of the ordinance.

The existence of Triad societies made the opium problem more acute. They had been a permanent feature of colonial life, but there was now a drive against them, following police complaints, and a committee, which included three Chinese Justices of the Peace, reported they were powerful and numerous, protected criminals, that they used blackmail and tampered with witnesses. They numbered 15,000, and government servants and even police were found to be members. The Chinese member of the Legislative Council was threatened with death, three Chinese who had informed against the Triads were found stabbed, and in December 1886 there was a plot to set fire to the jail. Strong action was taken against them and the problem became less serious.

Sufficient has been said to show that this period of the eighties was a formative period in the development of the colony. Both Bowen and Des Voeux were ending their careers, neither was very robust, and neither remained in the colony long. Bowen left his mark on the constitution, in education and defence arrangements, but it is impossible not to share the opinion of the Colonial Office that his contribution to the colony was not quite so outstanding as he believed. Des Voeux must bear the chief responsibility of the failure to move the Services from the city centre, to undertake the central reclamation as a public work and to stand up to property interests in sanitary legislation.

CHAPTER XIX

SIR WILLIAM ROBINSON, 1891-98

'. . . *under the protection of the British Government, Hong Kong has become a Chinese rather than a British community . . . and Chinese settlement . . . has been one main element in its prosperity.*'

Lord Ripon to Sir William Robinson, 23 August 1894.

SIR WILLIAM ROBINSON began his career as a clerk in the Colonial Office in 1854 at the age of eighteen, and after a series of promotions became Governor of the Bahamas in 1874. As with his two immediate predecessors, the Hong Kong governorship came as the climax of his career. He was very much a Colonial Office man, anxious to keep it well informed, and to be guided by its instructions.

The failure fully to implement the findings of the Chadwick Report due to opposition from property owners and the Chinese community, and in spite of the clearest warnings, has already been noticed. The plague of 1894 was needed to secure action.

Plague was endemic on the China coast; in May 1894 it attacked the colony, and by 15 May 130 cases, mostly fatal, were reported. There was no law requiring the registration of deaths among the Chinese and knowledge of the plague came almost by accident, when it was observed that many deaths were occurring in one street, and by 28 May the deaths were 450, and were increasing.

There was little scientific knowledge of plague; a permanent committee of the Sanitary Board was set up to recommend the necessary bye-laws, upon which vigorous action could be taken. These covered the cleansing and disinfecting of infected areas, compulsory removal of the sick, organization of additional hospital room, house-to-house visitation, and the recruitment of additional staff. Three hundred troops were brought in to assist, but after five cases had occurred among them, this number was reduced by half. Later bye-laws gave power to declare dirty and insanitary buildings to be a danger to health, to order their cleansing, and to declare buildings unfit for human habitation and remove their occupants. Hong Kong was declared an infected port.

There was deep Chinese prejudice against Western medicine, and against government interference and intrusion upon their privacy, and much complaint against the house-to-house visitation, carried out generally by the military. The Tung Wah made strong representations to take over completely the treatment of Chinese victims, but Robinson refused to give in. Placards appeared in Canton, warning Chinese women against going to the colony, and even accusing Western doctors of scooping out the eyes of newly born children for use in the treatment of plague. These rumours were believed, schools were emptied, and thousands fled to the mainland. One difficulty was the Chinese habit of secreting the dead and deserting the dying, and 109 plague-stricken bodies were collected in one day in June; 350 houses were condemned, 7,000 Chinese were dislodged from their homes, and much of the Tai Ping Shan district was cordoned off and closed. The hospital ship *Hygeia*, the Kennedy Town glassworks, and the recently completed pig depôt were converted into temporary hospitals. Anti-foreign feeling in Canton ran high, and a charitable institution sent junks to Hong Kong offering to remove all cases and dispose of all bodies; Robinson at first refused, but later, as a concession, allowed 170 cases to be sent to Canton.

Ships avoided the harbour and prices began to rise. Robinson thought the remedy was to pull down all insanitary property, about one-tenth of the city, and have a stringent buildings ordinance, and increase the water supply. Half the cases were from Tai Ping Shan, and a special Tai Ping Shan Resumption Ordinance was passed, resuming land in this area, and plans for the Tai Tam Water Works extension were sent home for approval. In January 1895 an ordinance was forced through by the official majority, dealing with insanitary property, cellars, mezzanine floors, and cubicles, and extending the powers of the Sanitary Board to enable it to make bye-laws before an emergency arose. Dr. Ho Kai and E. R. Belilios both strongly opposed the ordinance, and the home government agreed to it only if it were administered with caution. A strike of coolies against the inspection of lodging houses, which was made obligatory under the ordinance, showed that caution was necessary. This further disrupted trade, and the Chamber of Commerce urged concession, but Robinson refused to countenance any action directed against the government. He banished some of the ringleaders, issued an explanatory notice to the Chinese, and the strike was soon over, fortunately without any violence.

In 1895 there were very few plague cases, but in 1896 and subsequent years, plague recurred to greater or less degree every spring. It was inevitable that the Sanitary Board should be criticized; Ayres, in his 1895 annual report, referred to its 'long, wordy, windy, desultory rambling discussions . . . ending in nothing being done'. It had an unofficial majority, and an elected element, but it depended entirely on the government for funds, and its bye-laws had to be sanctioned by the Legislative Council, which was ultimately responsible for the sanitary policy pursued. The Sanitary Board was not therefore an independent body. It was decided to appoint a Medical Officer of Health for the colony, and the question arose whether he should be a government officer with a seat on the Board, or be an official of the Board, and be present at its meetings to advise, but not to vote. The appointment was, in the end, a government appointment, and all the unofficial members of the Board except one resigned in protest. In 1895, the Board was nearly defunct; it had become a committee of the heads of the government departments principally concerned. Robinson accepted a proposal by the Retrenchment Committee that it should be abolished, but the Colonial Secretary, Chamberlain, would not agree, as the question of constitutional reform had come up, by which the Sanitary Board might become a municipal council. Robinson and other opponents of the Sanitary Board felt that the government should take direct responsibility for sanitation through an official, the Medical Officer of Health. Meanwhile, an ordinance was passed allowing the Board to act through a committee, and the Director of Public Works, the Acting Colonial Surgeon, the Captain Superintendent of Police, and the Acting Medical Officer of Health carried out the functions of the Board as a temporary arrangement. The unofficial members of the Legislative Council all opposed the abolition of the Sanitary Board, and Robinson reversed his previous decision, and attached the Medical Officer of Health to the Sanitary Board, and not to the head of the Medical Department. The newly constituted Board aroused criticism and in 1896 Robinson took a plebiscite among the British community on the question of giving the Board an official or unofficial majority. The voting showed a preference for the latter by 331 to 31. This drew from Chamberlain the remark that 'it is inconsistent with Crown colony government to seek the guidance of a plebiscite', and Chamberlain suggested leaving any further change in the composition of the Board to the next Governor. In the meantime plague had returned to the colony in 1896 in all its violence, with 1,193 cases up to 31 August, of which 1,088 were fatal; in 1897 only 17 cases were reported, but 1898 was more serious, and two English nursing sisters succumbed to the plague in the course of their duty.

Japanese medical men showed keen interest in plague, and claimed to be the first to isolate the plague bacillus, but the connection with rats was not proved until a few years later. The Chinese resisted the measures taken; there was little incentive to report cases because it meant them having to vacate their houses for nine days while the cleansing process took place. In 1896, the plague epidemic was serious in Canton, and as a concession to Chinese prejudice, plague cases, and later, corpses, were allowed to be taken to Canton, and Robinson estimated one in four bodies were removed in this way. Each house in the Chinese quarter in Hong Kong was searched once every ten days, and the disturbance can be easily imagined. In 1896 two Italian Sisters of Charity died from the plague. Robinson saw that overcrowding was at the root of the disease, and after prolonged debate, fresh legislation was passed dealing with this and compulsory drainage of houses by the Public Works Department.

The plague had wider repercussions. It affected education policy, because it was now realized how little the Chinese had been affected by the ideas of the West, and it led to a demand for more teaching of English. The Medical Department was reorganized, but this was partly due to the Retrenchment Committee. Dr. Phineas Ayres, who had been Colonial Surgeon since 1873, retired in 1897. Described by Robinson as 'having a rather foolish manner, but he is in perfect possession of his senses', he had warned the colony continuously of the evil sanitary condition. The Colonial Office suggested his retirement so that the Medical Department could be reorganized with a Principal Civil Medical Officer. For the moment the Medical Officer of Health was placed under the Sanitary Board.

Chinese medicine and particularly the Tung Wah Hospital came under criticism, for if Western medicine failed to arrest the plague, that of China was equally impotent. The Tung Wah Committee asked that house-to-house visitations should cease and that it should be allowed to treat all Chinese victims and to send them to Canton. Robinson refused, but the committee was allowed to have some plague cases in hospitals under its control, subject to government medical supervision. In 1896, after Ayres had left, government medical officers demanded the abolition of the Tung Wah and its replacement by a government pauper hospital. This led to a commission of enquiry into the Tung Wah; its report in December 1896 recognized that good work for the Chinese sick and poor had been done, but recommended supervision by the Medical Department, with Western medical treatment allowed on a voluntary basis and the appointment for this purpose of a Chinese resident surgeon, trained in Western medicine. The Tung Wah directors were opposed to all government interference, and after two meetings reluctantly acquiesced in the appointment of Dr. Chung, a licentiate of the Hong Kong Medical College and Resident House Surgeon at the Alice Memorial Hospital, and then only on condition he was paid by the government. Daily inspections were made by a European medical officer. The Chinese proved not to be so prejudiced as was thought; in the first month of the new arrangement seventeen Chinese elected Western treatment, and by the end of the century the numbers were approximately half and half, and, curiously enough, the mortality rates did not at first favour Western methods. The new Principal Civil Medical Officer, Atkinson, stigmatized Chinese medicine in the Tung Wah as 'empiricism and quackery', but the Colonial Office in London resisted all attempts to have the Tung Wah closed.

The plague added also to the colony's existing financial difficulties. These had arisen because of the programme of extraordinary public works, which would in any event have taxed the colony's resources; it was added to by military defence works, and by the doubling of the military contribution in 1890; in addition, all salaries had been increased to compensate for the losses on sterling remittances, and increased cost of living. At the same time revenue from opium was threatened. The depreciation of silver made all sterling payments automatically heavier, and before Des Voeux left, the temporary suspension of all public works had been ordered.

The home government became alive to the evils of the opium traffic, and in October 1891 Lord Knutsford had demanded that the colonial government should take over direct control of opium with a view to diminishing its consumption. He ordered close co-operation with the Opium Commission sitting at Calcutta and advocated lessening the trade even at the cost of the revenue. Again, in April 1892, Knutsford urged a policy of raising the price to restrict consumption, as a question in the House had referred to the excessive number of divans in Singapore and Hong Kong.

Robinson faced a minor financial crisis, and in his first speech to the Legislative Council suggested a committee to report on the question of a loan to tide over the colony's financial difficulties. He changed the system of accounting to bring all accounts in respect of any one year in that year; the existing practice was to put accounts of the previous year settled in January, in the following year. This meant additional expenditure of $170,000 of a book-keeping nature for 1892. The loan committee recommended the arrangement locally of bank overdrafts at five and a half per cent as and when required, and thought that the colony should meet the difficulty by selling more land, though land was just then fetching low prices. The home government agreed to a loan of £200,000, in stock and not debentures, but told Robinson that he would have to publish better financial estimates or he might not be able to borrow cheaply, and the stock was merged with the outstanding stock of the 1886 loan. The revenue proved resilient, and it is very doubtful if this loan was necessary. Certain definite works, the praya reclamation, the new central market then being built, and the big water and sewage schemes were charged to the loan; all other works and charges were to be defrayed from current revenue. In addition, certain less urgent works were postponed to reduce expenditure, and economies were also effected by the cutting down or amalgamation of government offices. The posts of Colonial Secretary and Registrar-General were amalgamated, and those of Captain Superintendent of Police and Jail Superintendent. One Magistrate and the assistant Harbour-master were dispensed with. All clerical posts were to be filled locally, and economies were made in the police by revising the conditions of pensionable service. The unofficial members proposed that the salaries of government officers should be reduced by taking away the recently granted increases, and in January 1893 they asked for a commission to enquire into the colony's finances. The Secretary of State naturally refused to agree that the officials should bear the brunt of the economies, besides it was the unofficial members who had in 1889 suggested raising the official salaries. Lord Ripon suggested a Retrenchment Committee of 'the unofficials and one or two other government officers'. When Robinson suggested an official chairman and three other officials as members in addition to the unofficials, the latter protested, and some refused to serve unless the Retrenchment Committee had an unofficial majority; Robinson reduced the number of officials to meet their objection and the committee reported in September 1894, and recommended the economies which had already been mooted; the abolition of the posts of Clerk of the Councils, one Magistrate and Superintendent of the Jail and the amalgamation of the posts of Colonial Secretary and Registrar-General. Judicial salaries were to be reduced and many departments were to have reduced staffs, but there was no suggestion of retrenching on public works.

On the question of government salaries, an exchange compensation scheme was suggested by which half the salaries were payable at 3s. 4d. to the dollar, and half at current rates, and this was adopted in principle. Actually the revenue proved to be buoyant, and in 1894, the plague year, it was $2,287,203, which was $279,995 over the estimate and $209,068 over that of the previous year. Additional stamp duties were imposed in 1895, and in spite of heavy additional expenditure, the deficit was only $11,892. On the vexed question of the military contribution, this was fixed in July 1895 at seventeen and a half per cent of the colonial revenue. Since the revenue of the colony increased yearly, the main result of the protests of the unofficial members was to saddle the colony with a heavier financial burden. The unofficials accepted this basis on condition that certain purely municipal revenue, and certain other revenue of a book-keeping nature, like the postal revenue which was collected and paid over to the Imperial government, should be exempted, but the home government ruled that it should receive seventeen and a half per cent of the total revenue.

In general the programme of public works was maintained. In 1892 Robinson suggested new government offices on the new reclamation; most departments had out-grown their accommodation, the Post Office in the old Supreme Court building was particularly cramped, and new departments like the Sanitary Board were badly off. In 1896 the plan to have new government offices was again put forward and was strongly recommended by the Council; two blocks were planned, the Supreme Court and Registry in one, and the Post Office and other government departments in the other, the cost being $900,000, but a proposed competition for the best design was vetoed by the Secretary of State. Robinson considered that the value of the Crown sites on the new praya plus the savings in rents of rented offices and the sale of existing offices would pay the cost, but Chamberlain was against the principle of earmarking the new praya lots for government offices, and it was not until 1898 that he accepted it.

The Tai Tam Water Extension Scheme was pressed on, the aim being to increase the reservoir capacity to 400 million gallons, and to serve Aberdeen and Shaukiwan as well. In Kowloon, which in 1891 had a population of 14,200, it was proposed to sink wells and pump water to a storage tank, but Kowloon was growing so fast that this small scheme proved quite inadequate. The new central market was completed in 1895 and the main drainage system was practically completed. The Secretary of State demanded a new jail or jail block because for many years the existing jail had been notoriously inadequate, and only seventy cells had been provided. Des Voeux had had to postpone this work, but Robinson found a great obstacle in the unofficials, who refused to agree to a new jail, and they were supported by Ho Kai, who argued that the separate cell system was not suited to the Chinese. Chamberlain reluctantly agreed to delay, and eventually Robinson proposed a new central police station and magistracy to allow the jail to be extended on its existing site.

The keen interest of the unofficial members in financial measures raised constitutional issues, and led to a demand for constitutional reform. Since Bowen's reforms, the Council voted all taxation and debated appropriations in its Finance Committee, and it is easy to see that the unofficial members thought these reforms would not have been made except on the basis of giving colonial opinion a greater voice in colonial affairs. The successful functioning of the Shanghai Municipal Council with wide powers of self-government was a challenge to the colony. Though the unofficial members did not have a majority, they could and did bring much pressure to bear, under a system of government by discussion. Trouble began soon after Robinson's arrival. In December 1892 the unofficial members voted to reduce all salaries of government servants to their 1890 level, and Robinson reported that this vote was caused by resentment at the increased military contribution and the insistence of the Secretary of State on new jail accommodation. He reported that a small knot of British residents, led by T. H. Whitehead, manager of the Chartered Bank of India, China and Australia, wanted constitutional change, and hoped to secure it by persistent opposition and the threat of the unofficials to resign in a body. The Appropriation Ordinance for 1893 was duly passed by the official majority, and the unofficials, led by Whitehead, alleged that this was unconstitutional since the officials were interested parties, voting themselves increases in salaries. Ripon admitted that the unofficial members 'may be regarded as in some degree the special guardians of the public purse', but he refused to support their protest, and suggested a Retrenchment Committee, the constitutional dispute over which has already been mentioned.

In 1894 a petition asking for constitutional change was sent to the Secretary of State by ratepayers led by Whitehead, Chater, Jackson and Ho Kai. They stated that Hong Kong's annual trade was worth some £40,000,000 per annum, and that this prosperity had largely been created by British merchants and shipowners, and yet they had only a small share in their own government. They said many Crown colonies were given representative institutions and they similarly wanted 'the common right of Englishmen to manage their local affairs and control the expenditure of the colony where imperial considerations are not involved.' They demanded the 'free election of representatives of British nationality in the Legislative Council' and that they should be in the majority. Robinson sent the petition home and commented that the best course was to add slightly to the unofficial element, and to admit unofficial members to the Executive Council, though he said he had, in practice, always consulted the unofficial members of the Legislative Council on local matters. Lord Ripon treated the petition seriously and in a long dispatch he reviewed the progress and constitutional development of the colony; he 'inclined to judge that it had prospered because it has been a British colony', since it had few life-long residents, European or Chinese. He asked if voters were to be of any nationality, if the British representatives were to be from the British Isles, or to be British subjects of any race, and he had little difficulty in showing that no complete scheme had been put forward. He was against the main proposal, as it meant setting up a small oligarchy, and he argued that the existing system would better safeguard the interests of the majority of the inhabitants, there being no distinction of rank or race, than 'a system of representation which left the bulk of the population wholly un-represented'. He suggested additional unofficials on the Legis-lative Council, in which case the official element should be increased too, or a second Chinese representative might be appointed, though this was not what the petitioners wanted; and thirdly, there might be an unofficial element in the Executive Council, but the petitioners had to bear in mind that any subject of the Queen might be appointed, not necessarily a European. With regard to a municipal council, Ripon said, 'I frankly say that I should like to see one established at Hong Kong,' and thought that the Sanitary Board might develop into one. But, he added, while the Sino-Japanese war continued there could be no change.

Whitehead urged his reforms in London, but without making Ripon change his mind. The unofficials were dissatisfied with the offer of a municipal council, and Ripon, in June 1895, then suggested that two persons might be nominated to the Executive Council as unofficial members, one of whom should be Chinese to avoid all racial distinctions, and in view of the sanitary prob-lems, he thought it would be wise to have one Chinese. He also agreed to increasing the Legislative Council by one official, and suggested the General, and by two unofficials, by adding some representation of a class or interest inadequately or completely unrepresented, such as 'retail traders, or skilled labour'. He thought the Chinese element clearly under-represented. Robin-son was against having any Chinese on the Executive Council, because he thought a Chinese would not be really independent. In July 1896 these changes were carried out, and J. J. Bell-Irving, of Jardine, Matheson & Co., and Chater became the first unofficial members of the Executive Council, Wei Yuk be-came an additional unofficial member of the Legislative Coun-cil, which now had two Chinese members, and the General became an additional official member in December 1896. In May 1895 Robinson reported that he could not discover 'any real desire among the inhabitants of the colony for any change in its constitution', and this was probably true. In the Sanitary Board elections in June 1894, though the plague created an alarming situation, only 25 out of 500 voters cast their votes. Another constitutional change was made at this time arising out of the troubled situation in the Far East. Chamberlain, after consulting Robinson, arranged that the General, and not the Colonial Secretary, should be the officer administering the government in the absence of the Governor. The tense international rivalry in the Far East made the demand for self-government in Hong Kong inopportune.

In the interest of honest administration, a ruling was given in October 1892 that no government official was to hold land or property in the colony except for his own dwelling, or to engage in commercial pursuits, or purchase shares in local companies.

There was in fact little dissatisfaction shown by the Chinese with the form of government as long as they were left alone. The Diamond Jubilee of 1897 was an occasion enjoyed as much by the Chinese as by the British. Chater was chairman of the Jubilee Committee and it was decided to mark the occasion by the erection of a hospital for women and children, and, in association with it, of an institution for the training of nurses, and also by the construction of roads around the island. The cost was to be borne by public subscription with a grant of $50,000 from the government.

The tense situation in the Far East made defence questions more urgent, particularly naval defence. Robinson made a last and fruitless effort to secure the praya extension along the naval and military area north of Queen's Road. The Admiralty decided in 1896 to extend the dockyard to build a graving dock, and to take the whole military area, the reclamation and some privately owned strips of land dividing the naval and military areas on the north side of Queen's Road. This was done, and the military moved its artillery barracks to Gun Club Hill in Kowloon, and bought a large hotel on the Peak, much to the annoyance of the dwellers there. Queen's Road was widened and slightly straightened, but the division of the city into two parts was not altered. The naval yard in Kowloon was also enlarged, and eventually all the roads in Kowloon, Robinson Road and Macdonnell Road had to be re-formed and re-named. The bickering between the colony and the War Office over the disposal of land in Kowloon was resumed and not settled until 1904. The fact of troops being moved to the Peak led General W.Black to demand a new military road,Black's Link, between Magazine Gap and Wong Nei Chong Gap. The Hong

Kong Volunteers, now consisting of artillery and machine-gun sections, languished, and in 1893 Robinson complained that 'every effort had been made to increase its numbers without result'. Its Headquarters building was completed, and a Volunteer Ordinance of that year reorganized the corps. In 1897 Sir J. W. Carrington, the Chief Justice, became Commandant, and brought new enthusiasm. The corps then numbered 159, the highest for some years, and in 1898 a drum-and-fife band was added. In the following year, during the trouble in taking over the New Territories, the Volunteers were mobilized for duty in Kowloon.

The greatest single measure of defence was the negotiating of the lease of the New Territories, but this is reserved for a later chapter.

The period was one of tension, and during the Sino-Japanese war, a policy of strict neutrality was observed. In the struggle for reform carried on by the Cantonese, Robinson refused to allow the colony to become the centre of any conspiracy against the Chinese Imperial government, an action he was bound to take. In 1896, Sun Yat Sen, educated in the colony, and a licentiate of the Hong Kong College of Medicine, was banished from the colony for five years for conspiracy against the Canton authorities. He had gone to Japan when the order was made, and he wrote a dignified letter asking if it were true, and threatening to appeal to the British public, and explaining that he was attempting 'to emancipate my miserable countrymen from the cruelty of the Tartar Yoke'. This led to a question in the Commons, and Robinson had to explain. The Governor was also warned by the home government against allowing Philippine nationalists to organize a Philippine Republic in the colony, or to organize an expedition against the Spanish colonial authorities.

Robinson left in the summer of 1898, having been Governor for a longer term than any of his predecessors, six years and two months without leave.

CHAPTER XX

THE DEVELOPMENT OF THE EDUCATIONAL SYSTEM IN THE LATTER HALF OF THE NINETEENTH CENTURY

'I regret that the number of children in school is not in-creasing in proportion to the population and I trust that renewed attention will be given to augmenting the number of children on the school rolls.'
Lord Knutsford to the acting Governor, 1 September 1891.

THE abolition of the Board of Education in 1865 has been interpreted as marking the introduction of secular education in Hong Kong, but this is only partly true. The Bible was not banished from the schools, but fewer Christian teachers remained to teach it because control of the government schools was taken out of the hands of the churches. Stewart found that there had been much deception by the Chinese schoolmasters over scripture teaching; he noticed that the school bibles were generally unsoiled and it was clear they were rarely used, yet they were always taken up when he entered a school as if their regular use were expected. Occasionally he found two or three chapters committed to memory, without any understanding. He therefore felt that bible teaching as given was useless, and that the curriculum should be purely secular; he made no effort to continue Christian influence in the schools and it gradually faded out. There was much criticism of this 'godless' education, but Stewart argued that because education was secular it was not on that account immoral, and that Confucianism was an excellent basis for moral training. He thought 'it was no part of government policy to convert the Chinese'.

The abolition of bible teaching did not affect the numbers of Chinese pupils attending school, and Stewart declared in his 1868 report that secular education was on trial and that if the denominational schools with religious teaching proved superior, the secular system would be amended. Religious influences dominated educational policy in England; opinion in the colony reflected this trend, and for some years condemned the education given in the government schools. The religious bodies began to build up their own schools and their success proved that the secularism in education owed more to European than to Chinese prejudice.

In 1866, there were thirteen government schools under Stewart as Inspector, with 623 pupils, of which the Central School had 222. The standard of attainment in these schools was very low. No arrangements for the training of teachers existed and Stewart was anxious to secure the best pupils of the Central School as teachers, but most of its students left early, attracted by posts obtainable outside, and a separate class and an additional master would have been needed. Until 1864 Stewart was quite alone, and had to take three classes at the Central School in addition to his work of inspecting village schools. There he found pupils could repeat the Confucian classics, but without any understanding. His insistence on class teaching, and the keeping of proper rolls and school sessions was resented as unnecessary interference, and he complained that the villagers regarded it as conferring a favour to send a child to a government school. The masters appointed to the village schools were a poor type, and the vast majority had to be dismissed. Stewart was shocked soon after his arrival when the master at Tai Tam Tuk was charged with highway robbery; in 1867 the master at Tung Lung Chau was dismissed for devoting to his own use the money granted for a monitor, and when the petition of the villagers for his reinstatement was refused, half the pupils were withdrawn.

In 1868 the experiment was tried of enlisting local support by helping the villagers to provide their own schools, and a new category of government-assisted village schools came into being side by side with the government village schools. The Board of Education had allowed villagers to choose their own schoolmasters, but this had been abused and was dropped; the Board appointed and paid the teachers, and began to provide school buildings. Under the new alternative scheme of 1868, villagers could have the privilege of choosing a schoolmaster, and the government paid half the salary, that is, $5 per month, the villagers finding the other half of the salary and the building. The system worked badly, and Stewart found that the villagers did not fulfil their side of the arrangement. The fact was that $5 a month for education was there for the asking, and there were rarely wanting claimants able to induce the villagers to petition for a school, probably promising parents a few cash for each child. Stewart could devote little time to inspection, and warning was given of his approach; he found that children were paid seven cash a day to sit in school with books until his visit was over. The Stanley schoolmaster shut up the school for days on end, and when he was caught out, his excuse that he was being persecuted by the villagers because he was a Christian was found to be untrue. There was trouble at Little Hong Kong in 1870, when the local tepo made the villagers petition to have his son as the schoolmaster. Stewart's report for 1868 was a despondent man's record of how little had been achieved. He was under no illusion; all he aimed at was to get children into a school of some kind to have the beginnings of discipline, to get order into the schools, and to attempt to get new buildings. New school houses were built at East Point and West Point to accommodate four schools, and other school premises were rented.

In 1872 Stewart reported that the Assisted Schools Scheme was not proving so beneficial because it was surmised that the half salary received from the government was the sole means of the master's support, and that the education given was 'far short of anything that would be dignified with the name of education in the West. Still it has been that or nothing since the establishment of the schools'. Stewart continued to build up the government school system, and in 1872 there were 30 government schools, 15 fully maintained and 15 assisted, with a total of 1,480 children. In 1878 there were still 30 government schools, of both kinds, with a total of 2,101 pupils. In 1872, Stewart tried the experiment of introducing English and Chinese on the Central School model into the Aberdeen School, but it was not successful and the school dwindled, although English was successfully introduced into three government schools in or near Victoria. In 1875, a system of bonus payments based on the results of the annual inspection was introduced to encourage the teachers to greater efficiency. They were to receive an extra $25 for the mark of very good, $15 for good, and nil for fair; if less than fair, they were to be dismissed.

The most important of the government schools was the Central School, of which Stewart himself was Headmaster. It began as an amalgam of four city schools, but soon developed into something different, because it taught both English and Chinese, while the village schools were purely vernacular, with the exception of the experiments just noted. Stewart was able to adopt Western methods, but he had great difficulties. He found only one text-book in the colony, and it had to serve all forms. He found English was accepted purely because it had commercial value, and boys left as soon as a smattering had been obtained. The school was in disfavour with the Chinese, because the boys 'by giving themselves airs, by affecting a superiority they do not possess, by forming clubs to the exclusion of those who do not know English . . . do not place the character of the school, and training which is attempted . . . in the light which we have a right to expect'. There was a lack of class-rooms, and classes were often three to a room. He secured a European assistant in 1864 and a second in 1869 and additional classrooms in 1863 and 1868. Under Macdonnell, the school was thrown open to all, but Stewart resisted pressure to vary on behalf of any racial group the curriculum of four hours English and four hours Chinese. The introduction of a system of examinations for the Imperial Maritime Customs made the school more popular as many students aimed at that service, but the critics thought it was not the colony's business to train students for China. Macdonnell was keen on science, and Stewart was able to equip a laboratory and to introduce some mathematics. Interest was stimulated by the grant of prizes, and in 1869 a speech day was introduced. By 1870 the students were beginning to take posts in California, Japan, and the Treaty Ports, as well as in business houses in Hong Kong. The pressure to take appointments was such that in 1870, 29 out of 36 in the top class left before the end of the year and 134 out of an average of 249 left during the year. There had to be continual promotion to keep the school full, and this retarded attainment. Stewart reported in that year that the school was more accepted by the Chinese, and he raised the question whether it should provide elementary education for the many or higher education for the few. By 1871 the school had increased in number to 440, including 88 non-Chinese, and new buildings became necessary; eighteen years were to pass before they were provided. In 1872 the Morrison Education Society, which was being wound up, offered $3,000 to found a scholarship, but the government could not accept the conditions laid down, and Stewart had once more to defend the school from the charge of being 'godless'. He declared its main aim to be the provision of a school where all could meet on common ground without offending the susceptibilities of any section. The education of girls remained backward after 'the melancholy results' of teaching Chinese girls English through the efforts of the Diocesan Female Education Committee and of Jane Baxter. There were only two government girls' schools, but the missions had more, and by 1877 a quarter of the pupils in inspected schools were girls.

The outstanding advance in this period was the introduction of the grant-in-aid scheme in 1873, by which government aid and inspection were extended to the mission and other voluntary schools. To qualify for grant, a school had to be conducted as a public elementary school, on a non-profit-making basis with an attendance of at least twenty, and satisfy the inspector in school organization and discipline. Secular instruction only, extending over at least four hours a day, qualified for grant, but the government undertook not to interfere with religious teaching. The appointment of teachers rested with the school as long as the government was satisfied as to their competence, and a quarter of the grant payable was to go to the teacher as a personal payment. For purposes of grant there were five classes of schools, according as they gave (1) a Chinese education, (2) a Chinese education with additional English, (3) a European education in Chinese, (4) a European education in any European language and (5) a European education in any European language with Chinese additional. The grant-earning subjects were laid down, and the syllabus to be covered was graded into six standards in each of the five classes of schools. Grant was paid on the result of an annual examination conducted by the Inspector of Education, or examiners appointed by the government; each successful child earned a grant varying from $2 in Standard 1 to $8 in Standard 6 for schools in classes I and II, rising to a maximum of $10 for schools in classes III, IV and V, with an extra half dollar in schools of class II and V, where a second language was taught. In each case a minimum of 200 attendances was required.

In essentials the scheme adopted the principle of payment by results, following the English education code of that time, except that English controversies over denominational education were avoided by keeping the secular principle as the basis of government aid, as Stewart had always recommended. The difficulty of applying the scheme to Chinese vernacular schools because of the lack of graduated text-books was acknowledged, and a committee was appointed to deal with this.

All the religious bodies at first applied for grant-in-aid for their schools, but the Catholics soon withdrew from the scheme because they objected to its secularism. The Victoria Boys' School, an undenominational school for Portuguese under a committee headed by prominent business men, came into the scheme, and the Baxter Vernacular Girls' School also applied. In 1873, six schools became grant-aided; they were St. Saviour's (R.C.), St. Stephen's (C. of E.), Wanchai Chapel School (L.M.S.), Tai Ping Shan Chapel Schools (L.M.S.), Victoria Boys' School (undenominational) and the Baxter Vernacular Girls' School. In 1874 there were nine schools, the Baxter Schools forming three separate schools instead of one, and the Basel Mission School coming in, and by the end of 1876 there were eleven schools receiving grant-in-aid, though St. Saviour's dropped out. The additional schools were St. Paul's College, St. Stephen's Church School, and Victoria Girls' School. Some modification was felt necessary in 1877 because of the temptation to push the pupils to take the higher standards so as to earn more grant. The scheme was accordingly amended in 1878 to take effect from 1 January 1879, by which class I and II schools were given additional grants ranging from $5 to $10; class III, from $6 to $12; class IV, from $6 to $16, and class V, from $6 to $16½. Increased capitation grants were paid on the 200 average attendances, and pupils were permitted to take additional secular subjects for grant-earning purposes.

Hennessy had very definite ideas about education, and surprisingly for a man who adopted a strong pro-Chinese line, he thought the Chinese should be taught more English and less vernacular. He criticized the whole educational system as inadequate and backward. He compared Hong Kong with its

average school population of 2,707 with the little larger Barba-
does which had a school population of 14,000. In the Bahamas,
one in twelve of the total population attended school, in Hong
Kong the figure was one in eighty-two. Such statistics had little
meaning in Hong Kong because of the continual shifting of the
population and its male preponderance. Hennessy was intensely
interested in the treatment of criminals and the incidence of
crime; of 7,998 convictions registered in 1876, he found that
three out of five were first convictions, and half the floggings
administered were to juveniles, and argued that this pointed
to some connection between crime and the lack of education.
He criticized the examination papers set in the schools, and
sympathized with the criticisms of the grant-in-aid scheme by
the religious bodies. The home government suspected all this
criticism and warned him to be cautious in making changes,
and in any case to submit detailed proposals before acting.
Stewart felt Hennessy's attitude to be hostile. It was clear that
administrative changes would have to be made because the
new grant-in-aid schools made the work of supervision too
great to allow the duties of inspector to be combined with those
of the headmastership of the Central School. The posts were
separated. Against the wishes of Hennessy, the home government in February 1879 selected Dr. E. J. Eitel of the London
Missionary Society and a noted Chinese scholar, as Inspector
of Schools, but without control over the Central School, which
was to be an independent department. Stewart now left the
education field; after home leave in 1879 he returned as acting
Colonial Secretary, and was succeeded as headmaster by Dr.
Bateson Wright.

In February 1878 Hennessy appointed a committee to consider the teaching of English in the colony; it supported the
Governor's view that the primary object of government effort
should be the teaching of English. At the Central School instead
of four hours each to English and Chinese, the time allotted
was changed to five to English and two and a half to Chinese
which was to be voluntary, and the standard of entry in Chinese
was raised in an attempt to maintain the standard of Chinese
in the school. The committee, with some dissentients, also urged
that English should be taught in all government schools. The
Colonial Secretary criticized these resolutions as too strong and

as 'making it appear that government can properly pay less attention to other matters of importance in the education of the Chinese.' Hennessy's policy was directed against Stewart, who had steadily upheld the view that secular education in the vernacular was the prime requirement. The removal of Stewart and the fact that the Governor was a Catholic, now encouraged the religious denominations to attack the grant-in-aid scheme as too secular, and to ask for more favourable terms. In 1877 Hennessy asked the religious bodies to formulate their criticisms and make suggestions. The result was that in 1879 the grant-in-aid code was amended; the offensive word 'secular' was dropped, and replaced by 'instruction in the subjects of the standards'; the word 'elementary' was dropped and the way was opened for higher grade schools. The request that the minimum number of attendances to qualify for grant should be reduced from 200 to 160 was refused, but the voluntary bodies secured building grants. Taking his cue from the Governor, Eitel suggested, in his first full year's report, that for 1879, a complete revision of educational policy; the government should set up elementary English schools and leave Chinese 'native schools' to themselves.

The Central School was again criticized. It produced no Chinese boy with enough English to qualify him for jury service. It had become a middle-class school, and yet the fees amounted to only a fifth of the cost and this cheapness tended to create difficulties for the middle-class voluntary schools. Boys of all nationalities attended the school, and the churches were much opposed to the absence of any Christian teaching there. The Rev. A. R. Hutchinson, of the Church Missionary Society, accused it of pandering to the Chinese by teaching a smattering of English for its economic advantage, and he criticized the 'flippancy and conceit' of the pupils. In defence, the school was overcrowded, the staffing was inadequate with four English teachers for 610 children. In 1880 the fees were increased. The plans for the new school were delayed because Hennessy appointed a Commission of Enquiry to examine the function of the school, and to consider raising its status to that of a 'collegiate character', by which it would take children from the district schools for more advanced education, a scheme which the Committee broadly accepted; it also recommended that five new schools should be built. The Secretary of State was annoyed and thought that if a new school were urgently needed in Kennedy's time, it was still more needed then. In fact, as long as Hennessy was Governor nothing was done to secure a new Central School.

In other respects, however, there was an advance due to the 1879 alterations in the grant-in-aid regulations, and to the separation of the inspectorate from the headmastership of the Central School. In 1878 there were 30 maintained and assisted government schools with 2,101 pupils and 17 grant-in-aid schools with 1,021 pupils, and it was estimated by Eitel that there were 2,494 pupils in Chinese and Roman Catholic schools (the latter were then outside the grant scheme) besides numbers of evening schools for English teaching. By 1882, the year Hennessy left, there were 39 government schools and 41 grant-in-aid schools, with 2,114 and 3,086 pupils respectively. Of these 80 schools under government inspection, no less than 64 offered Chinese only, though some of the grant-in-aid schools had Christian teaching in Chinese, 2 schools, both girls' schools, gave a European education in Chinese, 2 a European education in Portuguese, 6 in English, and 8 schools taught both English and Chinese. Hennessy's attempt to insist on more English teaching was only partially realized; about 6 of the government village schools included English as well as Chinese, the master getting an extra $5. Eitel reported that the standard attained in the government schools was well below that of the grant schools, and it is clear that Hennessy's sympathetic attitude towards the missionary bodies led to a great expansion in their educational work.

Hennessy's plan of creating an English-speaking Chinese community in Hong Kong led to the setting up in 1881 of a normal school for the training of teachers, since recruitment of teachers from England was too expensive. May, the third master at the Central School, became Headmaster, with one Chinese assistant. Ten students, nine of them from the Central School, were selected for training and given an allowance of 48 dollars per year for the three-year course. Unfortunately, Hennessy omitted to take the precaution of submitting the scheme to the Secretary of State, who in the absence of a full explanation, demanded that the money voted for it should be cancelled, but on the urgent telegraphic representations of Hennessy, allowed the plan to go on pending a full report as to the vacancies expected for teachers, the full cost and the whole purpose and the nature of any bond demanded. He allowed the students to have their allowance for the first year, but forbade it for the second and third years of the course. It transpired that they were to be lodged in the school at the government's expense. Hennessy had not reported this, and Kimberley agreed that this should continue temporarily too. May's salary was reduced. Hennessy left the colony in April 1882, with the teacher training scheme in this unsatisfactory state. When a bond to teach five years at $25 per month salary at the conclusion of the course was insisted on, three promptly left, leaving seven, and in September 1883 this first experiment in teacher training came to an end. Only four students remained, two became teachers, one became a government interpreter and four of the original class went to Tientsin Medical College. It was hoped that a reorganized Central School would provide teachers more cheaply.

Bowen arrived in 1883 and was very keen to build the new Central School, and expand the education services. He too advocated that English should be taught in all government maintained schools, partly because he wanted to introduce examinations in the medium of English for appointments to government clerical and other minor posts. Derby again urged that encouragement of English should 'not result in the neglect of vernacular education'. Bowen also suggested the Central School should be called Victoria College, in recognition of the more advanced standards to be aimed at, to keep up with the religious bodies which called their best schools colleges, and because the pupils were generally older than those in the district schools. Its status in China was shown to be high when Bowen announced at the Speech Day in 1884 that twelve pupils had been invited to fill posts in the Chinese Imperial Service. There was criticism that the colony should be called upon to pay for education for the benefit of China, but Bowen thought it would strengthen British influence there. In 1885 the new building was held up nearly a year through a misunderstanding between Bateson Wright and Price, the Surveyor-General, over the needs of the school, and in 1886 financial stringency led to another suspension of building. The foundation stone was laid in April 1884, but the school was not completed until 1889, when it opened as Victoria College with 960 pupils.

The troubles of the school were now nearly over. There were continual quarrels between Bateson Wright and Eitel over the school's examinations, for which the Inspector was still jointly responsible, and in 1894 the school was removed from the purview of the Inspector, and placed under a Board of Governors. The Chinese side was now closed. It had been compulsory for the masters to learn and teach Chinese, but this had been done unsatisfactorily, and all teaching was now in English, except that Chinese as a subject was retained. In 1894 its name was changed to Queen's College, but though most of the pupils were older it covered much the same ground as other free government schools in spite of its high-sounding name, and its fees.

Government schools tended to have few girls, who were usually sent to the mission schools, where they were taught by ladies. In 1888 Eitel suggested a government school for girls comparable to that of the Central School for boys, and it was decided to rent premises until it could be seen whether the Chinese would send their daughters to be taught in English. The first headmistress arrived in January 1890 and the school was opened on 1 March 1890 with thirty-four pupils; there were by December forty-five, and the school soon needed new premises. In August 1889 Belilios had offered $25,000 for a building to bear his name, and after some demur his offer was accepted and the new school, called Belilios School, was opened in 1893. It catered for girls of all nationalities and was organized in two departments, English and Chinese; it prospered and by 1898 had 539 pupils, of whom 233 were English.

During his short stay, Bowen introduced in 1884 two government scholarships confined to pupils from three schools, Central School, St. Joseph's and St. Paul's, for the study in England of Medicine, Law or Civil Engineering. The first scholar was W. Bosnam, a Eurasian, who went to England to do Civil Engineering, though some difficulty was experienced in getting him to go where he was sent and to return to the colony when his period of study was over. In 1887, the examination for the scholarships was entrusted to the University of Cambridge and thrown open to the whole colony. The scheme was dropped in 1894 as Eitel reported that there were few suitable candidates and that the colony had not gained because there was no condition that the scholar had to return to the colony. In fact, one settled in Natal, one on the China coast, and one remained in England.

Progress in education continued to be very slow. The government-maintained and -assisted schools were often mere hovels, particularly in the villages, and in 1887 it was reported that only ten or twelve schools out of 204 in the colony were in decent buildings. Standards of attainment remained low, though the Central School (Victoria College), St. Joseph's, St. Paul's and the Diocesan Schools were now beginning to aim at standards above those of elementary education. The grant-in-aid schools set the standards in attainment and in buildings, and the government village schools began to lose ground.

In 1883 Stewart as Registrar-General used the district watchman to conduct an enquiry into all Hong Kong schools and found that there were 180 schools with 7,758 pupils; of these 39 were government and government-aided schools with 2,080 pupils, 48 were grant-in-aid denominational schools with 3,517 pupils and 103 outside government supervision with 1,161 pupils. He reported that most schools were overcrowded and in hovels, and calculated that only a third of the children were in school. This report led to a demand for compulsory education, but this was thought unsuitable for Hong Kong. Commenting on the education report for 1888, Lord Knutsford complained that it was unsatisfactory that more than half the children of Hong Kong should be without education; he suggested, in place of compulsion, the employment of school attendance officers, and asked for an enquiry into the state of education for the Chinese in Hong Kong. In 1890 Knutsford again complained that it was 'evident that no great progress is yet being made to a condition of general education' and that it was essential 'to do everything possible to promote school attendance'. Various suggestions were made; a 'ragged boat' school scheme, compulsory attendance for servant girls, and juvenile labour laws. An amendment of the grant-in-aid regulations in 1883 reduced the basis of examination for grant from

200 attendances to 100, and further encouraged the grant-in-aid schools.

By 1890 there were 112 schools with 7,170 under the Education Department, including 76 grant-in-aid denominational schools with 4,656 and 36 government schools with 2,514 pupils. In the district of Victoria there were 71 schools with 5,856 on the roll, 17 in Kowloon with 525, and 24 in the villages on the island with 789 pupils. There was a school within reach of everyone, and every hamlet with more than 20 children had its own school. The amount spent on education was 2·8 per cent. of the total budget. There were 86 schools giving a Chinese education (many with some Christian teaching in addition) 3 giving a European education in the Chinese language, 4 giving an English elementary type of education in Portuguese, 8 schools with an English education in English with some secondary education, and 14 Anglo-Chinese schools giving elementary English education combined with Chinese. The number of girls in the schools rose from 18 per cent of the pupils in 1880 to 32 per cent in 1890. Des Voeux helped the villages by taking over some of the assisted village schools, abolishing fees, and providing furniture and better conditions; this was done partly to meet the charge that Hong Kong education reached only the middle classes. All schools in Victoria tended to take pupils of any nationality as part of the effort to remove unnatural distinctions of race and creed and as a force against 'the unbridged chasms' that existed between the races (1887 report). Most government and grant-in-aid schools were free, the Central School and other middle-class schools and private schools charged fees.

Under Sir William Robinson, progress in education was slowed down. Great expense regarding defence and the increased military contribution together with the heavy cost of public works and the plague led to retrenchment. The scholarships to England were discontinued in 1894, and the plague outbreak of that year virtually emptied the schools, partly because of the incredible rumour that the livers and eyes of children were needed as a cure for the plague. The need for retrenchment led to a reduction of educational expenditure. With this in view Robinson declared in his speech to the Legislative Council in November 1892, 'our aim is to extend the grant scheme in every direction and encourage educational enterprise'; in other words, his object was to shift some of the burden of education on to the religious bodies. All government schools with less than twenty-five pupils were closed, unless there were no other school near, and by this ruling ten were closed. Eitel argued that this was beneficial because the grant-in-aid teachers were more efficient as their salaries depended in part on the results of the examinations. The grant code was revised in 1893 to allow for grant to Standard 7, and thus further prepared the way for secondary education. Two classes of schools were dropped from the code, leaving three classes: (a) vernacular schools, (b) those giving a European education in Chinese, and (c) those giving a European education in a European language. After the plague outbreak in 1894, Robinson, faced with Chinese intransigence over sanitary measures, determined to encourage more English in the schools with the aim, as Eitel said, 'to elevate the Chinese people of this colony by means of English rather than Chinese teaching'; in 1895 it was announced that no new boys' school would receive a grant unless it gave a European education in the English language, but this policy was too difficult to implement. There was a strong claim for a separate school for English children, and in 1898 a scheme for such a school in Kowloon was formulated. Compulsory education was not adopted, but in 1893 an attendance inspector was appointed, though the coming of the plague the next year made it impossible to judge his effectiveness. Cambridge Local Examinations were introduced in 1887, but this had the result of pushing on English pupils at the expense of Chinese.

The Chinese continued to support their own vernacular schools in which the traditional Chinese education could be given without government grant or inspection. In 1898, the Tung Wah had six such free schools for the poorer class, and there were 102 Chinese schools in which fees were charged. These 108 schools outside government inspection had nearly 2,500 pupils.

The missionary schools showed the greatest development, particularly when the grant was given on more acceptable conditions. In 1898 there were 115 schools under government inspection, 100 grant-in-aid with 5,882 pupils, and 15 government schools with 1,445, of which 539 were in Belilios. The grant schools were now making the greatest contribution. Of the grant schools 74 were class I, vernacular, 3 gave a European type of education in Chinese, and 23 were class III schools, generally giving an education in English. In 1898, the chief voluntary societies were the American Board Mission, Basel Mission, Church Missionary Society, the London Missionary Society, Roman Catholic Mission, and the Wesleyan Mission. A Female Education Society was founded in 1885 to continue the work of Jane Baxter, who died in 1865, but whose schools continued. Bishop Raimondi was instrumental in expanding the Catholic schools and securing concessions from the government in the grant regulations. St. Joseph's College was founded in 1875 out of a reorganized St. Saviour's School, and in 1876 the Anglican Bishop Burden revived St. Paul's College as a school after it had died as a seminary in 1867. The Diocesan Orphanage, founded in 1860, eventually grew into the Diocesan Boys' and Girls' Schools. These with Queen's College, St. Joseph's and St. Paul's, were the chief schools of the colony at the end of the century.

In August 1897 Eitel retired after serving eighteen years as Inspector of Education, having been appointed when that post was separated from that of the Headmaster of the Central School in 1879. It had been intended to make the school a separate department, but the mistake was made of making the Inspector and Headmaster jointly responsible_for the annual examinations, with the result that Eitel and Bateson Wright were involved in continual disputes. Eitel never gained the confidence of the Colonial Office, who ruled that he was not a Director of Education but an Inspector of Schools, and as early as 1894 made enquiries about his possible retirement. He was succeeded as Inspector by a cadet officer, A. W. Brewin, who was then serving as assistant Registrar-General.

CHAPTER XXI

SOCIAL AND ECONOMIC CONDITIONS, 1882–98

'It is extraordinary—not to say discreditable—that after fifty-five years of British rule, the vast majority of Chinese in Hong Kong should remain so little anglicised.'
Sir William Robinson, Speech to the Legislative Council,
25 November 1895.

IT remains in this chapter to give a general outline of economic and social developments during the later nineteenth century, other than those relating to sanitation and education which have been given above.

The Chinese and foreign communities still lived apart and the unpopularity of the pro-Chinese Hennessy tended to widen the gulf. Hennessy had allowed the Chinese to move into Queen's Road Central and adjoining districts, which up to that time had been reserved for Europeans by restricting the type of houses that could be built there. Land for Chinese houses was more valuable than that reserved for European dwellings, because, on the former, houses could be more crowded together, and it was thus an economic proposition to pull down European houses to replace them by Chinese. The increased Chinese population, too, restricted the space available for Europeans who demanded that the Peak should be reserved for them. A European Reservation Ordinance, in 1888, created a European reservation in the Caine Road district. No racial discrimination was technically involved, and Chinese were free to reside in the area, in which only the type of housing was restricted to comply with certain standards. Legislation directed against the Chinese as such continued to be contrary to Imperial policy and the home government was vigilant. The remission of the fines on the coolies who refused to unload French ships in 1884 has already been mentioned. In 1886, following the opium agreement with China ending the customs 'blockade' (see page 213), an ordinance was passed aimed at armed smuggling, by which all Chinese were forbidden to carry arms. Lord Stanhope's

R

reply was, briefly, 'for the word "Chinese" substitute "persons",' to make the ordinance of general application. Again, Lord Ripon refused to accept an ordinance passed in April 1895 restricting Chinese entry into Hong Kong in time of plague, on the ground that the ordinance should not be directed against the Chinese alone. Following Hennessy's governorship the status of the Chinese community steadily rose, helped by permanent representation on the Legislative Council. An important reform came in 1897 when the system of night passes for Chinese which had been in existence since 1843 was abolished and the Chinese were put on the same footing as others. An ordinance of that year arranged that night passes were to be required only as ordered by the Governor. Again, in deference to Chinese feelings, an ordinance was passed in 1899 preserving the Sung Wong Toi, a rock inscription which had special associations for the Chinese since it commemorated the flight of the last Sung Emperor, and which was threatened by quarrying. Complaints were heard that the Chinese were not so subservient as they had been. In 1895, during the coolie strike against the health regulations for plague prevention, Granville Sharp, one of the speakers at a public meeting called to urge the government to make concessions, complained that 'years ago, all coolies doffed their caps and stood on one side; now they don't . . .'. Yet he admitted in the same speech that 'we need the Chinese'. Russell, as Registrar-General, was most competent and won the esteem of the Chinese community before he was raised to the bench in 1888 as Chief Justice of the Supreme Court. In 1888 the Registrar-General was given powers over processions, theatres, registration and watchmen; at the same time, the special powers granted him by an ordinance of 1858 as Protector of the Chinese, were repealed since they had never been used.

One difficulty arose over the proposed introduction of the British practice of registering births, marriages and deaths, which came up in the discussion of the health legislation required by the Chadwick Report. Lack of registration made it impossible to secure statistics of Chinese deaths except in the Tung Wah Hospital and the French and Italian Convents where European doctors were available. Ayres had suggested in 1892 a scheme of Chinese medical practitioners working in

free government dispensaries, and thought that the licentiates
of the Hong Kong Medical College could be used to secure the
necessary information. The Registrar-General thought that the
Chinese would object to any enquiry into the cause of death
because of the prejudice against Western medicine, the strength
of which was revealed by the absurd rumours over the plague
remedies alleged to have been employed by European doctors.
There was a similar rumour over the Tai Tam tunnel scheme in
1886. In 1891 there had been 4,075 deaths of Chinese, of which
over sixty-three per cent were without any certificate as to cause.
In 1896 the marriage law was amended to allow of civil marriage
before the Registrar-General, if monogamous; before that one
of the parties had to be a Christian. At the same time the law
regarding the registration of births and deaths was tightened;
particulars of the birth of a child admitted to public or charitable institutions were to be given and authority was required
for the removal of a body. Robinson felt that was as far as he
could go, consistent with the traditional British policy of respect
for local custom.

Since Hennessy's governorship, many Chinese wished to
acquire British nationality. No easy procedure then existed, and
naturalization could be granted only by private act of parliament. The practice grew up beginning with Dr. E. J. Eitel in
1880, of proceeding by local ordinance which conferred British
nationality only in the colony. From 1880 to 1900, fifty-three
such ordinances were passed, and of these only three related
to persons not bearing Chinese names.

The Tung Wah Hospital remained the most important
Chinese charitable institution. Marsh complained in March
1882 that its committee acted as a kind of tribunal to which
Chinese addressed petitions and stated their grievances and
that it dealt directly with Canton officials and with the Japanese
government. Lord Kimberley urged caution in the process of
recalling it to its true charitable function. In August 1883, the
Tung Wah Committee sent a deputation asking for stronger
action against gambling; it also wanted an ordinance by which
married women running away from their husbands should be
declared guilty of a criminal offence, and it had to be told that
it was impossible to pass such a law restricting private liberty;
this in any case could not be done because of the doctrine of

repugnancy by which no law could be passed by a colonial legislature repugnant to the law of England. In the spring of 1886, the Tung Wah directors collected for the Kwangtung Province flood victims and were ordered by the Canton officials to hand over $31,000. They refused and complained to Marsh that their families were threatened; the Chinese provincial treasurer was thereupon warned not to demand any money from the Tung Wah. The plague epidemic faced the Tung Wah with its greatest test, from which, as has already been described, it barely survived. (See page 219.)

An important charitable institution, the Po Leung Kuk, came into existence during this period to combat the evil of *mui tsai*, the purchase of girls for child servitude. This had already been the subject of enquiry in 1878, when Sir John Smale, the Chief Justice, had charged that *mui tsai* were slaves and that the system of selling children was contrary to British law. This practice was a recognized Chinese custom, but unfortunately a great deal of abuse had crept in. Young girls were bought for immoral purposes, for Hong Kong or for shipment abroad; parents were induced to give up control over their daughters by fraud and there was much kidnapping. To counter this, the leading Chinese had in 1880 formed a society, the Po Leung Kuk, for the protection of women and children against kidnapping. By helping to combat abuses they hoped to retain the custom. Hennessy keenly supported the society and offered it a valuable plot of land worth $150,000, but he left before fulfilling the promise. It was found impossible to incorporate the society as the Tung Wah had been incorporated, but rules were agreed upon with the government, and the Po Leung Kuk officially came into being in August 1882.

Russell, the Registrar-General, in 1883 produced a full report on child adoption, which had been demanded by Lord Kimberley, who expressed the home government's anxiety on this matter. Russell had reported that child adoption accompanied by money payment was common in China. A male child was adopted because of the necessity of having an heir, a female child for domestic servitude or for subsequent disposal. The deed of sale was more usually referred to as a 'deed of gift', the price being one dollar upwards. Kimberley had suggested the registration of all adopted children, and that child

9. Typhoon damage in 1874.
(Public Record Office C.O. 129/181/94)

10. Ng Choy, the first Chinese Member of
the Legislative Council.
(Ernest Benn Ltd.)

11. Hong Kong in 1908.
(From *Twentieth Century Impressions of Hong Kong* edited by Arnold Wright. Lloyds Greater Britain Publishing Co.)

12. Victoria from the Peak, looking east to North Point, 1955.
(Photograph by Paul Tay)

adoption should not depend on a money payment. Russell recommended that the powers of the Registrar-General should be increased and that he should work with the committee of the Po Leung Kuk to prevent abuses, and that all purchases of children should be void. Bowen agreed, and a Chinese deputation which asked to have the custom of *mui tsai* retained, was told that 'if they deliberately chose for their own purposes to dwell on British territory, they must, while entitled to the protection of the English laws, learn to obey those laws'.

In May 1885, a bill giving the Registrar-General the necessary powers was delayed because the Attorney-General thought the powers excessive, and the existing laws against kidnapping adequate. Lord Derby demanded action by ordinance in consultation with the Chinese and the Po Leung Kuk, and in April 1887 an Ordinance for the Better Protection of Women and Children was passed, and accepted by him. A Refuge for women and girls was now needed. In August 1890, the Chinese community presented a memorial against some clauses of this ordinance, on the ground that the clause protecting girls under the age of sixteen interfered with Chinese custom in the choice of a concubine who might be under that age and Ho Kai defended this view in the Legislative Council. Lord Knutsford ruled that the ordinance should remain as it was, and that though every discretion would be used in bringing prosecutions under the act, no undertaking would be given that Chinese taking concubines under that age would not be prosecuted.

It was now decided to build a Refuge for the Po Leung Kuk, and a two-storey building was erected in 1891, the upper floor being the Home and the lower floor comprising five shops, the rents of which it was hoped would pay the cost of the Home. The Po Leung Kuk wanted the rents of the shops as assistance towards running the Home, but the government insisted on the rents being paid into the treasury and was willing to help in the maintenance of the Home only if private subscriptions were not adequate. The Society then refused to take over the Home. Lord Knutsford replied that he wanted something done as soon as possible and criticized the muddle. In 1892, Lockhart, as Registrar-General, took a more generous view, and reported favourably on the work of the Po Leung Kuk, which now wanted to be incorporated by ordinance like the Tung Wah.

A bill was introduced to do this in April 1892, but there were so many questions that a committee of enquiry into the Po Leung Kuk was set up. This gave Whitehead, an influential unofficial member of the Legislative Council, a chance of opposing the Society as he had the Tung Wah. The Po Leung Kuk Ordinance was eventually passed in May 1893. The Society was governed by a board of directors with the Registrar-General as President, and a Chinese member of the Legislative Council chosen by the Governor as Vice-President. The Society agreed temporarily to occupy the space above the shops in New Street, and in 1895 they were sold for $8,600, having cost the government $7,900. The government gave $20,000 and Chinese subscribed $30,000 towards a new Home in the resumed Tai Ping Shan area, which was completed in November 1896. The Society continued to do good work; during the period 1888–95, 5,543 persons were helped in returning home, or found husbands, or adopted into satisfactory homes. The evil of child adoption in virtue of a money payment continued and was not declared illegal until the British Parliament passed a resolution to that effect in 1922 and the issue was not finally settled until the ordinances of 1928 and 1929.

Gambling continued, despite ordinances against it and the Chinese had presented a memorial in 1883 alleging that there had been a great increase and that much suicide resulted. Bowen set up a commission of enquiry, but little was done. In 1890 a question was asked in the Commons on the subject. Des Voeux was of the opinion that gambling should either be allowed or thoroughly suppressed, and stopped secret money payments as it encouraged informers. Gambling in Chinese private clubs was untouched by any legislation. Gambling had developed on a large scale in Chinese Kowloon, free launches and refreshments being provided, and Knutsford wanted an ordinance against this evil. In Hong Kong, gambling continued to flourish underground with police protection, and came into the open only when something went wrong with the bribery, for example in 1886, when the proprietors of gambling houses gave information against the police. An inspector and interpreter were hidden on the premises and watched fifty-three Chinese constables receive money. They were all prosecuted and fined, but on appeal the sentences were quashed on the technical point that the police regulations had not been proved. In the following year there was another commission of enquiry into gambling. In 1897 a raid on a gambling house led to the discovery of a list of names of police in receipt of hush money. As a result of enquiries two European inspectors and one European sergeant were suspended, and twenty-two Chinese detectives were banished. The 1887 Commission had led to no action against gambling, and few believed it was serious; the police scandal of 1897 came therefore as a shock, and led to many dismissals and a complete reorganization of the force.

Other social events of this period can be reviewed only briefly. An epidemic of smallpox became serious in 1887, and in February 1888 an ordinance for compulsory vaccination of children was passed. Ayres, also, in his annual report for 1887 criticized the hospital staff who worked long hours for low pay, and usually stayed a very short time; the wardmaster had been jailed for taking property belonging to patients. It was decided to try female nurses, and five nurses of St. Vincent de Paul were appointed, but they were not trained for special duties and there were not enough for night work. On Des Voeux' suggestion in 1890, English nurses were sent out and proved successful; in 1895 the recruitment of Chinese nurses was suggested.

The founding of the Hong Kong College of Medicine for Chinese in 1887 was a notable factor in extending Western influence. The College arose out of the question of free hospital treatment for the Chinese on Western lines, and out of the problem of providing death certificates. Dr. W. Young of the London Missionary Society began a free medical service for Chinese at the Society's chapel in Tai Ping Shan, and in 1882, he and Ho Kai, a Chinese who had just returned from England where he qualified as both barrister and doctor, formed a committee to advocate a free public hospital for Chinese. This scheme broke down. On the death of his English wife, Alice, Ho Kai decided to build a hospital as a memorial, to be handed over to the London Missionary Society, to be supported and managed by them as a free public hospital. At the same time he expressed the hope that a clinical school would be founded in connexion with the hospital, with a three-year course in Western medicine, the students being assisted by the Belilios

Scholarships. The scheme was dependent for teaching on the active support of European medical men in the colony, among whom was Dr. P. Manson, who had already conducted medical research into parasitology in Amoy; he and Drs. Young, Hartigan, Jordan and Cantlie offered their services.

At the laying of the foundation stone of the Alice Memorial Hospital in June 1886, it was announced that 'it is proposed to attach a school of European medicine and surgery for the instruction of Chinese students' to be 'similar to the one established at Takow in Formosa.' A similar medical school had already been set up in Tientsin. The London Missionary Society gave $14,000 towards the College, Dr. Chalmers of the Society collected $8,000, and Belilios gave $5,000 besides his scholarships, and the College came into being. The support of the local medical men had been essential, but tended to obscure the equally vital contribution of the London Missionary Society. The College was set up in 1887, with two students, one of whom was Sun Yat Sen. The doctors gave their services and the College remained a private institution; the government stood aloof and gave no official recognition or assistance, and though Robinson did put $2,000 for the College into the financial estimates for 1894 the grant was not made. In its constitution, the College followed Scottish precedents; it was controlled by an elected Rector and Court, and a Dean and Senate were responsible for the instruction; there was also an Advisory Council consisting of all teachers, officers, licentiates, benefactors and others associated with the work. It was centred in the Alice Memorial Hospital, where students resided and teaching was done, with some help later from the Nethersole Hospital. Fees were $60 a year, later reduced to $40, but there were scholarships founded by Belilios, and the government gave three to third-year students. Equipment was largely provided by the Tung Wah.

In 1891 the Anglican church was finally disestablished when the Colonial Chaplain, Rev. William Jennings, retired, and the cathedral was handed over to a Church Body who became responsible for the fabric and the salary of the cathedral chaplain. Des Voeux brought up the question of Sunday labour and suggested the reintroduction of a proclamation of 1844 forbidding Sunday labour on government work; this had been disregarded, but had not been repealed. The Surveyor-General objected that it would add ten per cent to the cost of all government work, and the proposal was dropped, but in 1891 an ordinance was passed against Sunday cargo-working, over the protests of the Chinese merchants, although its working was mitigated by exemption permits at a fee. The Queen's Jubilee, 1887, was marked by the usual processions, by the setting up of a Chinese Chamber of Commerce and by a Jubilee Memorial statue of the Queen, unveiled in 1896. In 1885, the draining of Happy Valley was completed and at the wish of the Legislative Council it was to be called Bowen Park, but the old name continued.

Relations with the Chinese government were smoothed by the settlement of the customs 'blockade' in 1886. Opposition to the appointment of a Chinese consul to reside in Hong Kong as suggested by Lord Derby in 1883 remained very strong. Bowen agreed that there was no valid reason to deny to China the right of consular representation, but thought that inconvenience might arise if the Chinese population looked to the Chinese consul and not to the English government. The proposal for a Chinese consul in Hong Kong was revived in 1891 and again aroused great opposition. Difficulty continued over the extradition clause in the Treaty of Tientsin, particularly as the British insisted on conducting an enquiry before handing over any criminal, and the refusal to hand over anyone against whom there was no prima facie evidence gave great offence to the Chinese. In 1886, eight uniformed Chinese landed and seized a man whom they charged with murder and piracy, though no demand for extradition had been made. The eight men were arrested and their prisoner freed. In 1886 Chinese officials seized a Chinese whom they wanted, on a British steamer, and again protests were made through the Foreign Office. In some cases, Chinese appealed to British courts against their extradition, and Des Voeux in 1887 suggested an alteration in the extradition arrangements since holding an enquiry involved the Canton authorities in costs of five to six thousand dollars for each case.

There were demands for opening China to a wider measure of trade. The Chamber of Commerce asked for the opening of the whole of the southern provinces to counteract French influence. In 1895 the West River was opened to shipping, but that concession was full of difficulty over customs arrangements.

Hennessy had popularized the colony among the Chinese and the population showed great increase over this period in spite of the plagues of 1894 and following years, and in spite of the restrictions on emigration which checked the flow. The first estimate of population made in the period in 1886, showed a total of 181,432, of which 10,142 were British and foreign, and 171,290 Chinese; by 1898 the total was 254,400, of which 15,190 were British and foreign and 239,210 Chinese. The fifty per cent increase in the former between 1895 and 1898 was due in part to the increase in the garrison, owing to the growing international tension. The Portuguese were slow to adopt British nationality; their number was given in 1897 as 2,263, of which only 51 claimed to be British, yet 1,214 were born in the colony and 931 in Macao. The shifting character of the population was equally marked. In 1887 Marsh reported that the Chinese were flocking to the colony and 'hundreds sleep in the streets' because the $2.50 a month they could earn in Hong Kong was more than they could get in their village.

Revenue and expenditure showed a comparable expansion though, as Bowen pointed out, taxation in the colony was of the lightest, amounting in 1886 to no more than $5.72, or £1 0s. 10d. per head per annum. This expansion was due partly to the government undertaking additional revenue-producing services, for example the post offices, lighthouses for which light dues were charged, and the great praya scheme. Expansion of the population meant more building, and more rates, land rents and premiums on sales. Revenue increased from $1,173,071 in 1884 to $2,025,302 in 1891 and to $2,918,159 in 1898. Revenue from the opium farm increased from $111,034 in 1884 to $447,600 in 1890 and then decreased to $357,666 in 1898, owing to the recommendations of the Opium Commission. Proceeds from stamps more than doubled during the period and the proceeds from rates rose from $263,988 in 1884 to $466,619 in 1898. In the latter part of this period much revenue was secured from the supply of subsidiary coins which were sent into China in large amounts, and in 1898 this source alone produced $148,044. Expenditure rose from

$1,595,398 in 1884 to $2,449,086 in 1891 and to $2,841,805 in 1898. This was due to debt interest, to new departments like the Sanitary Department, to the increase of the cost of the military contribution, to seventeen and a half per cent of revenue and also to the fall in the value of the dollar. The military contribution rose from $111,034 in 1884 to $519,274 in 1898.

The economic life of the colony was adversely affected by the political tension resulting from fear of Russian designs, from the Sino-French War of 1884–85, the Sino-Japanese War of 1894–95, the rivalry of the European powers, and the Boxer anti-European movement in 1900. There was also tension in Korea, Siam and the Philippines. Early in the period there was a trade recession following the boom in Hong Kong of 1881, and a more serious recession during the 1890's, partly due to the speculation in mines of 1889. The colony retained its position as a great commercial port, and in 1884 Bowen called it the greatest port of the Empire next to London and Liverpool. No statistics of trade are available. A proposal was made in 1892 by Lord Knutsford that an imports and exports valuation should be made, but Robinson replied that the Chamber of Commerce and local opinion were against it because of cost and of the fear that the junk trade would be frightened away, and he pointed out that the trade was largely transit trade and not real colonial imports and exports.

A feature of this period was the gradual decline of British trade with China relative to China's total overseas trade, and in particular Chinese exports to Britain declined. Yet the colony handled a greater proportion of China's trade. In 1890 55 per cent of China's imports and 37 per cent of her exports passed through the colony, and in 1900 the corresponding figures were 42 per cent and 40 per cent. This meant that the colony's entrepôt trade was broadening to include greater trade from Europe and America and was less dependent on Great Britain. The entrepôt services were now becoming more international, and this tendency continued into the pre-war and inter-war years. This tendency reflected the expanding economic interests of Germany, Russia, France, northern European countries and Japan in the Far East. British trade with China, if the British Empire is included, was still the most important of any single country, but the old British economic domination was passing.

Hong Kong had to adapt itself to the new balance of economic forces.

The returns of shipping using the port give some indication of over-all trade. In 1883 6,785 ships of 6,882,381 tons entered and left, of which 74 per cent were British; in 1891 8,707 ships, 70 per cent British, of 10,279,943 tons entered and left, and in 1898 11,058 ships, 66 per cent British, of 13,252,733 tons. These figures refer to ships engaged in foreign trade. Junk trade which engaged in the coastal distributive trade, showed no spectacular increase. Foreign-going junk trade amounted to 24,258 arrivals of 1,851,239 tons in 1883 and 29,466 arrivals of 1,814,281 tons in 1898. The total arrivals in these years were 27,657 of 5,301,662 tons in 1883, and 39,815 of 8,648,274 tons in 1898; that is, foreign ocean-going shipping more than doubled in this period, but the junk trade remained fairly stationary. The explanation usually offered was the ring of customs stations around the colony, permitted by the 1886 agreement. In 1884 the junk tonnage was 49 per cent of the European tonnage arriving, but in 1897 it was only 28 per cent. The Chinese customs returns showed an increase in the junk tonnage using the colony, of 30·37 per cent between 1887 and 1897. Rumsey, the Harbour-master, in a long report on the junk trade in his 1898 Annual Report, said that many junks came and went without trace, as he had only two junk inspectors. He also showed that river steamers and steam launches were competing more successfully. In 1893, 74 per cent of the cargo of the ships calling was discharged and 36 per cent [sic] was in transit. In 1897, 59 per cent was discharged and 42 per cent [sic] in transit. This appears to show that the volume of junk trade was stationary because more ships were shipping cargoes direct. In 1893 junks exported 845,177 tons of merchandise, or 31 per cent of the imports, and in 1897, 684,320 tons or 26·3 per cent of import cargoes. Certainly the junk trade was hit by the recession of the early 1890's and again by the plague in 1894 and 1896. Rumsey thought the junk trade was closely related to the rice trade, and he gave a graph in the 1898 Report showing a close correspondence. The junk trade was probably confined to certain trades predominantly Chinese, and the increased shipping found other channels of distribution. The Chinese gave the junk trade with China as 33,441,526 taels in 1888, and

39,991,611 taels in 1897, an increase of 19 per cent in ten years. The complaints against the Chinese customs as the great hindrance to trade does not seem justified.

In 1898 the chief imports were calculated by Rumsey to be coal, 817,967 tons; cottons, 36,611 tons; flour, 103,544 tons; kerosene, 122,522 tons; rice, 747,355 tons; sugar, 267,422 tons and timber, 46,599 tons. Junks exported kerosene to the amount of 23,931 tons; rice, 284,747 tons; and general commodities 465,391 tons. These figures were all very tentative and gave no account of the direction of the trade, and, as Rumsey admitted in his 1898 Report, they 'depended on the gratuitous information compiled together without any special staff or machinery'. He was criticized by the Chamber of Commerce for making these attempts to correlate reports on shipping with trade, which he began in 1893. The Chamber, in pointing out some errors, questioned if the returns were of any value; and Rumsey had little co-operation from the commercial community.

A very important trade was the trade in Chinese passengers. For the years from 1883 to 1898 inclusive, 991,568 emigrated from Hong Kong to ports other than China and Japan, chiefly to North America, Australia, and after 1888, to the Straits. The number was 57,438 in 1883, and gradually increased to 96,195 in 1888, then fell to almost half because of restrictive policies in America and Australia, and gradually rose to 60,432 in 1898, the intervening figures varying according to the plague. Over the same sixteen years, immigrants from overseas to Hong Kong totalled 1,570,332, steadily rising from 73,767 in 1884 to 105,441 in 1898, the maximum being 119,468 in 1896. They brought each year considerable treasure, up to ten million dollars a year and even more.

There was, in addition, a great movement of people in and out of Hong Kong quite apart from these migrants who were registered under the Chinese Passengers' Act. In 1887, for example, 629,532 came from Chinese and Japanese ports, and 617,893 left for them; 57,675 arrived from Macao and 54,898 went there. In 1898 the movement in and out of the harbour was given as follows; arrivals and departures in British ships 130,176 and 139,574; in foreign ships, 65,820 and 62,665; in river steamers, 579,012 and 565,627, and in ocean junks 124,909 and 128,326; and 1898 was not an abnormal year.

The proportion of British ships using the port declined. In 1891 German shipping amounted to more than all the rest of the non-British ships put together, and was thirty per cent of the British figure. During the Sino-Japanese War of 1894–95 Chinese ships were transferred to British and German flags. After 1896 the Japanese increase was remarkable, 1898 showing for them an increase of half a million tons upon the previous year.

The increased shipping led to the demand for an additional lighthouse on Gap Rock, and in 1886 Sir Robert Hart agreed that the colony should pay one-third of the cost. There was so much delay over the terms, that the colony offered to pay the whole of the cost estimated at $90,000. The Chinese were against any cession of the rock and insisted on its control by the Kowloon customs commissioner, who was to pay $7,500 towards the cost, and $750 a year for the upkeep. Fleming, the acting Governor, laid the foundation stone on the 1 September 1890; the cost to the colony eventually came to $150,000.

The opium trade was still important, providing a sixth of the colony's revenue in 1893. After the agreement with China ending the customs 'blockade', the Import and Export Department provided an annual return of the trade. Hennessy had been very much against the opium trade, and when he returned to Britain he alleged in a public speech that the opium trade in Hong Kong was worth one million pounds a month, besides breeding a criminal class engaged in smuggling. This was denied by the Chamber of Commerce, who put the value of the opium handled by the colony at £200,000 a month, and the whole China opium trade at £10 million a year, and denied that Hong Kong was the centre of opium smuggling. In 1883 for a short period, the opium farm was given up, and the sale of opium in the colony was regulated by licences, but the revenue fell off, partly because a duty of $2.25 a ball on prepared opium was driving the boiling trade to the Straits. In 1885 the system was dropped and the farm was reintroduced and let for one year at $159,000; and the following year it was sold to a Singapore syndicate for $182,400 a year for three years, to break the Hong Kong monopoly.

The agreement with China ending the 'blockade' provided for control of armed frontier smuggling and also the control of the movement of all opium for the purpose of supplying the Chinese customs with information. In 1887 an Opium Ordinance was passed to implement this agreement. In that year, by the additional article under the Chefoo Convention, the Chinese secured the full control over the import of opium, and the arrangement of the Treaty of Tientsin which placed the opium duty on a treaty basis was dropped. Smuggling continued and collisions occurred on the frontier between Chinese customs and armed bands of smugglers, and the farmer complained that he was losing. In 1891 came the first serious attempt to limit the trade in opium. In Britain, the Society for the Suppression of the Opium Trade secured the passing of a resolution in Parliament condemning the trade, and later, the setting up of a commission of enquiry into it. In October 1891, Lord Knutsford, as a consequence of the resolution, asked Robinson to consider directly taking over the control of opium by the Hong Kong government. He thought that only by abolishing the farm and getting direct control could the evil be attacked, because it was to the advantage of the farmer to sell as much as he could; Knutsford suggested direct control with a view to restriction, by raising the price and reducing the number of divans. Robinson opposed the abolition of the farming system, as he thought this would lead to an increase of consumption; he criticized the views of the anti-opium society, and said the farmer restricted the consumption of opium by charging high prices and checking smuggling.

In supplying evidence to the Royal Commission on Opium, Robinson estimated consumption in Hong Kong at three chests a day, and the farmer was allowed to boil a maximum of 1,800 chests a year. Ayres, the Colonial Surgeon, supported the opium trade, while the farmer, curiously enough, gave evidence against opium. Estimates of the number of smokers in the colony varied from ten per cent to seventy per cent of the Chinese population and so were valueless. The limitation in the sales of opium affected trade and revenue. The proceeds of the opium farm fell from $447,600 in 1890 to $357,666 in 1898. The trade in opium fell; in 1889, 67,429 chests were imported, 61,808 exported and 12,306 chests were in transit but handled by the colony. In 1898 the corresponding figures were, 39,292; 37,828, and 15,482. Lord Knutsford had at least secured a diminution. One of the main hindrances to trade was the depreciation in the value of the dollar. In December 1883 the sterling rate for the dollar was 3s. 8¾d., in 1891 3s. 1d., and in 1898 1s. 11½d. This created difficulty for importers and militated against English trade. The expansion of the population tended to create currency shortages, and in 1884 Bowen wrote home regretting that the mint had been abandoned and suggested that the Hongkong and Shanghai Banking Corporation should increase its issue of notes with full metallic backing. Lord Derby, in April 1885, replied by proposing that the Hong Kong government should issue its own dollar notes, but Bowen thought it better to expand the subsidiary coinage. Des Voeux in 1890 began to order large amounts of subsidiary coinage to meet needs. Soon after Robinson arrived the fall in silver was more serious. A British dollar, minted in England, was recommended by a currency committee in 1894 and was introduced in 1895; and after much discussion, the proposal to introduce the Japanese yen as legal tender was rejected. Mexican dollars were in circulation as they had always been. In 1897 Robinson announced that he would adopt the plan of meeting currency requirements by importing subsidiary coinage from England in large amounts and at considerable profit.

Bank note issues helped. In 1883 the circulation by the banks averaged $5,099,661, in 1893 it was $6,344,454. In 1886 coin in circulation was $1,421,487 of dollars and half dollars of the old Hong Kong mint, and $1,983,811 of subsidiary coinage of twenty, ten and five cent silver pieces, and one cent pieces and cash in bronze. In 1893 the coin in circulation was $9,720,125. The Oriental Bank failed in 1884, but the government had been warned and all official deposits had been withdrawn. The Hongkong and Shanghai Banking Corporation had trouble in Manila over its status there as an agency and not a branch, and the result was that an ordinance was passed allowing the Bank to establish branches anywhere. The Bank played a notable part in providing finance for the Chinese government, and between 1874 and 1898 it negotiated nine such loans totalling £13,288,656. In 1896 and 1898 the Bank, in association with a German Bank, negotiated two loans of

£16 million each with the Chinese government. Jardine, Matheson & Co. made one official loan to the Chinese government of one million taels (at three taels to the pound sterling). In 1884 a savings bank was established in connection with The Hongkong and Shanghai Banking Corporation.

Local industries and manufacturers were given a fillip by the depreciation of the dollar. Shipping was the basis of local industry as it was of commerce. Ships chandlery, rope making, docks and ship-building all developed. In 1893, for example, forty-two steam launches totalling 2,605 tons were built. Robinson first set out deliberately to encourage local industry, which he did in his first speech to the Legislative Council. Robinson argued that the colony should be less dependent on trade, and would be more independent if it developed its own industries. He argued partly from the fall in the dollar which made imports more costly. In his farewell speech to the Legislative Council on 25 October 1897, he referred to the developments which had taken place; two large kerosene oil depots, feather dressing, match factories, soap, coal, briquette and rattan works, extension of the docks, sugar refineries and cement works were all 'standing monuments of that development'. Green Island cement works moved from Macao in 1897, and in the same year with Robinson's encouragement, the first company for cotton spinning was formed.

Other achievements were the opening of the Peak Tramway, called the Upper Level Tramway, in 1888. In 1890 street lighting by electricity brought a reproof from the Secretary of State that this should not have been done without his prior saction. One great beneficial reform came in 1898, the 'penny' post.

One further reform of the greatest significance came in May 1898 recalling the old dispute about land. Chamberlain ordered that all new leases of land should be for 75 years and not 999 years. Des Voeux had earlier tried a scheme for the commutation of premiums on land by an increase in the annual rent, but the experiment was not supported. The new short leases aroused great protest, but the only concession Chamberlain agreed to make was to make them renewable for one term.

s

CHAPTER XXII

THE NEW TERRITORIES

*'It was assumed that the knowledge of the just treatment of
the Chinese inhabitants of Hong Kong and British Kowloon
would induce the population of the leased area to accept the
jurisdiction of Great Britain with equanimity if not with
pleasure.'*

Sir Henry Blake to the Legislative Council,

11 October 1899.

SIR WILLIAM ROBINSON left for home in January 1898; his
successor, Sir Henry Blake, arrived in the following November,
and in the interval Major-General Black administered the
government. Blake's most important task was to take over the
new territory leased by China to Great Britain in June 1898,
and still called the New Territories. The extension of the
colony's boundaries took its origin in the fear of Russian
aggrandizement in the Far East, and of the French, who after
their acquisition of Tongking following the Sino-French War
of 1884–85, threatened to control China's southern provinces.
It also arose from the altered balance of power in the Far East
as a result of the Franco-Russian alliance of 1893, and the
claims of Germany for influence in the Far East. Rivalry
between the great powers was thus intensified.

The situation had long been foreseen, and demands for the
extension of the boundaries of the colony to meet possible attack
by a European power had been made from time to time. In
November 1884 Bowen reported that the Major-General,
Sargent, proposed to the War Office to acquire all Kowloon
Peninsula, to the summit of the range of hills to the north,
together with Lamma and some smaller islands. Bowen had not
been consulted and was against the plan. The Chinese were
engaged in hostilities with the French, and Bowen thought it
might lead to 'a sort of scramble for their territory', and in any
case the boundary along the high ridge would be difficult to
defend. The next general, Cameron, proposed in 1886 that the
small promontory on the Chinese side of Lyemun Channel

should be ceded. The Colonial Defence Committee in London rejected these schemes since they considered the defence of the colony entirely 'from the point of view of an attack by a European Power'. So little danger was thought to come from China, that the Colonial Defence Committee did not proceed with the planned extensive fortifications in the British part of Kowloon.

In 1895 the *Hong Kong Telegraph* urged an extension of boundaries for defence, but the Colonial Office advised that this was not a reputable paper and could be ignored. In September 1895 the Chamber of Commerce urged the extension of the boundary and the opening up of the West River, and the unofficial members of the Legislative Council strongly supported these representations. Robinson endorsed them in a vaguely phrased telegram sent in September 1895. The Foreign Office commented: 'Sir William Robinson seems a somewhat impulsive gentleman,' and added that Sir Neville O'Connor, Minister at Peking, had the matter of the boundary in hand. The Colonial Office commented, 'Can he so far have lost his head that he wants to annex Canton?'

The capture of Manila in May 1898 by the United States navy operating from Mirs Bay close to the colony, brought renewed nervousness regarding defence, and the Chamber of Commerce again urged that security demanded an extension of the boundary. At home, the China Association and the Navy League made similar demands. The main factor was the pressure of events following the Treaty of Shimonoseki of 1895, which ended the Sino-Japanese War. Intervention by the three powers, Russia, France and Germany, deprived Japan of some of the fruits of victory. Russia secured valuable railway concessions in Manchuria, and this, renewing Russian diplomatic initiative in the Far East, brought increased international tension. Germany occupied Kiaochow in November 1897 and in March secured the lease for 99 years. Russia followed with a similar occupation of Port Arthur. Great Britain was forced to abandon her traditional liberal open-door policy and keep pace by securing the lease of Weihaiwei, which had been in Japanese occupation, in April 1898. In this same month, France secured the lease of Kwangchowan on the Kwangtung coast, the right of building a railway from Tongking to Yunnan and other concessions. To meet this threat to British interests in South

China, the extension of the colony's boundary was claimed. In June 1898, the New Territories were leased for 99 years dating from 1 July 1898. This new acquisition formed a sort of rectangle extending from a line joining Deep Bay and Mirs Bay in the north, to Lamma Island in the south, and added 355 square miles to the colony.

News of the cession came on 11 June 1898, and caused great jubilation in the colony, but when *The Times* summarized the terms there was disappointment over the Kowloon City reservation. This stated that 'within the City of Kowloon, the Chinese officers now stationed there shall continue to exercise jurisdiction except so far as may be inconsistent with the military requirements for the defence of Hong Kong'. The precise northern frontier and the continued operation of the Chinese customs stations were left for further negotiation. The question of the administration of the leased territory had also to be decided. It was some time before the territory could be taken over and it was decided to do nothing while the American fleet remained in Mirs Bay. Lack of co-operation between the Foreign Office and the Colonial Office led to some misunderstanding by the Chinese officials over the administration of the leased area, and in July 1898 the Viceroy at Canton, on his own authority, issued regulations regarding the leased territory under the mistaken idea that Chinese authority would still be maintained there. Until the outstanding questions could be negotiated, there had to be some delay in the actual takeover. This delay produced a serious problem. Sir Henry Blake arrived on 25 November 1898, and a month later he sent a telegram home complaining that Hong Kong Chinese were buying up land cheaply in the leased area by spreading rumours that the British would seize all the land there. Lockhart, Colonial Secretary and Registrar-General, had been sent into the New Territories to report on the area, and he reported in October 1898 that there were conflicting accounts of the disposition of the inhabitants. As a result, Black suggested a separate administration for the New Territories under Lockhart, but Chamberlain ruled that it should be joined to the colony for administrative purposes.

Lockhart and Wong Tsun Shin[1] were appointed negotiators to fix the northern boundary. Wong agreed to the Shum Chun

[1] Huang Tsun-hsin, in Mandarin.

river line, but objected to the British claims to Shum Chun itself across the river and to Shataukok on Mirs Bay. On these two claims there was delay while reference was made to Peking, and it was not until 14 March 1899 that the boundary was settled. The claim to Shum Chun was renounced, and at Shataukok a compromise placed the boundary along the middle of the main street. There was much negotiation over the continued operation of the Chinese customs in the leased area, since the agreement of 1886 ending the customs 'blockade' by which all movement of opium was reported to Chinese customs officials in Chinese Kowloon, was now threatened. At the same time there was the usual hostility to any customs stations on British territory. In September 1898 Black reported that Ho Kai and Wei Yuk, the Chinese unofficial members of the Legislative Council, had found Chinese opinion in Hong Kong was against Chinese customs being allowed to operate in the leased territory. There was also much discussion over Kowloon City and the Chinese military garrison there.

On 3 March 1899 Chamberlain telegraphed asking when the New Territories would be taken over, and Blake replied that this would be as soon as the northern boundary was fixed. This was done on 14 March, and the Governor decided to proceed to the occupation without waiting for the other points in dispute to be settled. Unfortunately opposition grew in the leased area. On 1 April 1899 Blake reported that British parties were threatened with death and that placards had appeared calling on the people to arm against the British. Blake hurried to Canton and induced the Viceroy to disavow the placards and guarantee protection to British parties in the New Territories, who were there to make arrangements to take over the administration from the Chinese. He threatened that if protection were not given by the following Wednesday, 5 April, he would take over the following day.

The trouble had occurred when May, Captain Superintendent of Police, had begun erecting a temporary police station at Taipo. This affected *fung shui* or Chinese prejudices regarding building sites in the place, and the workmen were stopped. May insisted on the work proceeding as a matter of principle, and then agreed to move to another site; but here work was again impeded. May returned to the island, leaving a small armed guard of two Indian and two Chinese police to guard the matsheds. The Governor decided that armed parties should not be kept in the new territory, and when May was sent with an escort of five Chinese soldiers and some unarmed police to withdraw them, he was fired on. He sent a message to say that he would hold the matsheds until dawn. Blake sent two hundred men to protect him, but on arrival they found that May and his men had retreated over the hills. May found that villagers were being mobilized. It was then decided in Executive Council to take over on 17 April 1899 and a proclamation to that effect was issued on the 7th. In response to representations, the Viceroy promised to send six hundred troops to preserve order. On 10 April the Viceroy wrote declining to hand over the leased territory because Chinese customs officials had been told to leave, though there had been no agreement on this. Blake replied that he would hoist the flag at Taipo at 1.00 p.m. on 17 April.

Lockhart went to Taipo on 14 April, and was warned by the elders that there were rowdies about, and that the matsheds needed protection. The result was that on the next day Blake sent twenty-five police and a company of the Hong Kong regiment to prepare for the take-over ceremony. They arrived to find the matsheds in ruins and came back reporting troops on the hills with prepared gun emplacements. On the 16th Blake sent troops to Taipo by the warship *Fame*, which opened fire to cover the landing, and the hills around Taipo were occupied. The General, Gascoigne, and Lockhart arrived, the flag was raised and the proclamation read. The take-over was thus hurriedly effected one day before the date announced.

Chinese opposition was due partly to official opposition from the Viceroy, who objected to the handing over before full agreement on the collection of the customs duties had been reached. Wong, who was deputed to be the official representative of the Chinese government at the transfer, attempted to raise again with Blake the question of the continued operation of the Chinese customs stations. Major Fung, the Chinese military commander, also later admitted that he had been told by the Viceroy not to interfere with the people's plans. Chamberlain had agreed on 12 April to allow the customs stations to remain, provided arrangements were made to remove them by October. The opposition appeared to be fairly spontaneous, though the Taipo elders, in appealing for clemency on 15 April, after burning the matsheds, admitted they had been led astray by designing people.

Having assumed control of the leased area, Blake ordered the withdrawal of all Chinese troops, including those of the Kowloon City Garrison, and British troops were ordered to advance to secure the occupation of the whole territory. During the next three days there was desultory fighting as the troops moved to the west. A body of 2,600 men was driven from Kam Tin and six guns were captured at Uen Long. Villages began to surrender, and on 26 April Blake was able to report that all resistance was at an end.

Blake held the Viceroy entirely responsible for the fighting, and demanded reparation in the form of an extended boundary to include Shum Chun, that the area should be ceded and not leased, and he asked for the Viceroy's recall. Lockhart thought the gentry of the leased territory were to blame and urged banishment and confiscation of their property, but regarding the local inhabitants, Blake thought it better to 'pass a sponge over the events'. Chamberlain protested to the Foreign Office about the Chinese lack of faith, but urged that any occupation of Shum Chun should be only temporary, without bloodshed, and only if the general were satisfied he could hold it. On 16 May Kowloon City and Shum Chun were occupied by British forces. The Viceroy sent an official to enquire why they had been occupied, but Blake refused to see anyone except the Viceroy in person.

The main problem of the take-over was not military but administrative. A land syndicate of Chinese among whom it was suspected Ho Kai was one, had bought land at a fraction of its value by spreading the rumour that the British would seize all land. Blake threatened to restore this property, but the land problem proved too baffling for him to carry out his threat.

The leased territory was incorporated for administrative purposes into the colony, except that certain Hong Kong ordinances were not to be applied. A local Communities Ordinance gave power to create district and sub-district courts with limited civil and criminal jurisdiction and allowed a levy on any area if crime were prevalent there. As a temporary measure, the Executive Council was empowered to collect revenue for one year. Blake wanted May to be Magistrate for the territory, but Chamberlain refused, and he also refused to appoint a political officer for the Shum Chun area.

In August the Governor toured the New Territories, to see the nine district and forty-seven sub-district committees at work and address their members. They were to be responsible for security and order and the regulation of affairs in the villages. He promised to respect Chinese usages, but all punishment was to be in accordance with law, and no money was to be collected except authorized rates and taxes. All occupiers of land had to register their holdings. Land rent was to continue, now payable as Crown rent, but all customs duties and other monopolistic dues were to be abolished. He promised protection for all, though he admitted that conditions were unsettled and that there was much armed robbery. He reported to Chamberlain that the people had been badly governed, the officials had 'squeezed' the people, and that clan fights were used to settle disputes. A further drawback was that malaria was common. He reported that the Shum Chun area, which had been occupied by the military, was without civil government, and suffered from robberies and murders, and decent people were terrorized. He asked that the question of compensation for the events at the take-over should be decided soon. Even in the leased area, robberies and piracies along the inlets forced Blake to increase the police and double the water-police crews, and for the year he estimated police expenditure alone at $146,093. In November, Blake was ordered to withdraw from Shum Chun, and though he had advocated that some compensation should be paid before withdrawal, the home government decided against all claims for compensation for the events of April. It was some time before the administration was set up in the New Territories. Lockhart returned to his duties as Colonial Secretary and Registrar-General, leaving three government cadet officers in charge, but he remained closely associated with the administration. The local courts were not proceeded with, and the local committees were left without chairmen. Measures of economic betterment were immediately discussed; Ford, of the Botanical Gardens Department, was asked to experiment with vine and camphor culture, and in improving the sugar-cane and mulberry. Jardine, Matheson asked for the concession of all coal in the New Territories, after lignite had been found at Deep Bay.

The inhabitants proved to be suspicious and unco-operative, and in January 1900 an ordinance was passed giving the government special powers to summon Chinese to the Registrar-General's office for questioning. There was much protest over these exceptional powers, and Chamberlain agreed only if they were limited to two years. The ordinance had been passed because of the refusal of village elders to attend when it was wished to consult them about land holdings. In March 1900 a land court was set up to deal with disputed claims to land to avoid the expensive procedure of the ordinary courts; it was expected to deal with some 5,000 cases. Two prominent lawyers, Pollock and Gompertz, were appointed members, with a staff of officials. In the meantime, a corps of surveyors arrived from India to carry out a survey of the whole area, and make a record of all the holdings claimed. The home government had ruled that the examination of claims to land was not to be too technical and that occupation and improvement were to be favourably considered. The land court found a mass of anomalies; many claimed large tracts though they had never paid any rent to Chinese officials; many were found to be paying an annual tax to certain well-to-do families under the impression that these sums were being accounted for to the district treasury, and these families were found to have title to very little areas or no title at all. Often to avoid registration fees and avoid all attention, land had been bought and sold using unregistered deeds, the vendor continuing to pay the tax. The land court found that one claim in twenty was disputed, but a great deal of work was necessary to get all claims carefully marked on the map. All unclaimed land was held by the Crown for disposal.

The question of Kowloon City was discussed with Li Hung-chang, Viceroy of Kwantung and Kwangsi Provinces, when he passed through the colony in July 1900. A Colonial Office official minuted on this, 'We have definitely decided not to allow the City to fall under Chinese jurisdiction, and have told the Chinese government so, and have passed an order in council including it in the New Territory, and the matter is at an end.' The Foreign Office arrangement of leaving Kowloon City as it was, was dropped, but Chinese opinion in Kwangtung Province continued to regard it as not forming part of the lease.

The work of the land court set up in 1900 was completed in 1904, by which date it had marked out 354,277 lots and had determined their ownership at a cost of $143,615. The New Territories were for some years a heavy financial burden; there was a demand that this cost should be met by a loan, but Chamberlain refused his consent. Settling the land problems, policing and building roads were major tasks, and expenditure was much in excess of the estimates. The detailed survey took some years, and showed all existing maps to be inaccurate. In June 1900, the boundary had to be adjusted because the meridian 113 degrees 59 minutes 9·7 seconds which formed the western boundary was found not to cut the Chinese coast at the expected point. Up to 30 June 1901 the total revenue collected was only $41,140, as against expenditure up to that date of $736,571.

The military claimed land opposite the Lyemun Passage and the navy asked that the area adjoining this should be reserved, but neither project was proceeded with. Defence of the colony was thought of in terms of the balance of power, and in the spring of 1900 when there was a danger of an uprising in Canton against the Manchus, Blake was ordered from home not to resist the passage of Chinese government troops through the New Territories.

It had been Blake's aim in administering the leased area that 'existing village organizations should be maintained and utilised.' In practice it was found that the village elders lacked authority, since appeal could be made to one of the resident British officials. The pattern of administration of the leased area was only slowly evolved. At first the main problems were law and order and the land revenue. There were three chief officials; the chief police officer, an assistant superintendent, combined his duties with those of police magistrate and was also responsible for collecting the revenue. Two assistant land officers dealt with land questions, one in the Kowloon area and in the islands and the other in the rest of the mainland area, which was called the northern district. In 1907, the police superintendent became known as the District Officer, Northern District, but he still remained responsible to different heads of departments in respect of his different functions. In 1909, the assistant Land Officer was placed under the District Officer with the title of Assistant District Officer. In 1910 a new department was created, the District Office. In February 1910, the assistant Land Officer, Southern District, became assistant District Officer and in July of that year became a police magistrate, and had the same powers as the District Officer, Northern District, except control of the police. In 1913 he became District Officer, Southern District, and part of the northern district as far as Tsuen Wan was added to his district. This organization remained in being until the Second World War. Committees of elders remained in being and proved useful, but up to that date it was not found possible to give them the authority which Blake had envisaged.

CHAPTER XXIII

HONG KONG IN THE
EARLY TWENTIETH CENTURY, 1898–1918

'Hong Kong cannot thrive in isolation.'
Lord Lugard.

THE period 1898 to 1918 was one of steady economic and administrative development, interrupted only by the Great War of 1914–18. There were four governors: Sir Henry Blake left on retirement in November 1903 after an administration described by Chamberlain as marked by 'ability, energy and success'; he died in 1918. His successor, Sir Matthew Nathan, remained in the colony for a short period only, July 1904 to April 1907, before going to Natal as Governor and thence on to a career of some distinction in the Civil Service. He was followed by Sir Frederick Lugard, July 1907 to March 1912, for whom this stay in Hong Kong was but a brief interlude in a brilliant African career. Sir Francis Henry May, July 1912 to February 1919, was the first Hong Kong cadet to become

Governor of the colony; and was perhaps the dominating figure of these years. He became Colonial Secretary in 1902 and was promoted to the governorship of the Fiji Islands, but relinquished the post after a few months to return to Hong Kong. It was written of him in 1919: 'He served the colony wholeheartedly . . . and its ever-increasing beauty and prosperity stand as a monument in record of his work.' He had served the colony, except for the few months in Fiji, for thirty-eight years, and died within three years of retirement.

There was little constitutional development and the additional representation secured as a result of the 1894 petition was widely accepted as reasonable. A short-lived Constitutional Reform Association in 1917 served mainly to reveal the absence of any widespread demand for reform. More persistent was the demand that the Sanitary Board should ripen into a full Municipal Council, on which subject a pamphlet appeared in 1901. The Sanitary Board had almost disappeared under Robinson, who wanted its functions taken over by the government. The Chamber of Commerce organized a plebiscite on the constitution of the Board with the result that in 1901 it was reconstituted with four officials and six unofficials, as it had been in 1887. The Principal Civil Medical Officer became president of the Board and was made responsible for all sanitary matters directly to the government, and the Board's functions became purely advisory. A Commission of Enquiry in 1907 condemned this lack of direct responsibility and in the following year the Board, shorn of its duties regarding the Buildings Ordinances, was again reconstituted with a cadet officer as president who was made directly responsible to the government for the work. The Board had more statutory powers of consultation regarding estimates and bye-laws, but its development into a municipal body seemed even more remote than in the time of Bowen.

The rule that the Colonial Secretary administered the government in the absence of the Governor was again revived in 1903. Chamberlain had suggested in 1895 that in view of tension in the Far East, the General should act as the Governor's deputy. Lockhart, the Colonial Secretary during this period, whose prospects were affected by the ruling, was consoled by his appointment in 1902 as first civilian Commissioner of

Weihaiwei. He was succeeded as Colonial Secretary by F. H. May, whose appointment was urged by telegram from all the unofficial members of the Legislative Council. The post at the same time was separated from that of Registrar-General, and in 1913 this latter officer became known as Secretary for Chinese Affairs. The colony had moved far from the days when control of the Chinese population had been based on their registration. In 1899, the higher government officers had their salaries raised and the posts grouped in four classes according to their importance; certain technical officers, such as the Medical Officer, the Director of Public Works, the Harbour-master and the Headmaster of Queen's College were given their own salary scales, and the Colonial Secretary remained outside. A new scheme of classification of junior officers with appropriate scales came into force in 1902. On the judicial side, a second magistrate was found necessary in 1900, and in 1912 the supreme court was reformed to meet the growing pressure of work. All departments showed expansion, but a Retrenchment Commission in 1909 was unable to suggest any serious reductions.

Relations with China were disturbed by the outbreak of the Boxer anti-foreign movement in 1900. In the south the feeling was anti-Manchu. The two Kwang provinces were seething with political discontent, and when Li Hung-chang was ordered to assume the viceroyalty of Chihli Province, Blake asked the British Consul in Canton to urge him to stay, as it was felt that without his restraining influence, Canton would be in a ferment. In 1900, a prominent Chinese reformer, K'ang Yu-wei, took refuge in the colony where he was given protection; the Colonial Office asked that this should be withdrawn, and he left voluntarily for Singapore. Li Hung-chang was in touch with reformers like Sun Yat Sen. Sun Yat Sen had been educated in the colony and had graduated from the Chinese Medical College in 1892; his Hong Kong experience taught him the value of much that the West had to teach and he became an ardent reformer, for which activity he had been banished from the colony in 1896 for revolutionary activity directed against a friendly power. In July 1900 Blake warned Chamberlain that Sun Yat Sen and a party of reformers were coming from Singapore to assist the reform party, that Li Hung-chang would probably want to meet him in Hong Kong, and that if he did, Blake did not propose to interfere or impose the banishment. Li Hung-chang passed through the colony on 17 July 1900 on his way north; Blake had been advised by some of the prominent Chinese in the colony that Li would probably have welcomed being detained, to provide him with a good reason for not going to the north until conditions were clearer, but Chamberlain ordered that his movements were in no way to be interfered with. In August Blake reported that Sun Yat Sen and K'ang Yu-wei were enlisting men for possible action in South China, and he wanted to promise support for any just demands, but the home government ordered him not to give any such assurances and not to allow any British subjects to enlist in any enterprise against the Chinese government. The rebellion in the south threatened the border, but there was little trouble in the colony, though there was much support among the Chinese for the reformers.

The Boxer rising was eventually suppressed, the foreign legations in Peking liberated, and China had to pay 'Boxer' indemnities to the foreign powers concerned. Tension in the Far East continued with the outbreak of the Russo-Japanese War 1904–05, and the British Far Eastern Fleet was reinforced with battleships, which were withdrawn in 1905.

The colony played an important part in providing capital for Chinese railway development. In 1898 The Hongkong and Shanghai Banking Corporation and Jardine, Matheson & Co. formed the British and Chinese Corporation to provide the capital required for any concessions obtained from China; this Corporation was given the right to build the Canton-Kowloon Railway in that year. It also, in the same year, made an agreement with the German Deutsch-Asiatische Bank limiting the areas in which railway concessions from the Chinese government would be sought. Railway building in China became the subject of fierce economic and political rivalry between the powers, in which British interests were largely represented by the British and Chinese Corporation which had been formed to represent Hong Kong interests. In 1899 the Corporation agreed to share in the American concession to build a railway from Hankow to Canton. The concession was eventually withdrawn, and in 1905 the Hong Kong government lent the Viceroy of the Hupen and Hunan Provinces £1,100,000 at four and a half per cent, repayable in ten instalments on the security of the opium revenue from the neighbouring provinces, for the purpose of redeeming the Canton-Hankow railway concession. The money was advanced to the colony government by the Crown Agents at four per cent, and in 1905 it was converted into a loan and increased to two million pounds to raise funds for the building of the Kowloon-Canton Railway.

The British and Chinese Corporation made agreements with the Chinese government to build the Shanhaikwan-Newchwang Railway, the Kowloon-Canton Railway (except the section in British-held territory, in which the line was taken over by the Hong Kong government), the Shanghai-Nanking Railway and the Shanghai-Hangchow-Ningpo Railway. It joined with the Germans in building the Tientsin-Pukow Railway, and with an international consortium in building the Hu Kuang Railways.

The outbreak of the Chinese Revolution in 1911 caused excitement in the colony, and led to an influx of Chinese fleeing from the unsettled conditions. The stringent Peace Preservation Ordinance of 1886 was promulgated and various measures taken to maintain security. The colony subscribed liberally to alleviate distress from flood in Kwangtung in 1908 and again in 1915.

In the matter of opium the British government showed its clear intention to support in Hong Kong the policy of China. The opium trade on which Hong Kong had so long battened was gradually suppressed. Evangelical opinion had frequently protested against the opium trade throughout the nineteenth century, and from the formation in 1874 of the Anglo-Oriental Society for the Suppression of the Opium Trade, pressure in and out of Parliament was almost continuous. In 1891 a vote in the Commons condemned the opium trade, and led to the setting up of a Royal Commission of Enquiry; its report in 1895 was disappointing, but the British government promised to control the opium trade and suggested confidentially to the colony government that the opium farm might be handed over to the Chinese government. The American Philippines commission of 1903 led to the abolition of opium smoking in the Philippines and encouraged the Society in England to renew the attack, now supported much more earnestly by the Chinese reformers.

In 1906 the Chinese government, acting on information that the Indian government might agree to end the opium trade, and on a resolution in the British Commons passed without a division condemning the opium trade on moral grounds, issued an Imperial decree to abolish opium within ten years. World opinion was also moving and an International Opium Commission was appointed by the principal countries interested to meet at Shanghai in 1909. To forestall criticism at home, the British government decided to reduce the export of opium from India by one-tenth each year from 1907, if China would reduce her home-produced opium by the same amount. In 1908, the government of Hong Kong was suddenly ordered to close the opium divans in the colony 'to act up to the standards of the Chinese Government'. Lugard pleaded for time to make the necessary adjustment in the colony's finances; in 1906 the opium trade had been worth over five million pounds, and government revenue from opium had amounted to over two million dollars. The abolition of prepared opium for export was followed by the closing of twenty-six divans on 1 March 1909, and the remaining divans were closed a year later. Loss of revenue was made up by a grant from the Imperial government, and also by taxes on liquor, tobacco and perfumes. In 1909 the export of prepared opium was forbidden to any country which prohibited its import, and was allowed to other countries only under permit. There was also strict control of morphine and cocaine. In the colony itself, opium was permitted and the opium farm was let for three years from March 1910 at $1,183,200 per annum, $225,760 less than had been obtained previously. In 1913 the government set up its own monopoly of prepared opium; the farm was renewed for one year only, and the amount of opium allowed was reduced from 900 to 540 chests for consumption in the colony, and to 120 chests for export. The use of opium in the colony was increasingly restricted, but not prohibited until the Second World War.

It was still impossible to produce accurate trade returns, but shipping figures show the colony enjoyed continued prosperity. In 1898 11,058 ships of 13,252,733 tons entered the port and cleared; in 1913 the figures were 21,867 ships of 22,939,134 tons. Hong Kong had become one of the most important ports in the world. By 1918, owing to the demands of war, the figures dropped to 19,997 ships of 13,982,966 tons. The total annual value of Hong Kong's trade was estimated by the Hong Kong Chamber of Commerce, on the occasion of Lord Beresford's commercial mission to China in 1898, at £50 millions. Trade with China alone in that year was estimated by the Imperial Maritime Customs to be $67,182,585. In 1897 the West River had been opened to trade, with Samshui and Wuchow as treaty ports, and Nanning was opened in 1899; but the colony's trade did not immediately benefit, because of piracy. In addition, in 1898 the British secured the opening of Chinese inland waterways, but the difficulty was that customs duties in treaty and non-treaty ports were collected by different Chinese authorities; and when Hart ruled that different steamers had to be employed, British steamers were temporarily withdrawn in 1900 from the West River. French armed vessels there caused great uneasiness in the colony and fear of French claims.

Estimates of the nature and value of the trade made in the annual reports show the expected large entrepôt trade. In 1901 and 1902, for example, export figures given for the following commodities were, in tons:

	Coal	Rice	Sugar	Flour	Kerosene	General	Total
1901	917,144	618,780	241,291	145,287	148,000	1,278,619	3,480,987
1902	1,040,906	819,919	268,268	107,826	114,861	1,480,003	3,963,463

Import figures were not given, but since all these commodities had to be imported, the extent of the entrepôt trade can be gauged. The opium trade before it was stopped was equally entrepôt, and was valued at £5,312,645 in 1906. The port gained through the enormous movement of the Chinese to America, the Pacific, South-East Asia and Australia. In 1898 60,432 left the port, and up to 1914 the numbers varied between 64,341 in 1905 and 142,759 in 1913; 105,441 Chinese returned from abroad in 1898, and up to 1914 arrivals never fell below this figure, reaching as high as 168,827 in 1914.

Waglan Lighthouse was taken over with New Territories on 1 January 1901, and the Cape D'Aguilar light was closed. It was transferred to Green Island and the Green Island light to Cape Collinson.

Hong Kong lived by commerce, but industries were growing.
T

Early industries associated with shipping, or the entrepôt trade such as rope, sugar and ship-building developed further. In 1899 a cement works was started, moved from Macao, and in this year the Hong Kong and Whampoa Dock Company employed 4,510; there were also reported to be five soap factories, and seven vermilion factories. The New Territories produced 4,466 tons of salt. The textile industry which had been set up in 1898 could not meet severe competition and moved to Shanghai in 1914. Iron and tin industries flourished for a short time. There was a host of small Chinese industries, rattan, camphor wood, vermilion, soya, preserved ginger, and tobacco. Fisheries were reported in the 1901 Annual Report as being unimportant.

Population in 1898 was 254,400, of which 239,210 were Chinese, 8,732 non-Chinese civilians and 6,458 in the Services. At the 1901 census it had increased to 300,660, of whom 280,564 were Chinese, and there were 10,536 in the armed Services, the increase reflecting the presence of troops for the Boxer Campaign. In addition the New Territories were estimated to contain 100,000. By the next census of 1911, non-Chinese civilians were given as 12,075, armed Services as 6,727, and the Chinese as 444,664; the civilians were made up as follows: Victoria and the Peak 219,386, in the villages 16,106, Kowloon 67,602, New Territories 80,622, afloat 60,984, total 456,739. By 1916, the population was estimated at 528,010, the result of fighting and political unrest around Canton; by 1917 the population had dropped 431,700, due in part to paucity of shipping due to demands of the war, and diminished trade.

Public revenue showed steady growth from $3,610,143 in 1898 to $8,512,308 in 1913 and $18,665,248 in 1918, and this in spite of the smaller revenue from the opium farm, which was partly offset by the home exchequer grants. The levy on imported liquors in 1909 meant that the port ceased for the first time to be an absolutely free port. Public expenditure showed a corresponding trend. Much of the expenditure was devoted to public works, which continued at high pressure. The central reclamation scheme was completed in 1904, the new Post Office and government offices in 1911 and the Supreme Court building in 1912. In 1901 some offices below Government House were extended and raised and became the Colonial Secretariat building. Additional water-supply was arranged for by the building of the Wong Nei Chong Gap reservoir in 1899, an additional reservoir at Tai Tam in 1904; the lower Tai Tam reservoir was begun in 1913 and the large dam there was begun in 1914 and completed in 1917. Kowloon water-works and reservoir were undertaken between 1902 and 1906. The period of tension in the Far East had finally induced the Admiralty in 1899 to take over the private and military lands on the north side of Queen's Road East to expand the dockyard and build a graving dock. Blake made unavailing attempts in 1901, and as late as December 1902, to induce the Admiralty to move the yard to the existing admiralty site at Kowloon, so that the city should not be cut in two. He suggested Quarry Bay, and thought the town site was too small for a naval dockyard. The plea was rejected, and reclamation work for the naval yard went ahead, though it was not completed in time to meet the crisis of the Russo-Japanese War. The Admiralty had proposed that the Hong Kong and Whampoa Dock Company should build a graving dock with the navy having priority in use, but the Company refused unless they were given a 999-year lease of their land. The result was that the Services were more strongly entrenched in the central area and the development of the eastern district hindered. The only advantage to the colony from the change was the securing of a strip of land to widen Queen's Road, which Robinson had arranged for in 1892. In 1900 Chater proposed an East Praya reclamation scheme, but it was decided in 1905 not to proceed with it. In 1901 the military contribution was increased from 17½ per cent to 20 per cent of the revenue and the depreciation in the value of the dollar added to the burden. Defence of Hong Kong was not only inconvenient but expensive and the defence contribution which had been $508,976 in 1898 had risen to $1,314,773 in 1904 and to $1,557,377 in 1913.

The completion of the Central Praya and the decision, however unfavourable, that the navy should remain in the city centre, at last allowed the tramway scheme to proceed, and in 1904 the service Kennedy Town to Shaukiwan was opened. It was intended that the same company would also construct a new peak tramway via Battery Path and Glenealy, but the project was dropped. Quite apart from such private works, public works of a non-recurrent nature ran into some two million dollars per year. The Mongkok Typhoon refuge was completed in 1915. The largest public scheme was the Kowloon-Canton Railway. Great efforts were made to induce the Chinese to enter into an agreement for working the line in co-operation, but without success. The British commenced the section from Kowloon to the border in 1905, and completed it in 1910, the Chinese section from the border to Canton was completed in 1912, but it was some years before the Chinese became co-operative over the working arrangements.

It has already been shown that the colony presented the great problem of sanitation, particularly in regard to plague, which became endemic, at least until 1924. Deaths from plague, for example, were 1,175 in 1898, 1,428 in 1899, 1,434 in 1900; in 1901 the epidemic was so bad that many Europeans lost their lives and many Chinese began to leave. The connection between rats and plague was suspected, yet in May 1900 a commission of enquiry into the connection between rats and plague was dissolved because the Medical Officer of Health said that it was 'more probable that rats caught plague from man rather than that men were infected through rats'. Blake made a genuine attempt to combat the menace and instituted a great campaign against rats. A payment of two cents a rat produced 43,000 in 1900, but it was suspected that the total was swollen for the sake of the reward by importations from China and the New Territories, which were free from infection. A special ordinance to make regulations regarding rats was passed, a bacteriologist was appointed, Japanese doctors employed to examine all rats, and Chinese licentiates were trained. Blake experimented with disinfecting, and made a thorough-going experiment in Tai Ping Shan area, without much success.

In spite of Blake's vigorous action and clear determination to find the cause of the plague, there was much dissatisfaction. The military once more complained of the insanitary state of the colony, and in 1901 the Chamber of Commerce made a strong protest, and complained that practically nothing had been done to carry out the Chadwick Report of 1882; it presented a petition supported by 1,000 signatures asking for a commission of enquiry into the sanitary state of Hong Kong. Blake complained that this was only propaganda for municipal self-government and wider powers for the Sanitary Board. Blake had in fact done much to improve sanitary conditions; he had brought back the old 1887 constitution of the Board and secured the election of two representatives on the Sanitary Board in 1899, had appointed more inspectors of nuisances and introduced drains inspectors. In 1899 he passed an Insanitary Properties Ordinance to deal with cocklofts and mezzanine floors and restricted the power to partition rooms into cubicles; but in 1901, the two elected members resigned to show their dissatisfaction with the powers of the Board, and no new nominations were made.

This demand for an enquiry led to the sending out of two specialists, Professor W. J. Simpson to deal with plague and malaria, and Osbert Chadwick to deal with sanitation, drains and housing. They came out in 1902 and Chadwick urged increased water supply, and drew attention to the serious overcrowding.

In 1902 there was still an average in the central district of 502 persons, and in 1904 608 to the acre. Chadwick advised there was no other remedy than to resume land and rebuild, and the Insanitary Properties Resumption Ordinance was passed to carry this out in stages. With regard to the plague, Simpson advocated bacteriological examination of all rats, and eight Japanese were employed in this work until local men could be trained. He advised that all houses should be made rat-proof. But population increased to such an extent that problems were being created as fast as they were solved, particularly after the flood of refugees in 1911 and 1912. The discovery that malaria was carried by the anopheles mosquito had led in part to the sending out of Simpson in 1902; he recommended nullah training and treating with a view to the control of mosquito breeding. There was one drawback to all this sanitary improvement; in 1907 a commission of enquiry into the working of the sanitary legislation discovered much irregularity on the part of the sanitary officials. Inspectors were found to be in collusion with the building contractors and the powers intended for use in public health were made the subject of private gain. These disclosures caused great scandal.

During this period great changes were made in the educational system, not without prolonged debate. Since Hennessy's time there had been much emphasis on English teaching and

western education, and Robinson had revised the grant code
to deny grants to any future schools unless they taught English.
The main problem that faced Hong Kong education was that
which faced educationists in India and elsewhere, viz., the
relative positions of English and the vernacular in a mixed
community. There were further complications; the introduction
of the Cambridge Local Examinations had forced some schools
to raise their standards to prepare the few candidates who were
generally English-speaking; and there was a demand by British
parents for separate schools for their own children. Another
problem was the distribution of the responsibility for schools
between the government and the voluntary bodies, chiefly the
missionary societies; for some years it had been Eitel's policy
to cut down government schools and encourage voluntary effort
by grants. In 1900, only 1·24 per cent of the colonial revenue
was spent on education. It was recognized, too, that Chinese
private schools were more popular among Chinese than the
free government schools giving a similar vernacular education.
In 1901 Brewin was made Registrar-General, and Irving came
from Perak as Inspector of Schools. He was keen on vernacular
education. In 1901, Europeans petitioned for schools for European children only, on the ground that the education of
Europeans and Chinese together held both back. At the
same time, eight leading Chinese petitioned for schools where
children of the better classes could be sent so as not to mix
with those of the lower classes.

Blake set up a committee of enquiry into education. Its report,
issued in May 1902, recommended separate schools for European British subjects, and 'English' schools for those non-
British children who required an education in the medium of
English; yet it suggested withdrawing the grant from the four
schools giving an education in Portuguese. It criticized Chinese
education on the ground that it was better to educate a few
Chinese well than to give a smattering to many. It criticized
the poor standard of English teaching, in the Anglo-Chinese
schools where English and Western subjects were taught to
Chinese students, and suggested they should not attempt higher
form work without British teachers. It suggested attaching
vernacular schools to Anglo-Chinese schools with one headmaster, so that a student could more easily pass from one stage

to the other. The report was implemented almost immediately in one respect. A prominent Chinese citizen, Ho Tung, later Sir Robert Ho Tung, had presented to the government a school in Kowloon for English teaching, open to all; it was now proposed to take this building for the British school and exclude other races. The donor agreed, but regretted the change of policy 'so much opposed to the spirit which prompted my offer of the school to the colony'. On the island, Belilios had just presented the colony with a reformatory school, but as there were no inmates this building was taken for a British school in Hong Kong.

Chamberlain, the Secretary of State, strongly criticized the report and condemned racial schools which were set up only for the British and condemned the misuse of the generosity of Ho Tung and Belilios. He thought that 'the first duty was to maintain the vernacular schools' which the committee seemed to threaten, and he was against restricting entry to Queen's College and Belilios Girls' School to any one race, and in the case of Queen's College the purely Chinese classes were to be restored. He sanctioned the Kowloon British school because parents had clearly demanded that sort of school, but he was against allowing the educational system of the colony to follow the lines of race, and he thought the committee was inconsistent because it suggested suppressing the Portuguese language schools. The committee's report was not accepted as the basis of the proposed reforms and the process of gradual change and experiment continued. In 1903, the grant code was amended in a radical way; the system of payment by results was abolished and the grants were now based on the result of the inspector's general report. Increased grant was given to schools with specially qualified European or other equally qualified staffs. Grant was to be payable for English and Chinese schools only and the Chinese schools were to be conducted on Western lines. The general result was to reduce the number of government and grant schools, but to increase the number of pupils and the cost. Nathan keenly advocated more education and established evening classes in engineering, science and commerce, which were organized in October 1907 as the Hong Kong Technical Institute, and which also undertook the training of teachers as part of its evening class work. Lugard was equally interested in education, particularly in the vernacular; in 1911 he set up a Board of Chinese Vernacular Primary Education, and the principle of encouraging vernacular education was not again seriously challenged. In 1913, a new education ordinance made it obligatory to register all schools with ten or more pupils and gave additional powers of inspection and of closing unnecessary or inefficient schools, subject to appeal; 620 schools with 11,909 pupils were now brought under control.

A significant event of the period was the founding of Hong Kong University. In 1878, when the education system of the colony was under critical examination, Hutchinson, of the Church Missionary Society, suggested that 'a well organised collegiate or university system like Calcutta', giving its own degrees was wanted. In 1887 the College of Medicine for the Chinese was founded mainly by the public spirit of some of the local medical practitioners, Drs. P. Manson, W. S. Young and J. Cantlie, and by the Rev. Dr. Chalmers, influenced by similar institutions already in existence in Canton and Tientsin and assisted by the London Missionary Society. The founders gave their services, but as they died or left, conditions became difficult and after 1891 appeals were continuously made to the government for financial assistance. In 1896, because of the plague and the need for Western medical training, a government enquiry was made with a view to taking over the college. Belilios had offered to build a college because he admired the work of the doctors, but withdrew his offer in 1896 because he thought the government should take it over. In 1901 a crisis was reached. An appeal to the government was finally successful and a sum of $2,500 per annum was voted as honoraria for the lecturers. By 1901 there had been twelve successful licentiates, twenty had failed or dropped out, and twenty-three were still in the college. Most of the licentiates found openings in Singapore and Malaya; one of the twelve was appointed medical officer to the New Territories when they were taken over, and the government began to make Chinese medical appointments in its own hospitals and in connection with the free dispensaries for Chinese which were just being set up, and which the college had urged for years. In 1907 the college was incorporated as the Hong Kong College of Medicine, and a Chinese, Ng Li Hing, offered $50,000 for a new building.

Lugard, at St. Stephen's College speech day in 1907, threw out the suggestion of a university. The university movement was strong in England, in British colonies and in India. The establishment of universities in China was also under discussion, and a United Universities Scheme based on an alliance between British universities and religious bodies working in China was put forward. Lugard opposed this plan, and thought that the universities, if set up in China, should be dissociated from Christian teaching and be practical and utilitarian because China needed such training; he thought Hong Kong ideally situated to assist China. He accordingly pressed the Hong Kong scheme. H. N. Mody, a wealthy Parsee who admired the Lugards, supported it and offered $150,000 for the building and $30,000 as an endowment. Lugard formed a committee to promote the scheme and suggested that there should be two faculties, medicine and engineering, to incorporate the already existing College of Medicine and the Technical Institute, with a faculty of arts to be added later. The proposal was not very popular among the foreign merchants, who thought it unnecessary, nor among the Chinese, whose distrust of education sponsored by the West was only recently beginning to break down, nor with the Colonial Office, who called it Lugard's 'pet lamb'. The Foreign Office agreed to help if the Chinese government contributed. Personal appeals by Lady Lugard brought in sums from British and Chinese alike before Mody's offer expired on 31 December 1909, by which date $1,279,164 had been subscribed or promised, and the foundation stone was laid in March 1910. The University opened in September 1912, with the Governor, Sir F. H. May, as chancellor and with 72 students—31 in engineering, 21 in medicine and 20 in arts—drawn from Hong Kong, the Straits, Canton and the Treaty Ports. Its stated aim was 'to provide close to China, education for Chinese, similar to that given in the British universities.' Ng Li Hing, besides presenting the money set aside for a new medical college, gave the anatomy building, and a Straits Chinese, Cheung Pat Sze, helped the arts faculty. Ho Tung endowed a chair of surgery in 1916. The British government provided scholarships. The weakness of the institution was that it was insufficiently endowed.

The discovery of the spread of malaria by mosquitoes had

one unexpected social result. It brought about a renewed demand for exclusive residential areas to be set apart for Europeans on the ground that the Chinese were not to be trusted to take the proper precautions. In 1902 a sub-committee of the Sanitary Board proposed to reserve an area of some 20,000 acres between Tsim Tha Tsui and the Kowloon City, partly on the ground of malaria control, and partly because rich Chinese forced up the rents, and the New Territories Land Court agreed to resume 119 acres already claimed in that area. Chamberlain agreed with the principle of a reservation 'where people of clean habits will be safe from malaria', but he objected to excluding Chinese of good standing so as to give Europeans low rents, and the reservation was to be open to all persons approved by the Governor. Using the same argument, the Peak area was reserved on the same conditions by the Hill District Reservation Ordinance of 1904.

Other social events can only briefly be referred to. The diamond jubilee of Queen Victoria was marked by a proposal to build a road around the island and also a jubilee hospital, a nurses' training centre and nurses' quarters. The road scheme was held up by military objections, and after prolonged delay the road around Mount Davis in the west of the island at the 150 foot contour was agreed to and set in hand. The nurses' scheme was equally muddled, as rising costs made the scheme impossible with the funds available. Eventually the Victoria Hospital for Women and Children was built and the nurses' institute dropped in favour of a nursing association to get private nurses in the colony. The accession of Edward VII in 1901 was marked by laying out part of a military site in Kowloon as a public park, King's Park, but the military refused to relinquish the necessary land, and the park remained only a small space for recreation.

Severe typhoons in 1900, 1906 and 1908 did great damage, and in 1906 the Anglican bishop, Hoare, lost his life attempting to save the lives of trainees he had on board his mission vessel, which was wrecked.

In the war of 1914–18 all races volunteered for the forces and to serve with the Volunteers, though 60,000 Chinese left for the mainland for fear of attack on the colony. There was liberal subscription to war charities, and a loan of $5 million was raised and handed to the Imperial government as a gift. In 1917 the Hong Kong Defence Corps was formed from the volunteers and compulsory military service was introduced. Only seventeen British ships remained on the coast. They were taken over by the British government, and normal commercial activity had to await the return of peace.

CHAPTER XXIV

THE INTER-WAR YEARS, 1919–39

'Afterwards I saw the outside world, and I began to wonder how it was that foreigners, that Englishmen could do such things as they had done, for example with the barren rock of Hong Kong. . . .'

Sun Yat Sen at the Hong Kong University Congregation, 1923.

THE 1914–18 War brought an aftermath of social and economic problems. There was dislocation of world trade, depletion of shipping and shortage of commodities; scarcity of rice caused an almost fourfold increase in its price and government had to take over its purchase and distribution to check looting of rice stores. Labour unrest produced a series of strikes, continuing until 1922, when a seamen's strike paralysed the harbour and spread, by intimidation, to other branches of labour including domestic servants.

The long-term effects of the war were more profound but not immediately discernable. Few then realized that the Versailles Treaty ushered in a changing world to which Hong Kong would be forced to adjust itself, and that a new chapter in the colony's history had opened.

Hong Kong had been born in the early Victorian era as a military, commercial and administrative centre of expanding British trade with China, and supplied those conditions under which commerce could prosper and which China herself was then incapable of providing. That era was the very heyday of Victorian *laissez-faire* economic individualism by which the individual was expected to fend for himself within the framework of the rule of law, which, in theory at least, was applied to all without distinction of race or creed. The port was an open port in which all were free to come and go. These conditions suited the merchant class, foreign and Chinese alike, which asked for no more than to be left alone.

In the years following the Versailles Treaties, the position of Great Britain changed. She still exercised a diplomatic leadership, but the old commercial and financial leadership had been impaired by the war effort. Germany had been eliminated as a Far Eastern power, and Russia was temporarily weakened by revolution. In their place Japan emerged as the principal British rival in the Far East. She had seized the opportunity of the war in Europe to present to China in 1915 the Twenty-one Demands which revealed an ambition to make China a Japanese dependency. After the war the claims of Japan delayed the Far Eastern peace settlement until the Washington Treaties of 1922. For Hong Kong, the most important of these treaties was that which provided for naval limitation restricting the fleets of Great Britain, the United States and Japan to a 5 : 5 : 3 ratio, since its effect was to give Japan a naval preponderance in the Far East where her fleet was concentrated. In the same treaty, the Pacific Powers agreed also to a suspension of further fortifications in their Pacific possessions east of the 110° meridian. This included Hong Kong; its ability to protect British commercial interests in the Far East was now therefore limited by treaty and its future strategic role was obscure. The colonial contribution in the war led to a demand for greater freedom, and the British Commonwealth of freely associated nations began to emerge; in addition, imperialism came under fire as a result of the rise of socialist theories and of the Labour Party. New doctrines of trusteeship of colonial territories were evolved, but the special position of Hong Kong in the changing Imperial structure was not clear.

There were important commercial and economic changes. The British share of industrial production and world trade steadily declined during the inter-war period because of the growth of industrialization in those countries formerly supplied by Great Britain, and because of increasing pressure by her industrial competitors. The inter-war years therefore saw in-tense commercial rivalry marked by high tariff barriers and by newly devised commercial weapons such as 'dumping', cur-rency manipulation, quotas and bilateral trading arrangements. Japan, by means of a devalued currency and low labour costs, was able to capture traditional British markets in the Far East. In 1931, following a great depression in trade, Great Britain was forced to abandon the gold standard and place the pound sterling on a 'managed' basis, and to relinquish the principle of free trade which had characterized British commercial practice for nearly a century, in favour of a policy of protection. This brought some advantages in that Imperial preferences were now possible, but they were offset by the strong economic nationalism which restricted over-all international trade. Hong Kong had held to free trade as the condition of its being and prosperity, and the new economic order posed a problem of adaptation because British commercial relations played such a dominant role in its commercial life. Hong Kong remained a free port, but only under increasing difficulty.

A further far-reaching change in this period was the increas-ing social legislation in Britain in the interest of the people which resulted from political enfranchisement, the spread of socialist doctrines, and from the great common sacrifices of the war, borne by all classes alike. The 'Welfare State' became the ideal, and nineteenth century *laissez-faire* which had rested on the virtues of unfettered private enterprise, became suspect. Yet it was private enterprise that had created Hong Kong, and so the colony reflected and embodied a social theory which was passing away, and was faced with yet another problem of adaptation.

The most significant of the changes taking place in the Far East was the emergence of a new China. The Revolution of 1911 overthrew the Manchu Empire in favour of a Republic, but there was no experience in China of the working of demo-cratic institutions and the problem was to find a stable form of government to take its place. The first President, Yüan Shih-k'ai, attempted to set himself up as Emperor in 1916, but died on the failure of his plans. The chief group of reformers, led by Sun Yat Sen, was the Kuomintang or National People's Party, whose strength lay in the southern provinces centred at

Canton; it was opposed by more conservative elements in the north who resented its radicalism as being too Western in character. Provincial rivalry and the ambition of military war lords held back a solution of the political problem. Sun Yat Sen's political leadership did not match his idealism or his ability to inspire his followers. He called in Russian advisers under Borodin in 1923 to train the Party's political cadres, and, by harnessing socialist ideas to the existing nationalism of the movement, made it a revolutionary party.

The death of Sun Yat Sen in 1925 allowed his successor, Chiang Kai Shek, to advance to the Yangtze Valley in 1926 and eventually to Peking, and on 10 October 1928 the National Government of the Republic of China was established, controlled by the Kuomintang, though it was some time before it could establish undisputed control of all the eighteen provinces. The prospect of a strong and unified China alarmed the Japanese because it threatened their ambitions in China. In 1931 the explosion of a bomb on the railway at Mukden was magnified into an international incident and resulted in the Japanese military taking over control of Manchuria, and setting up the puppet state of Manchukuo under Pu-yi, the head of the Ch'ing royal house. Intervention by the League of Nations proved ineffectual. In January 1932 the Japanese attacked Shanghai, and next year they seized Jehol and part of Chahar preparatory to control of Inner Mongolia. In 1935 they sponsored a North China Autonomous Regime, by which the northern provinces were to be detached from China and placed under their control. The Japanese militarists were encouraged because China was weakened by faction and by civil war against the Communists, and because the rise of Fascist and Nazi parties in Italy and Germany forced the other Western powers to concentrate their attention on Europe. The incident at Marco Polo bridge in July 1937 led to hostilities between Japan and China, which conflict merged into the World War of 1939–45.

The Chinese struggle for unification was accompanied by growing nationalism, calling for equality of status with other powers and stridently demanding the abrogation of the unequal treaties, the abolition of exterritoriality, foreign concessions, settlements, and foreign control of the Chinese customs. The

German concessions were renounced in 1921 as a result of her defeat, and by 1928 some twenty treaties had been signed with various powers by which the special privileges were either ended or modified, or arrangements made to modify them. In 1928 China regained tariff autonomy. Great Britain renounced the Hankow and Kiukiang concessions in 1928 and the lease of Weihaiwei in 1930. In 1929 the Kuomintang government asked Britain, the United States, France and Japan to agree to the removal of all treaty restrictions on Chinese sovereignty, and later decreed the termination of all exterritorial privileges as from 1 January 1930. Britain and the other powers could not accept immediate abolition, but accepted the principle of their gradual and progressive extinction as from that date.

All sides of Hong Kong life felt the impact of these new conditions which have just been outlined, for a great commercial centre must necessarily be sensitive to those external factors upon which its prosperity depends.

Unrest and disturbance in China led to the usual flow of immigrants, and it is not surprising that population increased during the whole period. At the 1921 census, the figure was 625,166, of which 610,368 were Chinese; in 1925 there were 725,100, an estimated increase of 16 per cent, of whom 706,100 were Chinese. In these years, wealthier people came in from Canton, frightened by the Kuomintang extremist element, and in 1923 alone three and a half million dollars were received in premiums on new Crown leases, chiefly in the rapidly growing Kowloon. At the 1931 census the population was 849,751, and in 1937 the estimate was 1,006,982, of whom 984,000 were Chinese. Japanese hostilities against China in 1937 and the fall of Canton in the following year led to a great migration. About 100,000 refugees entered the colony in 1937, 500,000 in 1938 and 150,000 in 1939, and the estimate of the 1941 population was 1,639,000, of whom 1,615,000 were Chinese. These newcomers posed great problems regarding accommodation, water supply, sanitation and relief; they sought only food and shelter; they had no loyalty to the colony and, under the Japanese attack, they hindered the island's defence.

Labour unrest and the seamen's strike of 1922 have already been noted above. Even more serious was the general strike and boycott of 1925–26. This was a political movement arising from popular feeling against the privileged status of foreigners. An anti-Japanese demonstration at Shanghai in May 1925 developed into an anti-foreign movement which became primarily anti-British because the British had the largest stake in China, and it quickly spread along the coast. In June, the Kuomintang radical element in Canton organized an economic boycott of British and Japanese goods, with the result that street fighting occurred in Shameen between demonstrators and British and French troops. An economic boycott of Hong Kong was then organized and taken up effectively in the colony, where opinion among the mass of Chinese was always sensitive to that of Canton. On June 30 all Chinese workers were withdrawn and work came to a standstill; essential services were maintained by volunteers assisted by the armed forces and the Hong Kong Volunteer Corps was mobilized to assist in the emergency. The strike gradually collapsed, but the boycott of British goods and shipping remained until October 1926, and a special loan had to be arranged to assist the foreign merchants of the colony until normal trading was resumed.

The economy of Hong Kong began to reveal new trends which flowed from the changing world economic conditions. Shipping figures during the period show the port to be one of the principal ports in the world. In 1919 21,257 ships of 18,474,996 tons engaged in foreign trade entered and cleared; in 1927 the figures were 29,052 ships of 36,867,745 tons, and in 1939, 15,021 of 28,840,566 tons; 1938 and 1939 were exceptional years, affected by war between China and Japan. The peak year for ocean-going tonnage using the port was 1935. The proportion of British shipping declined from 60 per cent at the end of the nineteenth century to 56 per cent in 1914 and it remained at approximately this figure down to 1939.

The colony's trade was affected by the 1925–26 boycott, the slump of 1931 and Japanese hostilities, but the table on the next page shows the trends clearly enough.

The figures are percentages of the total imports and exports respectively, measured by value.

Imports from China remained high, but exports to China fell sharply, declining from H.K.$432·6 million in 1921 to H.K.$243 million in 1931 and to H.K.$90·3 million in 1939.[1]

[1] Taken from D. M. Kenrick, *The Economy of Hong Kong*, Hong Kong, 1954.

HONG KONG TRADE[1]

	Year	United Kingdom	British Dominions	China	Other Countries
IMPORTS	1921	10·24	10·79	19·12	59·77
	1931	9·94	8·88	27·84	53·34
	1939	6·62	7·03	37·95	48·40
EXPORTS	1921	·91	9·99	64·65	24·45
	1931	·89	9·09	51·67	38·35
	1939	5·23	13·93	14·83	66·01

This decrease reflected the drop in British trade with China passing through Hong Kong. The entrepôt trade with China was decreasing in importance relative to the whole trade of the colony. Trade with South-East Asia and the Western Pacific was increasing, particularly the rice and flour trade between Siam and America, and also the trade with Malaya and with Japan.

Trade statistics must be read in conjunction with the changing value of the currency. The Hong Kong silver dollar varied in value with the price of silver. In 1919 its sterling equivalent varied between 5s. 2d. and 3s. 0¾d., and next year, 1920, between 6s. 2d. and 2s. 11d. After 1921 it never exceeded 3s. 0d. and even dropped to below 1s. in the 1931 slump. There was clearly a need for currency reform.

In 1931 a currency commission was appointed by the Secretary of State for the Colonies to enquire into the Hong Kong currency, and recommended that Hong Kong should remain on the silver standard as long as that obtained in China, that all bank-notes should be convertible into silver bullion, and made unlimited tender, and that a Hong Kong Currency Board should be placed in charge of the note issue and the reserve of silver bullion. The Commission thus believed that Hong Kong was still so closely linked in trade with China, that the advantage of keeping the silver standard as long as China did outweighed the advantage of stabilization based on gold. This view was endorsed by the Hong Kong Chamber of Commerce in its Annual Report of that year, but the latter urged that

[1] ibid.

since China was estimated to hold two-thirds of the total Hong Kong note issue, such a wide circulation of Hong Kong notes in China made government control of the currency undesirable.

In 1934 United States purchases of silver led to an increase in its value and to the export of silver bullion, so that next year China was forced off the silver standard. Hong Kong had to follow with the result that all silver coins were called in and export of the metal prohibited, as a preliminary to complete currency reorganization. The Currency Ordinance of December 1935 set up a managed currency, linked with sterling; the note issue was backed by bullion, foreign exchange and sterling securities, and the dollar was stabilized at approximately 1s. 3d. Silver coins were replaced by cupro-nickel coins and supplemented by additional notes. At the same time the government took over the issue of dollar notes and the three issuing banks were restricted to the issue of notes of ten dollars and upwards. For the first time the colony's currency ceased to be linked with that of China. This severance was a decisive break with the past, but the advantages of a stable currency were to prove themselves beyond doubt.

Similar reforms and the institution of a managed currency in China by which the dollar would have been stabilized at 1s. 2½d., were suggested in 1935 by Sir F. Leith-Ross, who had been sent to Nanking to advise the Chinese government on its currency problem. If he had succeeded China and Hong Kong would again have been in step, but Japanese pressure in North China, their reluctance to see any financial reform which would strengthen China, and the outbreak of hostilities shortly after, resulted in the failure of his scheme.

In 1931 Great Britain was forced off the gold standard, and had to abandon her traditional free-trade policy. By the Ottawa Agreements of 1932, a system of Imperial preferences was introduced by which goods using a minimum of 50 per cent of Empire materials or labour were given a preference in the British and Dominion markets. In the case of Hong Kong, the percentage had to be modified because the colony produced so few raw materials itself. In the matter of imports, the colony made some slight concessions, for example, non-Empire motor-cars had to pay a special import licence fee and Empire brandy was allowed in at less duty. The status of the port as a free port was not therefore seriously impaired, and Hong Kong remained until 1941 outside the sterling area. Yet the change was serious in that the colony now had stronger economic links outside China, and the principle of the open door was to that extent affected.

Hong Kong banking, insurance and market facilities were still an important source of revenue to the colony. Before the 1914–18 War, various countries established banks in China, often with political support, to compete for railway and government loans, and mining and other concessions. In face of Japanese ambitions, Britain, the United States and France in 1921 established a Consortium with Japan, collectively to supply China with capital 'for a programme of economic reconstruction and improved communications', though this was done without the assent of the Chinese. The British and Chinese Corporation, which had been set up jointly by The Hongkong and Shanghai Banking Corporation and Jardine, Matheson & Co. in 1898, had been the main instrument in the supply of British capital to China for railway development and government loans, but it now operated on a more limited scale. The Hongkong and Shanghai Banking Corporation acted as one of the three foreign banks appointed to receive Chinese customs revenue after the Revolution of 1911, and in 1926 it became the sole Bank into which these revenues were paid until China secured tariff autonomy in 1928.

Significant of the changing times was the development of industry in the colony. The textile industry was reintroduced, and by 1939 the spinning and weaving factories were employing 5,867 people, mostly women. Hong Kong's oldest industry was ship-building and repairing; it employed 16,000 Chinese and 280 Europeans. In 1939 the Taikoo Dockyard at Quarry Bay, opened in 1908 by Butterfield & Swire, completed two ships of nearly 10,000 tons each. In 1934 a memorandum of the Hong Kong Chamber of Commerce on Hong Kong industries in relation to Imperial preferences listed the following manufactured or processed goods in Hong Kong: preserved and dry ginger, soya products, sugar refining, knitted wear, rattan furniture, rubber shoes, flashlight torches and batteries, rope, cement, perfumes, soap and fire-crackers.

The colony had been founded on its unrivalled harbour

facilities; it was not equally endowed by nature to meet the challenge of the air, yet it became one of the world's great airports. The air-field at Kai Tak came into being in 1928, and eight years later, Imperial Airways linked the colony with Britain via Penang, and in the same year Pan-American Airways began proving flights across the Pacific and China National Airways Corporation provided an air link with the mainland.

There were constitutional and administrative developments during these years, but no change of principle by which official majorities controlled the Executive and Legislative Councils. The demand for greater devolution of power in the post-war Commonwealth combined with the traditional British policy of cautious constitutional advance to give wider representation to local Hong Kong opinion. A Chinese member was added to the Executive Council in 1926, making the third unofficial member of that body, which, with the six official members, now numbered nine. In 1929 the Legislative Council was increased from eight officials and six unofficials to ten and eight respectively, including the Governor. Of the unofficials, two were elected respectively by the J.P.'s and the Chamber of Commerce, three were to be Chinese, and one also represented the Portuguese community. In 1922 the term for which an unofficial seat could be held was reduced to four years and the corresponding term in the Executive Council was fixed at five years. Attempts were made to mobilize public opinion and in 1920 a Kowloon Ratepayers' Association was formed followed by a Peak Residents' Association in 1922.

Sir Henry May was succeeded as governor by Sir Reginald Stubbs, who remained from September 1919 to October 1925, when he retired; Sir Cecil Clementi was Governor until February 1930, when he became Governor of the Straits Settlements and High Commissioner for Malaya. His successor was Sir William Peel (1930 to 1935), who was followed in December 1935 by Sir Andrew Caldecott. In 1937 he went to Ceylon as Governor, and Sir Geoffrey Northcote took his place in October 1937, to be followed by Sir Mark Young, who arrived in 1941.

There was some expansion and reorganization of the administrative services. The colonial treasurer was replaced in 1938 by a financial secretary who assumed control of all financial administration. The Secretary for Chinese Affairs lost his title of Protector of the Chinese, but with the growth of the Chinese population this office increased in importance and its holder, like the colonial secretary and financial secretary, was an ex-officio member of the two councils. Recruitment from overseas to the senior grades of the civil service caused much criticism, partly on account of costs; a Retrenchment Commission in 1932 urged more local recruitment, and in 1936 it was agreed to consider qualified local candidates before a government vacancy was filled. The police force, which had had such a stormy history, now settled into its modern form. The title Captain Superintendent of Police gave way to Inspector-General, and then in 1937 was changed to Commissioner of Police.

The educational system continued to evolve with typically British flexibility. In 1921 a Board of Education consisting of officials of the Education Department and representatives of the community was set up with advisory powers. At the end of 1921, the old grant code for voluntary schools was abandoned, except in the case of five schools under European management which had specially recruited overseas staffs; these schools later increased in number to twelve. Other schools needing public help were subsidized by the payment of monthly subsidies, subject to the reports of inspectors, missionary and secular schools being treated alike. The compulsory registration of schools was applied to the New Territories. In 1922, school medical inspections began and a schools medical officer was appointed in 1926. In 1923, in the urban areas, there were 471 schools with 24,000 pupils, of which 164 with 9,397 pupils were subsidized. In rural areas there were 192 schools with 4,665 pupils of which half were subsidized. It was estimated that 90 per cent of the peasants of the colony could neither read nor write. Schools for European children were provided and those over the age of nine were concentrated in the Kowloon school which became the Central British School. Teachers' training was carried on at the Technical Institute, and, for vernacular trainees only, at the Man Ho Temple and at Belilios Public School; in 1925, the training of teachers for the rural schools was begun at Taipo, and the Northcote Training College was opened in 1939 for training teachers for both Anglo-Chinese and vernacular schools. Queen's College catered for

Chinese boys of all ages, and the demand for admission was such that a second similar school, King's College, was completed in 1926. An administrative cadet officer remained as director of education until the retirement of G. R. Sayer in 1938.

The Hong Kong University held its first congregation for granting degrees in 1916 in the presence of the Governor of Kwangtung; in addition to twenty-three graduands, the occasion was marked by the conferring of honorary degrees on five distinguished local figures. The University's income soon proved inadequate to its needs, and government assistance became necessary in 1920. In 1922, the Rockefeller Institute endowed the three chairs of medicine, surgery and obstetrics, and in 1929 the Fung Ping Shan Chinese library was built and endowed by the family of the man whose name it bears. Women students were admitted in 1921. In that year, Sir Charles Eliot was made ambassador to Japan, and Sir William Brunyate succeeded as vice-chancellor. In 1939 a science faculty was added. The only honours degrees were those awarded by the engineering faculty, which for many years remained the largest faculty, as Lugard intended.

Following the example set by Britain, there was greater interest in social welfare. Plague had been a scourge since 1894, but now years of anti-plague measures began to have effect, and from 1924 it virtually disappeared from the colony. Malaria was brought under control, nullahs were trained and treated and a malaria bureau was set up in 1930. The influx of refugees beginning in 1937 brought more infection, however, and there were serious outbreaks of smallpox and cholera in 1937 and 1938. A new Building Ordinance 1935, provided for improved standards of lighting and ventilation, but overcrowding persisted because of the refugees. In 1935 the Sanitary Board which had consisted of five official members including a military representative, and five unofficials, was abolished and replaced by an Urban Council, still with only advisory functions, having power to frame and operate bye-laws subject to their acceptance by the Legislative Council. The medical and health services were combined under one head, the director of medical and sanitary services, and he became vice-chairman of the council, and controlled its health staff. The Urban

Council consisted of five official members and eight unofficial members, of whom two were elected by those whose names appeared on the jury lists, and six were appointed by the Governor, of whom three had to be Chinese. Medical services expanded; the government civil hospital moved to Pokfulam in 1937 and became known as the Queen Mary Hospital, the Kowloon hospital was opened in 1926, and the Tung Wah expanded and built another hospital at Sokonpo. The question of *mui .tsai* was finally settled in March 1922, when it was declared illegal by the British government; legislation against child servitude was passed in the colony in December of that year, by which child adoptions were subject to strict regulation; registration of *mui tsai* became compulsory in 1929.

A beginning was made with factory legislation. In 1923 an ordinance protecting children employed in industry began a series of factory ordinances which extended as the colony became increasingly industrial, and a Labour Officer was appointed in 1938 to deal with general conditions of labour, strikes, organization of trade unions, and arbitration in trade disputes.

The programme of public works included chiefly water schemes, roads and reclamation. The Tai Tam water scheme had been virtually completed in 1918, when Sir Henry May opened the Tai Tam Reservoir, and incidentally caused offence by urging civil servants to drink more of its contents. In 1928 the Shing Mun Valley water scheme was commenced and in 1937, the Jubilee Reservoir, named in honour of the jubilee of George V's reign, was completed, the 285 feet dam being the highest in the British Empire at that time. Yet population tended to outstrip water supply because of unrestricted immigration rather than through lack of foresight in the Public Works Department. The last section of the road around the New Territories was completed in 1920, the road to Shek O in 1923, and that to Repulse Bay from Wong Nei Chong Gap in 1924. The road to the Peak and Stubbs Road were completed and new roads in Kowloon. A reclamation scheme in Wanchai, which had been talked about ever since the great central reclamation had been completed, was begun in 1922, and further reclamations were carried out at Kai Tak, Shamshuipo and Laichikok.

Public loans were issued, to finance public works or convert existing loans, in 1934 and 1940, additional to the trade loan of 1925. In spite of the continual setbacks to trade due to un-settled conditions in the neighbouring provinces, public revenue showed its accustomed buoyancy. Additional taxation was im-posed after the first World War, in 1921, but it was not until the opening of the second World War that direct taxation was introduced in the form of a tax on income, property, salaries, profits from trade and corporation profits. Revenue showed steady increase except for the years following the 1931 slump. In 1921, revenue was $17,728,000; in 1931, $33,549,000 and in 1939, $41,478,000. In 1940, as a result of special war taxation, it had risen to $70,175,000. Expenditure increased from $15,739,652 in 1921 to $37,949,000 in 1939; over the same period military expenditure increased from $2,318,654 to $6,051,926, police expenditure more than doubled, but the chief rises were in the social services: education costs went up from $589,325 to $2,336,865 and sanitary services from $536,438 to $1,148,034.

This period of economic, social and administrative expansion was brought to an abrupt close by the war of 1939–45, when, in December 1941, the colony fell to the Japanese.

CHAPTER XXV

DEFEAT AND RECOVERY

'I had no illusions about the fate of Hong Kong under
the overwhelming impact of Japanese power. But the finer
the British resistance the better for all.'
                        Winston Churchill: The Second World War
                        Vol. 3, p. 562.

BRITISH preparations for the war that came to Europe in September 1939 were already well in hand and included arrangements for the Colonies, for whose defence Britain was responsible. British emergency legislation, which mobilized the nation's human and material resources behind the war effort, were not forced on the Colonies but they were never-theless expected to support Britain by enacting the necessary measures, following models sent for their guidance from London.

In Hong Kong, as in all Colonies, a mass of emergency legislation was passed, usually in the form of regulations based on existing, or new or amended ordinances. Yet significantly, the power of concurrent legislation by the Crown was invoked in matters vitally important to the conduct of the war, for example the main Emergency Regulations of September 1939 in Hong Kong were issued by the Governor acting alone, as representative of the Crown, and not by the Governor in Council. Hong Kong's emergency measures included a censorship, mining the harbour approaches, assuming powers to requisition ships and aircraft, marking out protected areas for defence security, requisitioning buildings, controlling trade to economise in shipping and controlling foreign exchange to conserve hard currency, the interning of enemy citizens and liquidation of enemy firms. Hong Kong's trade, being that of a free commercial entrepot, proved difficult to control and the Colony was treated sympathetically as a special case; indeed, no satisfactory scheme of control was worked out before the Japanese attack made any further attempt superfluous. The Colony was useful in purchasing Chinese metals like tungsten and molybdenum to prevent them falling into Japanese hands.

There were also difficulties about exchange control since Hong Kong currency freely circulated in southern Kwantung Province, but this was offset by the large number of Hong Kong firms which had their headquarters in London and so easily came under British controls. Eventually in June 1941, the deteriorating war situation demanded much stricter exchange regulations which forced Hong Kong, for the first time in its history, to link its currency with sterling.

The Colony's manpower too had to be organized to ensure its most efficient use. Conscription for male British subjects of European birth, between the ages of 18 and 55, was introduced in June 1939, Hong Kong being the first British overseas territory to follow Britain's lead in this respect. Those fit for active service age 18 to 41, were allocated to the Hong Kong Volunteer Defence Corps (H.K.V.D.C.), or Hong Kong Naval Defence Force (H.K.N.D.F.); those in reserved occupations received training but were not allowed to volunteer for the armed forces without permission, and the less fit were posted to one of the auxiliary defence services. Appeals were allowed in case of hardship. Conscientious objectors were very few and were allocated to one of the defence services. Dominions citizens were given three months to volunteer, after which the ordinance was applied to them; large numbers of friendly European nationals volunteered and 450 local Chinese also volunteered. The Hong Kong Volunteer Defence Corps was placed on a more effective footing, under a professional soldier as commandant with compulsory parades and camps, and men over the age of 55, with military service, formed a static defence unit, nicknamed the 'Hughesiliers' after its first commander, A.W. Hughes. Auxiliary Defence Services were organized—for example, the Auxiliary Police, the Auxiliary Nursing Service, the Auxiliary Fire Service and the Air Raid Precautions Department (A.R.P.)—and Essential Services were defined. The A.R.P. started in 1938 and rapidly expanded after 1939, particularly after the decision not to build public shelters for the masses was reversed in June 1940.

The Chinese in Hong Kong generally held themselves aloof, pursued their normal lives and generally left the fighting to the British. Proposals to arm the local Chinese were turned down partly because British policy was to avoid as far as possible giving offence to the Japanese. Many Chinese, particularly those with European associations, joined the Volunteers, or enlisted in the British regular forces for such duties as drivers and orderlies. Shortage of manpower for the Auxiliary Defence Services led to recruiting campaigns among university students and others with some knowledge of English, which continued up to the eve of the Japanese attack.

Rapid expansion and dilution of the Civil Service created problems and a public enquiry into the A.R.P. Department revealed serious corruption and malpractice, and that into the Immigration Department, set up in 1940 to restrict the flood of Chinese immigrants, chaos and inefficiency. The threat of a Japanese attack on the Colony in June 1940 led to the abrupt evacuation of 3,474 expatriate women and children to Australia, an unpopular move resulting in Government being accused of favouritism, racial discrimination and callous inefficiency.

The cost of the Emergency measures was covered by special war Budgets additional to those for normal expenditure, in which direct taxes on salaries business profits, corporation profits and property were levied. The proposal to impose a full income tax met with the bitter and combined opposition of Chinese and Europeans alike, and was dropped.

Japan, taking advantage of the pre-occupation of the Western Powers with the War in Europe, and having failed to win American acquiescence in her plans for the Greater East Asia Co-prosperity sphere, suddenly attacked Pearl Harbour in December 1941, crippled the American fleet, and engulfed the whole Far East in war by simultaneous onslaughts on Hong Kong, the Philippines and Malaya.

The lapse of the Washington Naval Limitation Treaties in 1938 freed Hong Kong from restrictions regarding its defence, and the Gindrinkers Line of defence was constructed, stretching thirteen miles from Gindrinkers Bay in the West, via Tide Cove, to Port Shelter in the east to protect the harbour from land attack, while heavy coastal guns pointed seaward. The War in Europe made it impossible to spare sufficient forces to man all these defence positions, and in 1939 the Gindrinkers Line was given up and defence was confined to the Island, one regiment being stationed on the mainland to hold it for two days to allow time for the necessary demolitions. With the arrival of two largely untrained Canadian batallions only three weeks before the fighting began, Major General C.M. Maltby, the garrison Commander, felt himself strong enough to revert to the earlier Gindrinkers defence Line, hoping to hold it for about a week. At no time was it intended to attempt to hold the New Territories indefinitely. Reports of Japanese troop concentrations on the other side of the border warned of impending attack and by the evening of 7 December 1941 all British troops were in position. They were organized in two brigades, each of three infantry batallions; one, comprising the 2nd Royal Scots, the 5/7 Rajputs and the 2/14 Punjabis on the mainland and the other comprising the 1st Middlesex, the 1st Royal Rifles of Canada and the 1st Winnipeg Grenadiers on the Island, altogether, including some 2,000 Hong Kong's own Volunteer Defence Corps and Naval Defence Force, some 12,000 men. The Japanese used one division, the 338th, of three infantry regiments the 238th, 239th and 230th, each of three batallions with additional artillery units, these numbering rather more than the defenders. They attacked at 8.0 a.m. on the morning of 8 December by crossing the river at Lo Wu, and dive-bombing the Kai Tak airfield. From the start the position of the defenders was hopeless. They lacked air power and the six obsolescent R.A.F. planes were mercifully grounded; there was no radar, they were inferior to the enemy in artillery, and some locally recruited men in the regular units proved unreliable. The sinking of the two capital ships, *Prince of Wales* and *Repulse* gave the Japanese complete control of the sea, and ruled out any relief of the garrison from outside. British intelligence had consistently and inexcusably under-rated the Japanese who were well trained, highly disciplined, efficiently handled, suitably shod for silent night work and made skilful use of artillery and air bombing. Japanese intelligence was excellent and every officer had a map pinpointing British military positions.

On the night of 9–10th they seized the Shing Mun redoubt on Smugglers Ridge, the strongest point in the Gindrinkers Line; General Maltby decided to withdraw from the mainland rather than risk losing men earmarked for the vital defence of the Island bastion and the last British units crossed to the Island in broad daylight on the morning of the 13th. The mainland had fallen in five days. On the 13th and again on the 17th, Japanese demands for the Island's surrender were summarily rejected.

The defence of the Island was now organized in two Brigades. East Brigade comprised the Rajputs, Royal Rifles and three companies of the H.K.V.D.C. West Brigade comprized the Punjabis, Winnipeg Grenadiers, four companies of the H.K. V. D.C. and the Royal Scots; each brigade was supported by artillery. The Middlesex, armed with heavy machine guns, manned pill-boxes along the east and south coasts.

After an intense barrage, the Japanese landed on the night of 18 December at three points all in the Rajputs' sector between Lyemun and North Point. They immediately advanced to the high ground, captured West Brigade headquarters at Wong Nei Chong Gap next day, and cut the defence in two by advancing to the Repulse Bay Hotel on the South Coast, forcing the East Brigade back on Stanley peninsula. Stubborn resistance by small isolated bodies of men only temporarily held up the Japanese advance and the defenders could not be concentrated in sufficient strength to challenge the Japanese who seized and kept the initiative. A determined and heroic defence ended on Christmas Day only when the resolute Governor was told that further resistance was useless. Force "Z", a small body mainly of Hong Kong Volunteers and trained in sabotage behind the enemy lines, had some success in blowing up enemy transport in Tsun Wan before escaping into Free China.

The Colony, now known as the 'Captured Territory of Hong Kong', suffered a harrowing Japanese occupation lasting three years and eight months. Over 7,000 Prisoners of War were concentrated in Shumshuipo Barracks until April 1942, when the Officers and Indians were put in separate camps; all were kept on a starvation diet giving rise to deficiency diseases such as beriberi and pellagra, while deaths from dysentry were common at first and treated by the Japanese camp authorities with callous indifference. Gross overcrowding was relieved when the younger men, chiefly regular soldiers, were drafted to labouring work in Japan, one party of which lost 1,092 men out of 1,816, when the ship they were travelling in, the *Lisbon Maru*, was torpedoed off the Chusan Islands.

Enemy civilians were herded, like cattle, men, women and children intermingled, into a civilian internment camp at Stanley, which lacked the basic essentials of a civilized life, and they barely survived on a starvation diet. Help was, however, received from some Chinese in Hong Kong.

There were a number of escapes to free China from the camps and among them, some Hong Kong men formed the British Army Aid Group, with headquarters at Kweilin and a main forward base at Waichow, which aided escapees, saved many lives by supplying medicines and gathered intelligence regarding conditions in Hong Kong.

During the occupation period, the Japanese reduced Hong Kong's population from 1,600,000 to under 600,000 mainly by driving them back into Kwantung, and often by harsh methods, mainly for reasons of defence and to save the import of food and calls on shipping. A Chinese Representative

Council of three members, later increased to six, and a Chinese Co-operative Council of twenty-two, later increased to twenty-six, represented Chinese views and interests. Some eighteen District Bureaux spread over the whole Colony kept the Japanese in touch with local opinion. Towards the end, American air raids and a tight American blockade created shortages which brought rice rationing and most public utilities services to a halt.

The Japanese accepted defeat on 14 August, 1945 and a week later, the Colonial Secretary, Mr. (later Sir), F.C. Gimson, left Stanley Camp with some senior officials and set up a temporary administration, and other internees emerged to help restore the public utility services. On 30 August, units of the British Pacific Fleet under Rear Admiral C.H.J. Harcourt entered harbour, raised the British flag, and brought the Japanese occupation to an end. In the evening, accompanied by Mr. Gimson and senior staff officers, the Admiral attended a solemn thanksgiving service at Stanley.

The resumption of British authority in Hong Kong did not pass unchallenged, particularly in the United States where anti-colonial sentiment was strong. President Roosevelt felt that clause 3 of the Atlantic Charter of March 1943 which urged the liberation of all peoples, applied as much to those of British colonies as to those over-run by the Germans and Japanese and he ' . . . once or twice urged the British to give up Hong Kong as a gesture of good will . . . .'[1] At the Yalta Conference in February 1945, Roosevelt was anxious to secure Russian help in the Pacific War and offered concessions at the expense of both Japan and China, and to mollify the latter, urged that Hong Kong should be given back to her.[2] British and Chinese representatives were excluded from that part of the negotiations relating to the Far East, and Churchill 'exploded' when he learnt that Britain's control over her colonies was being questioned.[3] In January 1943, the United States and Britain each made a treaty with China renouncing all concessions, settlements and special privileges attached to

---

[1] R.E. Sherwood, *The White House Papers of Harry L. Hopkins*, 1948, pp. 718-19. Lord Halifax, British Ambassador in Washington at the time has confirmed this in his memoirs.
[2] Sherwood. op. cit. p. 854.
[3] Ibid.

the treaty port system; Chiang Kai-shek therefore had some hopes of taking over Hong Kong, or at least the New Territories, though Britain explained that the treaty related only to such privileges as were inherent in the treaty port system.

The Allies set up military administrations in their territories recovered from enemy occupation, under the Supreme Allied Commander of the territory, who was to be guided in his civil policies by the Government which had exercised control there before the war, and assisted by military Civil Affairs Officers appointed by that Government. A Planning Unit under D.M. MacDougall, a senior Hong Kong Government officer who had escaped on the day of the surrender, had been set up in July 1943 by the Colonial Office in London to prepare plans for restoring British authority in Hong Kong, and it naturally formed the nucleus of the Civil Affairs staff of the Military Administration which Admiral Harcourt was ordered to set up. The Civil Affairs officers began to arrive on 7 September and the Military Administration began to function as planned with MacDougall as Chief Civil Affairs Officer, in place of the administration headed by Mr. Gimson who left for home on 16 September.

A difficulty arose over the Japanese surrender in Hong Kong as the Colony came within the war zone controlled by General-issimo Chiang Kai-shek, to whom therefore the surrender should have been made. This was surmounted by the Admiral receiving the surrender at Government House on 16 September on behalf of both China and Britain.

Rebuilding a viable community life in Hong Kong presented monumental problems and since peace came suddenly, before the War Office could organize and send civilian supplies, improvisation had necessarily to be the order of the day. This situation allowed the Chinese, flocking back at the rate of 100,000 a month, to show their characteristic resilience. Food and fuel were first priority and officers were sent to Canton, Borneo, India and Japan to secure food and supplies at virtually any price. The Government was forced into bulk buying, rice was rationed according to stocks available and subsidized; and general price control introduced. Private trading was restored on 23 November 1945 mainly at the request of the Chinese who were supplied with credit by American firms, but many British business men took Government posts until normal commercial dealing could be resumed. Trade and foreign exchange controls were introduced to conserve hard currency and to prevent scarce supplies needed in Hong Kong being sent to more lucrative markets abroad.

There were many other problems left over from the war. The prisoner of war camps and Stanley internment camp had to be wound up and those domiciled abroad repatriated. The Hong Kong Volunteer Defence Corps and Hong Kong Royal Naval Volunteer Reserve were demobilized; those who were prisoners throughout the occupation were given full pay, leave and allowances, those who escaped and rejoined the Allied forces were treated according to their service, those who escaped and remained in Hong Kong were treated as being demobilized 98 days after their escape. Many local men felt they should be given free passages to and from Britain the same as the Europeans alongside whom they had fought. War cemeteries were contructed at Stanley and Sai Wan.

Then there was the problem of accommodation. War damage to property made 72 per cent of the foreign community homeless and 160,000 flat dwellers lost their homes; the shortages were more acute by the commandeering of private property for the needs of the swollen armed Forces. The shortage of building materials, the refusal by Government to rebuild war-damaged property at public expense as a legitimate war charge, and the very high prices ruling which were confidently expected to fall, all resulted in much delay in rebuilding and caused great dissatisfaction with Government. Rebuilding got under way in 1948, and until then pressure on accommodation led Government to requisition empty property, use all accommodation to capacity and delay the passages of families. Local hotels helped by packing three persons into a single room.

Converted lorries were used as buses, and the Services did much to keep the public utilities going until new equipment arrived. The substitution of trolley buses for trams was discussed and turned down, and similarly, the suggested change to driving on the right was rejected. Recovery in road traffic was so rapid that in 1948 a one-way street system had to be introduced into the Central District.

There was much recrimination over collaboration with the Japanese. Influential Chinese had little option under strong Japanese pressure but to work with the victors, besides which, they naturally wanted to assist their own people. Much lower in the social scale were those who served under the Japanese and particularly those who assisted the Japanese Kempeitai in apprehending and torturing those suspected of espionage or of being in contact with Allied Forces. Over 50 suspects were held to face committal proceedings on a charge of treason; after the first trials, the others were charged under the Emergency Regulations with committing acts with the intent to assist the enemy, a charge which did not carry the death penalty. Altogether 30 persons were tried, 5 were hanged, 22 were imprisoned for various periods ranging from fifteen years to six months, 2 were sentenced to one day, one was acquitted, and one escaped.

At the same time, the War Crimes Trials of Japanese accused of war crimes were held in special British Military Courts, and not in Hong Kong's Courts. The two were quite different, but the tale of atrocities in each gave them a decided similarity. Altogether 21 Japanese were given the death sentence, 85 were imprisoned for various terms, 14 were acquitted and charges against the remainder were dropped.

CHAPTER XXVI

NEW ADMINISTRATIVE PATTERNS

'Your return, Sir, we hope and believe, marks a new epoch in the history of the Colony. . . . It signifies the birth of a new Hong Kong.'

Sir Man Kam Lo in the Legislative Council,
16 May 1946

THE peace inevitably brought changes in colonial policies, and in Hong Kong, particularly after the British humiliations in the War, there could clearly be no simple return to the past. The call for common war sacrifices had brought the fact of appallingly low colonial living standards starkly into the open

and helped to produce a 'new angle of vision' in the Colonial
Office, advocating colonial self-government within the Commonwealth and economic development to give higher living
standards and general social betterment.

Significant of the this new spirit, Sir Mark Young's first
announcement, when he landed at Queen's Pier on 1 May 1946
to resume his interrupted governorship and restore civil
government, promised the Colony's inhabitants 'a fuller and
more responsible share in the management of their own affairs
. . . the fullest account being taken of the views and wishes of
the inhabitants', and he proposed a Municipal Council to
which some important functions of government would be
transferred. After inviting the views of representative bodies
and individuals, the Governor, in a broadcast address on 26
August 1946, outlined his proposals which became known as the
'Young Plan'. Briefly, he proposed a municipal council, elected
one-third by Chinese voters, one-third by non-Chinese and
one-third equally by Chinese and non-Chinese representative
organizations, with its own finances which would give it some
independence in its policies over the wider sphere of administration entrusted to it. Comments were again asked for, and in
July 1947, a simultaneous announcement in London and Hong
Kong broadly approved the Young Plan.

Sir Mark Young left on retirement in May 1947 and was
succeeded by Sir Alexander Grantham, High Commissioner
for the Western Pacific, who had earlier served thirteen years
as a Hong Kong cadet officer, and who began a ten year
governorship often referred to as the Grantham era in tribute to
his personal leadership. Three Bills setting out the Young Plan
in detail were published in June 1949. However, the Plan
was still-born. The Unofficial Members of the Legislative
Council, who had already criticized the Plan at the Budget
debate in March, now carried motions to reject the Plan, and
despite petitions by some Chinese organizations for more
far-reaching reform, the Plan was dropped, and simultaneous
announcements in London and Hong Kong in October 1952
declared the time inopportune for constitutional changes of
a major character. It has remained inopportune ever since.
The Plan foundered because of the enormous influx of refugees
which transformed the character of the people of Hong Kong.

Minor constitutional changes have been made. The Executive Council was restored along with civil government in May 1946 with seven official, five of them *ex officio*, and four unofficial, and in 1948 there were six official and six unofficial members and in 1966 the latter were increased to eight, four of them Chinese. The Legislative Council was restored on 1 May 1946 with nine officials and seven unofficials, increased in 1951 to nine and eight respectively, and in June 1964 to twelve and thirteen respectively, the Governor having, as President, an original and a casting vote. The Chinese element among the unofficials increased until in 1971 eleven were Chinese and only two European, the latter nominated respectively by the two nominating bodies, the Hong Kong General Chamber of Commerce and the Unofficial Justices of the Peace. Thus the Chinese have a majority on the Council's sixteen-member Finance Committee.

The Urban Council was revived with five official and six unofficial nominated members under an official Chairman who became also Director of Urban Services in 1953. Elections were resumed in May 1952 when the Young Plan was dropped, and the elected representatives were increased from two to four in 1953 and the electoral roll increased to some 18,500. In 1956 there were sixteen unofficial members, half elected and half nominated, increased to twenty in 1965, retaining the same proportions. The registered electorate had increased to 37,788 in 1971, only a small fraction of the community, and even of the number entitled to register as voters which was estimated to be roughly 350,000. Elections brought two political bodies into being, the Reform Club in 1949 and the Civic Association in 1955, each advocating more direct representation of the people on the Legislative Council.

More significant was the policy of local recruitment for the civil service. Government posts which up to 1946 had been reserved for European officers were then opened to local officers, and expatriates were to be appointed only if suitable local candidates were not available. Beginning in 1961 local officers were sent abroad to gain qualifications to fit them for higher posts. The first Chinese administrative class officer was appointed in 1946 and in 1952 a local appointee reached the position of head of the Medical Department. In 1951 there were

54 locally recruited officers in the Administrative and senior professional classes, or 10.75 per cent of the total. In 1971 there were 2,874 professional and administrative staff of which 1,609 were local, that is just over 52 per cent. New administrative departments, such as Resettlement, Labour and Mines, Information Services, Transport, Social Welfare, Statistics and Planning and Immigration, and the renamed Secretariat for Chinese Affairs which became the Secretariat for Home Affairs, all testified to Government's increased awareness of social problems and interest in Welfare. The Judiciary has been greatly expanded to include a Chief Justice, Senior Puisne Judge, six Puisne Judges, eight District Judges, and eleven magistrates. More important, Hong Kong became virtually autonomous, administratively and financially, in 1958, as was announced by Sir Robert Black, the Governor from 1958 to 1964, in the Legislative Council in March of that year; while Britain still exercises sovereignty, she has in practice restricted herself to control of Hong Kong's external relations.

The central feature of Hong Kong's post-war history has been the appearance of a vast new immigrant population from the mainland, following communist successes in the Civil War and particularly their capture of Canton in October 1949, which by May 1950 had brought 700,000 refugees into Hong Kong. The population of 1,600,000 at the end of 1946 had swollen to an estimated 2,360,000 by the end of 1950 and to 2½ millions at the end of 1956. The newcomers made their homes on roof-tops, in stairways and in crude insanitary shanty towns on the hillsides, and subjected community and public utility services to severe strain. It was quite impossible to absorb so rapid an inflow and in May 1950 entry from China was restricted at the frontier by a quota system to make those entering roughly equal to those leaving. A serious squatter fire on the evening of Christmas Day 1953 which made 53,000 homeless forced Government into large resettlement schemes and the adoption of a policy of integrating the squatters into the community. This policy, coupled with the new British colonial policy of improving social and economic conditions, led the Hong Kong Government gradually to embark on new and wider fields of social welfare, mostly in alliance with voluntary welfare agencies operated by the religious bodies.

Huge housing estates have been perhaps the most spectacular of Government's achievements. Beginning in 1954, squatter clearance and rehousing in huge Resettlement Estates has proceeded without remission. Speed and cheapness demanded the minimum acceptable standards in uniform seven-storey blocks with communal washing and other facilities; these conditions have been gradually improved in later types of resettlement blocks. At the end of 1970 the Resettlement Department had housed nearly 1,100,000 persons, Government Low-cost Housing estates for those with monthly incomes of under $500 contained 187,789 in rather better accommodation, and the Government Housing Authority, set up in 1954 and comprising mainly the Urban Council, to cater for those earning between $400 and $1250 monthly, had re-housed 205,044 persons. Voluntary agencies such as the Hong Kong Housing Society were subsidized, so that by the end of 1970 some 43 per cent of the population lived in government or government-subsidized accommodation. The noted town-planner, Sir Patrick Abercrombie, visited the Colony in 1947 and urged in his report more attention to zoning, more open spaces, the removal of the armed services from the central district, which has been partly achieved, and a harbour tunnel, the construction of which began in 1970 and was completed in 1972.

A Social Welfare Office, set up in 1948, became an independent department in January 1958 and dealt with youth services and child welfare, work amongst women and girls, probation and correction, relief and community development. It worked with the voluntary agencies, mostly organized under the Hong Kong Council of Social Service through the medium of subsidies. In 1971, it introduced a cash relief scheme for the very poor, but its attitude has been a cautious one of not undermining the cohesiveness of the Chinese family and of directing social welfare assistance to making individuals more self-supporting.

The Government set out to improve the conditions of labour and living standards. The immediate post-war period saw great labour unrest because wages were not adjusted to meet the highly inflated cost of living, partly due to the employers' belief that prices would fall to more normal levels. Government employed an experienced trade unionist from Britain to organize a trade union movement on British lines, but with little success. Trade unions developed strong political affiliations, and in any case surplus labour weakened the bargaining power of the unions. Nevertheless, wages steadily rose to give the Hong Kong industrial worker the second highest standard of living in Asia in 1971. A Labour Officer attached to the Secretary for Chinese Affairs headed an independent Labour Department in 1946 which was responsible for much labour legislation to protect the worker. Hours of labour for women and young persons were restricted to eight daily,[1] and night work for women was abolished in 1970 but allowed to continue under stringent conditions in a few of the larger cotton spinning factories. An Ordinance in 1961 gave compulsory holidays with pay for industrial workers and paid sickness leave, and a Workmen's Compensation Ordinance of 1953 has, with a number of amendments, arranged for compensation in case of industrial accidents, for which the Labour Department has assisted the worker in making his claim. In 1970 all manual workers and non-manual workers earning up to $1,500 monthly became entitled to four rest days per month in addition to the statutory holidays. In addition, attention has been paid to industrial health, safety and conciliation in industrial disputes.

There has been growing concern over public health and medical services. Total hospital beds represented 4.03 per thousand of the population in 1970 compared with 1.65 in 1957, and was backed by free clinics for tuberculosis, social hygiene, leprosy and infant welfare, while free floating clinics for the boat people, free mobile dispensaries for remote villages and a free vaccination service were developed. A School Medical service at $7 per year set up before the war was treating 42,803 students in 1970. Legalised opium smoking divans supplied by a government monopolist were finally abolished after the war, but the vast over-crowding, the pressures of a harshly competitive society and maladjustment to urban conditions have led to a severe drug addiction problem responsible for a large percentage of the prison population. Malaria disappeared except for certain rural areas because of

[1] 8 hours 20 minutes a day and 50 hours a week in 1971 and 8 hours a day and 48 hours a week from December 1971.

the draining, clearing of nullahs and treatment of streams by the Anti-malarial Bureau.

Education had virtually to be rebuilt from scratch after the war because many schools were destroyed or requisitioned, and because of the expansion of the population in which some 43 per cent on average were of school age. One building was made to serve two schools in separate morning and afternoon sessions. Again, as in the social welfare field, much was achieved by a partnership between Government and aided and subsidized schools under voluntary agencies. In 1946 there were about 53,200 receiving education, and some 60,000 were estimated to be without education; in 1970 total enrolment in all types of schools was 983,495, and the goal of free primary education for those who wanted it, was achieved in 1971, while in the same year a cautious beginning was made with compulsory attendance subject to enquiry by officers of the Education Department. Recently some 46,000 new primary places have been needed each year, roughly a large school of over 900 places every week. About 17 per cent have gone on to aided or provided secondary schools, and in 1971 Government began to organize three years' secondary education for all on a fee-paying basis.

The University of Hong Kong expanded from the pre-war 400 to 2,283 in 1970 and the new Chinese University of Hong Kong, comprising three autonomous Colleges, set up in 1963 mainly for students of the Chinese language Middle Schools, had an enrolment of 1,928. A Technical College set up in 1946 had 13,417 students in seven departments, and technical education was being expanded at lower levels, while three Colleges of Education catered for teacher training.

The old City Hall site was sold and after some pressure Government built a new City Hall in 1961 on reclaimed land on the north side of Connaught Road which proved popular with all sections and became a focus for cultural activities.

The cost of these policies have been met partly out of increasing taxation yields, but in 1947 the old war taxation was revived, and while a full income tax was again avoided, somewhat equivalent taxes on salaries and wages, property, business profits and corporation profits were imposed. But Hong Kong has remained a free port with no customs duties except the duties charged on luxury items such as wines, spirits, perfumes and tobacco etc., whether imported or locally produced, though rates are not uniform.

A significant social development has been the movement towards racial equality brought about by the war, by the entry of many more Chinese into the learned professions, under the stimulus of the higher professional and administrative posts in Government being thrown open to them, and partly due to the academic distinctions gained by Chinese students in Universities and institutions abroad. In addition the Chinese have tended to dominate local commerce and industry and have become the wealthier section of the population. The working class have not fully shared Hong Kong's prosperity and rioting in 1956 and 1966 may have indicated an underlying malaise. In fact some at least of Hong Kong's problems would seem to be related to greater, rather than less, mass prosperity and leisure in a cramped environment.[1]

[1] During the 1960s real wages in the manufacturing industry rose at an average of 5.7 per cent a year.

CHAPTER XXVII

A PROBLEM OF PEOPLE AND THE RISE OF INDUSTRY

'Hong Kong's economic survival was due to the expansion of, and a revolution in, its industry; and this was made possible in some measure by the three gifts which some of the refugees brought with them from China; the first, a surplus of labour, the second new techniques from the North coupled with a commercial shrewdness and determination . . . and the third new capital seeking employment and security.'

Hong Kong Annual Report, 1956, Ch. 1.
'A Problem of People'

THE Hong Kong Government tried to be friendly towards China after the war; for example captured Japanese ships were handed over to it before the agreed time, pre-war restrictions on entry into the Colony were dropped, and more important, in 1948 the Chinese National Maritime Customs were given the right to set up collecting stations in the Colony and patrol the Colony's waters. The Government assisted China with measures to establish her new Gold Yuan currency, and in 1948 sent 10,000 tons of rice to Shanghai on loan to relieve food shortages there. British and Chinese officials met at the border in 1948 to restore the boundary stones removed by the Japanese. Unfortunately in this year, the Hong Kong Government's proposal to remove squatters from the old Kowloon walled city led to riots inspired by Canton elements who had never ceased to regard that City as subject to Chinese jurisdiction. The Kuomintang regime soon fell; its civil war against the communists, always latent, resumed in earnest after the War and by 1 October 1949 the Communists had captured enough of China to proclaim the Chinese Peoples' Republic.

In Hong Kong, there was tension and fear of attack when communist troops appeared on the frontier and the garrison was increased and roads and bridges strengthened to permit the movement of heavy armour. Leftists showed their delight by holding long snake dances in the streets of Wanchai. Britain recognised the new Peking regime in February 1950 a lead which was perfunctorily received by the Communists, and which few other nations followed.

There were incidents in which shipping was fired on in Hong Kong's local waters from communist-held islands and from Chinese armed vessels, and the Courts had to adjudicate on the disposal of Chinese property such as state commercial aircraft which had been flown to the shelter of the Colony. The tension eased when the Communists showed themselves punctilious in respecting the Colony's boundary and British troops were kept away from the border where conditions remained peaceful enough. Tension was renewed by the War in Korea which began in June 1950 when the Communist regime in North Korea attacked the United States-supported regime in South Korea and was rescued from defeat by Chinese intervention. British troops served with the United Nations' forces in Korea and tension remained until the cease-fire in 1953. All Hong Kong residents were required to have identity cards and, in September 1951, a Compulsory Service Ordinance directed all British subjects into the local Volunteer armed forces, or Police, or Auxiliary Defence Services unless exempt by work in an essential occupation. This Ordinance remained until suspended by Proclamation as from 5 August 1961.

The Korean War adversely affected Hong Kong when the United Nations placed an embargo, with which Hong Kong had also to comply, on trade with China in a wide range of strategic goods. Worse, the United States, in December 1950, placed an almost complete embargo on Chinese trade which fell with particular weight on Hong Kong which was treated as part of China for this purpose. The Colony was badly hit and was described by a visiting American journalist in 1951 as 'this dying city', with its trade cut off by the fiat of outside nations engaged in a struggle against communism.

From this state of depression, Hong Kong was saved by the colossal immigration of Chinese refugees. Many from Shanghai brought capital and industrial expertise; most brought only themselves and formed a reservoir of labour that became one of Hong Kong's greatest assets, because they were industrious, frugal, unversed in trade union restrictive practices, forced to look for jobs, and many of them intelligent enough to be trained in the highest skills. Enterprising industrialists quickly saw that industry, particularly that in which labour was an important factor of production, could be brought in to absorb the labour supply, and industrialization, already given some fillip in the war when normal sources of supply were cut off, began to expand and flourish. Hong Kong had little raw materials, no local sources of power such as oil or coal, no tariffs behind which a growing industry could shelter, and there was a shortage of land and of water. It was nevertheless able to benefit greatly from this influx because, besides its magnificent harbour, it had a comparatively stable and honest government with the minimum bureaucratic interference, efficient banking, insurance and shipping services, a vast supply of labour, and the existence of Commonwealth preferences, and low and stable tax rates.

Industrial growth was rapid. From 1,050 industrial undertakings, employing 64,000, in 1947, the figures rose to 17,239 and 589,505 respectively in 1970. Many more worked in unregistered factories or as outworkers. Most factories were small family concerns, using self-generated capital, and often employing clansmen. In 1958, out of 4,906 factories, 3,225 employed under 20 workers, and 4,182 under 50 workers. Even in 1970, 75 per cent of all Hong Kong's industrial production came from factories with a hundred workers or more. Textiles, chiefly cotton, woollen knitted goods, made-up garments and since 1968, man-made fibres, dominated, employing 30 per cent of the total work force in 1954, and 40 per cent in 1970. Plastics developed early and in 1970 supplied 12 per cent of exports, the electronics industry was introduced in 1959 and in 1970 supplied about 10 per cent of all exports. In 1947, domestic exports were 10 per cent of the total exports, compared to 81 per cent in 1970.

The success of industry in Hong Kong has been due partly to relatively low wages, but also to the intensive use of the most modern equipment for 24 hours per day and the use of the latest automatic machinery needing less manual skill, while wages have been supplemented by the provision of meals, medical facilities, dormitory accommodation, and assistance with education.

Raw materials had to be imported and manufactures exported, and as the import-export entrepot machinery was already there, its adaptation to the new commerce was relatively easy. At first Hong Kong exported domestic products to developing countries, for example Indonesia was its best customer in 1956 taking 16 per cent of its total domestic exports. But the developing countries were eager to promote their own industry and the Colony moved into more sophisticated markets. In 1970 the United States and Britain took 54 per cent of the total domestic exports, with the German Federal Republic taking 8 per cent and Japan next with 4 per cent. The search for new outlets to avoid a dangerous dependence on two markets led to the setting up of the Trade Development Council in 1956 with eleven offices abroad. The Hong Kong Export Credit Insurance Corporation, set up in 1966, covered about 8 per cent of Hong Kong's exports in 1970. Another statutory body, the Hong Kong Productivity Council, was set up in 1967 to increase the productivity by training and disseminating information, and some 60 professional or experienced men were employed, usually on a short-term basis, to give instruction in the necessary skills and operating techniques.

The impact on developed countries of Hong Kong's exports, particularly textiles, resulted in the imposition of quotas in Britain, the United States and most other developed countries, by which Hong Kong's exports have been limited to prevent industrial dislocation in the importing countries, generally within the United Nations' General Administration of Trade and Tariffs (GATT) arrangements, and the United Nations Conference on Trade and Development (UNCTAD) in which Hong Kong has been accepted as a developing country.[1] British entry into the European Common Market will mean the end of preferences in the British market, but Hong Kong has been accepted as an associate member of the Market, entitled to preferences except in the case of textiles and footwear.

The entrepot trade has remained important, accounting for 19 per cent of Hong Kong's total combined exports. The trade with China which had been the staple of Hong Kong's commerce, being 40 per cent of its total trade before the war declined relatively, but she remained the leading source of the Colony's imports for twenty years up to 1968 when she was overtaken by Japan. The import of food, of which China supplied 46 per cent of the total food imports, ensured China an important place in Hong Kong's trade, and she retained a significant place in the re-export trade, supplying 24 per cent of the total re-exports.

The Japanese Yen was abruptly withdrawn from circulation on 13 September 1945 and replaced by the Hong Kong dollar tied to sterling at 16 to the pound. Bronze coins replaced the one cent and ten cent notes in 1949 and cupro-nickel coins replaced the Hong Kong Government one dollar notes in 1960, though HK$1 are still occasionally issued at Chinese New Year. Foreign exchange control was imposed immediately after the War and has remained in force, but Britain tolerated a free market in foreign exchange based not upon official parities but upon supply and demand, partly because the funds involved were Chinese remittances to relatives in China passing through Hong Kong, partly because funds came in by secret channels from South-East Asia and because Hong Kong was allowed to retain hard-currency earnings from trade with

[1] Hong Kong is usually treated as a borderline or special case as between developed and developing countries.

America, and also because Hong Kong was a net earner of foreign exchange. Britain also permitted a gold market restricted to Chinese operators.

The three chief British Banks had their note-issuing powers restored in denominations of $5 and upwards. Banks proliferated, cashing in on the boom in land-values until 1966 when some bankruptcies occurred due to over-investment in real estate, the value of which temporarily declined abruptly, and the Government was forced to impose stricter controls by a Bank Ordinance and appoint a Commissioner for Banking in 1967 to supervise its working.

Generally, from the middle 1950s boom years followed in virtually unbroken succession. Hong Kong's total trade, including both imports and exports, increased from $5,852 million in 1954 to $32,845 million in 1970. Government revenue has increased from $396,881,967 in the year ending April 1954 to $2,480,657,388 in that ending April 1970. Increasing population, to over four millions in 1971, meant prosperity for the building industry, and new industrial suburbs came into being at North Point, and To Kwa Wan in Kowloon, and completely new industrial townships were created such as that of 500,000 at Kwun Tong, built largely on reclaimed land, and that of Tsun Wan with 350,000 to which will be added the new township of Kwai Chung. Real wages have increased substantially, but even so, it is doubtful if the worker has shared proportionately in Hong Kong's prosperity. Pressure on available land has necessitated vast reclamation schemes, such as the Central reclamation begun in 1962 which added land stretching from the Naval base to the Macao Ferry Wharf. Even more striking is the virtual filling in of the north-eastern end of the harbour.

Industrial expansion has been successfully backed by the infrastructure; electric and gas companies, transport by sea, land and air, and telephones have all kept pace with an ever-increasing demand. Water-supply for some years lagged behind, and each winter restrictions in supply were enforced. A severe drought in 1963–4 reduced these to four and even three hours' supply every four days, and tankers were chartered and brought 2,436 million gallons from the Pearl River. The Tai Lam Chung reservoir completed in 1956 added 4,500 million gallons to the storage capacity, the Shek Pik Scheme on Lantau Island, completed in 1964, added another 5,390 million. But population expansion demanded more far-reaching schemes, and Plover Cove in Tolo Harbour was drained and sealed off in 1967, to add another 30,000 million gallons to the Colony's storage capacity. At present it is being enlarged, by raising the dam by 12 feet, to take 50 million gallons. An agreement with the Kwangtung Provincial authorities in 1960 brought water from the Chinese East River to supply the Colony with 15,000 million gallons yearly. The High Island water scheme, with a storage capacity of 60,000 million gallons, the largest scheme so far, was begun in 1970, and after its completion the Colony is likely to have to rely on desalination of sea-water. For this purpose a pilot desalination plant is being installed.

Government's policy has been to interfere with the economy to the minimum, consistent with ensuring sanctity of contract and law and order, and subject to legislation to deal with weaknesses, although it plays a large part in it. Land has been auctioned publicly to secure the most economic use, and to secure for Government part of the increased value due to the prosperity created by the community, and rents have been subject to some minor restrictions. But broadly, private capitalistic enterprise has reigned supreme. However, on occasions it has used its massive public works programme to even out boom and slumps in the economy, especially in the past decade.

CHAPTER XXVIII

HONG KONG IN THE MODERN WORLD

' . . . but Hong Kong has a record of overcoming its difficulties and there can be no doubt that the industry, intelligence and resilience of its people will ensure that this tradition will not be broken.'

Hong Kong Annual Report 1970.

THE Far East scene had undergone great changes since the Second World War, and Hong Kong had to face a problem of adaptation to a new post-war world in which the conditions which brought it into existence and nourished it for a century had virtually disappeared. Hong Kong was always regarded as a peculiar place, as *sui generis* as Phineas Ryrie (Legislative Councillor 1867–92) used to say, while Sir Hercules Robinson noted that 'its position is in many ways so grotesquely anoma-, lous'. The anomaly has continued.

In the first place Hong Kong has remained a British crown colony at a time when colonialism has been everywhere in retreat. The British accepted the fact of Asian emancipation and began in 1947 to negotiate the independence of her territories; Holland had to recognize an independent Indonesia in 1949 and in the same year, the French, after losing the 'impregnable' fortress of Dien Bien Phu had to agree to an independent Vietnam. The United States had already granted independence to the Philippines in 1946. Hong Kong has therefore been exceptional in remaining stranded by the tide of history, the one remaining visible reminder of what the Chinese call the 'unequal' treaties. The Kuomintang authorities in Canton naturally eyed the Colony jealously, and just after the war, their representative here occupied an influential position among the local Chinese and became the focus of the demand for its retrocession, though this demand never became a community-wide agitation. Britain has continued to shed her imperial responsibilities and announced the withdrawal of her military presence east of Suez by 1971, except for Hong Kong where a small garrison, including the remaining Gurkha units was retained mainly for civil defence. Though this decision was amended by a conservative Government to retain a token force in Malaysia and a rather larger garrison in Hong Kong, it has virtually meant that Britain will not seek to retain Hong Kong by military force.

Secondly, there has also been the relative weakening of British strategic influence in the world. The United States and Soviet Russia emerged from the War as the two super-powers and they were soon in a state of bitter rivalry resulting in a cold war. Britain had to pay a heavy price for her all-out effort in the War and was in no position to re-assume her role of a world power. Japanese militarism was checked at least temporarily, and Japan's conquests have since become more economic in nature. China on the other hand has become a potentially formidable world power, especially after joining the nuclear club, and despite periods of isolation such as that during the cultural revolution, she has tended to seek greater influence in the world. It has always been true that decisions affecting Hong Kong have been made outside the Colony, but it has become apparent that the voices of Peking and Washington will be more influential in the future. In seeking to join the European Common Market, Britain has looked to Europe and her overseas policies will be conditioned by that fact, and the anomaly is that by the accident of history, Britain retains sovereignty in Hong Kong despite her power in the Far East having passed.

In the third place, despite the trend towards colonial self-government, Hong Kong has remained a crown colony in which democratic machinery has been conspicuously absent. It had always been a predominantly Chinese community, and even more so after 1950 when the closing of the frontier has led to the Chinese remaining permanently there. The great majority were refugee newcomers and their families, to whom it was practically impossible to hand over political power. At the same time, it was impracticable to give that power to the comparatively small number of old-established Hong Kong families, Portuguese, Eurasians, Indians, Chinese and others, without creating an undesirable oligarchy.

Again, it is clear that China would not consent to Hong Kong's independence, nor would it be possible to introduce self-government using normal democratic elections which might be interpreted as claiming sovereignty. Chinese tradition has never been democratic, but Hong Kong has contrived to preserve much personal freedom, which many newly independent countries have sometimes failed to do, which has tended to dispel any impression of government dictatorship. British control has therefore been more or less accepted by the majority of the Chinese. Yet the anomaly is that Hong Kong has become internally autonomous under a British Governor appointed by the London authorities and subject to their instructions, but, at the same time, having to pay attention to constitutional consultative machinery designed to allow the Chinese majority to make their wishes known.

The Hong Kong Chinese have remained thoroughly Chinese in outlook, loyal to the great Chinese tradition rather than to any particular regime. A Hong Kong citizenship based on a loyalty to the local community and characterized by a fusion of European and Chinese traditions which might have been expected, has entirely failed to materialize, and the population of Hong Kong has remained divided into a number of clans or communities, all of which have a degree of loyalty from their respective members.

Finally Hong Kong has had to adapt itself to fundamental changes in its economy. The old entrepot trade with China was a clear-cut economic activity which Hong Kong was seen to be best situated to perform. When this entrepot trade was almost destroyed by outside factors, industry grew up to fill the vacuum. This has brought Hong Kong into direct competition, in textiles at least, with the world's industrial centres. In spite of this competition, most countries have a vested interest in Hong Kong's survival, because it is used by them as a centre for business operations in the surrounding area and indeed as a valuable market for several of their own products. In addition, Hong Kong is now the largest source of free foreign exchange for China itself, which has therefore a strong economic interest in the *status quo*.

In the past, the economy was self-regulating in the sense that people came to Hong Kong mainly for economic reasons and stayed if successful or returned home if not. Now with the closed frontier and the prevailing climate of welfare, Government has had to raise living standards and give the worker more protection. Yet, Government has pinned its faith on the virtues of private enterprise and free competition in industry and its welfare programme has been limited by its policy of maintaining Hong Kong's competitive position. Hong Kong therefore anomalously remains an oasis of the capitalist system in a world of increasingly planned economies. Yet the scale of its industry has been too small to permit of research into new industrial techniques and its future must increasingly rely on joint-venture projects with firms of the advanced industrial nations. But free capitalist enterprise has undoubtedly led to increasing wealth, whatever may be said about the distribution of that wealth. Perhaps the greatest anomaly has been the

growth of an economically dynamic society despite the fact
that it faces an uncertain political future. Hong Kong in essence
remains what it has always been, a market place. Economic
pursuits are its life blood and its sole justification, and men in
the market are concerned not so much with the future as with
conditions as they are.

A SELECT BIBLIOGRAPHY

Official Government Sources:
  Admiralty Records
    Series Ad 19 and Ad 46.
  Colonial Office Records (Public Record Office, London)
    Series CO 129. Governor's Dispatches and Replies from the Secretary of State for the Colonies.
    Series CO 130. Hong Kong Ordinances.
    Series CO 131. Minutes of the Hong Kong Executive and Legislative Councils and Sessional Papers.
    Series CO 132. Hong Kong Government Gazettes.
    Series CO 133. Annual Blue Book of Statistics.
    Series CO 809. Confidential Prints.
    Series CO 403. Dispatches from the Secretary of State for the Colonies to the Governors of Hong Kong.
    Series CO 323. Various documents, commissions, warrants, etc.
  Foreign Office Records (Public Record Office, London)
    Series FO 17, FO 223 and FO 228.
  Hong Kong Government Publications
    Hong Kong Government Annual Reports.
    Hong Kong Hansard, Printed Proceedings of the Legislative Council from 1844.
    Historical and Statistical Abstract of the Colony of Hong Kong, 1932.
    Chinese Law and Custom in Hong Kong. Report of a Committee appointed by the Governor in October 1948. Hong Kong, February 1953.

Newspapers:
  Canton Register, 1828–43.
  China Mail, since 1845.
  Chinese Repository, 1832–51.
  Dixon's Hong Kong Recorder, 1850–59.
  Friend of China, 1842–61.
  Hong Kong Register, 1844–58.

Some Printed Sources:
  Anonymous, *Events in Hong Kong and the Far East, 1875–84*, Hong Kong, 1885.
    —*Guide to Hong Kong*, Hong Kong, 1883.
  Belcher, Edward, *Narrative of a voyage Round the World, performed in H.M.S. 'Sulphur'*, 2 vols., London, 1843.

BIBLIOGRAPHY

Bernard, W. D., and Hall, W. H., *Narrative of the Voyages and services of the Nemesis*, 2 vols., London, 1844.

Bingham, J. E., *Narrative of the Expedition to China*, 2 vols., London, 1842.

Cunynghame, Capt. A., *An A.D.C.'s Recollections of Service in China*, 2 vols., London, 1844.

Des Voeux, Sir William, *My Colonial Service*, 2 vols., London, 1903.

Mayers, Dennys and King, *Treaty Ports of China and Japan*, Hong Kong, 1867.

Oliphant, L., *Narrative of the Earl of Elgin's Mission to China and Japan*, 2 vols., London, 1860.

Sirr, H. C., *China and the Chinese*, 2 vols., London, 1849.

Smith, Albert, *To China and Back*, published privately, 1859.

Smith, Rev. George, *A Narrative of the exploratory Visit to each of the Consular Cities of China, and to the islands of Hong Kong and Chusan*, London, 1847.

Various:

Allen and Donnithorne, *Western Enterprise in Far Eastern Economic Development*, Allen and Unwin, 1954.

Carrington, C. E., *The British Overseas*, Cambridge, 1950.

Eitel, E. J., *Europe in China. The history of Hong Kong from the beginning to the year 1882*, Hong Kong, 1895.

Endacott and She, *The Diocese of Victoria*, Hong Kong, 1949.

Fairbank, J. K., *Trade and Diplomacy on the China Coast*, Harvard, 1953.

Fox, Grace, *British Admirals and Chinese Pirates*, London, 1940.

Gull, E. M., *British Economic Interests in the Far East*, London, 1943.

Ingrams, H., *Hong Kong*, H.M.S.O., London, 1952.

Norton Kyshe, J. W., *The History of the Laws and Courts of Hong Kong*, Hong Kong, 1898.

Orange, James, *The Chater Collection. Pictures relating to China, Hong Kong, Macao, 1655-1860*, London, 1924.

Sayer, G. R., *Hong Kong. Birth, Adolescence and Coming of Age*, Oxford, 1937.

Wood, Winifred A., *Brief History of Hong Kong*, Hong Kong, 1940.

APPENDIX 1

List of Governors of the Colony of Hong Kong

Capt. Charles Elliot	Administrator	Jan.–Aug. 1841
Sir Henry Pottinger	Administrator	Aug. 1841–June 1843
	Governor	June 1843–May 1844
Sir John F. Davis		May 1844–Mar. 1848
Sir S. George Bonham		Mar. 1848–April 1854
Sir John Bowring		April 1854–May 1859
Sir Hercules Robinson		Sept. 1859–Mar. 1865
W. T. Mercer	[Administered]	Mar. 1865–Mar. 1866
Sir Richard Graves Macdonnell		Mar. 1866–April 1872
Sir Arthur E. Kennedy		April 1872–Mar. 1877
Sir John Pope Hennessy		April 1877–Mar. 1882
W. H. Marsh	[Administered]	Mar. 1882–Mar. 1883
Sir George F. Bowen		Mar. 1883–Dec. 1885
E. Marsh	[Administered]	Dec. 1885–April 1887
Major-General N. G. Cameron	[Administered]	April–Oct. 1887
Sir William Des Voeux		Oct. 1887–May 1891
Major-General Digby Barker	[Administered]	May–December 1891
Sir William Robinson		Dec. 1891–Jan. 1898
Major-General W. Black	[Administered]	Feb.–Nov. 1898
Sir Henry A. Blake		Nov. 1898–Nov. 1903
F. H. May	[Administered]	Nov. 1903–July 1904
Sir Matthew Nathan		July 1904–April 1907
Sir Frederick Lugard		July 1907–Mar. 1912
Sir Francis H. May		July 1912–Feb. 1919
Sir Reginald E. Stubbs		Sept. 1919–Oct. 1925
Sir Cecil Clementi		Nov. 1925–Feb. 1930
Sir William Peel		May 1930–May 1935
Sir Andrew Caldecott		Dec. 1935–April 1937
Sir Geoffry Northcote		Nov. 1937–May 1940
Sir Mark Young		Sept. 1941–May 1947
Sir Alexander Grantham		July 1947–Dec. 1957
Sir Robert Black		Jan. 1958–Mar. 1964
Sir David Trench		April 1964–Oct. 1971
Sir Murray Maclehose		1971–

APPENDIX 2

List of Secretaries of State for the Colonies

Ministry		Secretary of State for the Colonies *Note:* Secretary of State for War and the Colonies until June 1854	
Peel, Tory	1841–46	Lord Stanley	Sept. 1841–Dec. 1845
		W. E. Gladstone	Dec. 1845–July 1846
Russell, Whig	1846–52	Earl Grey	July 1846–Feb. 1852
Derby, Tory	1852	Sir J. Pakington	Feb.–Dec. 1852
Aberdeen, Coalition	1852–55	Duke of Newcastle	Dec. 1852–June 1854
		Sir George Grey	June 1854–Feb. 1855
Palmerston, Whig	1855–58	S. Herbert	Feb. 1855
		Lord John Russell	Feb. –July 1855
		Sir William Moles- worth	July–Oct. 1855
		H. Labouchere	Oct. 1855–Feb. 1858
Derby, Tory	1858–59	Lord Stanley	Feb.–May 1858
		Sir E. Bulwer-Lytton	May 1858–June 1859
Palmerston, Whig	1859–65	Duke of Newcastle	June 1859–April 1864
Russell, Whig	1865–66	E. Cardwell	April 1864–June 1866
Derby, Tory	1866–68	Earl of Carnarvon	June 1866–Mar. 1867
Disraeli, Tory	1868	Duke of Buckingham	Mar. 1867–Dec. 1868
Gladstone, Liberal	1868–74	Earl Granville	Dec. 1868–July 1870
		Earl of Kimberley	July 1870–Feb. 1874
Disraeli, Tory	1874–80	Earl of Carnarvon	Feb. 1874–Feb. 1878
		Sir M. Hicks Beach	Feb. 1878–April 1880
Gladstone, Liberal	1880–85	Earl of Kimberley	April 1880–Dec. 1882
		Lord Derby	Dec. 1882–June 1885
Salisbury, Tory	1885–86	Sir F. A. Stanley	June 1885–Jan. 1886
Gladstone, Liberal	1886	Earl Granville	Feb.–Aug. 1886
Salisbury, Unionist	1886–92	E. Stanhope	Aug. 1886–Jan. 1887
		Lord Knutsford	Jan. 1887–Aug. 1892
Gladstone, Liberal	1892–94	Marquis of Ripon	Aug. 1892–June 1895
Rosebery, Liberal	1894–95		
Salisbury, Unionist	1895–1902	J. Chamberlain	June 1895–July 1902
Balfour, Unionist	1902–05	J. Chamberlain	July 1902–Dec. 1905
Campbell-Banner- man, Liberal	1905–08	Earl of Elgin	Dec. 1905–April 1908
Asquith, Liberal	1908–16	Earl of Crewe	April 1908–Nov. 1910
		L. Harcourt	Nov. 1910–1916